D0872291

INTERPRETATION
A BIBLE COMMENTARY FOR TEACHING AND PREACHING

James Luther Mays, *Editor*
Patrick D. Miller, *Old Testament Editor*
Paul J. Achtemeier, *New Testament Editor*

LEO G. PERDUE

Proverbs

INTERPRETATION

A Bible Commentary
for Teaching and Preaching

John Knox Press
LOUISVILLE

Library of Congress Cataloging-in-Publication Data

Perdue, Leo G.
    Proverbs / Leo G. Perdue.
        p. cm. — (Interpretation, a Bible commentary for teaching and preaching)
    Includes bibliographical references.
    ISBN 0-8042-3116-8 (alk. paper)
    1. Bible. O.T. Proverbs—Commentaries.   I. Title.   II. Series.

BS1465.3.P45 2000
233'.7077—dc21

00-032712

© copyright Leo Garrett Perdue 2000
This book is printed on acid-free paper that meets the American National Standards Institute Z39.48 standard. ∞
00 01 02 03 04 05 06 07 08 09—10 9 8 7 6 5 4 3 2 1
Printed in the United States of America
John Knox Press
Louisville, Kentucky

SERIES PREFACE

This series of commentaries offers an interpretation of the books of the Bible. It is designed to meet the need of students, teachers, ministers, and priests for a contemporary expository commentary. These volumes will not replace the historical critical commentary or homiletical aids to preaching. The purpose of this series is rather to provide a third kind of resource, a commentary which presents the integrated result of historical and theological work with the biblical text.

An interpretation in the full sense of the term involves a text, an interpreter, and someone for whom the interpretation is made. Here, the text is what stands written in the Bible in its full identity as literature from the time of "the prophets and apostles," the literature which is read to inform, inspire, and guide the life of faith. The interpreters are scholars who seek to create an interpretation which is both faithful to the text and useful to the church. The series is written for those who teach, preach, and study the Bible in the community of faith.

The commentary generally takes the form of expository essays. It is planned and written in the light of the needs and questions which arise in the use of the Bible as Holy Scripture. The insights and results of contemporary scholarly research are used for the sake of the exposition. The commentators write as exegetes and theologians. The task which they undertake is both to deal with what the texts say and to discern their meaning for faith and life. The exposition is the unified work of one interpreter.

The text on which the comment is based is the Revised Standard Version of the Bible and, since its appearance, the New Revised Standard Version. The general availability of these translations makes the printing of a text in the commentary unnecessary. The commentators have also had other current versions in view as they worked and refer to their readings where it is helpful. The text is divided into sections appropriate to the particular book; comment deals with passages as a whole, rather than proceeding word by word, or verse by verse.

Writers have planned their volumes in light of the requirements set by the exposition of the book assigned to them. Biblical books differ in character, content, and arrangement. They also differ in the way they have been and are used in the liturgy, thought, and devotion of the church. The distinctiveness and use of particular books have been taken into account in decisions about the approach, emphasis, and use of space in the commentaries. The goal has been to allow writers to develop the format that provides for the best presentation of their interpretation.

The result, writers and editors hope, is a commentary that both explains and applies, an interpretation that deals with both the meaning and the significance of biblical texts. Each commentary reflects, of course, the writer's own approach and perception of the church and world. It could and should not be otherwise. Every interpretation of any kind is individual in that sense; it is one reading of the text. But all who work at the interpretation of the Scripture in the church need the help and stimulation of a colleague's reading and understanding of the text. If these volumes serve and encourage interpretation in that way, their preparation and publication will realize their purpose.

The Editors

AUTHOR'S PREFACE

Biblical wisdom literature, which includes the book of Proverbs, was produced in an ancient society that interacted politically, socially, and religiously with cultures in the ancient Near East. Among the non-biblical literature ancient Israel engaged were the sapiential writings of ancient Near Eastern sages, the themes and literary forms of which are quite similar to biblical wisdom texts. These sages were at home in a variety of social realities (family, court, and school) that paralleled those in which the wise men and women of Israel lived and functioned. Indeed, ancient Near Eastern wisdom literatures influenced, both directly and indirectly, biblical wisdom traditions. Israel's sages were cognizant of the existence and importance of ancient Near Eastern sages and traditions, drew at times from their literature, and even compared themselves and their literary forms to them. Israel's recognition of the validity of ancient Near Eastern wisdom literature is unique when compared to the often-exclusive views of Israelite prophetic and legal texts. The Israelite sage's attribution of validity to non-Israelite textual traditions and the teaching of ancient Near Eastern sages leads us to understand the universal character of wisdom, including its views of God, creation, the nations, and human nature. This universal character of wisdom contrasts with the Israelite election traditions at home in their prophetic, narrative, and legal texts, which affirm that God has chosen Israel from among the nations to be the recipient of revelation and both the beneficiary and the instrument of divine salvation. Consequently, any proper understanding of Israelite wisdom literature, including the book of Proverbs, must take into account the universal character of wisdom, the influence of ancient Near Eastern wisdom on the traditions and forms of Israel's sapiential texts, and the same social settings and literary forms that give expression to the teachings of the wise.

Proverbs consists of eight separate collections of sapiential literary forms composed at different times by a variety of sages. Our introductions to these eight collections orient the reader to the major historical, social, literary, theological, and ethical elements to be encountered in interpretation. In the commentary, each collection is divided into its constituent parts and customarily interpreted in four categories: "Introduction: Date and Provenance," "Literary Structure and Interpretation," "Conclusion," and "Theology." The date and provenance of each collection are difficult to determine, but the efforts to locate each collection in the history and social world of ancient Israel remind us that wisdom texts, including even two-line sayings, do not transcend the historical and social settings that produced them and provided the context in which they continued to function. Wisdom, including the collections in Proverbs, is not to be understood in the categories of philosophical idealism, which implies that what is said and taught is universally true regardless of time and space. Rather, wisdom texts, including Proverbs, are to be interpreted in the categories of philosophical realism, which intimates that texts, including individual sayings, have their primary meaning(s) in the concrete reality of the time, space, and social world in which they were produced and continued to function. This is true of all biblical literature, and wisdom texts are no exception.

The category "Literary Structure and Interpretation" notes the fact that sayings and other forms of sapiential literature were generally placed within larger literary sections that provide a compositional context for interpreting what is taught by a smaller unit. This means we are encouraged as modern readers to interpret wisdom sayings, teachings, and poems within a larger literary context, moving from the specific wisdom form and content to the larger literary unit of the subunit, to the collection, to the book, and finally to the wisdom corpus itself. In addition, interpreting wisdom texts within larger collections enables us to see the aesthetically shaped dimensions of the book and to understand how literary expression and interpretation are inseparably entwined.

The "Conclusion" brings together the salient points of date, content, text, and literary structure into a convenient interpretative whole that concentrates on the meaning of the larger subunit and collection.

Finally, the "Theology" of the collection enables us to recognize that the sapiential texts set forth a theology of creation of the cosmos and humanity and a moral ethic that shapes human character according to the ideals of sapiential virtues. It is from this section that we may reflect on the relevance or invalidity of wisdom teachings for theological and ethical understandings of the social realities and issues of the modern world.

CONTENTS

Introduction

The Place of the Book of Proverbs in the Canon

The book of Proverbs is found among the "Writings," the third and final section of the canon of the Hebrew Bible, which also includes the "Law" and the "Prophets." In the Hebrew Bible, the Writings comprise some thirteen books: Psalms, Job, Proverbs, Ruth, Song of Songs, Qoheleth (Ecclesiastes), Lamentations, Esther, Daniel, Ezra, Nehemiah, and 1 and 2 Chronicles. In contrast to the Law and the Prophets, which have a reasonably coherent basis for their assemblage into two major groupings of texts, the diversity of the various books in this third section makes it difficult to identify common features of content and genre. Thus, the Writings contain such disparate literature as narrative history and legend, psalms for use in temple worship and private devotion, secular love songs, apocalyptic visions, and wisdom literature. Subjects addressed include the history of Israel and Judah, God's acts in creation and history, human suffering and divine redemption, human love between a man and a woman, visions of the end time, moral behavior, the questioning of divine justice, and the destruction of Jerusalem.

Attempts, even detailed investigations, to date the book of Proverbs or its parts (from individual sayings to collections) have produced no consensus, nor, for that matter, any major trends among scholars. Most interpreters see the book as the product of many "authors" and editors of collections over at least several centuries, beginning during the monarchy (tenth to sixth century B.C.E.) and continuing until the final form of the book was shaped, perhaps as late as the third century B.C.E. (see Whybray, *Proverbs,* 5–7; Murphy, *Tree of Life,* 18–19). Quite a number of scholars have undertaken efforts to date each collection in Proverbs and occasionally even a particular saying, instruction, or poem. Some scholars have argued that the concise, less elegantly crafted saying that represents an observation based on human experience and lacks theological reference is early, that is, from the time of the early monarchy or perhaps even shortly before, whereas the didactic genre of the instruction, the poems on Woman Wisdom found in Proverbs 1—9, and sayings that are strongly theological in content are later (mostly postexilic). The primary assumptions behind

1

this method of dating are that there is a chronological development from short forms to lengthy ones and that early wisdom exudes a somewhat more humanistic spirit than after the tradition enters Judah's religious and theological mainstream in the exilic and post-exilic periods. The majority of scholars have concluded that the final collection to be written, edited, and added to the others is Proverbs 1—9, likely put together in the postexilic period, though important voices have opposed this conclusion (Murphy, *Tree of Life*, 18–19). This evolutionary schema has often been criticized, especially since brief sayings, including ones with considerable insight and literary beauty, continued to be spoken, written, and collected long after the final composition of the book of Proverbs (e.g., *Pirqe Aboth*). In addition, brief sayings, poems, and lengthy instructions existed in ancient Near Eastern collections of texts, including wisdom ones, long before the emergence of early Israel, and there is some evidence that these collections may have influenced those of the book of Proverbs (e.g., *Instruction of Amen-em-Opet* and Prov. 22:17—24:22). Nevertheless, there may be some merit in seeing in the literary and intellectual sophistication, especially of poems and perhaps even instructions, evidence of a later theological and literary polish and skill that came with the increasing education of sages through the generations of Israel's and Judah's schools.

Outside the superscriptions of collections that mention Solomon, Hezekiah, Agur, and the mother of Lemuel, there is very little other concrete historical data on which to formulate dates. Even in these cases, the historical value and trustworthiness of the superscriptions is open to question. Agur and Lemuel are otherwise unknown and thus provide no clear historical clues. While a literary tradition incorporated into the Deuteronomistic History about Solomon's great wisdom developed in Israel as early as the sixth century B.C.E. (1 Kings 4:29–34), few scholars would see this as anything more than patronage of the great king (see von Rad, *Old Testament Theology* 1:48, 55, 140, 316, 425, and 429), and some consider it to be completely legendary, without any real basis in history (see Crenshaw, *Old Testament Wisdom*, 35–44). Solomon himself ruled from around 961 to 922 B.C.E. Agur, apparently a sage, and Lemuel, a ruler, may have been Arabians, but their dates cannot be precisely identified. In addition to Solomon, only Hezekiah of the late seventh and early sixth centuries B.C.E. can be identified precisely (715–687/6 B.C.E.). This means that much of the wisdom corpus, including the book of Proverbs, cannot be placed with precision within the known framework of Israelite history, although intimations of literary form, social institutions and customs, and content at least suggest plausible but still general chronological periods in which the various collections may have been produced. While scanty historical and especially social-historical information exists, these fragments of data should not be ignored. From the bits of data still extant, it is apparent that the book of Proverbs developed from the period of the early monarchy (tenth century B.C.E.) into postexilic times (fifth–fourth centuries B.C.E.). The scarcity of specific historical references, however, does not mean that the sages were ahistorical and considered wisdom to consist of timeless teachings that were always true, regardless of time and circumstance. The sages were well aware that the authenticity of a saying or teaching was intrinsically connected to the concrete specificity of time, place, and conditions in which a teaching was considered for guidance in a sage's decision making and behavior.

The Book of Proverbs among Biblical Wisdom Literature

Wisdom literature includes three books in the Hebrew canon—Job, Proverbs, and Qoheleth—and two more in the deuterocanonical or apocryphal literature—Sirach (Ben Sira) and the Wisdom of Solomon. Some scholars have argued that additional texts in the Hebrew Bible were written, redacted, or at least influenced by the sages who wrote and compiled the wisdom literature. These claims are based on sapiential language (vocabulary and literary forms) and content that are thought to be detected in books outside the traditional corpus of the wisdom books mentioned above. How pervasive or how limited the presence of wisdom in the Bible may be is determined largely by the criteria used to make the argument. On the one hand, very general criteria, while allowing one to include more within the wisdom corpus and the literature influenced by the wise, are often too broad and imprecise to be convincing. On the other hand, criteria can be so restrictive that almost nothing, even some of the books normally accepted as part of the wisdom corpus, could be said to be the product of the sages. One may best account for the presence of wisdom in nonsapiential literature (e.g., Jer. 17:5–11) by noting that the scribes who redacted the various books of the Hebrew Bible were probably educated in wisdom schools, thus leaving their indelible mark on what they edited.

The Meaning of Wisdom

Wisdom (*hŏkmâ*), a feminine noun that explains in part its presentation as a woman in Proverbs 1—9, has received many definitions by scholars over the years (Crenshaw, "Prolegomenon," 3–5; *Old Testament Wisdom,* 1–15). To define wisdom, one should begin by noting

3

that it refers to a body of literature found in the Hebrew canon (especially the books of Proverbs, Job, and Qoheleth) and in the Apocrypha (in particular Sirach and the Wisdom of Solomon). These texts are characterized by the presence of common literary genres, language, and themes. Later examples of extant Jewish texts to be counted among the burgeoning wisdom tradition include Baruch 3:9—4:4; *Pirqe Aboth;* the *Testament of the Twelve Patriarchs;* and some of the writings among the Dead Sea Scrolls. In texts belonging to other types of canonical literature (e.g., the Law and the Prophets), some wisdom fragments have been preserved that reflect the editorial activity and influence of wise scribes (e.g. Jer. 17:5–11; and the wisdom psalms).

Moving beyond this literary definition to a more conceptual one, one may also say that wisdom in ancient Israel and early Judaism includes at least six important elements: knowledge, imagination, discipline, piety, order, and moral instruction.

Wisdom as knowledge

The sages' understanding of wisdom as knowledge includes: (1) a distinctive collection of texts that formed a tradition; (2) the means to obtain and understand this knowledge (memory, sense perception, reason, experience, and imagination); and (3) the process of instruction and learning by which teachers transmit this tradition to their students.

Wisdom literature embodies knowledge, a growing tradition that was incorporated eventually into five main canonical and deuterocanonical writings—Proverbs, Job, Qoheleth, Ben Sira, and the Wisdom of Solomon—and that was influential in shaping the language and content of other collections of literature: psalms (Pss. 1, 19a, 19b, 32, 34, 37, 49, 73, 112, 119, 127); certain prophets (e.g., Amos, Isaiah, and Jeremiah); and particular narratives (e.g., the Joseph story in Genesis 37—50 and the succession narrative in 2 Samuel 9—20; 1 Kings 1—2). In addition, the sages appear to have played an important part in the editing of nonsapiential books, some of which entered into the canonical literature of the Hebrew Bible (e.g., Deuteronomy). The forms and themes of Israelite and Jewish wisdom impacted in significant ways on apocalyptic literature (e.g., the Enoch texts), early canonical and noncanonical Christian writings (e.g., the *Gospel of Thomas* and the epistle of James), and rabbinic texts (e.g., *Pirqe Aboth*). Wisdom literature especially influenced the formation and content of subsequent sayings collections and ethical instruction that provided part of the content for character formation and the moral life in early Jewish and Christian communities.

4

The wisdom tradition possesses distinctive literary, social, theological, and ethical features. Literary forms or genres include a variety of sayings (proverb, beatitude, riddle, question, numerical saying, admonition, and prohibition), instructions, dialogues or disputations, didactic narratives, and poems. This tradition likely arose within several social contexts, in particular the court, royal and temple schools, and the family. Counted among the sages were not only teachers but also officials and scribes at work in the major social institutions of the court and temple, as well as parents and elders who were members of extended households and clans and were responsible for the instruction and socialization of their families, especially the children. Through their teaching, the sages developed and passed on orally and in writing an evolving sapiential tradition that, from these various settings, merged into what became the extant wisdom books.

Most of what survived from the course of study in the schools and the teachings and customs of the households of Israel is embodied in the Hebrew canon and apocryphal literature of early Judaism. Due to the nature of the canon as largely a theological and ethical collection of literature concerned with faith, worship, and morality, it is not surprising that the surviving literary tradition of the wise is also largely theological and moral in nature. One can well imagine, however, that some highly educated sages who passed through the royal schools not only studied Hebrew and eventually Aramaic but also came to master the variety of other ancient Near Eastern languages (Canaanite, Egyptian, Akkadian) needed to carry out diplomacy and international commerce. Some also would have studied mathematics, diplomacy, economics, and law (see Sir. 38:24—39:11). It was sapiential theology and ethics, however, taught first in these schools and eventually adapted for the instruction of a broad public audience, that entered the canon of the Hebrew Bible and therefore was preserved.

The content of the wisdom literature is largely moral and theological, but this does not mean the teachings were considered to be divine fiats of eternal truths that transcended time and place. The wisdom tradition was considered by its teachers to be authoritative, at least in a qualified way, for it represented the best and tested insights of the sages who studied the divinely established order of the world and of human society and who reflected on their observations and experiences, recorded their insights in their writings, and passed their learning on to successive generations. Some sayings even were presented as indicating that an action was pleasing or abhorrent to Yahweh, thus giving certain sapiential affirmations the imprimatur of divine authority (Crenshaw, "Wisdom and Authority," 326–43).

5

This did not mean, however, that the wisdom tradition was inflexible and incapable of contestation. The theological and ethical knowledge of the wise was fluid and subject at times to challenge, dispute, and reformulation, when not confirmed by experience carefully tested by reason. The sayings and teachings of the sages were not considered, even in the days of ancient Israel and early Judaism, to be moral absolutes about which there were no disputes or doubts. Indeed, much of what we in the contemporary world read in Proverbs sounds bizarre, sexist, and, epistemologically speaking, just plain wrong. To recognize the limits of the teachings, however, is not at all contrary to the nature of the wisdom tradition itself. Certainly Agur (Proverbs 30), Job, Qoheleth, and even the aphoristic materials attributed to Jesus contested previous sapiential teachings and observations (Williams, *Those Who Ponder Proverbs*). The tradition of the sages invites critical review, dialogue, and reformulation. To do so today is to be in keeping with the nature of the wisdom tradition itself. To turn the teachings and sayings of the sages into moral absolutes is to corrupt the wisdom tradition into inflexible dogma and thus to undermine its dynamic character. Wisdom allowed for no stasis that would lead to stagnation and inauthentic existence. Indeed, the dogmatic positions of the wise "friends" (actually opponents) of Job contradicted wisdom's openness to critical scrutiny.

After critically engaging wisdom teachings, the sages used these sapiential insights and understandings to form human character and then to guide actions and speech. Carefully rendered in human behavior, sapiential teachings led to success, if they were actualized at the proper time and place in the social order. Only the truly wise person, whose character was duly shaped by the virtues of wisdom that were present in the sapiential literature and continually reformulated by critical engagement, could determine the correct time and place to act on the basis of sapiential instruction. There were times and circumstances when even the wisest of actions and the most persuasive and articulate speech were sure to fail. For example, there was a time not to answer a fool according to his or her folly and a time to respond to foolish talk and action (Prov. 26:4–5). Only a sage could determine when and where to answer or not to answer a fool. In some situations, the wise taught that patience and restraint were the better part of valor, waiting for a more auspicious time and circumstance when success was more likely to occur (von Rad, *Wisdom in Israel,* 138–43). And there were times and circumstances when a saying or instruction was not given the ring of authenticity and acted on. Rather, the sages were taught to assess critically the validity of what the saying or instruction taught them, to negate or to affirm the teaching by reference to reason and experience, and to recognize that time and circumstances could substantiate or disconfirm what was taught. It was inconceivable for the sages to think there were moral absolutes that were unconditionally and eternally true, irrespective of the concrete situations of life.

Learning, at least at a sophisticated level, involved more than rote memorization and the unquestioning acceptance of what was taught. Critical engagement, including even the possibility of rejecting the teaching, and reformulation were an integral part of the process of the transmission of wisdom. Students were expected to honor the ancestors' traditional teachings, but only if and when they correlated with their own experience (Job 15:17–18). This process of transmission meant that the tradition was assimilative and pliant rather than systematic and inflexible.

According to the wise men and women of Israel, creation was sustained by both divine action and humans living in conformity with the moral order of the cosmos (Perdue, "Cosmology," 457–78). Social institutions and individuals were expected to reflect these norms of justice governing the structures of existence. Ultimately, God is the source of true wisdom that creates and sustains life and provides insight into reality (Job 9:4; 12:13; 15:7–8). At creation God used divine wisdom to permeate the cosmos with a moral order of justice that continued to sustain and govern all life (Job 28:23–27; Ps. 104:24; Prov. 3:13–20; 8:22–31; Jer. 10:12). This divine wisdom, which is all encompassing (2 Sam. 14:20), oversees the moral order of cosmic as well as social reality, brings punishment to the wicked and blessing to the righteous, and shapes the future that leads to life (Isa. 31:1–2). The sages spoke also of social institutions, including government, family, commerce, and law, that received their legitimation and support by a just and nurturing creator as long as they were guided by divine wisdom. God also imbues individuals with the organs of perception and gives or teaches them wisdom to allow them to observe reality and its undergirding moral order, to shape their observations into a transmittable tradition, and to live in conformity with its teachings (Pss. 51:6 = Heb. 51:8; 90:12; Prov. 2:6–8 and 20:12). Woman Wisdom, the personification of divine wisdom incorporated into the teachings of the wise, issues the invitation to the "simple" or "unlearned" to take the path to insight that obtains favor from Yahweh and leads to life (Prov. 8:32–36).

The sages derived their understandings of God, reality, and human existence from three sources: natural reason and the powers of observation, the gift of divine wisdom that provided the means to

7

reason and think, and the sapiential tradition inherited from wise ancestors. This contrasts to the more direct revelation claimed by the prophets who in states of ecstasy received the word of the Lord and to the divine knowledge of the priests who obtained the sacred oracle during times of theophany or from the ritual of casting lots. This more indirect way of receiving divine revelation and insight meant that the sages had both the freedom and the responsibility to subject the teachings of their ancestors to critical assessment based on their own experiences of life and insights into the nature of reality. While on occasion they claimed divine authority for the integrity and truth of what they taught (2 Sam. 16:23), they normally avoided a dogmatism that made their teachings absolute, unyielding, and unresponsive to the times, specific circumstances, and human experience. They admitted there were limits to their knowledge, for they were readily aware of inexplicable contingencies that were at variance with what they normally experienced to be true.

Wisdom as imagination

Wisdom is not limited to knowledge derived from observations of cosmic and social reality that continued to be refined by reason and tested and tested again in the arena of human experience (see Perdue, *Collapse of History*, 263–98, and *Wisdom and Creation*). In their linguistic portrayals of God, humanity, and the world, the sages were also aesthetes who activated their imagination to project a reality of order and beauty in which human society was to be a microcosm of justice and symmetry, present both in creation and in the nature and character of God, and who used their language to construct artistic and compelling literary worlds of beauty and delight. They invited the unlearned to take up the study of wisdom and enter these worlds of imagination, where well-being was to be had. Those who took up wisdom's path to understanding entered a symbolic universe of order, goodness, and artistry, a universe constructed by the imagination of learned sages.

To speak of God's presence in this world of wonder and order, the sages turned to the metaphor of Woman Wisdom. Woman Wisdom is both an architect who orders and sustains the regularities of the cosmos and a sage whose teachings offer the bounty of life to her students. She also is God's child whose delight and rejoicing in the world of human habitation provide the communal bond between creation and its creator (Prov. 8:22–31). Elsewhere she is the fertility goddess who builds her palace, initiates her reign, and invites the simple to partake of her banquet of life (Prov. 9:1–6). In Prov. 8:12–21 she is the

8

queen of heaven by whom kings and princes govern the earth and are blessed by her bounty. Finally, Wisdom becomes the revelatory voice of God heard both in the tradition of the wise and in the creation that calls the simple to insight and life (Prov. 8:32–36; see Camp, *Wisdom*).

Yet even with the free rein of their imagination, the sages did not claim to remove the veil from many mysteries that resided beyond their ability to understand (Prov. 21:30; 25:2; and 30:1b-4). This lack of comprehensive knowledge was especially true of divine reality and activity. In their imagination, the sages portrayed God as the creator and sustainer of reality who transcended creation and yet could be known indirectly through its beauty, operation, and life-sustaining orders (see von Rad, *Wisdom in Israel,* 144–76). Wisdom as the instrument of divine creativity represents on occasion in the sapiential literature the transcendence of God the Creator and providential Judge. Yet the immanence of God was also expressed in the metaphor of Woman Wisdom who, in the symbolic world of sapiential imagination, personified the divine justice, truth, nurture, insight, and instruction that were embodied in the wisdom tradition. This entrancing and commanding figure went in search of the unlearned and offered them the means by which to come to a knowledge of God and thus to experience the blessings of life. Even so, God remained to a large extent enigmatic. This ready acknowledgment of divine mystery, along with the admitted limits to their knowledge of God as well as of other matters, provided the sages their rationale for inexplicable contingencies in reality and offered some rationalization for the questions of injustice, righteous suffering, and theodicy.

Wisdom as discipline

The sages speak of wisdom as "discipline" (*mûšar* = Gk. *paideia*), that is, education that includes both a course of study embodied in "teachings" or "instructions" and the moral formation of character (Prov. 1:2, 3, 7, 8; 3:11; 15:33; and 23:23). Study and character formation are to lead to "sagehood," the wise person's successful integration of knowledge, character, action, and speech (Prov. 8:33; see Brown, *Character in Crisis*). Needless to say, this quest "to become wise," regardless of how intensely undertaken, is a lifelong endeavor that never is fully and perfectly achieved (Prov. 1:2–7).

Nevertheless, there were stages of life through which the sage passed in moving from ignorance to wisdom. Socialization into the duties of adulthood, marriage and family, and scribal careers, and the final transition from life to death, involved mastering and implementing in word and deed a body of knowledge concerning wise behavior,

9

responsibilities, and expectations. Wise teachers instructed students in scribal schools in order to prepare them to meet their moral requirements once they reentered life at a new level of social responsibility. Parents taught children the duties and obligations expected of adults, including those of husbands and wives after their households arranged and formally concluded their marriages. These teachers and parents were "significant others" whose own character was to provide an exemplar for the moral life and whose teachings were to become part and parcel of the character of the student or child. Personal example and teaching provided a *nomos* for living, that is, a moral structure and guide for responsible behavior.

The goal of the sage was to use these teachings and their incorporation into human character to master or control (*māšal*) the various situations encountered in life and to enter the state of blessing that included honor, prosperity, good health, contentment, love, longevity, and success. Stated in a negative way, the sage through wisdom sought to avoid premature death, dishonor, unhappiness, poor health, anger, conflict, and failure. By achieving these goals, the sage lived in harmony with God, creation, the human community, and the self.

Wisdom as piety

The sages did not dichotomize between faith and rational inquiry or between the practice of religion and moral behavior (Perdue, *Wisdom and Cult*). This is seen in their repeated affirmation that "the fear of [Yahweh] is the beginning of knowledge" (e.g., Job 28:28 and Prov. 1:7). "Fear of Yahweh" is the attitude of reverential piety that the one seeking and then finding wisdom was to possess, and this piety became the essential theological foundation of wisdom (von Rad, *Wisdom in Israel*, 53–73). The sages believed that Yahweh was the creator of the world and the sustainer of the orders of life, and subsequently Yahweh received both their awe and their adulation. This fundamental confession and worship provided the foundation for understanding and interpreting the character and activity of God, the nature of reality, and the significant values that were seen as the goal of the wise and prudent life. Even early wisdom was not a secular enterprise devoid of theological affirmation and cultic observance.

Wisdom as order

Central to the understanding of wisdom is the concept of order in the cosmos, in human society, and in human life. Order not only expressed regularity and continuation but also connoted the moral idea of justice or righteousness. For the wise, God established a cosmic order of justice at creation and continued to maintain it through righteous rule. This just order was rooted in the character of God, activated by divine will, and expressed in divine action. Thus order did not operate mechanically on its own, nor were humans through their behavior and language automatically rewarded or punished. While the sages' understanding of order accommodated the doctrine of retributive justice, they did not separate its operation from the free will and activity of God. For example, Yahweh's blessing, not human effort, makes a person wealthy (Prov. 10:22). Humans may make plans, but it is Yahweh who directs their steps (Prov. 16:9). Entrusting one's actions to Yahweh leads to the establishment of one's plans (Prov. 16:3). It is Yahweh who punishes the arrogant and has even made the wicked for the "day of trouble" (Prov. 16:4–5). Thus, while God was expected to punish the foolish and the wicked and to reward the wise and the righteous, divine freedom was not compromised. The creator was not only a God of justice but also a deity of compassion and mercy who could choose to forgive or to wait before enacting judgment. In addition, the suffering of the just could be understood as a process of purification and refinement of virtuous living and was not necessarily an indication either of punishment for evil behavior or of divine caprice. Likewise, the well-being of the foolish or wicked did not signal divine impotence or caprice. Justice would assuredly be meted out, but in God's own good time. The sages affirmed both the justice and the freedom of God in holding sway over the cosmos, although the ways of the Almighty were not always immediately apparent in their intention and design (see Boström, *God of the Sages*, 90–140; Koch, *Um das Prinzep der Vergeltung*; and Rankin, *Israel's Wisdom Literature*).

Order as righteousness (*şĕdāqâ*) was also to permeate and sustain the life of human communities. The sapiential tradition continued to shape and reshape the meaning of social justice and the virtues of the moral life, which, if followed and implemented in communal existence, led to the well-being of the whole. The moral law of God was contained in the teachings of the sages and was to be actualized in society's institutions of the extended family and clan, jurisprudence, and government. Human actions and speech, whether good or evil, righteous or foolish, directly impacted for better or worse on both society and the larger cosmos. No human actions were isolated and self-contained, either in their performance or from their results. The sages taught that all actions and language had an effect, whether positive or adverse, on the human community and even on the order of creation.

The person whose behavior and speech embodied order was the

11

"righteous one" (ṣaddîq). The sages did not consider this moral order of justice to be intrinsic to human nature but rather to be learned and realized through actions and words informed by wisdom. The sage sought to live in harmony with God, the cosmos, human society, and the self and, through actions and speech, undergirded, constituted, and enhanced the orders of life in their cosmic, social, and individual dimensions. This means the moral life not only imitated the justice present in the character of God, observable in the cosmos, and actualized in society but also helped to create and sustain a just order in all dimensions of existence. The sages sought to incorporate themselves into this sphere of cosmic and social life, to live in harmony with creation and the human community, and to experience well-being in life (Perdue, "Cosmology," 457–78).

Not all sages believed in a moral order presided over by God. Qoheleth denied the existence of justice in reality that could be perceived by even the wisest of sages. Further, he argued that God was a hidden and capricious power who could not be known but who certainly was to be feared. Still other sages, especially the wise opponents of Job (Eliphaz, Bildad, and Zophar), denied the attribute of freedom to God and portrayed divine justice as a system of mechanical retribution for the punishment of the wicked and the reward of the righteous. This view, of course, is repudiated by the poetic dialogues of the book of Job, including the speeches of God.

Wisdom as moral instruction

Wisdom in Proverbs is primarily understood as moral instruction. The features of this instruction include the following. First, moral instruction in Proverbs consists primarily of material that is traditional and unoriginal. This is largely due to the static view of world order and the conservative bent of the teaching by sages who sought to uphold a social reality that would not be easily open to change. Thus, unlike some of the literature of marginal prophets (e.g., Amos and Jeremiah), the moral discipline of wise teachers does not advocate for social change but rather seeks to legitimate the existing social reality and the worldview that sustains it. Second, moral instruction is applicable to a variety of life situations and individual circumstances. Thus, general precepts provide guidance for the ones taught, who then apply those precepts to the various situations in which they find themselves. Third, moral instruction seeks to stimulate the memory of those who have been taught in order to exhort them to act on the basis of what they already know (Perdue, "Paraenesis and the Epistle of James," 241–56).

12

Although archaeological and literary data are rather sparse, most scholars have argued for the family, court, and school as the social settings in which moral instruction occurred (see Crenshaw, *Education;* Davies, *Wisdom in Ancient Israel,* 199–211). The similarity of Israelite and Jewish wisdom to the moral teachings of sages in adjacent cultures (Egypt, Mesopotamia, Greece, and Rome), however, suggests that the sages were a social class of wise teachers whose moral teachings provided guidelines for behavior in the court, family, legal arena, and cultus. Consequently, one may suggest that the life settings of moral instruction include a variety of situations in which teachers, be they parents, tutors, or masters of a profession, instruct disciples, that is, the "simple," in the content of traditional teachings. Thus the school, the teaching of youth by parents, and professional guilds offer moral discourse to those who are seeking to enter new roles in the social order. These teachers are significant others who desired to transmit the moral world they have received and helped to shape those who are being elevated to a higher social position with new responsibilities. These social positions include, in particular, career, family, and marriage.

Victor Turner describes this elevation as a rite of passage that includes three phases: separation from the social structure, liminality in which past associations with the culture are being transcended, and incorporation into the social structure at a new level or into a new social group (*Ritual Process;* Perdue, "Liminality as a Social Setting"). Even sages, already advanced in their social standings, are urged to reflect on their formative passage to their present locations. What obtains in moral discipline is an experienced teacher and immature novices who are being initiated into a new status or a new social group.

The social functions of moral instruction include socialization, that is, the induction of an individual into the social reality of the teacher. The one who teaches is the "significant other," a teacher with whom the students have formed a strong emotional bond. Once socialization is complete, the novices have begun to create a "generalized other," or a social reality that their behavior incorporates and sustains. The reality of the new social world is achieved by an ontological refashioning of the taught by means of exhortation, appeals to reason and experience, and even verbal and physical chastisement. This new social reality is legitimated in such ways in order to sustain a worldview that is in conflict or competition with the social worlds of other groups. The identity of the world-creating group is sharpened and given cohesion by moral teaching that is inculcated into behavior. Thus, socialization and the refashioning of the character of the unlearned are the two primary purposes of this literature.

13

The Universal Character of Wisdom

The wisdom tradition of ancient Israel developed within a cultural world in which this type of literary expression and moral teaching flourished (see Gammie and Perdue, *Sage in Israel;* Clements, *Wisdom in Theology,* 40–64). Indeed, wisdom literatures from Egypt, Mesopotamia, and the Hellenistic world may have influenced the development and formation of a similar tradition in ancient Israel and early Judaism. The sages of Israel and Judah acknowledged the authenticity of wisdom from other nations, meaning, then, that the sages prior to Ben Sira (see Sirach 24) admitted to the universality of their knowledge. The Old Testament recognizes that wisdom is not limited to the people of ancient Israel and early Judaism and their teachers, scribes, and kings. Indeed, the Deuteronomistic historians recognized in particular two regions as being renowned for their wisdom: Egypt and the "people of the East," the latter probably Arabia (1 Kings 4:30–31). Elsewhere, Edom, one of the Transjordan countries, is recognized for its cultivation of wisdom (Jer. 49:7; Obad. 8–9). It is true that in the eventual accommodation of its wisdom tradition to the larger national epic Israel came to claim that its wisdom and sages (at least the idealized Solomon and his remarkable wisdom) were superior to those of other nations (1 Kings 4:29–34; Sirach 24; and Wisdom of Solomon 11—19). Yet the recognition of the wisdom of other nations may have emerged in the earlier history of the wisdom tradition, prior to the period of the exile (sixth century B.C.E.). The sages of Israel perhaps were influenced by and may have even borrowed from and then transmitted some wisdom texts from foreign cultures (cf. Prov. 24:23–34, which may have been adapted from the Egyptian text *The Instruction of Amen-em-Opet;* the characters in Job who are portrayed as non-Israelites and perhaps are Edomites; "The Sayings of Agur" in Prov. 30:1–33; and "The Sayings of King Lemuel's Mother" in Prov. 31:1–9).

This attribution of authentic wisdom to peoples outside Israel is grounded in part in the recognition that the knowledge and insight obtained by wise men and women derive from the organs of perception and reason, which are part of a common human nature that is divinely created. In addition, wisdom's reservoir of understanding is filled in large measure by the sages' observations of the revelatory character of the world and human society and by their common human experience, astutely assessed. Further, the deity of the sages in Israel is a universal God, not a tribal deity. Until Ben Sira in the early second century B.C.E., the Israelite and early Jewish wisdom tradition

14

contains no acknowledgment of any special divine revelation limited only to Israel and Judah that provides their sages with a unique knowledge of the world, of human society, and of God. Indeed, there is no claim that God, even when named Yahweh, has elected Israel as the chosen people. In the wisdom literature of ancient Egypt, the "god" is frequently mentioned. This deity is a universal being, a deity of creation and all peoples, not merely a national or ethnic deity of a particular people. This monistic, perhaps henotheistic tendency in Egypt, while not monotheism, is more than likely attributable to the universal character of wisdom that transcends the confining boundaries of nationalism. Thus we find in wisdom an early expression of natural theology.

The Social Locations of the Wisdom Tradition

The final decision of what to include in the Hebrew canon, including the wisdom books, rested in the hands of Jewish rabbis in the early common era, though by this time tradition, including the use of texts in worship, already had largely filled out, at least informally, much of the literary corpus, leaving for the most part only the determination of which books to include in the Writings. After the Great Revolt against Rome that essentially ended with the fall of Jerusalem to the Roman general Titus in 70 C.E., the major sect among the Jewish groups that continued to survive and thus largely shaped formative Judaism was the Pharisees. It was among these learned Pharisaic rabbis, teaching in the synagogues of worship and the houses of learning scattered throughout Palestine, that the Hebrew canon received its final shape. These rabbis, who represented the formation of one major stream of the earlier biblical wisdom tradition and thus were the descendants of the early sages, were teachers concerned not only with the preservation of what they considered to be the proper representations of the Israelite and Jewish religious and moral heritage but also with issues of the prophetic inspiration of texts and their conformity with the Torah. What they preserved were materials they considered worthy of instruction for their own contemporaries who were the practitioners of early Judaism.

Even so, in working back through the canonical literature and other surviving texts that these rabbis did not include in the canon, one may detect and outline the traces of a variety of social locations for the formation of the diverse traditions of wisdom. These social locations prior to the work of teachers in the synagogue likely included the family household, the royal court, and schools (Gammie and Perdue, *Sage in Israel;* and Perdue, *Wisdom and Creation,* 69–74).

15

Wisdom in the clan and family household

One social location for the wisdom tradition was the Israelite and Jewish household, which typically included several families whose members could span linearly several generations (great-grandparents, grandparents, parents, children) and could also extend laterally (uncles and aunts, cousins, unmarried brothers and sisters, and widows; see Perdue et al., *Families*). Marginal members of the household at times included foreigners, sojourners, day laborers, and slaves.

The senior male was the instructor who taught the household's members the traditions of the family and larger clan, other males their responsibilities as household members, and older sons the skills and knowledge for future livelihood, for example, farming (Prov. 1:8; 4:1; 6:20; and 10:1). The senior female taught young children (sons and daughters) and instructed older daughters in the duties associated with their social roles in the family household. The teaching of the "father" and "mother" was authoritative (see Prov. 1:8; 6:20; 10:1; 15:20; 20:20; 23:22, 25; 28:24; and 31:26, 28), and both carried, especially when they were the senior parents in the household, the responsibility for teaching their families their social and religious traditions (Fontaine, *Traditional Sayings in the Old Testament*).

Some senior males also assumed public roles in the villages (largely populated by clans), tribes, and league of tribes as "elders." They were believed to possess the wisdom necessary to make various military, economic, and legal decisions for the larger social units. After the rise of the Israelite monarchy, these elders also served as counselors to kings, though many of their roles external to the family and some even internal to the households were taken over by royal officials and their appointees (see Num. 11:16–30; Josh. 9:11; 2 Sam. 17:4; 1 Kings 12:6–11; 21:8). Indeed, the social and political pressure exerted on clan households by the monarchy led to the royal dispossession of much family patrimony, the undercutting of their social and religious mores, and the removal of necessary farm laborers to perform work as corvé workers on royal projects. The monarchy, before its demise at the hands of the Babylonians in 586 B.C.E., not only rivaled but also seriously threatened the Israelite and Judahite household.

This familial (clan, tribal) wisdom pointed to the extended household as a community in which social roles and traditions were learned. The value system was relational, based on intimacy, in contrast to a moral system that within the larger society emphasized the virtue of loyalty to palace and temple. It is difficult to say how much of this household and tribal wisdom made its way into sapiential literature

16

preserved in the canon and Apocrypha, including the book of Proverbs. The rivalry between the household and its oral culture on the one hand and the royal court in which the literary texts were written and flourished on the other undoubtedly led to the dissipation of much of the rural, familial tradition. It is true that in ancient Near Eastern schools familial titles referred to teachers and students, and this may be true at times in the book of Proverbs as well. While the social context of households and clans likely contributed at least in a small way to the content and setting for some of the sayings and instructions of Proverbs and other sapiential texts, it is doubtful that any folk wisdom directly entered the developing sapiential tradition that eventually was formed into larger collections and books. The literary artistry of the various sayings, instructions, and poems appears too sophisticated for a largely uneducated and unsophisticated clan wisdom to have produced. The most one can say is that perhaps the sages of the court and schools reshaped popular sayings into aesthetically pleasing, often intellectually compelling, literary, polished proverbs that they eventually included in the book of Proverbs. One probable example of the influence of the household on literary wisdom is the less pronounced patriarchy and sexism one finds in wisdom texts prior to Ben Sira. While the senior male exercised great power in the ancient household, the senior female also played a significant role of influence and responsibility. Thus, while hierarchy, based largely on gender, age, and standing in the social structure of the family, is present in Proverbs, sexism and patriarchy are somewhat mitigated by the importance of the mothers of Israel in teaching in the family household.

The royal court

With the rise of the Israelite state, and in particular the United Kingdom of David and Solomon in the tenth century B.C.E., the monarchy required officials and scribes to organize and carry out the various governmental functions of the royal bureaucracy. In addition, some type of royal school would have been necessary to educate princes, officials, and scribes for governance, building projects, the development of a standing army and other military objectives, and administrative responsibilities (see 1 Kings 3—10). Among the literature produced for the education of the children of the royal house and the landed nobility, courtiers, and bureaucrats would have been wisdom texts that provided instruction in moral formation, albeit largely reflecting a class ethic. This explains why much in the book of Proverbs appears to derive from a largely, though certainly not exclusively, male upper social stratum that values wealth, possessions, long life, family, honor,

17

and status. It also explains why a hierarchical ethic at times may be seen as providing the basis for charity and other dimensions of the moral life. The fact that one gives out of the excess of one's accumulated resources indicates that it is those of substance and social prominence whose perspective is at work, not that of the poor. Royal wisdom represents the interest of the ruling, landed class, from king to nobles related by blood, marriage, or treaty. While the sages and their students are exhorted to perform acts of charity, the wealthy are not admonished to divest themselves of their possessions.

Significant extant textual evidence indicates that women were among the sages of Israel (2 Sam. 14:1–24; 20:14–22; Proverbs 31; the metaphor of Woman Wisdom in Proverbs 1—9, Sirach 24, and Wisdom of Solomon 10—19; and the references in instructions to "mothers" who teach their "children," Prov. 1:8; 6:20; 10:1; 31:1; and 31:26). Further, the images used to describe Woman Wisdom and the representation of the ideal wise woman in Proverbs 31 point to women of prominent social position and wealth in Israelite and early Jewish society. While Solomon's father, David, is flattered by the wise woman of Tekoa for having insight "like the wisdom of the angel of God to know all things that are on the earth" (2 Sam. 14:20; cf. v. 17), the larger narrative indicates that she, not David, is the true sage (cf. 2 Sam. 20:14–22, the wise woman of Abel of Beth-maacah).

The monarch is presented on occasion as the ideal wise man (e.g., Solomon in 1 Kings 3—11). It is Yahweh, or Woman Wisdom, who chooses kings to rule and provides them with counsel and wisdom to govern the kingdoms of the earth (Prov. 8:14–16). The divine gift of wisdom provided kings with the ability to rule their domains in ways that would bring about peace and prosperity (1 Kings 3:1–14; Isa. 11:1–9; cf. 9:5).

This important role of the kings and the royal court in the development of the wisdom tradition is suggested by a variety of literary sources, including especially the Solomonic narrative in 1 Kings 3—10, the superscriptions of several collections of wisdom teachings in Proverbs (1:1; 10:1; 25:1; and 31:1), and several of the collections themselves. For example, the royal mother of King Lemuel (Prov. 31:1–9) issues her son an instruction on how to rule wisely and well. Some scholars have also argued that texts such as Prov. 16:1—22:16 and Proverbs 25 are instructions for royal officials.

The notoriety given to Solomon and the lauding of his legendary achievements in the Deuteronomistic History likely derive from a scribal clientele enjoying the largess of the continuing royal patronage of the house of David or from claims of earlier royal legitimation as

18

part of a Solomonic "enlightenment" in which humanism and especially reason displaced an earlier mythic cosmology of direct, miraculous, divine participation in the world. This type of flattering portrayal
of an ancient Near Eastern ruler whose accomplishments were
attributed to his election by the gods and to god-given virtues, including especially wisdom, is frequently found in other cultures in the
region (e.g., Sargon, Hammurabi, Assurbanipal). Solomon is notably
depicted as the "wise" king whose divine endowment with "an understanding mind" (1 Kings 3:1–14) enabled him to rule justly
(1 Kings 3:16–28) and to bring prosperity and international prominence to the empire of his father, David (1 Kings 10:1–29). Indeed,
Solomon's reorganization and administration of the Israelite state into
a royal kingdom ruled by the monarchy (1 Kings 4), his employing the
help of Phoenician architects to build the magnificent edifices of the
temple and palace (1 Kings 5—9), his active role in the creating of wisdom literature (1 Kings 4:29–34 = Heb. 5:9–14), and the unparalleled
development during his reign of great prosperity, not only for himself
but also for his kingdom, are attributed to his God-given wisdom
(1 Kings 3:1–15; 10). His wisdom is described as exceeding that of "all
the people of the east, and all the wisdom of Egypt" (1 Kings 4:29–34),
while his wealth and wisdom are said to have excelled "all the kings of
the earth" (1 Kings 10:23–25). Piety, wealth, prominence, justice, and
wisdom, virtues so conspicuously displayed in this legendary narrative,
find their direct correspondences in the wisdom corpus, including the
book of Proverbs. It is likely that the scribes who shaped the materials
in 1 Kings 3—10 did so in large measure for reasons of royal propa-
ganda designed to legitimate the Davidic monarchy and thus were not
writing descriptive social history. The association of Solomon and the
house of David with wisdom suggests that these scribes, some of
whom may have been active as officials within the kingdom, sought to
legitimate this dynasty through its writings and to curry favor with its
reigning monarchs.

The association of Solomon with the wisdom tradition is also represented by three superscriptions in the book of Proverbs—1:1, 10:1,
and 25:1—as well as by the attribution to him of the books of Qoheleth
(Ecclesiastes), the Song of Solomon (Song of Songs), and the Wisdom
of Solomon. As noted above, the legendary narrative of Solomon presents him as a wise man engaged in the creating of sayings, songs, and
lists (1 Kings 4:29–34 = Heb. 5:9–14). Historically speaking, however,
there is no plausible basis for directly associating Solomon with the literary collections in Proverbs or with the books of Ecclesiastes, Song of
Songs, or Wisdom of Solomon. The superscriptions in Proverbs that

19

attribute three collections to Solomon imitate the dedicatory colophons attached to some ancient Near Eastern wisdom literature and in addition, perhaps, indicate royal patronage of the tradition by the house of David.

Although the impact of a Solomonic "enlightenment" has perhaps been exaggerated by some scholars, the rise of the royal state did require the formation not only of an efficient bureaucracy but also of a new ethos to provide an intellectual climate conducive to shaping a legitimizing royal tradition (see Brueggemann, "The Social Significance of Solomon as a Patron of Wisdom"). Royal officials and scribes, some of whom may have been foreign imports, began to recast the older household and clan traditions into new Near Eastern genres and to provide them with transformed understandings. Those high-placed officials who were not of foreign origins likely would have come from increasingly powerful indigenous families whose alliances with the house of David gave rise to a class of nobility that accumulated significant wealth and power. High-placed royal officials provided kings counsel, namely, well-laid plans and insightful advice to produce well-being and success in all areas, including the judiciary, military, international relations, the political arena, and the economy (cf. Jer. 18:18).

In addition to highly placed cabinet officials, wise scribes served in a variety of roles in the royal administration: secretaries, heralds, architects, lawyers, recorders, and teachers. The role of royal and, later, colonial scribes in shaping most of the literary tradition of Proverbs is apparent not only from the superscriptions of the collections but also from some of the book's content. For example, the two Solomonic collections in 10:1—22:16 and 25—29 suggest a socially conservative class ethic for aristocratic youth that included a code of decorum for the royal court and loyalty to the ruling government.

Solomon is the king to whom the book of Proverbs and several of its collections are attributed (Prov. 1:1 = chaps. 1—9 or 1—31; 10:1 = chaps. 10:1—22:16; and 25:1 = chaps. 25—29). Two other superscriptions ascribe collections to royal origins: "These are other proverbs of Solomon that the officials of King Hezekiah of Judah copied" (25:1 = chaps. 25—29) and "The words of King Lemuel [of Massa]. An oracle that his mother taught him" (31:1 = chaps. 1—9). The first of these (25:1) points to a social group of royal scribes who were active as the men of Hezekiah, king of Judah (reign 715–687 B.C.E.). This superscription intimates that these royal scribes were involved in the collecting, editing, copying, and transmission of sayings. If these scribes were indeed a part of the royal administration or at least enjoyed royal patronage, it may be they or their superiors were actively involved in important diplomatic efforts during this critical period in history, when Judah struggled to survive the tyranny of the Assyrian Empire (see Isa. 5:18–25; 29:14–16; 30:1–5; 37:14; and 39:1). The craft and profession of the royal scribe may have been transmitted within hereditary families. This seems true of the family of Shaphan, the "secretary" of Josiah (2 Kings 22:3–14; 2 Chron. 34:8–20), whose descendants were also important figures in the royal government (Ahikam, his son, 2 Kings 22:12, 14; Jer. 26:24; and Ahikam's son, thus Shaphan's grandson Gedaliah, the ill-starred governor of Judah who was assassinated by revolutionaries, Jer. 39:14 and 40:5). Two other sons of Shaphan, Elasah (Jer. 29:3) and Gemariah (Jer. 36:10–12), were also politically prominent.

The school

It is likely that the setting for much of the wisdom tradition, including Proverbs, was a school where young males and females would have been educated for scribal, administrative, teaching, and governmental careers. Ben Sira, a famous sage and teacher who resided in Jerusalem in the early second century B.C.E., issues his invitation to the uneducated to come and take up residence in his "house of instruction" (Sir. 51:23). More than likely Ben Sira operated a boarding school that was designed to educate Jewish youth for a variety of social roles and careers in Hellenistic Judah.

The existence of schools in the surrounding ancient Near Eastern cultures is well documented, though literary and archaeological evidence for royal and temple schools in Israel and Judah is surprisingly meager. Thus, the evidence for schools in Israelite and later Jewish society is largely inferential. Beginning with the monarchy, some formal education likely took place within royal schools, established to instruct children of elite and powerful families to assume powerful positions and other youth to become officials and scribes to administer the kingdom. This may explain what may have been the patronage of wisdom by Solomon (see 1 Kings 3—10) and the association of his name with sapiential literature for many centuries (e.g., the Wisdom of Solomon, a Greek text composed in Alexandria of Egypt and written in the first century B.C.E.). At least some of the wisdom tradition, including several of the collections of Proverbs, may have originated within royal schools, where the tradition would have provided youth instruction for ethical behavior, character formation, proper decorum for their social roles, and the artistic use of language (reading, writing, and oratory). Thus Proverbs may have served as a school manual for the teaching of ethics and language skills to an elite, educated class in

21

Israelite and later in Jewish society. This group would have included royalty and powerful families throughout the administrative districts and tribes of the kingdom. While not all the sages were counselors and royal and temple officials of substantial positions, they would have assisted such powerful and influential people in the carrying out of their responsibilities.

When Jerusalem was sacked by the Babylonians and the reign of the house of David came to an end in the early sixth century B.C.E., Israelite royal schools probably came under the oversight of governors appointed by foreign rulers in a succession of empires (Babylonian, Persian, Greek, and finally Roman). Colonial governments in Judah also would have required educated officials to carry out administrative functions, and former royal schools, or at least the remnants that had survived through the exile, most likely would have filled this need. In addition, with the separation of the priesthood from the control of the house of David, schools may have enjoyed the patronage of the Jerusalem priesthood, especially in producing temple scribes needed to create and edit literary texts (e.g., the Torah), maintain records and archives, and carry out the substantial economic activities of tithes, gifts, and sacrifices (cf. Ben Sira's substantial concern with cultic activities and devotion to the priesthood). These priestly or temple schools explain the close connection between the priesthood and the sages and scribes of the postexilic period. Indeed, the emphasis on the primacy of the Torah (Pentateuch) in religious teaching and as the basis for the faithful life during the Persian period also enters the wisdom tradition in the postexilic period, as noted by the presence of Torah psalms (1, 19b, 119), Sirach, and Bar. 3:9—4:4. Indeed, wisdom and Torah are at times equated. Schools under the patronage of the priesthood during this period would be one explanation for the centrality of the Torah in sapiential teaching. Another would be the growing influence of the Zadokite priesthood and their legitimization in the legal traditions. A third reason would be the overall prominence of the Torah in the postexilic Jewish community as Judaism moved toward becoming a religion of the Torah.

Educational institutions, especially among prominent Jewish communities in the Diaspora, also shaped their own unique literary traditions that included wisdom texts, most notably the first-century B.C.E. book the Wisdom of Solomon, likely written in Alexandria by an unknown Jewish sage who was strongly influenced by popular versions of Hellenistic moral philosophy. Some sectarian movements that conflicted with the colonial powers of temple priests and foreign appointed governors formed their own schools and literary traditions that included some wisdom texts. The most conspicuous of these sectarian communities was the Dead Sea community of Qumran, which likely was the center for the sect of the Essenes. With the appearance of the synagogues at least as early as the first century B.C.E., the learned teacher or rabbi carried on in local communities the scholarly and scribal tradition of Pharisaic Judaism. The synagogue and its house of study became the place where moral instruction, including the use of wisdom texts such as Proverbs, would have been redirected to the general Jewish populace. Rabbis eventually began to take the place of scribes. The synagogue and the house of study were largely responsible for the democratization of wisdom, along with other Jewish religious traditions. Learning and the inculcation of sapiential virtues no longer were the mainstays of an exclusive class ethic for royalty, nobility, educated priests, and scribes but became accessible once more to Jewish households, including even their marginal members.

The Sage

The social identities and functions of the sages have long puzzled modern scholars. The answers are not readily apparent, though the following portraits may be drawn and supported in part from the evidence of biblical and comparative ancient Near Eastern texts.

The sage as parent

The village society of ancient Israel, based on the ideal of kinship, provided one setting in which familial wisdom was cultivated and transmitted (see Perdue et al., *Families in Ancient Israel*). In this largely nonliterate setting that did not have formal schools or professional teachers, oral tradition, transmitted from parents to children, was the means by which the customs, laws, values, and religious teachings of the households, clans, and tribes were passed along. Fathers, and in particular the senior male or head of the household, taught boys and young men the body of knowledge and skills required for farming and tending sheep, goats, and small cattle, while the senior female and other mothers instructed girls and young women in parenting, food preparation and preservation, cultivating gardens, and producing textiles.

In the family household, education went beyond the pragmatic necessities of labor to include social customs, moral values, and religious beliefs and rituals. These teachings shaped a social world for a community that enabled it to sustain its identity, spirit, and bondedness. Both senior parents, who exercised authority and discipline (cf. Prov. 13:24; 19:18; 23:13–14; 29:15, 17), taught familial, clan, and

23

tribal traditions, laws, and customs to their own children and presumably to others who lived in the household (Deut. 6:7; 11:19; 32:46–47), as well as moral behavior and religion (Exod. 12:26–27; 13:14–16; Deut. 4:9; 6:7, 20–25; Josh. 4:6–7, 21–23; Prov. 1:8; 6:20; 30:17; 31:1; cf. Prov. 10:1; 15:20; 20:20; 23:22, 25; 28:24; 30:11, 17). Some male heads of households were selected to be clan and tribal elders who made legal, economic, and religious decisions affecting the associations of extended families (Deut. 21:1–9; 25:5–10; cf. Prov. 31:23). How much of this folk wisdom of households and clans was taken into the literary traditions of wisdom is impossible to say. Some of the sayings and teachings of wisdom refer to the household and agricultural life of villages and towns, and the familial titles of teachers (fathers and mothers) and students (sons and children) on occasion reflect the family household. None of this means that any of the sayings and teachings of Proverbs necessarily originated in the teachings of households and clans, but it is a likely possibility that many did. In any event, at least this part of Israelite social life is the object of significant sapiential reflection and teaching (see Perdue et al., *Families in Ancient Israel,* 172–73).

The sage as scribe

Another understanding of the sage is that of a scribe, whose primary skills were reading, writing, and oratory. But scribes could be more than mere accountants and copyists. Our best portrait of the scribe or scribes comes from Ben Sira in the early second century B.C.E. (Sir. 38:34—39:11), though it must be acknowledged that this depiction is quite late. Indeed, Ben Sira's description of the sage here and elsewhere in his book may be a self-portrait, though the picture conforms nicely with the ideal wise person found even in the older portions of the book of Proverbs. The sage is a counselor to kings and other great people (Sir. 39:4; cf. Prov. 14:35 and 25:15), a person of piety (Sir. 18:27 and 39:5; cf. Prov. 14:2 and 15:29, 33), a keeper of secrets (Sir. 8:19; 9:18; cf. Prov. 10:19 and 12:23), a person who avoids adultery and controls other appetites (Sir. 31:12–21; cf. Prov. 20:25–26; 23:26–28; and Sir. 42:12–14), and one who is kind and charitable (Sir. 4:1–10 and 29:81–83; cf. Prov. 11:17, 24–25).

The role of the sage as a wise counselor to kings and other people of power is prominently displayed in the Old Testament (Prov. 11:14; 15:22; 24:6; 25:15; Isa. 19:11–12). The task of the counselor was to formulate well-laid plans that would enable rulers to succeed in their efforts and others to experience life and well-being (Deut. 32:28–29; Isa. 16:3 and 41:28; and see Ahithophel in 2 Sam. 16:20 and Hushai in

24

2 Sam. 17:6–14). Counselors renowned for their wisdom also included women, for example, the wise woman of Tekoa (2 Samuel 14) and the wise woman of Abel Beth-maacah (2 Samuel 20).

Wisdom in Ben Sira as well as in Proverbs involves not only ethics and skilled rhetoric but also cultivating the social graces, polite conversation, comportment in the presence of the great and powerful as well as with the opposite sex, and even proper table manners. These interests, along with Ben Sira's emphasis on the need for leisure to have the opportunity to become a wise scribe, the fact that he owned land (Sir. 7:3, 15, 22) and slaves (Sir. 7:20–21; 33:25–33; 42:5), and, like his forebears, his valuing of wealth (Sir. 14:3–19; 30:21–25), suggest that at least the most prominent scribes belonged to the upper socioeconomic class.

Added to these features is the emphasis that Ben Sira places on the sage's reverence for and study of the Torah, which he equates with divine wisdom (Sir. 24:23; 39:1; cf. Sir. 6:37; 19:24; 23:27; and 29:11–13). This piety of the sage that incorporates the study of and obedience to the commandments of the Torah compares to the so-called Torah psalms (Pss. 1, 19b, and 119), which were perhaps the literary creations of the sages along with the other so-called wisdom psalms. One should note, however, that in Ben Sira the sage is also one who travels in foreign countries (39:4; cf. Sir. 31:1–31; 32:1–13), perhaps in the role of a diplomat or emissary, and is open to contact and conversation with foreigners. Ben Sira's portrayal of the sage suggests a knowledge of and receptivity to foreign cultures that would prohibit a strict adherence to the dietary laws of the Torah. This receptiveness even extended to his occasional use of Greek literary genres and ideas. This openness to the insights of other cultures was indigenous to the wisdom tradition from very early times (1 Kings 4:29–34 = Heb. 5:9–14), and it implies that the sages possessed a knowledge of other ancient Near Eastern and later Hellenistic and Latin literatures, values, ideas, politics, and, of course, languages.

The sage in Ben Sira is also a jurist who functions at times as a lawyer and at other times as a judge involved in the interpretation and administration of secular, Israelite law (38:34; cf. 10:1–5). It is clear that during the period of the reign of the house of David (1000–586 B.C.E.) a royal judiciary developed, charged with administering and overseeing the law of the state. Judges and lawyers would have transmitted the growing corpora of laws and precedents that accrued over the centuries. This legal tradition of the royal state would have existed alongside the religious legal corpus associated with the temple and its priesthood. After the fall of the monarchy in the early sixth century

25

B.C.E., this royal tradition largely disappeared, though fragments of it found their way into the Hebrew canon.

The role of some sages as lawyers would explain why at points the content of the wisdom tradition compares to that of the Israelite legal tradition (e.g., the prohibition against moving the boundary stone, Deut. 19:14; Prov. 22:28; 23:10) and why there is some similarity in form between the sapiential admonition and case law. Apodictic law (imperatives and prohibitions) is frequently found in Israelite legal corpora and formally and, occasionally, thematically compares to the admonition in wisdom literature. Case law in Israelite legal codes combines an imperative or prohibition with a general situation and either a result or motive clause that justifies the authenticity and appropriateness of the ordinance in much the same way that admonitions and prohibitions are rationalized in wisdom literature. Some scholars have even argued that the so-called law codes in the Torah are really not meant to be law codes at all but rather were didactic teachings that sought to educate Israelites in moral behavior. While much of the Torah may consist of the traditions and laws of the priests (Jer. 18:18), the "laws" in Deuteronomy, at least, may have been written and interpreted by the same wise scribes who also helped to put together the sapiential collections of wisdom (Deut. 4:5–8; Jer. 2:8; 8:8–9).

Ben Sira notes that the sage is a scribe who not only engages in the study of the Torah but also seeks out the wisdom of the past, studies the prophetic tradition, preserves the speeches of notable people, and interprets the meanings of sayings and parables (39:1–3). These remarks indicate that the sage was involved in the collection, redaction, and transmission of Israelite literature, including not only wisdom materials but other types of literature as well. One of the clearest examples of the scribal and redactional activity of the sages is found in the epilogue to Qoheleth. This sage, in addition to teaching the people knowledge, also weighed, studied, and arranged proverbs with great care (Eccl. 12:9). A purpose of the collection of the sayings is to motivate people to wise action and to provide stability and continuity in human behavior (Eccl. 12:11). Much of wisdom literature, therefore, likely reflects the professional ethics of sages.

The sage as teacher

It is clear that Ben Sira regards himself as a teacher, and the frequency of didactic instructions in his "book" clearly underscores this social role of the sages. In Sir. 51:23–30, he issues an invitation to the untaught to lodge in his school and to receive instruction (cf. 39:8). This role of the teacher is perhaps the most common one for the sages of Israel and early Judaism. In addition to the parents teaching their

26

children, sages most likely taught students moral instruction in various schools. While these schools may well have included a curriculum that would have educated students in various professions, ranging from an official to a scribe to a lawyer, part of what was transmitted was moral instruction and proper social decorum that grew into what became the wisdom books.

The Language and Rhetoric of Wisdom Literature

The sages not only emphasized the importance of proper and elegant speech; their texts also provided eloquent testimony to their skill in the writing of polished and captivating language. Together, the content of what the sages taught and observed and the artistry of their language, both spoken and written, shaped a world of beauty, order, and delight into which they entered, took up residence, lived, and invited others to join them. Through their imagination they shaped a world of beauty and delight and a social reality that embraced virtue and both expected and valued proper decorum.

The sages cast their teachings in a variety of literary genres, ranging from the proverb to the wisdom poem. Most of their speech forms, however, were placed under the general term *māšāl* (1 Sam. 10:12; 24:14; Prov. 1:6; 26:7, 9), while the plural of this word, *měšālîm*, is the name of an edited collection of wisdom materials (Prov. 1:1; 10:1; 25:1). The *māšāl* included "sayings" (1 Sam. 10:12; 24:14; Ezek. 12:22–23; 18:2–3), wisdom psalms (Pss. 49:4 = Heb. 49:5; 78:2), sapiential poems (e.g., Isa. 14:4–10), and even parables (Ezek. 17:2; 21:5; 24:3). The verbal form of the noun *māšāl* has several meanings: "to rule" (*qal*, Prov. 16:32; 17:2; 19:10; 22:7), "to be like" (*niphal*, Isa. 14:10; Pss. 28:1; 143:7), or "to compare or liken" (*hiphil*, Isa. 46:5). The first meaning corresponds to the goal of the sages to master life, that is, to control the various situations in which they find themselves, to anticipate possibilities and contingencies, to know the proper time to act, and to respond in appropriate ways that will culminate in success and well-being. The second and third meanings of the verbal form of *māšāl* issue from the sages' understanding of an order underlying and integrating the world and what it contains. They sought to find associations and connections between various entities in order to better understand the nature of reality and the place each thing had in the larger scheme.

Sayings

Included among the wisdom sayings are the proverb, the comparison, the beatitude, the better saying, and the numerical saying. Each of these sayings was superbly crafted into a minute aesthetic that gave form and elegance to the content of what was taught or observed.

The most frequently encountered *māšāl* is the literary proverb, which usually consists of two parallel lines of poetry. These lines may be synonymous, that is, the second line parallels, though does not simply restate, the thought of the first; instead, the second line extends or develops the first line in some fashion (e.g., Prov. 21:12; 22:7, 8, 14). Antithetical proverbs, in which the second line contrasts with the first, include Prov. 10:4, 5, 12; 14:3, 5, 6, 8, 9; and 21:31. In synthetic proverbs, the second line continues to develop the thought expressed in the first line and does not really parallel it in literary technique or in content (Prov. 15:3; 21:6, 7, 21, 22, 25). Normally, the proverb is presented in the indicative mood, both stative and active, which presents what is considered to be a state or action regarded as authentic and true and confirmed by common experience (e.g., Prov 15:1, 2; 20:1, 3, 4, 8). This confidence in the authenticity of what is stated also includes the religious and ethical sphere (10:6, 9, 27–30; 11:11, 20, 25, 28; 13:25; 14:1; 15:25, 33).

Another type of *māšāl* is the comparative saying, which points to two subjects, often dissimilar at first appearance, that are said to resemble each other in some way (Prov. 10:26; 11:22; 19:12; 20:2; 25:3, 13, 14; 26:7–11). This type of saying reflects the search of the wise for a common underlying structure or order that regulates and provides continuity for the various components of reality. One specific kind of comparative saying applies the principle "If this, then how much more or less this" (see Prov. 15:11).

Four other kinds of sayings are present in Proverbs and in the other wisdom books. The better saying is a *māšāl* that evaluates two things, concluding that one is of more worth or value than the other or at least is to be preferred over the other (e.g., Prov. 15:16, 17; 16:8; 19:1, 22; 21:9, 19). Beatitudes, or happy sayings, normally begin with the predicate adjective *'ašrê* (happy), which points to a state of well-being and contentment. This type of saying pronounces people "happy" who are wise and righteous or who, having demonstrated some actualization of sapiential virtue, have entered a state of well-being and joy (Prov. 8:32, 34; 4:21; 16:20; 29:18). Numerical sayings begin with a title line and then provide a list of two or more things that hold some feature or features in common with the beginning (Prov. 30:15–16, 18–19, 21–23, 24–28, 29–31). Finally, the abomination saying echoes priestly language that points to perverse actions of ritual impurity as well as ethical corruption (Lev. 18:22, 26, 27, 29; Deut. 25:16). Borrowing this language from the priests, the sages point to unethical actions that are detested by Yahweh and thus are sure to corrupt not only the perpetrator but also the larger community. These

28

detestable persons and the terrible actions they perform are sure to fail due to Yahweh's abhorrence and rejection of them. Abominable actions are harmful to the community and threaten both its cohesion and its viability. At the same time, actions that are abhorrent to Yahweh are contrasted with those that Yahweh approves, indicating that righteous deeds may offset the destructive and defiling power of perverse wickedness (Prov. 3:32; 6:16; 8:7; 11:1, 20; 12:22; 13:10; 15:8, 26; 16:5, 12; 17:15; 20:10, 23; 21:27; 24:9; 28:9; and 29:27).

Questions and riddles

The question and the riddle are also succinct, sometimes related wisdom forms. Often the question is rhetorical or perhaps even catechetical, expecting an obvious or known answer (Prov. 20:9, 24; 22:27). Some interrogatives, however, pose "impossible questions," that is, questions that have no answers, or at least no ready answer (cf. the questions of Yahweh addressed to Job in Job 38—41). Related to the impossible question is the riddle (*ḥîdâ* "dark or hard saying"), which appears at one time to have been a type of wisdom saying used by the sages (Ps. 49:4 = Heb. 49:5; Prov. 1:6; and 1 Kings 10:1 = 2 Chron. 9:1), though none is found in their literature. The only one that has survived in the Old Testament is proposed by the mischievous Samson (Judg. 14:12–18; see Num. 12:8; 1 Kings 10:1–3; Ps. 49:4 = Heb. 49:5). Unlike the proverb that strives for clarity about reality based on human experience, the riddle is intentionally obscure, even paradoxical in its intent. The goal, at least at first, is not clarity but rather puzzlement. This type of saying describes in a concealed manner a feature or characteristic of a topic, though one or more clues are present. The goal is to guess what is being described. The sage was then to use his or her knowledge to guess the answer (see 1 Kings 10:1–3).

The instruction

In addition to the saying in its various literary manifestations, the second major wisdom genre is the "teaching" or "instruction" (*mûsār* and *tôrâ*; see Prov. 1:3; 8:10, 33; 24:32). The *mûsār* (= *tôrâ*) articulates proper behavior for the moral life within the following literary structure:

1. Introduction: Using the second person, the teacher (father and/or mother) addresses the student(s) (son, children) and exhorts him/them to listen to his or her instruction.
2. The Teaching Proper: In the second person, the teacher directs to students a list of admonitions (imperatives) and

29

prohibitions that are normally coupled with one or more clauses (result, motive, conditional, purpose, and causal) and exhorts the students to act according to particular sapiential values, to become virtuous, or to avoid vices, foolishness, or evil deeds and people.

3. The Conclusion: Some instructions conclude with a characterization of the results of wise or foolish behavior, with a saying that summarizes the teaching, or with an inclusion that points back to the beginning. The conclusion is often in the third person.

Even a quick glance allows one to notice that the book of Proverbs contains numerous instructions (e.g., 1:8–19; 2:1–22; 3:1–12, 21–35).

The teaching proper, found after the introduction, contains two related forms: the admonition and the prohibition. Admonitions exhort or seek to persuade, rather than to command, the hearer to act wisely according to a sapiential virtue and to incorporate it in their character (Prov. 4:23–26; 5:1; 8:10). Prohibitions are admonitions plus a negative ("no," "not") that exhort or attempt to persuade the hearer to avoid foolish or evil behavior or people (Prov. 3:28–31). Although admonitions and prohibitions were considered to possess an intrinsic authority, they are not direct commands as are apodictic laws that do not need reasons or justifications. The admonition and prohibition may be coupled with one or more clauses (result, motive, conditional, purpose, and causal). A motive clause states the reasons or incentives for doing or for avoiding something, while the result clause points to the consequence or consequences of behavior (see Prov. 3:3–12). A conditional clause sets forth a situation in which an action or speech is appropriate or not appropriate, while a purpose clause establishes the reason or reasons wise behavior or speech is to be practiced. A causal clause sets forth a circumstance or set of circumstances that precipitate a course of action or speech. On occasion, an admonition or prohibition occurs independently within the collection of sayings and not as a part of a larger instruction.

The didactic narrative

Sages composed stories that created narrative worlds in which readers and hearers were invited to take up residence and dwell. The narrator normally assumes the stance of a third person, omniscient storyteller, who knows even the secret thoughts of the story's characters, including the mind and activity of God. The main character is the protagonist who embodies a sapiential virtue and thus is a sage or, through the unfolding of the plot, becomes one. After negotiating successfully a series of tests and even overcoming an antagonist who challenges the validity of this virtue and behavior based on it, the hero is vindicated and the opponent is vanquished. Though no didactic narratives have been preserved in the book of Proverbs, two examples elsewhere in the Bible are the prologue and epilogue of Job (Job 1—2; 42:7–17), as well as, perhaps, the Joseph Story in Genesis 37—50 (von Rad, "Joseph Narrative," 292–300) and the Succession Narrative in 2 Samuel 9—20; 1 Kings 1—2.

The book of Proverbs contains another type of narrative where, in the first person, the storyteller, a sage, relates an observation in a brief story form and then draws a conclusion that points to an insight into the nature of reality and wise human behavior. In Prov. 7:6–27, the sage (or perhaps Woman Wisdom herself) tells of observing a simpleton seduced and brought to destruction by Woman Folly, who, as the "strange woman," is dressed in the guise of a harlot. At the conclusion of the drama, the sage admonishes his or her students to avoid the embrace and charms of this seductress, for folly leads surely to death. Other examples of sapiential first person narratives include Ps. 37:35–36 and the first part of the book of Qoheleth.

The sapiential poem

Among the literary repository of the sages were poems of various kinds, some of which imitated features of the psalms used in worship (Psalms 1, 19, 34, 37, 49, 73, 111, 112, 119, 127, and 128). These poems are artistically crafted into several strophes that are tied together by the repetition of images, words, and motifs. Running through the poem is a central theme that articulates one or more sapiential virtues. Among the best-known sapiential poems are those that speak of Woman Wisdom as a teacher or goddess who dispenses life to those who accept her invitation to follow her teachings (Prov. 1:20–33; 8:1–31; 9:1–6; Job 28; and Sirach 24).

The dialogue

Dialogues or debates also are found among the literary forms of sapiential discourse, though not in the collections present in the book of Proverbs, with the possible exception of the "Sayings of Agur" and his traditional respondent (Prov. 30:1–6). The best-known example occurs in the book of Job, where Job and three sages debate the issues of the righteous sufferer and the justice of God.

The collection

An important genre of wisdom literature is the collection, which brings together in a literary unit various types of sapiential language (see Eccl. 12:11). Eight separate collections of different lengths comprise the book of Proverbs. All but the last one are introduced by a title or superscription:

1:1. "The proverbs of Solomon son of David, king of Israel" (1—9 as well as the entire book)
10:1. "The proverbs of Solomon" (10:1—22:16)
22:17. "The words of the wise" (22:17—24:22)
24:23. "These also are sayings of the wise" (24:23–34)
25:1. "These are other proverbs of Solomon that the officials of King Hezekiah of Judah copied" (25—29)
30:1. "The words of Agur son of Jakeh [of Massa]" (30)
31:1. "The words of King Lemuel [of Massa]. An oracle that his mother taught him" (31:1–9)
31:10–31. No title. A poem in which the subject is the "woman of worth" (31:10–31).

Collections not only contain subunits of sayings or other literary forms but also provide evidence of artistic crafting and at times demonstrable thematic coherence.

Rhetoric

The largely poetic genres of wisdom literature reveal a high level of artistic sophistication and elegance. The literary creation of the sage, whether a saying or a didactic poem, engages the audience not only by the appeal to common experience and reason but also by the entrancing allure of beauty. Indeed, the sage uses the art of well-crafted and polished language to render meaning. Artistry and content are inseparable in the sapiential genres.

Artistic features that are common to sapiential literature include repetition, especially, but also parallelism of poetic lines, the fashioning of couplets for most succinct sayings, and the use of strophes (self-contained units of two or more lines that express a common theme). The larger structures of poems on occasion are arranged in various patterns, including acrostics and chiasms. In addition to ordinary repetition of words, wisdom poetry contains anaphora (the repetition of an initial word or words of several clauses, lines, or strophes); refrains (repeated words or phrases at the end of strophes or other subunits);

interweaving words or phrases (*mots crochets*) that blend together the entire unit or major subunit; and inclusions (the repetition of the opening word[s] or image[s] at the close of the unit, thus marking the unit's literary boundaries). Other features remind us that wisdom poetry was meant to be heard as well as read. Alliteration, the correspondence of sounds at the beginning of words, is often present, as is assonance, the correspondence of the sounds of accented syllables.

The highly artistic nature of wisdom poetry demonstrates that the various genres, even the brief poetic saying, are meant to be slowly savored rather than quickly devoured. The literary and phonetic qualities of a saying or poem are designed not only to provoke the imagination and to move the audience to reflection on the content of what is written or said but also to understand that truth and virtue include both reason and insight as well as beauty and symmetry. Content and elegance of form in even a brief saying craft a minute aesthetic of meaning to be understood, prized, embodied in character, and activated in the moral life.

The Imagination of the Wise

The refined rhetoric of the sages points to their attempt to construe imaginatively the nature of reality and the moral character of sapiential life. This is suggested by Ben Sira's invitation to the simple to take up residence in his "house of instruction" (51:23), both a reference to a wisdom school and a metaphor for a world of human dwelling created and inhabited by means of sapiential imagination.

Definition of imagination

Humans have the capacity to form images in the mind that derive from sense perception. The most elementary form of the act of human imagination is to fill in the fragmentary data of the senses. Imagination, based on experience as well as expectation grounded in experience, is needed to complete the unfinished picture of what the senses perceive: the hearing of thunder leads to the assumption of impending rain; the viewing of the external facade of a house suggests the internal presence of rooms and furniture; and the smell of smoke indicates the presence of fire.

Sapiential imagination moves beyond this basic act by observing inanimate objects, such as trees, stones, and rivers; animate objects, such as ants, birds, and serpents; and social groups, such as families, kings, and teachers, to note the typical and recurring patterns of appearance, nature, behavior, and action. Through these observations the sages searched to discover what was typical, recurrent, and consistent

33

in order to develop a pattern of expectations concerning the nature and character of the many phenomena that were present in their environment. Different objects of study were expected to be consistent and predictable. The objective of these observations by the sages, however, was not primarily to make scientific or social-scientific classifications of type, genus, and species. Rather, the sages as moral teachers drew on these observations and on their own common experiences in order to set forth ethical teachings that encapsulated proper ways of being and doing in concert with the order of creation and the divine paradigm for society. In their view, there was an underlying order to reality, an order that was characterized by consistency, recurrence, correspondence, and patterns. What is more, they viewed this order as having a moral quality. Thus the order that permeated creation, society, and human character was named "justice" (*mišpāṭ*) or "righteousness" (*ṣĕdāqâ*). All things, including humans and nonhuman creatures, existed within a reality of order in which its constituent parts somehow related to one another in ways that were life-sustaining. God the Sage was the creator who established this just order at creation and continued to maintain its functioning through life-enhancing blessing and punishing judgment.

From these observations of the world and what it contained, the sages used their imagination to liken and to differentiate various things that, in contemporary Western thinking, might not intimate a reasonable basis for comparison or contrast. Israelite and Jewish sages, however, saw an underlying order or common structure to the whole of reality and sought to incorporate these into sayings that led to life. Thus very different things were scrutinized in order to discover some underlying common features. Different objects of observation, having no seemingly obvious connection, were examined to find an intrinsic order or pattern. Thus, in the numerical sayings in Proverbs 30, the way of a man with a woman is compared to the wonderment and mystery of the movement of the flight of an eagle, the crawling of a serpent, and the passage of a ship (vv. 18–19), while Sheol, the barren womb, the dry earth, and fire share the same characteristic of insatiability (vv. 15b–16).

Sapiential imagination moves beyond mere perception and observation to the articulation of the apprehension of reality on a much grander scale, that is, to the shaping of a worldview that is theologically coherent, aesthetically attractive, and morally compelling in character. The sage asks, "What does this image mean for understanding God, the world, and human behavior?" And the answer is given not through concrete definition but rather through the rational process of deduction, analogy, and inference; through imaginative enactment that conceives and projects; through the entrancing attraction of the beauty of sight, sound, and speech; and through the admission of contingencies and mystery. Sapiential imagination moves from the arrangement and categorization of images, to the description of their nature and character, to extrapolation in order to understand the nature of creation, society, the moral life, and God, and to the construction of a comprehensive worldview that makes sense of reality. Sages derived instruction for human living and orientation to the world of creation and of faith from such simple observations as the behavior of the ant (Prov. 6:6–11) and the flight of an eagle (Prov. 30:19). They observed orders of life and of nature from which they construed insight not only for the awareness of how creation and its creatures operated but also for how they might give direction to wise discourse and righteous behavior of human beings (e.g., Isa. 28:23–29).

The sages concluded that human beings are drawn as much by the attraction of engaging images or striking metaphors as they are by profound ideas. It is true that images and metaphors stand at the center of sapiential thinking and that the discourse of the sages embodies and articulates the meaning of images and metaphors. Indeed, the content of the image is set forth and explored. But the discourse provides not straightforward definition but rather an aesthetically nuanced set of rhetorical devices (e.g., similarity of sounds, antithesis, comparison) that awaken in the hearer a receptivity to teaching through the engagement of both content and beauty.

Features of sapiential imagination

The imagination of the wise involves several major features that, taken together, point to a way of knowing that was unique in ancient Israel and early Judaism.

Tradition and memory.

The teachings of the wise drew on the traditions of their forebears and those of ancient Near Eastern sages that were passed down for centuries (Job 15:17–19). What one finds in Israelite wisdom is a confluence of both the sapiential teachings from the royal court, which cultivated international learning, and the folk tradition that was indigenous to the households, clans, and tribes of rural villages and towns. Through the corporate memory of the circles of sages, these traditions merged and were transmitted through successive generations to construct worlds of faith and life for future generations.

Engagement and reformulation of tradition.

Israelite and Jewish sages, however, did not rest content with simply transmitting the teachings of their ancestors. Rather, they entered the world of these traditions, not merely to live them out in a new time and perhaps a different place but also to engage critically their affirmations through reasoned analysis and present experience. The teachings of old wisdom were critically examined with a view to either affirming or reshaping their insights for a new and changing world.

Envisioning of the world.

The sages sought through their teachings to construct a view of the world that made sense, corresponded to their experience, was true to a directive yet pliant tradition, called for prudent and righteous human participation, and rewarded with well-being those who lived in conformity with the dictates of wisdom. This world of the sages, which encompassed both creation and society, was beautiful and good, but it was not fully realized. Through wise behavior and decorous language the sages lived this world into being. There were at times, however, a dimension of the tragic and the presence of inexplicable incongruity that defied understanding and eventually led in periods of crisis either to the outcry of pain and protest in the book of Job or to the subdued pessimism and resignation of Qoheleth.

Positing God at the center.

The God of the sages of Proverbs is Yahweh, whom they believed to be the one, universal God who created the world and providentially sustained all life. Thus Proverbs, and all other Israelite and Jewish wisdom literature, is strongly monotheistic and places God as creator and divine providence at the center of reality. Yahweh is assumed by the sages of Proverbs to be omnipotent and omniscient.

For the sages, "the fear of Yahweh [God] is the beginning of wisdom." The word *beginning* (*rē'šît*) means that "fear of Yahweh," that is, belief in and reverence before the God who created and continues to sustain the world, is the necessary precondition of wisdom and its human quest. *Rē'šît* also means the "foundation" of the sapiential tradition, indicating that the teachings of the sages are based on the foundation of religious piety and devotion to the Creator and God of wisdom. The wisdom tradition, even in its earliest stage, is not a humanistic or secular enterprise by which intelligent people seek to come to a knowledge of the world. The fear of Yahweh in Proverbs refers not to terror but rather to wonderment before the all-wise Creator who originated and continued to maintain the orders of existence.

God stands at the center of the teachings of the sages. This means that God provides the wise their insight and ability to understand and know the world but also authenticates the validity of what is taught. The God of the sages is primarily the God of the present, who blesses human life receptive to and guided by the divine gift of wisdom while punishing the wicked and foolish who do not live in concert with the just order of creation and society. This God is the creator and sustainer of the world and human society who actively maintains the righteous order of life by rewarding the wise and just and, at the same time, by bringing into judgment and punishing those who through their foolishness and evil undermine justice in the cosmos and society. For the sages, God is not personally present in the world, not even in the sacred sphere of the temple in Jerusalem. Rather, God is transcendent, existing beyond time and space. Eventually, it was the personification of divine wisdom, according to the sages, that came to embody and represent God's active presence in the world.

The revelation of God in Proverbs is like a winding river with various tributaries, coursing its way through the passage of many centuries. The primary mode of revelation through these many years, at least for the sages, was creation. Through innate reason and the powers of trained observation common to all peoples, the sages believed they could come to an understanding of the character and activity of God through the nature and operation of creation. Indeed, the knowledge of creation was not different from the knowledge of God. From the orders of life that were seen by the astute observer, the life creating and sustaining powers of a caring God could be inferred. This may have been the earliest view of divine revelation that the sages developed (von Rad, *Wisdom in Israel,* 144–76). While this view continued to find its way into the thinking of later generations of wise men and wise women, some later sages eventually came to think that God gave divine wisdom to the "God-fearers," meaning that only by being such could one come to an understanding of the Creator and other divine mysteries (see Ben Sira and the author of the Wisdom of Solomon). Others described revelation as a kind of intellectual eros and metaphorically depicted wisdom as the incarnation of divine insight who, like a beautiful and intelligent woman teacher, called the simple to embrace her, to learn from her the pathways to life, and to come to a knowledge of the Creator. Finally, some of the sages reached the more pessimistic conclusion that their experiences and observations

37

did not always correlate with sapiential teachings. These are the ones who spoke of the mystery of the hidden God, who could not be known but certainly was to be feared (e.g., Qoheleth).

For the sages, it was important to affirm both the freedom and the mystery of God. Retribution was not viewed as an automatic system that forces God to act in predetermined ways. Nor was it a teaching that removed God's participation from the world of creation and the lives of its creatures. It is simply not the case that the sages of Proverbs believed that the relationship between human deed and its outcome was automatic, that is, that each thought or act contained a seed that germinated in good or ill fortune. The sages were quick to affirm divine and human freedom. Still, they argued that God oversees both social and individual human existence, judges human actions, and may determine as an act of divine freedom whether or not to bless or to punish. God shapes human life but, while possessing the power to do so, does not irrevocably determine its character and outcome. God forms life in the womb and guides those receptive to divine teaching throughout their lives, giving them the tools of the senses, perception, reason, and imagination to understand divine teachings and purposes. God forms creation, permeates it with order (righteousness, justice), and ensures its life sustaining orders. God is not, however, the God of the future who draws humans toward a final culmination in history or beyond history. Neither is God the Lord of Israel's history, a national story of a chosen people. The description of the God of the sages is not even specifically Israelite and Jewish in character. God is, however, the just deity who will act to punish the wicked and to bless the wise and righteous. Even so, the wisest of the sages cannot come to a complete knowledge of God, for God transcends the limits of human observation and the contours of human experience. Until Ben Sira in the second century B.C.E. brings the teachings of the sages within the arena of Israel's salvation history, the God of the sages is known only through the order of creation and the teachings of savants of the past and the present.

The sages did not depict God by numerous names that suggested something of a mythical reality of wonder and miracle, born of a polytheistic background. Rather, in addition to the name Yahweh, Israel's special name for God, the sages chose metaphors from human life to portray the God of wisdom. Metaphors for God in Proverbs range from a divine judge who sits in judgment of human behavior, to an artisan engaged in creating a work of beauty and delight, to a parent who conceives or impregnates and then gives birth to and raises a child, to a teacher who instructs students in the traditions of prudence and life.

Metaphors like these engage the imagination and allow divine nature and activity to be construed in ways that make sense of who and what God is and does.

Imagining human existence, character, and behavior.

The sages' moral instruction is an invitation to the unlearned to follow their teachings, to incorporate them in everyday existence, and to experience well-being in all phases of life. The sages commonly depicted life as a path or road along which humans traveled, though it eventually took two different directions, one of wisdom and the other of folly. Those who followed wisdom embarked on a path that led to success, longevity, and well-being, whereas fools and the wicked undertook a journey toward destruction (Prov. 2:20–22; 4:10–19). Without wisdom, humans were bound to lose their way and face an untimely end. With wisdom as the learned guide, however, the sages who feared God received the directions needed to reach the destination of a full and joyous life.

For the sages, no one was born wise. Certainly all humans, by nature, possessed the tools of reason and sense experience that, properly developed, could lead them to acquire something of the knowledge of God and the proper course for human life. Yet some sages came to argue that only those limited few who, fearing God, took up the invitation to learn from the teachers of Israel would receive true wisdom. This led to the view that wisdom was a divine gift, but it came only to those who were receptive to its offering. While all humans were capable of gaining wisdom, most did not accept either it or its discipline for life. In creating humanity, God provided people with the organs of perception (especially hearing and seeing) and of thinking (*lēb*, the "heart"; Prov. 13:16; 14:33; 15:14; and 17:24) that would enable them to pursue, discover, gain, and sustain wisdom. While the heart was the organ both for thinking and reflecting and for acquiring knowledge and insight, trust was to be placed in wisdom that originated with God, not the heart, for it could also be the receptacle of false certainty and foolish thinking (Prov. 28:26). Wisdom was a divine gift, provided to those who feared God and undertook the course of study leading to its refinement and continuing implementation in character and in life.

The sages of Proverbs typically divided humans into two primary, antithetical pairs. One is the contrast between the wise on the one hand and the foolish and the simple on the other. The second antithesis is drawn between the righteous and upright on the one hand and the wicked and scoffers on the other. The wise are guided by wisdom

39

and knowledge accessed by their hearts (= minds), whereas the fools pursue the folly of the intimations of their emotions (Prov. 13:16; 14:33; 15:14; 17:24). The wise master their passions and emotions, whereas the fools lose their self-control (Prov. 12:16; 21:24; 29:8, 11). The wise shun evil, for it leads to destruction, whereas the wicked possess an affinity for evil (Prov. 13:19; 14:16). The wise master speech that is used to create communal order and sustain social life, whereas the wicked engage in foolish talk that destroys community and brings death (Prov. 10:18–21; 12:19; 14:7). Most important, the sages of Proverbs teach that the behavior of people, both wise and foolish, has significant consequences for the human community in which they dwell. Through their actions and language, the wise are those who establish and sustain the peace of the community, contribute to its well-being, avoid conflict and effectuate reconciliation among its members, and are generous with their resources to those who are in need. The love of God is actualized through the love of the neighbor (2:5–8, 9–11; 3:1–12, 21–35; 14:21, 27, 31; 19:17; 22:9; 30:1–14). By contrast, the fools do not restrain themselves, either their emotions or their speech. Through their behavior and language they sow discord that disrupts and threatens the harmony and peace of the larger human community. The major difference between the wise and the foolish is that the former promote their own well-being and that of the community through their speech and actions, whereas the latter, while not necessarily those who are deficient in intelligence, lack restraint and do not realize that their senseless actions and witless language have dire consequences not only for themselves but also for the larger society.

The "unlearned" or the "simple" were invited by the sages to take up the quest for wisdom. The call to come and study wisdom is expressed on occasion by the metaphor of Woman Wisdom as a teacher (Prov. 1:20–33) or as a fertility goddess who sends out her maidens (Prov. 9:1–6). This likely reflects the invitation of teachers to potential students to come and pursue their course of study.

Another major antithesis is that of the righteous or upright and the wicked. The behavior and actions of the righteous and the upright that contrast with those of the wicked are described in such texts as Prov. 2:21–22; 12:5; and 29:7. The deeds and cogitations of the righteous create an order of well-being for the community as well as for themselves, whereas the activities and thoughts of the wicked undermine the social order and bring harm to both its members and themselves (Prov. 17:23; 21:7, 10, 15; 25:19). The righteous avoid harm and enable others to do so, whereas the wicked suffer its ill effects and damage others, including the upright (Prov. 13:17; 28:15; 29:10). The righteous use language as a creative force to sustain life, establish and maintain important relationships, and promote the common good, whereas the wicked misuse speech to harm others and themselves and to create discord (Prov. 10:21, 31–32 and 15:28). Yahweh acts on behalf of the righteous but does not respond to the needs of the wicked (Prov. 10:3 and 15:29). The righteous may expect to experience well-being and salvation, whereas the wicked enjoy only the destructive consequences of their own actions (Prov. 11:21; 13:15). What is interesting to observe in Proverbs is that the capital crimes of murder and theft are left to be addressed by the courts. Rather, the sages take up the variety of virtues and vices and their implementation in character leading to wise and righteous behavior and speech. And characteristics of language and action are addressed not only in terms of private morality but also in view of public consequence.

Human virtues comprising the character of the sage include especially wisdom and understanding (1:2), prudence (1:4), discretion (1:4), righteousness and justice (1:3), restraint in speech (13:3), control of passions (14:29), forbearance (18:14), avoidance of strife (20:3), and generosity of spirit (19:17). These virtues are embodied in the character and activity of the sage, who lives among a community of people. These virtues at work in the lives of the wise impact, in positive and life sustaining ways, not only on their own well-being but also on that of the entire community. By contrast, human vices to be avoided by the sage that characterize the life and behavior of the fool and the wicked include especially foolishness (26:1–12), wickedness (12:3), indolence (26:13–16), contentiousness (16:28), maliciousness (26:23–28), loss of control of the passions (14:16–17), pride (16:8), deception (26:27), violence (21:7), foolish and unrestrained talk (10:19), and callous disregard for the poor and lowly (21:10). The actions of the wicked and the foolish, who give unrestrained rein to anger and other passions, not only bring evil on themselves but also constitute a threat to the well-being of the community in which they are active.

Through the inculcation of wisdom a person's character was formed, allowing him or her to act in concert with the moral order of the world and human society. The behavior of the sages, which was guided by self-control and proper speech, allowed them entrance into the realm of divine blessing that led to well-being. While the accoutrements of wisdom included material blessings, for example, long life, riches, a family with many children, health, other, less tangible rewards were obtained: contentment, peace, joy, and respect. Beyond the well-being of the individual, just and wise behavior contributed to the life and blessing of social groups and the larger community and aided in constituting the righteous order of creation. The communal and cosmic character of a righteous order means, then, that wisdom in Proverbs does not represent individual utilitarianism or a crass eudaemonism limited to the well-being of one's own particular fortune.

Recognition of mystery and contingency.
The sages realized that there were major limitations to their wisdom and that there were many things beyond their capacity to know (von Rad, *Wisdom in Israel*, 97–110). These sages did not enter into the speculation of attempting to know the entirety of the mind of God or to predict the future that rested in God's hands. They were content to know what God revealed to them in their observation of the world and society and from their own experiences. This admission of the limits to wisdom's claims to know God in a complete fashion resides behind the theme of the "fear of Yahweh," that is, reverence toward and devotion to the Creator and Sustainer, who, while partially revealed in and through creation and the teachings of the sages, still remains to some degree hidden and mysterious.

The teachers of Israel and early Judaism also recognized the presence of contingencies that could not be anticipated, much less mastered. They attempted to come to an understanding of the "times," that is, periods in which righteous and wise acts would be successful or settings where even prudent behavior would court disaster if pursued. Yet this acknowledgment of mystery and the inevitability of unexpected contingencies did not absolve the sages from their sustained efforts to know, to understand, and to act righteously, wisely, and appropriately.

The Message of Proverbs for the Contemporary Church

The church's appropriation of the book of Proverbs

Throughout the history of Israel and the early history of both Judaism and the church, collections of sayings were assembled to provide guidance for the moral life. Several of these collections have been compiled in the book of Proverbs and have helped shape the ethical teachings of the synagogue and the church for many centuries. The modern interpreter standing within the context of the church begins by attempting to understand the words of the wise assembled in the book of Proverbs, both in terms of their expanding literary context (the collection, the book, the wisdom corpus, the Writings, and the Hebrew Bible, or Old Testament) and in regard to their placement in the early social and historical settings of ancient Israel and early Judaism. This

42

is a difficult task but one that needs to be undertaken before any serious talk of a modern re-presentation of the book's meaning for the contemporary world can authentically occur. The book of Proverbs—its collections, individual sayings, teachings, and poems—was not addressed to us. These were moral instructions addressed to ancient audiences long since gone. We must honor the past by attempting honestly to listen to its voices and by giving them a full hearing before engaging them with our own questions and responses that lead to modern articulations of meaning.

The church needs to claim, through critical interaction and assessment, a new re-presentation of the message of the moral life proclaimed by the voices of ancient sages, too often silenced by unforgivable neglect. Not all of Proverbs is to be reclaimed, but neither are all its teachings simply to be forgotten. To ignore the teachings of Israel's sages in Christian proclamation hinders the church's efforts to articulate ethical instructions that provide moral guidance for contemporary life. Kerygma must find its implementation in moral living. Without the order and direction of didache, kerygma simply becomes affirmation that, failing to take root in everyday life, becomes like the seed cast on stony ground, withering away and dying.

Even though Proverbs instructs its audiences in the moral life, it is invalid to construe the sayings and teachings of these ancient collections as divine fiats and ethical absolutes that somehow transcend both the constraints of time and space and critical interaction between text and interpretation. Wisdom represents an open, not a closed, system of understanding that invites engagement, testing, reformulation, even negation. The teachings of the ancient sages, to be appropriated by later audiences, must be tested in the arena of human experience to be authenticated. And these teachings must be examined with a view for their appropriateness for particular times and places. To follow at all the teachings of the sages means to develop their same critical, inquiring spirit, along with the virtues of prudence, insight, and knowledge that allow one through discipline to study and to embody the moral life of the sages. The teachings of the sages are not unbending rules for life or moral absolutes that remain unchallenged but rather bear the weight of authority only when assayed and affirmed by the experiences and reflections of succeeding generations. Transformation and even negation always remain possible alternatives.

The affirmation of the value of a full and integrated life   43

Proverbs teaches the church that existence is not a vale of tears, from which death and resurrection offer final redemption, but rather a value of incomparable worth, if lived wisely and well. What immediately strikes one in reading Proverbs is the emphasis placed on the value of present human life and the desire to experience the fullness of its bounty. Longevity, health, meaningful work, significant human relationships, family and descendants who would continue to carry the name and memory of the deceased into the future, love and charity, access to the goods necessary for survival and even wealth, and honor and respect are the important elements of a full life that is offered by wisdom. Present life is not a burden to be endured but rather a value to be affirmed and a joy to be celebrated. Proverbs presents no pessimistic view of human existence, no feeling that life is an oppressive bondage from which the escape of death offers a desirable release. This means, then, that those living in poverty and neglect become the responsibility of the larger community that is to extend its network of care to eliminate injustice and to provide the necessities that make life not only possible but also joyful.

Proverbs does not set forth a belief in an afterlife to be enjoyed by the deceased through resurrection or by an immortal soul that continues beyond death. The ideal goal is to live a long and satisfying life, one filled with the joy of meaningful work and loving human relationships, and then to die at a ripe old age surrounded by loved ones and offspring whose descendants will continue to honor one's memory.

The fundamental message, then, of Proverbs is the quest for a full and complete life that exists in harmony with God, one's human community, and the order of creation. Life is both the gift and consequence of wisdom that originates in the mind and character of God. A full life is the goal of the reflective sage who actualizes the teachings of the wise in his or her character through discipline and study.

The quest for wholeness in life through discipline

The sages of Proverbs taught their students to engage in the quest for the wholeness of life through discipline. Life is integrated and made whole when human character is formed by insight and imbued with virtue; when personal piety grounds the quest for wisdom in active faith; when knowledge is gained from study, reflection, and meditation; when language creates order and well-being for the community; and when behavior contributes to the common good. The church, in following wisdom's lead, is to teach its members to inculcate in themselves the piety and wonderment of human response to divine creation and redemption, to incorporate moral virtue in their characters, and to engage throughout life in the discipline of study and reflection that leads to the increase of ethical knowledge and its implementation in human behavior.

44

The discovery and constitution of justice

The sages of Israel teach the church that justice is the constitutive order of reality, not only in terms of regulating the social organization of human interaction and governing individual behavior but also in the operation of creation. By means of the gifts of perception, reason, reflection, and insight, the sages observed and then construed through their teachings a just order that, originating in the character of God the Creator, permeates all creation, undergirds and guides the social life of the human community, and provides the center for individual existence. This order is far more than an objective force that holds all things together in a consistent continuum or a pattern of regularity that can be counted on when engaging in human actions. Rather, this order is a moral force that undergirds and then penetrates the fabric of all existence. Indeed, this order holds together the components of reality, but it operates not as a natural law or as a series of natural laws held together in a system but rather as an ethical power that creates and sustains life. This ethical power is not self-operative. Rather, it is activated by and operates according to the will of the Creator, who brought all things into being and continues to sustain their existence. This same divinely directed moral order operates to keep the forces of chaos and destruction at bay, though not without intense struggle. The church also is called on to embody the moral values of wise teaching that are grounded in the justice of God, while knowing that struggle, not ease, is required for the ethical life.

Wisdom, both divine and human, in the form of the teachings of the sages, becomes the means by which life triumphs over death, good over evil, and well-being over fragmentation and dissolution. Wise actions constitute and sustain life in creation, society, and the individual and draw on the enduring and sustaining force of justice. In wisdom literature, death and evil are not vanquished once and for all in the realization of some new eschatological world, as envisioned by the apocalyptic seers, but they can be constrained through the actualization of justice incorporated in sapiential behavior. Evil can be avoided even though death ultimately is unavoidable. Yet death is not the feared enemy; rather, a foolish existence and the threat of a premature demise, from which only wisdom offers the possibility of escape, evoke the greatest dread.

The justice of God and the moral imperative

45

The sages of Israel teach the church that God is the Lord of justice who issues moral imperatives that are to govern individual life as it interacts with and sustains both the human community and the larger creation. Social justice is primary in living a life in response to moral imperatives that derive from divine instruction embedded in sapiential teaching. Existing in harmony with creation means for the church that respect for all life and sustaining the environment that makes existence possible are fundamental components of morality.

An obvious question to ask the sages of Proverbs is their basis for responding yes or no to their audience. Their answer is that all sapiential teaching, and thus every moral imperative or prohibition, is grounded ultimately in the justice of God. For the sages, justice is a divine, moral power that enables creation, society, and the reflective life to cohere in a way that leads to well-being for all elements of life and their harmonious integration. Wise actions and language promote and sustain this order of justice that brings about life, underscores the consistency and expectation of action and behavior, and promotes the beneficence of human beings. What endangers the cosmic and social order sustained by this moral power is human behavior that is not in concert with the teachings of wisdom, tested to be authentic and true. When the instructions of the wise, validated by new reflection, are not acted out in everyday life and in social arrangements, the well-being of the community is threatened, even harmed, and the individual miscreant experiences injury and perhaps complete ruin.

It would be wrong to assume that the blessings accruing to the community and the individual from wise and righteous behavior and speech or the harm resulting from foolish and wicked action and language occur automatically within some mechanical system of retribution. Rather, the operation of justice in the world and its consequences are brought within the sphere of divine responsibility and activity. God is the one who establishes and acts through this moral order of justice, choosing on the basis of divine freedom if and when to act. The sages' strong affirmation of the justice of God, however, and of the divine undergirding of the moral order present in the world, human society, and the individual person leads them to postulate the conviction that the wise and righteous will be blessed with well-being in its specific expressions of long life, health, honor, and so forth, whereas the foolish and wicked are threatened with injury and ruination. At the same time, the sages of Proverbs, while affirming openly their confidence in the moral order grounded in the ethical integrity of God, recognize that there are inexplicable contingencies of life that resist neat placement in a simplistic formulation of a scheme of retribution. Indeed, serious doubts about the moral order of reality grounded in the justice

46

of God reach an acute state in the critical wisdom tradition, represented in particular by the books of Job and Qoheleth (Ecclesiastes).

Aesthetics: *The coherence of order and beauty*

The order perceived by the sages to be intrinsic to the character of God, the operation of the cosmos, the social organization of human communities, and the nature of human beings is not only a moral category. Order also includes the dimension of beauty, which shapes both the appearance of the elements of nature and the form of human language. In the crafting of a saying, for example, the sage constructs a minute aesthetic that combines the elegance of language with the moral content of human observation and behavior. The saying engages the imagination of the hearer not only by the persuasiveness of what was said but also by the artistry and symmetry of the linguistic conveyance of the meaning. Literary form and moral content are inextricably one (Perdue, *Wisdom and Creation*, 63–69).

This means for the church that beauty of expression in the proclamation of the word, in its articulation in teaching, and in its arrangement in liturgy is not a rhetorical enhancement to embellish the tapestry of human language but rather an intrinsic and necessary part of the word-event, that is, the divine word that goes forth to create the world, calls communities into being, and promotes justice in society, among its members, and throughout the cosmos.

God as creator and sustainer

The sages of Proverbs give early and clear expression to what become the church's fundamental affirmations of God as creator and divine providence. Creation theology in Proverbs takes shape in two traditions that are found in the larger Old Testament. The older of the two, appearing in the wisdom texts emanating from the period of the monarchy, is the teaching that God is the creator of humanity in general and individual human creatures in particular (Prov. 14:31; 16:4, 11; 17:5; 20:12; 22:2; 29:13). God enables conception to occur, nurtures the fetus in the womb, aids in the delivery of the newborn, and continues as the personal deity who, like a parent, providentially guides the child through life (Job 10:8–12). The other tradition, developing later in the exilic and postexilic periods in the Old Testament and in wisdom literature, is cosmology, that is, that God is the creator of heaven and earth who, through divine wisdom, brings the world and its creatures into being, establishes the arrangements that provide structure and give continuity to the world's various elements, and then

47

continues to sustain and guide this reality through active participation and nurturing oversight (Prov. 3:13–20; 8:12–21, 22–31; 30:1b-4; see Westermann, *Creation*).

What is particularly surprising in Proverbs is the omission of the major traditions of salvation history so prominently displayed in most other biblical texts. These distinct complexes of traditions, eventually redacted and brought together to form what many scholars have viewed as the primary faith of ancient Israel (see Deut. 26:5–9), are the liberation of Israel's ancestors from Egypt in the exodus and divine sustenance and guidance in the Sinai wilderness; divine revelation, presence, and issuance of the corporate law at Mount Sinai; the conquest of Canaan; and the choosing of the house of David to reign over Israel-Judah and of Jerusalem to be the city either of divine presence or of theophany. God's election of the mothers and fathers of Israel (Sarah and Abraham, Rebekah and Isaac, and Rachel, Leah, and Jacob) and covenant with them form another important tradition of faith. These traditions shape Israelite belief in God and Israel's own identity and purpose as the elect. Now it is true that the later books of Ben Sira in the early second century B.C.E. and the Wisdom of Solomon in the first century B.C.E. incorporated these traditions of salvation history into sapiential creation theology, perhaps following the lead of the theological synthesis of Second Isaiah, the prophet of the exile. But the book of Proverbs affirms only the theological traditions of God's creation of the world (cosmology) and humanity (anthropology) and of divine providence, where, through blessing, the structures and forces of life are maintained; human community is enhanced; and the wise and the righteous experience well-being. Through punishment, the foolish and the wicked eventually meet their ruin. It is likely that the sages of Proverbs did not refer to the traditions of salvation history, the promise to the house of David, and the election of Zion because these were limited to Israel alone. Wisdom operates, at least until Ben Sira in the second century B.C.E., within a universal framework where God is the God of the world, not only of a specific people.

This emphasis on creation and providence, along with their framework of universalism, provides an important corrective and counterbalance to inadequate formulations of Christian theology that restrict God to residing and acting within the boundaries of the church and do not allow God to reach beyond these margins into the unlimited horizons of a universal domain. Furthermore, the sages of Proverbs teach the church that creation and its bounty are not only divine gifts for human consumption and use but also are precious in their own right and are to be preserved against exploitation and misuse. A theology of

48

human stewardship of divine creation is a principal imperative to the church from Israel's ancient sages.

The feminization of wisdom

It is clear that women were counted among the ranks of sages in ancient Israel and early Judaism. Two of the best biblical examples outside the wisdom corpus are the wise woman of Tekoa in 2 Samuel 14 and the wise woman of Abel Beth-maacah in 2 Samuel 20. The task of the first unnamed woman sage was to follow the instructions from Joab, David's military chief, and to use her persuasive skills to argue by analogy with her contrived story about her sons that the king should forgive and receive back into his good graces his son Absalom, who, in avenging the rape of his sister Tamar, had murdered his half brother Amnon. The ruse worked, and Absalom was allowed to return home to Jerusalem and then, after two years, to come into the king's presence. The second unnamed wise woman used her diplomatic skills to assist in saving her town from the attack of Joab and his army by persuading the town's leaders to execute the traitor Sheba. These counselors fit well the sapiential ideal of persuasive, diplomatic speech that induces kings and other leaders to make wise, even pragmatic decisions.

Proverbs points to the teaching of mothers who either were the senior females in households responsible for instruction of children and older girls or teachers in wisdom schools and royal courts who bore this honorific title in the same way that male teachers were called "fathers." Indeed, one of the instructions comprising a small collection in 31:1–9 is attributed to the mother of Lemuel, king of Massa, a kingdom in Northwest Arabia. This instruction sets forth important elements of behavior for a ruler who would be a successful king: the avoidance of promiscuous sex, especially with women who would betray him; the practice of sobriety; and advocacy on behalf of the destitute, who have no voice.

Other social roles attributed to women, in addition to being sages, teachers, and counselors, include those of the senior female in the household, who managed many of its economic and social affairs; the wife, lover, and counselor of the husband; and the adulteress and prostitute. The wise woman is described in some detail in the didactic poem in Proverbs 31, and her social, economic, and educational roles demonstrate not only that she held high status in postexilic society but also that she became an exemplar for those who sought to embody the virtues of sapiential life and to enjoy the fruits of wise living. Residing in a large and prosperous household and on its estate, this wise woman is the counselor of her husband, the prudent manager of the assets of

49

the household that gain in value, an industrious worker in preparing cloth and food, an astute assayer and buyer of real estate, a merchandiser who sells her fine garments to merchants, a sage who teaches wisdom, a generous spirit who is charitable to the poor, a pious worshiper who fears the Lord, and a mother and wife who is honored by her family.

What is most striking about the feminization of wisdom is the personification of Woman Wisdom as a metaphor, along with her opponent, Woman Folly. As already noted, in the four didactic poems on Woman Wisdom (Prov. 1:20–33; 3:13–20; 8:1–36; and 9:1–18) she is presented as the instrument by which God created the earth, the daughter in whom he takes delight, the queen of heaven who elects kings and dispenses wealth and success to her royal devotees, the goddess who inaugurates her school of instruction, and the sage whose teaching brings life to her followers. Ultimately, she is the voice of God, who reveals the divine character and will in creation and in her teaching, and she embodies the sapiential tradition that finds its authentication in the insights of the savants of Israel's past and present. This representation of wisdom as a woman was more easily constructed because the Hebrew word for wisdom is a feminine noun. More than grammar is at stake here, however. Israel's gradual development of monotheism becomes expressed clearly for the first time in the period of the exile (see especially Isaiah 40—55). While making the national God Yahweh into a deity of creation and providence who ruled over all nations, this development opened the door to numerous theological quandaries. The problem of evil could no longer be easily explained by reference to any divine power save Yahweh. The fortunes of the people of Israel could be directed only by Yahweh and not by any other power, human or divine. And the earlier portrayal of Yahweh primarily, though not exclusively, in male terms raised the question of the adaptability of Israel's theological representations, largely patriarchal, to include elements of the feminine. Pagan religions solved this issue with divine pairs, male and female. Israel chose to address the dilemma in various ways, including the personification of Israel and Jerusalem as a woman (wife, daughter) and, for the sages, the metaphor of divine wisdom as a woman, as both the daughter and the consort of God. This feminization of wisdom reached its climax in the sapiential tradition, with even divine characteristics and roles being assigned Wisdom (Sirach 24; Wisdom of Solomon 7—9 and 10—19). In Prov. 8:22–31, Wisdom is the first of divine creation and is presented as the beloved daughter of God, in whom God takes delight. Indeed, in the Wisdom of Solomon she is described in terms that represent her as the consort and divine reflection of God (chaps. 7—9).

Finally, the presence of didactic poems in Proverbs 1—9 and 31 provides the overarching inclusion for the entire book. This feature represents more than mere literary enhancement. Rather, it is clear that the wise woman in the concluding poem represents the human incarnation of Woman Wisdom in a striking manner.

The prominent position that Proverbs gives to women in both the household and larger society reinforces for the church the important positions women are to hold in both the church and the larger culture. The feminization of wisdom directly challenges and undermines the sexism of modern culture, its unfortunate infusion into the church's understanding of clergy and lay leadership, and its frequent reinforcement of patriarchy in the family and other social institutions.

The feminization of divine wisdom as Woman Wisdom also provides the church with important theological language and insight for portraying the feminine character and activity of God. God in feminine language becomes the creator and giver of life, the one who conceives and nurtures the creature in the womb; the handmaiden who assists with the delivery of the child; and the mother who loves, cherishes, and nourishes her offspring. Wisdom also takes on the divine roles of providence and redemption. In the language of providence, Wisdom is the queen of heaven, who chooses the leaders of nations and provides them with the tools needed to rule and the coveted gifts of her benevolence. She is the one who providentially redeems and guides the ancient ancestors and the people of Israel. All of this means, then, that this element of Proverbs and the other wisdom literature equips the church for a more rounded, inclusive representation of God in faith and practice and theologically shatters the sexist portrayals of God so prominent in much Christian theology for two millennia and that remain embedded in much contemporary faith language.

The revelation of God in creation, experience, and reason

The sages of ancient Israel and the book of Proverbs teach the church that God is known primarily through creation. The God of the sages is a transcendent deity who oversees the operations of the world, the workings of human communities, and the behavior of individuals. The sages observed an order of justice and blessing that provided for the continuation of the existence of both human and nonhuman creatures. Divine blessing sustains life, enhances its vitality, and makes it abundant. In their observation of the world and human existence, the sages believed they obtained insight into the will, character, and

51

activity of God. They concluded, then, that God was orderly, just, compassionate, and beneficent and that the justice and life-sustaining order that could be observed in the world emanated from divine will and compassion. The sages tested what they observed in the arena of their own experience, critically assessed their observations in the light of past understandings, constructed teachings that were to embody truth in a formative tradition, and transmitted that tradition to those who took up wisdom's path and began the journey toward sagehood.

Divine immanence or presence in the world and in human community was metaphorically depicted in the person of Woman Wisdom. Woman Wisdom, imagined as the child of God, became the ideal teacher who called the simple to learn of her, set up her school, sent forth her maidens to issue her invitation to life, and gave her instructions of insight and life to the simple. The wisdom active in the creation of the world becomes the voice of God that speaks through the wisdom tradition, calling the simple to take up the quest for life.

Thus the sages, while avowing the authority and authenticity of their teachings as anchored in the nature and will of God, claimed no direct divine revelation either in the form of theophanic experiences in cultic celebrations (as did the priests) or in a "thus saith the Lord" of prophetic imagination, when God spoke to the prophets or transported them into the world of future vision. The sages remind the church that there is an important place for understanding God by appeal to natural revelation, both in the operations of the world and in the testing of human experience by critical and reflective reason.

Wisdom and moral instruction

The church requires moral guidance that implements the content of its proclamation. Kerygma is not enough. Didache is also necessary in following the moral life. Proverbs and other wisdom texts have much to do with moral existence and provide the church with instruction for moral transformation and shaping character. This does not mean that sapiential morality works out of the same theological framework as the gospel, but it does mean that serious reflection on the moral life must be fashioned into ethical teachings for the church. Proverbs at least provides a model for how this is to be done, even if some of the content does not fit the life situations of the church and its theology.

The acknowledgment of mystery and ambiguity

52

The sages teach the church to avoid a deadening dogmatism that issues from exaggerated claims of the human capacity to know the mind and activity of God. They concluded that God resided beyond the ability of even the wisest to know totally and completely. And they reached the conclusion that there were limits to their understanding in every area, including especially the knowledge of God. The recognition of the limits to their knowledge did not mean the sages would even think of abandoning the quest for clearer insight into reality or that they entered a world of pluralism in which competing claims could not be assayed by appeal to tradition, experience, and reason. They did require, however, that what they taught always be examined in the world of new insight and varying experiences. And they realized that a degree of mystery, especially as concerns the workings of God, would continue to preclude a total, complete, and final revelation.

The sages also acknowledged the reality of ambiguity. For the sages, ambiguity could mean uncertainty or doubt about a matter, but more importantly, ambiguity pointed to the realization that something could be understood or interpreted in various ways. Wisdom, carefully cultivated, provided important insight into the understanding or interpretation of a matter. But wisdom did not always guarantee even the most astute sage the one and only correct understanding. Time and circumstances, as well as limits to understanding, always figure into interpretation and application.

For the church, then, a ready admission of the circumscription of the knowledge of God, the incompleteness in understanding the divine will for the moral life, the ambiguity of various beliefs and ethical actions, and the openness of the tradition to debate, transform, and even negate various theological and ethical affirmations should prohibit the hardening of entrenched theological and ethical positions that polarize and divide. Indeed, the sages teach the church to tolerate difference and to accept diversity in the expression of its faith and in the living out of its moral life.

The First Collection

"The Proverbs of Solomon
Son of David, King of Israel"

PROVERBS 1—9

Date and Provenance

Proverbs 1—9 is the most aesthetically composed and theologically incisive of the collections of wisdom in the book of Proverbs (see Whybray, *Proverbs*, 23–30). Most of the instructions and didactic poems in the book of Proverbs are assembled and aesthetically arranged here. The overwhelming majority of modern interpreters have concluded that the first collection not only is the latest compilation in Proverbs but also consists of later materials largely deriving from the early Persian period. This postexilic dating is based on several hypotheses.

First, as literary forms, brief sayings, while often artistically shaped as they are here, largely incorporate simple human observations. This suggests that they are a more archaic genre than lengthy instructions and didactic poems, which require greater intellectual prowess and literary sophistication.

Second, the detailed theologizing and nationalizing of wisdom, leading to its incorporation of the definitive religious traditions of Israel (e.g., the exodus from Egypt, the law and covenant at Sinai, and the dwelling place of Yahweh in the temple at Jerusalem), are not fully evidenced until Ben Sira in the early second century B.C.E. The climate for the sages' strong impetus toward theological and religious wisdom appears to have been provided by the events and circumstances of the early Persian period (von Rad, *Old Testament Theology* 1:441–453).

Third, the personification of wisdom occurs elsewhere in sapiential literature in the Persian and Hellenistic periods (cf. Job 28; Sirach 24; and Wisdom 10—19; see Ringgren, *Word and Wisdom*).

Fourth, the closest literary parallels to the book of Proverbs are found in literature from the late sixth and fifth centuries B.C.E. These include Deuteronomic, Deuteronomistic, and late prophetic literature (cf. Jeremiah, Deuteronomy, Second Isaiah, and Malachi). The absence in Proverbs 1—9 of the legitimation of wisdom by reference to the Torah, however, suggests that the latter had yet to achieve its central position in Jewish piety, beginning with Ezra in the fourth century B.C.E. The dating of the literary materials and the redaction of Proverbs 1—9 in the early Persian period (late sixth and fifth centuries B.C.E.) appears to be the most plausible possibility from the very limited evidence we possess. The interpretation that follows, then, understands this initial collection as deriving from sages active in early postexilic Judah when it served as a colony in the Persian Empire (538–332 B.C.E.; see Perdue, "Wisdom Theology and Social History in Proverbs 1-9").

Postexilic Judah and second temple Judaism did not represent a homogeneous society and unified religion (see Albertz, *History of Israelite Religion*). Geographically, significant Jewish communities developed not only in Judah but also in various regions of the Diaspora, including Egypt and Babylon in particular. Jewish communities in foreign lands faced the task of preserving their heritage while integrating into the dominant cultures. Religion especially became the means of preservation of the past and provided the peculiar definition of what it meant to be Jewish outside Israel. In the colony of Judah, the major challenge was to reshape in vital and effective ways the restored Jewish community's social institutions and religious expressions in view of the social, economic, and religious collapse occasioned by the Babylonian exile and captivity (586–539 B.C.E.), and to adapt to the new social, economic, and cultural infusion necessitated by inclusion in the massive Persian Empire. Here, as elsewhere, religion played a vital role in preservation of the past and continuation into the future. Even in the tiny colony of Judah, however, this challenge was met in many, often-conflicting ways.

In Judah, where times were hard during Persian rule, significant tension developed between the indigenous population who had remained in the homeland during the Babylonian captivity and the Jewish exiles who, leaving Babylon, returned to Judah and sought to reclaim and then rebuild the country as a Persian colony. The returnees eventually were to prevail in this struggle to shape the identity of the Jewish community, largely because they enjoyed the support of the Persian authorities. Even so, competing factions and strife continued throughout the postexilic period.

The Persian authorities maintained political control over the colony of Judah and encouraged peace through the appointment of governing officials, who carried out imperial policies by exacting unswerving loyalty to the ruling Achaemenid family, the collection and payment of taxes to the empire, and the creation of local social and economic stability. The Persian authorities achieved these goals in part by allowing the colony to have and maintain its own social and religious institutions with their distinctive values and beliefs, as long as the empire's political control and economic interests were duly acknowledged and supported. Temples like the one that was rebuilt in Jerusalem not only provided ideological legitimation of Persian rule and reinforced the colony status of the province but also funneled economic contributions to the empire through the collection of taxes. Persian support for the rebuilding of the temple was not at all an early and unusual expression of religious tolerance but rather a means by which local stability, the collection of resources, and the social construction of reality could be achieved in the interests of the empire. If tolerance and local support did not achieve their desired ends, the Persian rulers could and would resort to more brutal methods to enforce their will, as they did in some of their other colonies.

While they themselves did not represent a unified group, the leaders among the immigrants who returned from Babylonian captivity, largely because they included Persian-appointed officials and descendants of the earlier Jerusalem civil and priestly leadership, soon emerged as the dominant political and religious power in Judah. This ascendancy was gained at the expense of local inhabitants whose families remained in Judah during the time of the Babylonian exile. The controlling faction of Persian-appointed officials and Zadokite priests, whose high priest received Persian legitimation, practiced a pragmatic politics of accommodation with Persian authorities. In addition to the exercise of political and religious control, economic issues became a major source of conflict in the Persian period and were expressed especially in terms of the composition of the family household and its patrimonial land. One of the major issues in this regard concerned intermarriage with non-Jews. It appears that the exiles had largely practiced endogamy, that is, many of the returning households had arranged marriages for their children within the ethnic Jewish population in Babylonia and had avoided intermarriage with other groups. By contrast, exogamy, marriage with other ethnic populations, some of whom had migrated to and taken up residence in the former kingdom of Judah, was more common in the homeland. The conflict over intermarriage was driven not only by the desire for uniformity among Jews in regard to custom and religion but also by political and economic ambitions. This issue was eventually resolved with Ezra's decision that Jewish males should divorce foreign wives and disinherit the children produced by this union, a measure designed not only to reject outside influence on Judaism but also to make clear that the inheritance of household property was to pass through exclusively Jewish offspring, primarily males (see Ezra 9—10). This decision helped solidify the hierocratic party's political and religious position by gaining the support of Jewish households and collecting from them tithes and offerings for the Levites, the priests, and the temple in Jerusalem (Neh. 10:32–39).

Quite different social, political, economic, and religious expectations gave rise to a rival movement that challenged the reconstituted order achieved by the hierocratic party after the return of the exiles. This movement of "visionaries" especially opposed the position and influence of the Zadokite priests and their control of second temple Judaism. Jewish apocalypticism first distinctly manifests itself in the Hellenistic period, although several of its major elements originated in older Israelite religion, including the prophetic emphasis on the "day of the Lord" that points to a coming time of judgment and the notion of a heavenly council of supernatural beings presided over by Yahweh (Job 1—2; Psalm 82). Paul Hanson has argued that the early roots of Jewish apocalyptic eschatology can be traced back to the first part of the Persian period and are discoverable in Isaiah 56—66, Zechariah 9—14, Isaiah 24—27, Malachi, and perhaps Joel (*Dawn of Apocalyptic*). Whether the people behind these texts are best classified as early apocalypticists or later prophets from whom apocalypticism would develop is a historical question that will not be addressed here. Hanson's major thesis, however, is a cogent and supportable one. According to Hanson, the Persian period witnessed a power struggle between the hierocratic movement and the visionaries. The former, led by the Zadokite priesthood, Persian-appointed governors, centrist prophets, and traditional sages who acquired the dominant political power, was able to shape the prevailing worldview and practice of second temple Judaism along the lines of a theocracy and to control the ritual practices and economic resources of the temple in Jerusalem. The latter consisted of peripheral prophets and critical sages who had a very different and contrasting social and religious view of the faithful community. While standing outside the circles of power and control of the temple practices and resources, the visionaries anticipated a new future centering on a Davidic ruler and a purified temple cult. In this struggle, the hierocratic movement prevailed, at least politically, through the Persian period. This did not lead, however, to the silencing of the "visionaries," who continued as political marginals to articulate their contrasting worldview for the Jewish community in Judah, which, shaped by future eschatology, was yet to be realized.

This group of visionaries, consisting of peripheral prophets and some of the Levitical families ruled by the Zadokite priesthood, developed a more inclusive view of second temple Judaism and focused their future expectations on Second Isaiah's (Isaiah 40—55) vision of the cosmic and social transformation of reality as largely unfulfilled. This prophetic vision, emanating from the community in Babylonian captivity, regarded the collapse of the Babylonian Empire as the act of Yahweh through his "anointed one" Cyrus. These visionaries shaped a future eschatology in which the final restoration would be rendered by a miraculous act of God that would culminate in a new sacral and social order ruled over by the messiah, who would be a descendant of David, and presided over, by a legitimate priesthood that would conduct proper rituals in a purified temple cult (see Isaiah 56—66 and Zechariah 9—14). This eschatological act of God thus would bring about salvation for the faithful remnant of visionaries, who would be honored with positions of prominence in the time of the new order. This largely disenfranchised group came to regard the existing temple cult as defiled and its priesthood as corrupt, pronounced judgment on Jewish civic leaders appointed by the Persians, argued that Yahweh would establish a new political order, and may have challenged the dissolving of marriages and families comprised of Jewish men, non-Jewish women, and their offspring. The visionaries would have been inclined to support the land tenure of families of mixed races who, faithful to God, could be included in the community of the restored Israel. As things developed during the Persian period, this group of visionaries was largely disenfranchised and held only a secondary status in the new order, which was dominated by the hierocratic party that cultivated and enjoyed the support of the Persian government. The leaders of the visionaries, however, were not themselves poor, dispossessed, uneducated, and socially on the fringe of Jewish culture and politics. Rather, they came from socially respectable families with means, if not power, and included among their leaders well-educated intellectuals. This movement of visionaries became increasingly pessimistic about the transformation of the current cosmic and social order and finally concluded that every vestige of present reality must be either radically reshaped or destroyed by a cataclysmic act of God before the creation of a "new heaven and new earth" and a purified universal kingdom could occur.

The sages were active participants in this struggle for power,

59

influence, and the opportunity to shape second temple Judaism in the Persian period (Perdue, "Wisdom Theology and Social History in Proverbs 1—9"). Theologically, the sages joined with Second Isaiah in articulating a theology of Yahweh's creation of the world and sustaining of the orders that made life possible, though they did not adopt the sacred traditions of salvation history until Ben Sira in the second century B.C.E. From the extant wisdom literature, however, it is clear that two distinct camps of sages emerged during the postexilic period: on the one hand, traditional sages who aligned themselves largely with the increasingly dominant hierocratic party of the Zadokite priests (Proverbs 1—9 and Ben Sira) and, on the other, critical teachers who, in challenging many of the conventions of the conservative wise and the priests with whom they were aligned, reached rather pessimistic conclusions about the evils of the current cosmic and social order. Some were "skeptics" in that they recognized all too readily the impairments of the current period, and yet they still hoped for a better world to emerge one day in the future (Job). While religiously and perhaps socially compatible with the party of visionaries, these critical teachers did not all share the hopeful anticipation of God's dramatic ending of the current reality and reshaping of a new social and political order. Some became cynics and possessed no human hope for the future (e.g., Qoheleth and Agur; see Crenshaw, "Birth of Skepticism in Ancient Israel," *The Divine Helmsman* 1–19).

After the return from exile, the social groups that emerged in the early Persian period included the sages whose literary artistry and editorial activity are represented by Proverbs 1—9. Finding their primary locus of activity in Jerusalem, these sages and their descendants quickly allied themselves with the hierocratic party of second temple Judaism that would become the dominant political and religious group among the Jews in the postexilic period. Although this alignment would not reach its full realization until the time of Ben Sira, elements already present in the first collection of Proverbs are compatible with the agenda of the hierocratic party. These compatible elements include the theme of a largely static and just cosmic order that is universal; the affirmation of Yahweh as the one true God; the insistence that justice is largely retributive and dispensed by a righteous deity; divine providence expressed through the theory of retribution as the justification for the possession of wealth and power by the dominant social group; the legitimation of wisdom teachings by grounding them in the just order of creation and by personifying the tradition as the daughter of God; the authentication of the rule of the kings of the earth by reference to their selection by Wisdom, the queen of Heaven, who embodies God's creative power and providential rule; the warning against the dangers of extra-Israelite culture and religion personified by the metaphor of the "strange woman"; affirmation of the social features of the traditional extended household, including the authority of the senior male and female, marriage limited to Jewish women, patrimony and heredity, and the value of children; the claims of the "righteous" to the inheritance of the land, over against those who dally with the strange woman; and the support of the sacrificial system of the temple.

The theological and ethical materials found in Proverbs 1—9 probably derived from several school settings in the early half of the Persian period: a temple school, family guilds, and civil academies. More than likely a temple school emerged in the Persian period to educate scribes to assist the priests in compiling, copying, and interpreting the Torah, written in Hebrew, to a populace increasingly dependent on Aramaic (the lingua franca of the Persian period); in codifying and arguing case law for civil and religious regulations and disputes; in administrating and recording the temple's vast economic resources; and in shaping the major case for legitimating the claims to power and influence of the ruling class. Guilds (most likely centered in family households) continued to train scribes for service in the government or in the temple (1 Chron. 2:55). Scribes also were needed by the Persian government at both the central (e.g. Ezra) and the provincial level to carry out administrative leadership and bureaucratic tasks, to maintain records, and to serve as notaries. These scribes perhaps were educated in civil academies supported by the central and provincial governments. Traditional sages sought through their writings and educational system to promote the interests of the prevailing social and religious order.

The critical wisdom tradition emerging in the Persian period is represented primarily by Job (the poetry), Qoheleth, and perhaps Agur (Proverbs 30), texts also likely produced by teachers as school literature (Crenshaw, "Human Dilemma and Literature of Dissent," 235–58). These sages were intellectuals who opposed traditional wisdom's social knowledge, which was used to support the political power and economic advantages of the hierocratic movement. These teachers were critical of earlier sapiential tradition and their conservative colleagues; questioned and at times even denied the justice of God; ranged from open criticism to a deepening skepticism concerning the teaching that justice permeated the cosmic and social order; doubted that a just order representing the larger justice of God could be discovered by astute observation and then implemented in a life that

61

would consequently experience success and well-being; held that God remained hidden, was capricious and unjust, or was engaged in a struggle for justice that was never completely won; viewed both religious and civic leaders as often corrupt; denied that the temple cult produced the dividends of blessing that the priests claimed; and witnessed a vitiated social order that oppressed not only the poor but even the righteous. Unlike their visionary contemporaries, however, these sages did not easily look to a future act of God that would transform heaven and earth and then constitute a reality of justice in which they would participate as leaders among the redeemed. Instead, either they retreated into a deepening cynicism that avoided speculation about a hidden, capricious deity, while teaching their students to "seize the day" when joy in one's labor and family is experienced (Qoheleth), or they concluded that moral living and resistance to the forces of chaos, while restrained and held in check by God, did not always promise the exemption of the righteous from their suffering or even their eventual justification (Job). While these critical sages questioned and thus would have undermined the epistemological and confessional assumptions undergirding and legitimating the current social world of Judah as a Persian colony, they were not, however, in agreement as to whether a new and just social order would one day emerge through righteous living and the intervention of divine justice. These teachers challenged the comfortable theological and ideological dogmas that promised advantages and privileges to students who persevered in their discipline of study and character formation, but they were not quick to offer in their literature of dissent a new, constructive vision of social justice that would reshape the current political order of Persian rule (Crenshaw, "Human Dilemma and Literature of Dissent," 235–58).

Literary Structure

It is clear from the artistic quality of the first collection that the sages who produced it possessed remarkable literary skills (see Skehan, *Studies in Israelite Poetry and Wisdom*, 1–47). The symmetrical shaping of the first collection of Proverbs, chapters 1—9, comprises a superscription (1:1) and general introduction (1:2–7) for both this collection and the entire book, ten instructions, and four related didactic poems whose subject is Woman Wisdom. The instructions are located in the first seven chapters (1:8–19; 2:1–22; 3:1–12; 3:21–35; 4:1–9; 4:10–27; 5:1–23; 6:1–19; 6:20–35; and 7:1–27; see Whybray, *Wisdom in Proverbs*, 33–71), while the four poems on Woman

Wisdom are strategically placed at the beginning and end of the collection (1:20–33; 3:13–20; 8:1–36; and 9:1–18) to form a literary *inclusio* that reconstitutes in the elegance of didactic poetry the themes and language present in the instructions. Indeed, the conclusion of the book of Proverbs, 31:10–31, is an exquisite poem on the "woman of worth" or "capable wife," who, while not a literary metaphor for divine wisdom, becomes the human incarnation of what Woman Wisdom teaches through her instructions about moral existence, the bounties of insight, and the fullness of life. Consequently, the crowning poem on the ideal wise woman offers an intricate integration of sapiential themes and provides a stunning symmetrical closure to the entire book.

The literary positioning of the poems in the first nine chapters underscores the centrality and essential role of (Woman) Wisdom in the origins of creation; in sustaining and enhancing the cosmos, society, and human life; in guiding or steering the moral behavior and skillful language that leads to the fullness of life for both the devotee of wisdom and the larger community; and in avoiding folly and evil, which threaten life in all its manifestations. In particular, Woman Wisdom, who embodies the sapiential tradition as divine instruction for life, is counterpoised to Woman Folly, who represents not only the evil and frivolity of foolish life that strays toward destruction but also both the allure of the "foreign woman" and her culture and the threat of the prostitute to the extended family (Blenkinsopp, "Social Context of the 'Outsider Woman' in Proverbs 1–9," 457–73).

In four didactic poems (1:20–33; 3:13–20; 8:1–36; and 9:1–18) and one instruction (4:1–9) in this initial collection, divine insight and artistic design are personified and metaphorically depicted as Woman Wisdom, employed in creating the cosmos, in guiding its human community, and, while representing a divine attribute of Yahweh, serving much like the personal goddess of the sage (Ringgren, *Word and Wisdom*). Woman Wisdom is the divine, creative force that originates and continues to permeate the cosmos; the social justice that shapes and provides a righteous character to human institutions; the enticing goddess and lover of the sage, who seeks to find comfort and exhilaration in her charms and life-giving embrace; a personal goddess who protects, exalts, honors, and crowns the aspiring sage who follows her; the darling daughter of God, whose endearment toward the child combined with her own delight in the world of human habitation form the affectionate bond between creator and human creation; and the powerful queen of heaven, who not only elects and enables the princes of the earth to rule successfully and well but also gives wealth to and

63

bestows honor on her royal lovers. But most of all, Woman Wisdom, through the teachings of the wise whose tradition she embodies, is the voice of God, whose invitation to come and learn of her and whose instructions revealing divine knowledge and insight direct the simple on the path to the fullness of life (Lang, *Wisdom and the Book of Proverbs*).

Ultimately, the voices one hears in Proverbs 1—9 are not limited to those of the wise teachers of Israel or even of Wisdom herself, who incorporates and articulates the sapiential tradition that is grounded in the order of creation. The audible undertone of the teachings and poems of the entire collection is sounded by the mouth of God, who reveals to the simple and the wise the pathway to life.

1:1

The Superscription: "The Proverbs of Solomon Son of David, King of Israel"

Date and Provenance

The superscription for both the first collection and the entire book reads: "The proverbs of Solomon son of David, king of Israel." The association of the book of Proverbs and its first collection with Solomon is based on what may have been a long-standing tradition that depicts him as the wisest of the kings, the creator of wisdom texts, and the patron of the sages (1 Kings 3—10). The earliest elements of this royal tradition about the wisdom of Solomon may have reflected a new spirit that was evoked by the transition from the old sacral orders of the period of the judges to the rise of the Israelite monarchy and its emphasis on an "intensive enlightenment" and a "Solomonic human-ism" (von Rad, *Old Testament Theology*, 1:48–56).

However ancient this tradition may have been, another factor may be at work in the sages' staking their claim to Solomon in the opening superscription and in two later ones. Sages in the Persian period sought to demonstrate that their teachings were a continuation of the tradition of the royal court, which was given its most culturally devel-oped expression, in the fiction of tradition if not in the reality of his-tory, by the renowned Solomon. The temple, Jerusalem, the Torah, and the Zadokites had not yet achieved their positions of prominence in developing Judaism and would not do so until the fourth century

B.C.E. and thereafter. The final accommodation of wisdom to these hierocratic elements is well illustrated in the wisdom of Ben Sira (ca. 190 B.C.E.). But the monarchy and creation were the two theological traditions the sages could exploit to legitimate their work and its resumption in the early Persian period. At a time when the fires of messianic expectation concerning the reestablishment of the dynasty of David were burning brightly, the sages of the period may have sought to lay claim to the dynasty's most famous ruler by associating their labors with him, thus expressing in a way that even suspicious Persian authorities would not find offensive their support for the reestablishment of the house of David. The sages were seeking to show that their tradition was firmly in line with the institution of the house of David, and in particular, its most esteemed representative. Thus, the sages not only may have lent their tacit support to the reestablishment of the royal dynasty associated with Solomon but also may have sought to legitimate, to a Jewish audience in the Persian period, the authority and authenticity of their own teachings and the prominent social position to which they aspired. This claim of royal association and continuity with the most famous king of Israel's past allowed the sages in the Persian period to align themselves with the developing hierocracy of the Zadokites without the risk of making any noticeable threat against the rule of Persia (Berquist, *Judaism in Persia's Shadow*).

Literary Structure and Interpretation

Wisdom collections are normally provided with superscriptions or titles. In addition to the first one, the collections in Proverbs have the following superscriptions:

10:1. "The proverbs of Solomon" (10:1—22:16)
22:17. "The words of the wise" (22:17—24:22)
24:23. "These also are sayings of the wise" (24:23–34)
25:1. "These are other proverbs of Solomon that the officials of King Hezekiah of Judah copied" (25—29)
30:1. "The words of Agur son of Jakeh [of Massa]" (30)
31:1. "The words of King Lemuel [of Massa]. An oracle that his mother taught him" (31:1–9).

The one unit that has no superscription, a lengthy poem on the woman of worth, is found at the end of the book: 31:10–31. An editor or editors also eventually provided Proverbs 1—9 a superscription that

65

came to be regarded as a comprehensive title for the entire book: "The proverbs of Solomon the son of David, king of Israel."

Superscriptions of wisdom texts were produced by editors who, at some point in the creation of collections, used a general term (*māšāl* = "saying" or *dābār* = "word" in the plural) to refer to the type of sapiential material the collection contains and provided the name or names and occasionally the titles of the patron(s), author(s), or redactor(s) who were associated with the collection in some way. The historicity of superscriptions in the Hebrew Bible (Old Testament) varies, from the general accuracy of many prophetic ones to the questionable authenticity of many of those provided for various psalms in the Psalter.

Scholars differ in their assessment of the historicity of the various superscriptions provided as headings for the different collections in Proverbs. It is doubtful that there is any direct historical association of King Solomon with Proverbs or any of the three collections that bear his name. This is also true of the other books of Qoheleth (Ecclesiastes), Song of Songs, and Wisdom of Solomon, all of which were written centuries after the death of this king. One might speak of these "Solomonic" superscriptions as similar to colophons attached to some ancient Near Eastern wisdom literature dedicated to a god or ruler; or it may be that these royal superscriptions that mention Solomon and, in one instance, Hezekiah suggest the royal patronage of the work of the sages by the Davidic monarchy. The one superscription that intimates some measure of historical authenticity is Proverbs 25:1, which refers to the copying of the materials in Proverbs 25—29 by the "officials of King Hezekiah of Judah."

Conclusion

Even though no scholar would suggest that the initial superscription reflects Solomonic authorship of Proverbs or even of the first collection, it may preserve some abiding memory of Solomon's association with the formation and patronage of court wisdom. This collective memory embedded in the sapiential tradition and the minds of its tradents continued to be reflected in the new literary creations of sages for a thousand years (1 Kings 3—10; Proverbs and three of its collections; Song of Songs; Qoheleth [Ecclesiastes]; Sir. 47:12–22; and the Wisdom of Solomon).

When examining this steady stream of literary creations by the sages, one sees that Solomon came to represent in ancient Israel and early Judaism a cultural symbol of a tradition that bore a unique character and outlook (Brueggemann, "Social Significance of Solomon as a Patron of Wisdom," 117–32). This does not mean that incongruities within the tradition were absent or that clashes in perspectives were avoided. Wisdom's openness to new understandings, reaction to changing historical fortunes of both the larger culture and its individuals, and tolerance of diversity precluded the formation of a unified tradition with singular and unchallenged views. The symbolization of much of the wisdom tradition by reference to Solomon, however, indicates that this continuing stream of literary works breathed its own creative spirit and articulated values that sought to claim the lives and devotion of students, some of whom would achieve for themselves positions of prominence in Israelite and Jewish society and would substantially shape that culture. The glories, achievements, intelligence, prosperity, success, and piety represented in the often idealized personage of Israel's legendary king (1 Kings 3—10) functioned to promote the major values of the wisdom tradition in a fashion not unlike the symbolization of the diversity of the faith and ethics of early Christianity present in the various depictions of Jesus in the canonical and noncanonical Gospels.

Theology

If there is some element of authentic cultural memory in the attribution of the book of Proverbs and its first collection to Solomon, it may be found in the fact that new forms of power in the rule of a royal dynasty required "new modes of knowledge" that would express, theoretically, the political and religious legitimation of the newly formed monarchy and, practically, the administration of the new empire. Von Rad called this new cultural era a Solomonic "enlightenment" that broke with the mythic-cultic forms of knowing reality in the formative period of the Judges (Iron I) and operated through a new epistemology that affirmed the value and authenticity of human reason and experience (*Old Testament Theology,* 1:48–56). This new cultural ethos required fresh and invigorating modes of knowledge and cultural expression that went beyond the social customs and sacred stories of familial and clan religion and life. Canaanite religion provided the new capital Jerusalem and its royal house a sacred, mythological cast that combined with the Israelite understandings of the divine election of the dynasty and God's perpetual covenant with David. The crown thus received its divine legitimation. Wisdom offered to this mix knowledge that derived from astute observation, rational inquiry, and testing in the arena of human experience. Wisdom's experiential, rational mode

67

of understanding was needed for administering and governing the empire; for developing a scientific understanding and implementation of the rules of agriculture, economics, warfare, and architecture; for establishing royal policies governing every aspect of life, from law to religion to economics to education to the military; and for planning future directions for the kingdom. The counsel of sages provided monarchs well-planned strategies for the various facets of successful rule. The learning of the wise enabled kings to engage in international diplomacy and to shape a body of learning that legitimated their rule by reference to Yahweh, who elected them and chose Zion/Jerusalem as the divine dwelling place. Even more, however, the sages developed an ethos of behavior grounded not in brute strength or unbridled passion but in the sense of cosmic justice, issuing from a class ethic of those of social prominence who keenly felt a sense of obligation and loyalty to the community as a whole, including its poor (Kovacs, "Is There a Class Ethic in Proverbs?" 171–89). Finally, this intellectual tradition of the wise was open to and even encouraged careful scrutiny, welcoming new insights that challenged, transformed, or even negated earlier teachings. It was this openness to new possibilities of understanding, regardless of their source, that allowed the indigenous traditions of Israel and Judah to be receptive, though critically so, to new learning that derived from any source, including even pagan cultures.

This symbolization in the person of Solomon of a new way of seeing the world is perhaps what is at the basis of the superscription's association of the book and its first collection with Israel's wisest king. Even the radical book of Qoheleth, which intimates that Solomon utters its narrative voice, reminds its audience by this attribution that wisdom, symbolized in the person of its patron saint, continues to be receptive to new and even radical propositions (see Kalugila, *The Wise King*).

1:2–7

Introduction: To Know Wisdom and Discipline

Date and Provenance

This general introduction to the first collection, and indeed, to the entire book, delineates the general types of knowledge, skills, and virtues required by the specific social roles and positions that the sages assumed in early postexilic society (teacher, counselor, jurist, scribe, and administrator; see Whybray, *Proverbs,* 32–36).

What is of particular interest in this introduction is the recognition of two very different groups who make up the audience to whom the first collection and the entire book are directed. The first group consists of the "simple" (*pĕtā'yîm*) and the "youth" (*na'ar,* v. 4). In wisdom literature, the "simple" or "unlearned" are those who lack sense, that is, the acumen of reasoned thinking, yet who, provided the opportunity, are open to instruction and learning (Prov. 1:22; 8:5; 9:4, 16). These simple are those whose gullibility and lack of a disciplined ethic often render them ill equipped to make prudent judgments and to engage in moral actions (Prov. 14:15), and whose lack of good sense leads them to acquire only folly and its disastrous fruits (Prov. 14:18). Untrained in the ways of wisdom, the simple are easily deceived by malefactors and seduced by the depraved (Prov. 1:32; 7:7; 9:6; and 22:3 = 27:12). Thus the mainstay of potential students of the wise teachers would have been young, naive, easily deceived and manipulated, lacking in maturity, at times succumbing to frivolous behavior (even debauchery), and certainly not prepared to take on the responsibilities of career and family. Since the study of wisdom is primarily limited to very intelligent young men and women who belonged to the leisure class and prosperous families (cf. Sir. 38:24), these simple are likely well-to-do "youth" (*na'ar,* v. 4) who have the opportunity of time and advantages of resources and social position to pursue the education offered by the sages. This means also that potential students, at least those outside family guilds, had to be recruited or enticed by the sages' rhetoric of persuasion and promises of success. One might well imagine that resources to support the wisdom academies came not only from the institutions of temple and government but also from the "tuition" paid by affluent families to educate their children.

Yet a second group of people is present, invited not to begin the study of wisdom but rather, through the hearing of its word and continued reflection on its teaching, to add to their reservoirs of knowledge and to acquire "counsel," so as to provide to kings and other leaders in the community well-thought-out plans that lead to success and life. Verse 5 offers to the mature sage, then, an opportunity to add to "learning" (*leqaḥ*) and to acquire the skill and knowledge of counseling. *Leqaḥ* is the "learning" or "received tradition" of the sages that is persuasive and convincing (Job 11:4; Prov. 9:9; 16:21; Isa. 29:24). The accomplished sage who hears these words of wisdom may "add to" or "increase" not simply his or her own learning but also, perhaps, even the received teaching of the wise (Deut. 32:2; Job 11:4;

69

Prov. 4:2; 9:9; 16:21; Isa. 29:24). Further, the intelligent and already well-informed person, through continued study of wisdom, may acquire the knowledge and skill of "counsel" (*taḥbūlôt*—NRSV, "skill") and thus receive from God steering, guidance, and direction for life and success in human endeavors (Job 37:12; Prov. 11:14; 12:5; 20:18; 24:6). *Taḥbūlôt* is a synonym for *'ēṣâ* (counsel), advice or direction that is well thought out and planned. This highly valued counsel guides the individual, often a ruler or person of high position, and his or her community to success and the enhancement of life. This inclusion of accomplished sages among the audience of students indicates that wisdom is not obtained once and for all but rather is to be pursued, cultivated, and deepened throughout life. This wisdom is not simply the knowledge of the intellect but the fiber of the soul. Continuing moral formation of character and the increase in knowledge and skill are strongly encouraged and even required by the sages in the course of their public and private lives.

Literary Structure and Interpretation

The literary structure of the introduction consists of six poetic lines, each of which consists of two equal parts (or half lines), and features five infinitive clauses (cf. introductions to *Instruction of Ptahhotep* 40—50, in *ANET,* 412; and *Instruction of Amen-em-Opet* 1:1–12, in *ANET,* 421). The reference to "wisdom" (*ḥŏkmâ*) and "discipline" (*mûsār*—NRSV "instruction") in the opening half line of verse 2 is matched by the concluding half line in verse 7, thus providing a literarily cohesive and thematically significant inclusion for the larger introduction. The inclusion underscores the sages' view that the receptive study of the first collection, and indeed, of the entire book of Proverbs, will lead to the development of the virtues and skills of wisdom (*ḥŏkmâ*), their embodiment in human character, and their actualization in daily living through the rigor of discipline (*mûsār*). Those who take up the study of wisdom will come to know it in intimate ways and will activate it in discourse and in living, while only fools "despise" wisdom, that is, regard it with contempt, and thus they refuse to take up the course of study that leads to its attainment through disciplined learning and reflective meditation. The declaration the "fear of Yahweh [the LORD] is the beginning of wisdom" in verse 7 provides an important inclusion not only for the first collection (cf. 9:10) but also for the entire book (31:30).

70

The first half line of verse 2 begins with the initial, all-inclusive statement of purpose for the collection and the larger book: to know "wisdom" (*ḥŏkmâ*) and "discipline" or "instruction" (*mûsār*). Wisdom is many things. In summary, one may say wisdom has to do with a tradition of learning produced by Israelite and Jewish sages, the human capacity to obtain and understand the knowledge transmitted by this tradition through reasoned reflection and the testing of experience, the process of instruction by which this tradition is transmitted, the capacity of the imagination to project a reality of order and beauty in the world, the establishment of justice and order in society, the formation of human character by sapiential virtues, and faith in the God who created and sustains the world in and by righteousness and calls on the wise to embody this righteousness in their lives and in their community. Discipline involves the rigorous study of and reflective meditation on wisdom, the embodiment of its virtues and attributes in human character, and prudent, moral behavior informed by sapiential ethics.

The second purpose of the study of wisdom in Proverbs 1—9 and the book of Proverbs as a whole, mentioned in the second half line of verse 2, is to develop the intellect and the capacity to understand those "words" or sayings of the sages that offer "insight" into the character and action of God, the operation of the world, and the proper and just functioning of human society. These insights are obtained by astute observation, critical analysis through the application of reason, comparison with the traditions of the ancestors, and the testing of what is affirmed by experience.

The third purpose articulated in the introduction appears to point not only to general virtues and skills desired by any student of wisdom but also, more specifically, to the role of jurist that some of the sages in the Persian period assumed (v. 3). After their formal education, some of the sages went into careers in religious as well as secular law, serving as both lawyers and judges in the judiciaries of the temple and the provincial government. These jurists were to pursue in the wisdom schools "discipline," that is, a course of study that allowed them to know and to embody in their discourse, arguments, and decisions "prudent consideration" (*haśkēl*—NRSV "wise dealing"), "righteousness" (*ṣedeq*), "justice" (*mišpāṭ*), and "fairness" (*mēšārîm*—NRSV "equity"). "Prudent consideration" is a learned skill of rulers and judges, who must pay careful attention to a particular, at times complicated case and in the end reach the proper and just decision (Job 34:34–37; Prov. 21:16; Jer. 3:15; Dan. 1:17–21; 9:13). "Righteousness" is the order of the society embodied in its legislation and in the rule and judicial decisions of its leaders (Prov. 8:15–16; 25:5; 31:9). "Justice" has to do with the formulation of words and deeds that promote the life and

71

well-being of creation and people in the community (Prov. 12:5; 21:7, 15; 28:5), with individual laws that together provide the legislation for adjudicating disputes and determining correct decisions in court cases (Deut. 33:10, 21; 1 Sam. 8:9, 11; Jer. 8:7), with the act of deciding a legal case (Deut. 1:17; 1 Kings 3:28; Prov. 16:33), with the process of litigation before judges (Job 14:3; Eccl. 11:9; 12:14), with the case presented for litigation (2 Sam. 15:14; 1 Kings 3:11), and with the decision itself (1 Kings 20:40; see also Deut. 17:11). *Mēšārîm* is the attribute of "fairness" or "equity" that judges are to possess in their administration of justice (Pss. 9:8 = Heb. 9:9; 58:1 = Heb. 58:2; 75:2 = Heb. 75:3; 96:10).

The teaching of the "simple" and the "youth" or "young" is the fourth purpose of the collection and the book (v. 4). They are to be taught three things: "prudence" (NRSV "shrewdness"), "knowledge," and "discretion" (NRSV "prudence"). "Prudence" or "sensibility" is the virtue that enables one to make sound and well-reasoned decisions, to speak judiciously and wisely, and to take proper action, because one has reasonably and carefully assessed the situation and the information at hand before speaking or acting. Prudence is the opposite both of naiveté, which makes one an easy target for deception and seduction, and of thoughtlessness, which leads to hasty, emotional, and heedless determinations and foolish conduct (Prov. 12:16; 14:8, 15; 22:3; 27:12). "Knowledge" is a common synonym for wisdom. In one sense, knowledge in wisdom literature is information about moral virtues for proper and ethical human conduct (Gen. 2:9, 17; Job 34:34–35), about the character and workings of God (Job 13:2; 21:14; 33:3; Prov. 2:5), and about the world, society, and human beings, established by observation and tested by experience (Prov. 11:9; 13:16; 22:12; 29:7). In another sense, knowledge is also the seasoned skill of discernment and the astute understanding of a situation that lead to wise speech and the proper course of action (Prov. 13:16; 15:2, 7, 14). The third virtue, offered to the simple and the youth who study wisdom, is "discretion" (*mĕzimmâ*). This virtue represents the ability to use one's judgment to discriminate, discern, and judge in a reasoned fashion the facts at hand and the situation that presents itself. The virtue of discretion allows the sage to know when and how to speak and behave in ways that are upright and beneficial both to the individual and to the larger community.

As noted earlier, among those who are invited to study wisdom are mature sages (v. 5). This is the fifth purpose of Proverbs 1—9 and the entire book. In deepening their understanding of wisdom, older sages have the opportunity to hear and then to add to the tradition, that is,

72

to create their own sayings, instructions, or poems that can be tested by time, assayed by other sages, and perhaps then included in the growing tradition. In continuing to study the wisdom offered in the first collection, and indeed, in the entire book, sages also may acquire "counsel," the much-valued commodity of knowledge and insight that enables one to construct carefully a considered plan of action that leads to a successful outcome for individuals and for nations. This plan may be one for war, for city planning, for diplomacy, or for many other necessary activities requiring the knowledge and skill of a clear, thoughtful, and well-informed mind.

The introduction then articulates the sixth purpose in studying the wisdom of Proverbs: to learn to use and interpret the teachings of the wise composed in the various genres of wisdom literature (v. 6). Those who study wisdom will comprehend and learn to utilize the diverse kinds of sapiential genres; will grasp the appropriateness and various turns of metaphors and know how to make and comprehend an "argument" (NRSV "figure"), will understand the "words of the wise," that is, the various collections they compose and redact; and will propose as well as grasp the disguised meanings of "riddles."

Discussed more fully in the introduction, the *māšāl* (proverb) includes "sayings" (1 Sam. 10:12; 24:14; Ezek. 12:22–23), didactic poems (Isa. 14:4–10), wisdom psalms (Pss. 49:4 = Heb. 49:5; 78:2), and parables (Ezek. 17:2; 21:5). Among the variety of sayings are the proverb (Prov. 21:12, 25, 31), the comparison (Prov. 10:26; and 11:22), the beatitude (Prov. 8:32, 34), the better saying (Prov. 15:16, 17), the numerical saying (Prov. 30:15–16, 18–19, 21–23, 24–28, 29–31), and the abomination saying (Prov. 3:32; 6:16; 8:7; 11:1).

The term *mělîṣâ*, "argument" or "figure," is difficult to define, due to its infrequent occurrence in the Old Testament (only here and Hab. 2:6), though its usage in later rabbinic Hebrew indicates it may mean either an "argument," that is, the ability to construct and debate a position persuasively and knowledgeably, or the interpretation of a "metaphor," that is, the capacity to grasp the meanings especially of poetic images that so enrich the artistry and content of sapiential language.

Those who study wisdom will also learn to understand and to use two other genres, "collections" (literally, "words of the wise") and "riddles." The different collections of the sages are known as the "words" (*dibrê*) or "sayings" (*mišlê*) of the "wise" or of a particular sage, for example, Qoheleth. Collections are characterized by repetition of common themes and literary expressions and images; are artistically crafted by means of strophes, repetitions of themes, images, and

73

words, and the variety of parallelism; and provide a ready compendium of sapiential genres for teaching and reflection. While "riddles" were at one time created and used by the sages, none remains in the wisdom corpus itself. Riddles were intended to confuse even the wisest of sages. In a test of wits, a sage who confounded his or her hearers was proven the wisest of them all, while the sage who answered an obscure riddle demonstrated he or she was to receive high honor from colleagues (see 1 Kings 10:1–3). Comparative literature from ancient and contemporary times shows that riddles were used for various purposes: entertainment, the acquiring of status and honor, wagers, and even serious contests that could involve life and death. The sole riddle preserved in the Bible, however, is that proposed and answered in the Samson narrative (Judg. 14:12–18; see Perdue, "Riddles of Psalm 49," 533–42).

The seventh and final purpose of studying wisdom is the formation and deepening of religious piety (v. 7). The "fear of Yahweh" (or "the LORD") or religious piety or reverence in Proverbs (1:29; 2:5; 9:10; 10:27; 14:26, 27; 15:16, 33; 19:23; 22:24; 23:17; cf. Job 28:28; Pss. 34:11; 111:10) is neither the terror occasioned by the supposition of a powerful yet unknown, even capricious deity, about which Qoheleth later speaks (see Eccl. 5:6), nor the awe evoked in the presence of the holy God who is wholly other. For Proverbs, the "fear of Yahweh" is the stance of the believer who confesses God is the creator and sustainer of life and the source and provider of all wisdom. This fear of Yahweh is called the rē'šît of knowledge, which may mean either "beginning" or "best" of wisdom; or perhaps the intimation is that both are intended. To take rē'šît in the first sense, "beginning," suggests that the entire enterprise of the pursuit of wisdom through the disciplined study of Proverbs is founded on religious piety or reverence. Thus the one who comes to the study of wisdom or who seeks to deepen his or her knowledge and skills as a lifelong pursuer of its bounty must come with religious conviction and reverence already in place. This piety recognizes that the true source of wisdom is God and that only through this acknowledgment may one come to its possession. To take the second meaning of rē'šît, "best," connotes the view that the discovery that is most valued and important to learn from the study or deepening of wisdom is reverence for its true source, the Creator and Sustainer of all that is. For the sage or sages who constructed this introduction, faith and reason, confession and experience, and analysis and reverence are not opposing polarities that require the negation or neutralizing of the one in order to engage in the other. Rather, these polarities

74

find their unity, even synergy, in the pursuit of wisdom, for not only does wisdom come from God, but the knowledge of God is wisdom's ultimate and culminating goal. Prayer, meditation, religious ritual, and reflection on the nature and activity of God, though not mystical union, were the spiritual disciplines in which the second temple sages of a traditional bent were engaged.

This combination of wisdom and piety appears to inform the wisdom movement and its literature from its earliest traceable beginnings (Perdue, *Wisdom and Cult*). While it is true that wisdom over the centuries developed an increasing interest and sophistication in theological content and a heightening in its specification of and expanding on religious subjects and practices (e.g., Torah, sacrifice, fear of God, temple, and priesthood in Ben Sira), it is not accurate to argue that early wisdom was a secular, humanistic, perhaps even alien enterprise that only later, in the postexilic period, was wedded to Israelite theology and the particulars of Jewish self-consciousness (against von Rad, *Old Testament Theology*, 1:418–41).

While the simple, the youth, and even mature sages are invited to take the path to understanding, those who reject the sages' invitation to come and learn of them are "fools" who "despise" or "hold in contempt" (cf. Prov. 19:16) wisdom and the discipline it requires to learn and embody it in living. Fools are frequently mentioned in Proverbs. Sages should not waste their efforts on them, because of their intrinsic resistance to learning and pressing orientation toward folly and wickedness (Prov. 15:5; 27:22). Fools are not necessarily lacking in native intelligence. Rather, they are inclined toward licentious behavior and thus easily seduced (Prov. 7:22), engage in strife that is disruptive to the community (Prov. 20:3), follow the lead of their passions instead of their reason (Job 5:2–3), and are lacking in the knowledge of wisdom and the will of God due to their contempt for instruction (Prov. 14:2; Jer. 4:22). The behavior of fools damages the order of justice that undergirds both human community and the creation, not only bringing harm to themselves but also extending it to others. Fools are those who eventually will experience the devastation of their own folly (Prov. 19:16).

Conclusion

In the words of the introduction (1:2–7), then, the overarching purpose of the collection and the larger book is to grasp "wisdom" (*ḥŏkmâ*) and to acquire the means to attain it, *mûsār*, that is, the "discipline" of

75

study and the formation of human character through virtue. This introduction serves as both a rationale and an invitation to pursue the study of wisdom (Perdue, "Wisdom in the Book of Job," 76–78).

Theology

The quest for wisdom, obtained through disciplined study and reflective meditation, is founded on reverence or religious piety (the "fear of Yahweh"), which is wisdom's most valued virtue. God is both the source and goal of wisdom. As will become clear in the later chapters of the first collection, this piety is both the confession of a righteous God who has created and continues to rule providentially the cosmos and the informed expression of the moral life rightly lived by embodying the virtues of wisdom. In the act of creation, this God uses divine wisdom to design and order a cosmos of justice and to shape and regulate human institutions. God has established orders for life that make existence not only possible but also worthwhile (Perdue, *Wisdom and Creation*). But the worthwhile quality of life, the fullness of its expression, and the joy of its living are not givens just for the taking. Rather, to plumb the depths of life and to celebrate its vibrancy requires the obtaining of wisdom and the implementation of its virtues in human behavior.

The sages are called on to shape and sustain this just order of reality in both creation and society through skillful word and moral deed. The attributes of wisdom, articulated in this general introduction, become the qualities of knowledge and discipline that enable the simple and the young to become wise and that provide the mature sages the opportunity to make their own contribution to the tradition, to enhance the moral order of creation, and to obtain life both for themselves and for those to whom they give counsel.

1:8–19

First Instruction: A Warning against the Enticement to Join Violent Men

Date and Provenance

76

The poetic unit in verses 8–19 is the first of ten instructions placed in the initial collection (see also 2:1–22; 3:1–12, 21–35; 4:1–9, 10–19,

20–27; 5:1–23; 6:20–35; and 7:1–27; Whybray, *Wisdom in Proverbs*). The literary form of the "instruction" (*mûsār*) dominates this collection and underscores the primary function of wisdom teaching: the formation of character through the discipline of study that enables students who eventually will enter the various scribal professions to actualize in their speech and behavior the moral life, which enhances their well-being as well as that of the larger Jewish community (Brown, *Character in Crisis*). This particular instruction advocates a conservative tendency in traditional wisdom by exhorting the students to support the existing social order by avoiding brigands and revolutionaries who practice violence. Articulated probably during the first half of the Persian period, this teaching underscores the legitimacy of the existing political and social order by grounding it in the "fear of Yahweh" (1:7, 29) that acknowledges the providential rule of God.

Literary Structure and Interpretation

This instruction contains the three typical features of the genre: the introduction, in which the teachers ("father" and "mother") admonish the student (their "son"; NRSV "child") to hear (i.e., obey) their teaching (vv. 8–9); the instruction proper, which consists of prohibitions (vv. 10–18); and the conclusion, which describes the results of wise or foolish behavior (v. 19).

While the character and authority of the social institution of the family is reflected in the titles "father," "mother," and "son," the more likely setting is that of a school: a temple school, a civil academy, or perhaps a household guild of scribes. In the first two types of schools, the familial titles would actually reflect the roles of teacher and student and not necessarily those of parents and children. The teacher stands in the place of the parent in becoming now the "significant other" who helps shape the student's moral character for both the scribal profession and righteous and proper living in the Jewish community. To "hear" means not only to listen to the content of the teaching but also to obey what is taught by incorporating its virtues into one's character and behavior through study, reflection, and practice. When the student finishes the course of study and leaves the teachers' daily guidance, then he or she is to have embodied the discipline of what was taught and no longer needs their presence to help him or her live the moral life.

The introduction also contains a motive clause that speaks of the great value of the instruction or discipline (vv. 8–9). In general, wisdom is offered as the source of life. Here two metaphors are used to express both the intrinsic value of "teaching" and "discipline" and their exhibition in the guidance and conduct of "life": they are an "elegant wreath" (NRSV "fair garland"; cf. Prov. 4:9) for one's head and "pendants" for one's neck (see Judg. 8:26; Song of Songs 4:9). These metaphors for the value of wisdom are adornments owned only by the wealthy. Wisdom's value is often expressed in terms of precious commodities, for example, silver, gold, and jewels (cf. Prov. 3:14–15; 8:11, 19). This metaphorical description of the value of teaching and discipline for living the moral life resonates with the images in Deut. 6:4–9 that portray the guidance of the commandments of the law, which are placed on the hand, the forehead, and the doorpost of the house.

The teaching proper (vv. 10–18) contains a warning against the enticement of "sinners" (defined in v. 19 as those "who get gain by violence"; NRSV "who are greedy for gain") to join them in their acts of violence against the innocent. "To entice" (*pātâ*) in verse 10 most often is a negative expression meaning "to seduce" (Exod. 22:16) or "to deceive" (Prov. 24:28; Jer. 20:7) and is used to contrast with the teacher's (or Woman Wisdom's) "call" or "invitation" to take up the course of study. The word for "sinner" (*ḥaṭṭā'*) literally means "to miss the mark" (Prov. 8:36) and is a general term that refers to any kind of violation of norms, particularly divine ones (Eccl. 7:26). The word may be used to refer to the violation of the just orders of life present in creation (Prov. 11:31) and incorporated in human society (Prov. 14:21, 34), and, due to divine retribution, sinners are expected to receive their just deserts (Prov. 13:21). These brigands who plot to rob and murder their victims and thus enrich themselves compare their insatiable greed to the voracious appetites of Sheol and the Pit, two terms for the underworld, whose ravenous hunger, along with that of Death, for the flesh of the living is prominently displayed in biblical literature (Job 18:13; Isa. 5:14; Hab. 2:5). In Canaanite mythology, Mot (Prince Death) is also described as having gaping jaws and a wide-open throat that continuously consume the living.

The beguiling speech of these brigands is "quoted," that is, formulated by the teacher's imagination as a diatribe where their arguments are used to entrap the unsuspecting student. The second part contains the teacher's motivation for not being seduced by the persuasive speech of these sinners: their acts of thievery and shedding of blood will lead to their own demise. This is one of the clearest expressions of retribution in Proverbs, and the most ironic: the means by which sinners work their evil is the same means by which they are punished, and in this case, destroyed.

The expression "to get gain by violence" (v. 19) is the major action ascribed to these sinners, and their own deeds of robbery and shed-

78

ding blood will come back against them to destroy them. In the early Persian period, this action of sinners could refer to those who sought to obtain from others, especially the weak and the poor, unjust gain through the misuse of political and social position (Isa. 10:2; Jer. 6:13; 8:8–10; Ezek. 22:27), to common criminals who robbed or committed financial crimes against others (Ps. 10:3), or to warriors or brigands who engaged in hostilities to obtain the booty of war (Num. 31:9, 53; Deut. 2:35; Jer. 20:5). Future sages, some of whom would obtain positions of prominence in political and social circles, were here admonished, then, not to abuse their power by engaging in violent deeds or fraudulent means to acquire wealth. In addition, the exhortation also may well be a warning against joining in acts of banditry and revolution against the Persian authorities and their colonial representatives.

The type of argument used by the teacher is casuistic, which sets forth the condition for a particular action or type of behavior: "if . . . , then." The content of this conditional (casuistic) argument is expressed in the hypothetical enticement of the student by sinners to join them in their villainy and in the teacher's exhortation to avoid this action: "do not consent" (v. 10), "do not walk" (v. 15), and "keep your foot from their paths" (v. 15b). The prohibition and admonition are followed by two motive clauses that speak of the wicked running to do evil and hastening to commit murder. The metaphor of walking on a path or road is commonly used by the sages to refer to the moral conduct one exhibits and the direction one takes in life (Prov. 4:26; 5:8, 21; 10:9; 14:2, 8, 12; 16:2, 7, 9, 17, 25; 19:3, 16; 21:2, 29).

Verses 17–19 form the conclusion, which sets forth what happens to those who practice violence to obtain unjust gain. In an undeniably clear expression of retributive justice, in which people are the recipients of the results of their own actions, those who practice violence will themselves be its victims and will lose their own life in the process.

Conclusion

This initial instruction seeks to deter students of wisdom from joining those who seek power and wealth through unjust acts of violence against the innocent. If this instruction is interpreted within the early decades of Persian rule, the intent may be to discourage the youth of Judah's prominent second temple households from resorting to political and social abuses of power or to engage in revolutionary acts against governmental authorities.

The expression "one who obtains unjust gain by violence" (NRSV all who are "greedy for gain") most likely refers either to revolutionaries who seek power and riches by violent means or to corrupt officials who

79

exploit others (v. 19). This instruction may have intended to discourage specifically those youth of the second temple period who came from prosperous families and had the option of substantial careers from either joining the militant bands of revolutionaries who were intent on overthrowing Persian rule and establishing once more an independent Jewish state, in which they would have prominent positions, or from exploiting their positions of prominence by acts of plunder and extortion. It is common that leaders of revolutions as well as prominent officials are from upper-class families. What was to discourage the youth of second temple families from joining these bands of brigands and revolutionaries or from profiting from their social and political positions was the "discipline" and "teaching" of the "parents" and the sure recognition of the disastrous end of such foolish action.

Theology

Whoever the "sinners" may be, whether corrupt leaders, social opportunists, common outlaws, or even revolutionaries, it is clear that this instruction, as well as the others to follow, expresses a social conservatism that more than likely emerged from a sociological paradigm of order. This paradigm saw creation and the social world of human beings as the entwined objects of divine action and providential control. To engage in violent acts against the innocent or duly appointed officials in a Persian colony in order to obtain unjust gain was a direct violation of this paradigm and, in the minds of the traditional sages, a negation of life-giving wisdom that was sure to lead to destruction for the perpetrators and harm for the community. Subsequently, the teachers of Proverbs 1—9, social conservatives that they are, warn their students to avoid joining this band of "sinners" and participating in their acts of violence. Divine providence, effectuated through retributive justice, will bring these sinners to destruction, for they will be destroyed by the very acts of deception and violence in which they engage.

1:20–33

First Poem on Woman Wisdom: Woman Wisdom's Invitation to the Simple

Date and Provenance

Proverbs 1:20–33 is the first didactic poem in this initial collection and thus in the entire book. Central to this poem, and to the ones to follow in chapters 8 and 9, is the personification of wisdom as Woman Wisdom, who is both an attribute of the divine character and a virtue to be sought, possessed, and then embraced by students and sages. Literary personifications are common in biblical literature. Examples include Jerusalem/Zion as the daughter of Yahweh (Jer. 6:26), Israel as the bride or wife of God (Jer. 2:2; Hosea 2), and Jerusalem and Samaria as sisters who are married, yet unfaithful, to God (Ezekiel 23; cf. chap. 16). Even so, the personification of wisdom as a woman is limited to the literature of the sages: Job 28, Proverbs 1 and 8—9, Sirach 24, and Wisdom of Solomon 10—19 (Murphy, *Tree of Life*, 133–49).

This literary figure takes on great theological and social significance in the literature of the sages. In these texts, wisdom is the active means and the righteous design of creation, the daughter in whom God takes delight, the royal queen who chooses rulers and brings them wealth and success, the teacher who gives instructions of life to her students, the providential guide of Israel and the faithful through the course of salvation history, the creative mist and divine word that took up residence in Zion and the temple, and the voice of God who declares divine instruction to those who would find life and well-being. This metaphor, then, serves to convey both the theological and the ethical content of wisdom, as well as the quest to discover and embody it. But the metaphor is also important in legitimating the existing social order, in which traditional sages served a variety of roles.

Set in the first part of the Persian period, this poem embodies the invitation of the sages to the "simple" of Judah's more prominent families to take up wisdom's course of study in one of the postexilic schools. What Woman Wisdom offered to these potential students was not simply mastering the knowledge and skill of a profession but a way of life that would lead to well-being and secure dwelling in what was, for the most part, an unsettled and difficult time.

Literary Structure and Interpretation

The poem consists of four parts: a third-person introduction in which Woman Wisdom issues her invitation throughout the various parts of the city (vv. 20–21); her first-person speech addressed to the simple, who are exhorted to listen to her reproof (vv. 22–23); her diatribe warning of the disaster that engulfs those who do not heed her invitation to learn of her (vv. 24–31); and her conclusion contrasting the secure dwelling and life of those who listen to her teaching with the death and destruction of complacent fools who hate knowledge and say no to her instruction (vv. 32–33).

81

Verses 20–21 depict Woman Wisdom as a peripatetic teacher, at least in her attempt to recruit the simple, for she goes to each of the major public arenas and thoroughfares of an ancient city in search of her students: the streets, the marketplaces, the tops of the walls, and the entrances to the gates. This does not mean these were the places where regular instruction occurred, but they are the contexts in which teachers could come and attempt to persuade potential students to learn from them. Presumably, the actual teaching and study would have occurred in schools located in public buildings or perhaps large private houses, including their courtyards.

The audience Wisdom primarily addresses is the "simple," those youth who have yet to take up the sages' course of study. Two other groups of people typically reject Wisdom's invitations (v. 22): "scoffers," who are unteachable (Prov. 13:1) because of their arrogance and contentiousness (Prov. 21:24; 22:10), and "fools," who do not restrain either their emotions (Prov. 12:16; 21:24; 29:8, 11) or their speech (Prov. 10:18–21; 12:19; 14:7). Because they lack the discipline of wisdom, both of the latter groups create discord that threatens and even disrupts a community's harmony and well-being (Prov. 15:18).

The youth reside not only in the city (presumably Jerusalem) but also in the towns and villages economically, politically, and religiously associated with this urban center. These simple ones are not necessarily opposed to the teaching that the sages offer but are young, lack prudence and sapiential knowledge, and have not acquired the discipline of study, critical thinking, and proper behavior (Prov. 1:22; 8:5; 9:4, 16). They are easily seduced by folly and led astray to experience disaster (Prov. 14:18). More than likely, the simple comprised intelligent young men and women from the very few well-to-do families (cf. Sir. 38:24) in Judah who could provide their offspring the opportunities for advancement through education and did not need them to remain at home in order for families to survive economically as households.

Woman Wisdom's diatribe (vv. 24–31) is a warning issued to the simple that the rejection of her invitation to come and learn of her will lead to their experiencing the same destruction that scoffers and fools are sure to encounter. Indeed, in times when fear and calamity engulf the simple, it will be too late then to seek the protection of life-giving counsel from Woman Wisdom and the school traditions she embodies. Only those who accept Wisdom's invitation, fear God and thus acknowledge Yahweh as the creator and providential sustainer of life, undertake the intensive and dedicated study of wisdom, and seek through discipline to incorporate its values to actualize in everyday life will have the means by which to face the times of calamity and panic that threaten them and their community. In a striking irony, it will be Woman Wisdom who mocks and derides the simple when they, in desperation, seek the safety of her teachings. These times of panic and impending destruction could range from major disasters threatening the existence of the larger community of Jews (e.g., pestilence, crop failure, and military invasion; see Jer. 18:17; Ezek. 35:5; Obadiah v. 13) to individual calamities of various types (e.g., illness, poverty, robbery, war; 2 Sam. 22:19 = Ps. 18:18 = Heb. 18:19; Job 18:12; 21:17; 31:3, 23). Without the guidance of counsel, that is, the careful planning designed to lead to success and to secure life, both the community and individuals could be vulnerable to the threats of disaster (de Boer, "The Counsellor," 42–71). This unprepared state of the simple, who do not fear Yahweh and, like fools, hate knowledge (v. 29; cf. v. 22), leads to devastation when calamity comes upon them. Thus, in the language of retributive justice, the simple who reject Wisdom's invitation will suffer the results of their own folly.

In typical fashion for instructions, the general conclusion (vv. 32–33) contrasts the fate of the foolish and the wise. The simple turn away from Wisdom's invitation and thus miss their opportunity for life-preserving instruction. The complacency of fools that makes them unaware of danger leaves them unprepared for the calamities of life. By contrast, those who heed the call of Woman Wisdom will dwell securely and be at ease (cf. Deut. 33:12, 28; Ps. 102:28 = Heb. 102:29; Jer. 23:6; 33:16). This promise of dwelling at ease in the land is especially appealing in a period of insecurity. For a people whose land in an earlier time had been conquered by the Babylonians and whose leaders had been exiled, this promise of peaceful inhabitation would have been particularly compelling.

Conclusion

The major purpose of this poem, in addition to the theological reasons given below, is to invite the simple to take up the course of wisdom. Woman Wisdom, assuming the role of the teacher in search of students, issues the reasons why the simple should accept her call (Malherbe, *Moral Exhortation*, 122–24). Included in her instruction are not only the benefits that the study of wisdom offers but also the destruction that comes to those who reject the invitation to take up this course of study. Socially, the sages are those who assume roles in the government, temple bureaucracy, and schools. These sages are the mainstay of Jewish life during the first half of the Persian period. Because of their key roles in Jewish society and conservative politics,

83

they as well as their families most likely enjoy not only the support of the presiding governor and the hierocracy of the Zadokite priesthood but also that of the Persian authorities. Thus, they are assured by Woman Wisdom, who embodies not only sapiential tradition but also speaks the voice of Yahweh, that they will dwell securely and be at ease in their country and in their homes, even during times of political and economic upheaval. By contrast, fools and scoffers who have rejected wisdom's invitation will experience calamity and panic when disaster strikes.

Perhaps these fools and scoffers should be understood as those who do not buy into the social world of Judah as a Persian colony that the traditional scribes help construct and attempt to legitimate. It is doubtful that those who reject the teachings of the sages and their invitation to enter their schools would be simply those who belong to families of common laborers and the poor. More likely, the fools and scoffers would belong to well-to-do households. As youth, they would have the opportunity and means to take up the study of wisdom. They would, however, likely be not those attracted to an alternative worldview of the "visionaries" but rather the youth of aristocratic families who lack either the desire or the conviction of the reality of traditional wisdom's worldview to engage in the rigorous study of the wisdom curriculum of the schools.

Theology

First person divine speeches, whether of Yahweh in the Old Testament (e.g., Isa. 42:8) or of gods and goddesses in other parts of the ancient world, were a common literary expression in religious literature. Bauer-Kayatz has pointed to important parallels between the speeches of Woman Wisdom and those about the Egyptian goddess Ma'at, the daughter of the sun god Re and the cosmic order of truth and justice that permeated reality (*Studien zu Proverbien 1–9*). In later texts, Isis, another Egyptian goddess, issues first person speeches that include an invitation, promises, and self-praise. The sage or sages who composed the speech of Woman Wisdom appear to have drawn on the discourse of goddesses from the ancient Near East to emphasize that the sapiential tradition, encapsulated in this striking literary metaphor, is the embodiment of the virtue of Yahweh's wisdom. This provides a compelling way of speaking of the divine authority of Yahweh, who seeks out the simple to lead them to life. Yet the voice of Yahweh not only offers salvation but also issues a dire warning: those who reject the teachings of wisdom will one day face disaster and panic that will engulf them and lead to their destruction. This is not unlike the sermons in Deuteronomy, where we find the "either-or" so typical of this preaching: obedience to the teachings of the law lead to life, whereas disobedience results in death.

The metaphor of Woman Wisdom also serves to give a concrete, albeit literary, form to divine immanence in the world. The increasing transcendence of Yahweh in exilic and postexilic literature raised the serious problem of how to depict divine presence in the world and among the chosen people. Woman Wisdom, who is God's virtue leading to life, provides one of the more concrete ways of representing divine presence. Moving beyond the metaphor, the sages are saying that God through wisdom not only is the teacher of the divine tradition but also is present in its articulation through the invitation to take up the course of study; in the knowledge contained in the teachings, sayings, and poems; in the actualization of what is learned in the formation of character; and in the behavior of the wise. Woman Wisdom and the tradition she embodies become the means by which the sages express the reality of divine presence. Divine immanence is given graphic though metaphorical expression in Woman Wisdom's assuming the role of the peripatetic teacher who goes throughout the areas of public gathering and discourse in the city (streets, marketplaces, tops of walls, and entrances to city gates) in search of students, that is, the "simple" who may respond affirmatively to her invitation of life.

Woman Wisdom also provides for the sages a means of speaking about divine revelation and thus gives flesh to the abstract understanding of the life-creating, life-sustaining, and life-redeeming word of God. The sages did not simply set forth their teachings on a take-it-or-leave-it basis, though they did encourage debate, examination, and testing to determine what was true. Even so, they argued that, to use their metaphor, Woman Wisdom was the voice of God who revealed the essential understanding for coming to a knowledge of God, for conducting the moral life, and for forming the character that would lead to well-being. Wisdom permeated the cosmos, was present in the social order, mediated between God and the cosmos, and took up her dwelling in the mind and moral life of the receptive sage. Through discipline, which included the study of the tradition of the wise, the observation of the order present in the world, and the formation of human character, students could understand in part the nature and will of God, who creates and sustains all life, the elements of the moral life, and the order of justice that permeates the world.

Finally, in a time perhaps not too many years removed from exile, the promise that those who took up Wisdom's call would dwell

85

securely and be at ease would have been an especially appealing one. This dwelling safely, presumably in the land of Judah, may at least suggest the promise that those who lived according to the dictates of wisdom would be confident of having a safe and secure place in Israelite society and would enjoy the protection and fruits of their household's patrimony (cf. Ps. 37:9–11; see Brueggemann, *The Land*).

2:1–22

Second Instruction: The Blessings of Wisdom and the Avoidance of the Strange Woman

Date and Provenance

The lengthy instruction in 2:1–22 is the second of this genre in Proverbs 1—9. In its present location, this teaching follows the didactic poem of Woman Wisdom (1:20–33), which serves as a speech of persuasion designed to induce Judah's youths to take up the study of wisdom and to warn them of the dire consequences of rejecting her invitation. This instruction also functions as a speech of persuasion, only this time it is uttered not by Woman Wisdom but by an implied teacher, neither named nor provided a title. The addressee is called the "son" (NRSV "child"), likely a youth considering entrance into a wisdom school's course of study. The major theme of this teaching is that wisdom, which is to be coveted and pursued like a valued treasure, still remains a gift from Yahweh. This means that, in the view of this instruction and, indeed, that of the entire first collection, wisdom is not simply available to rational inquiry and human observation. While these indigenous talents are necessary for obtaining and sharpening the understanding of the comprehensive variety of topics the sages examine and enfold into their teaching tradition, they are not enough. Ultimately, wisdom is a divine gift bestowed on a select few who fear Yahweh. This gift provides the necessary basis for the pursuit of discipline and its shaping of human character. Even the recipients of divine wisdom and the most disciplined of the sages still recognize the limits of what they know, not only of the world but also of God.

Among the important benefits of the possession of wisdom is its ability to protect the student from entrapment by the "strange woman" (vv. 16–19; NRSV "loose woman"). The metaphor of the strange woman appears several times in Proverbs 1—9 and is the opposite of Woman Wisdom. The identity of the strange woman, here and elsewhere in Proverbs 1—9, has often been debated and presents one of the major challenges for interpreting the first collection (5:3–14, 19–20; 6:24–35; 7:1–27; and 9:13–18). The two primary expressions for this woman, "strange woman" (*'iššâ zārâ*) and "foreign woman" (*nŏkrîyâ*), have a variety of connotations. The word *zārâ* is a feminine participle often used as an adjective or noun to refer to one who is estranged (Job 19:13; Ps. 78:30); is unknown to a person or group (Job 19:27; Prov. 27:2); belongs to another household (Deut. 25:5; Job 19:15; Prov. 6:1; 11:15; 20:16; 27:13), tribe (Num. 1:51), and nation (Hos. 7:9); is a foreigner (Jer. 5:19; Hos. 7:9; 8:7); is a prostitute (Prov. 22:14); or is a devotee of a pagan fertility goddess (Prov. 7:5). The feminine noun *nŏkrîyâ* is a synonym of *zārâ* and refers to a foreigner or foreign group (Deut. 17:15; 1 Kings 11:1, 8), a prostitute (Prov. 23:27), and one who is unknown (Eccl. 6:2). The proposed interpretations of the strange woman and her activity in Proverbs include adultery, common prostitution, cultic prostitution in devotion to a pagan fertility deity, foreign culture and religion, and folly, the opposite of wisdom (see Prov. 9:1–18). It is likely that the sages of Proverbs understood the strange woman to represent all these identities (Blenkinsopp, "Social Context of the 'Outsider Woman' in Proverbs 1–9," 457–73).

The other important topic in this instruction is the promise that the upright will inhabit the land, whereas the wicked will be uprooted. The promise of the land and continuing to inhabit it is a major theme in the Old Testament, and represents, perhaps, the major blessing of Yahweh poured out over Israel and Judah and its family households to whom the land was parceled out (Brueggemann, *The Land*). The loss of the land was perhaps the greatest curse, both for a household and for the nation, for this led for all practical purposes to their demise. This theme was particularly of concern during the period of the Babylonian destruction of Judah, the return home of the descendants of the captives from exile, and concomitant issue of the hereditary rights of the families who returned over against the possession of those who were left behind.

Literary Structure and Interpretation

This instruction may be subdivided into the following, typical parts: the address (v. 1a, "My son"), the teaching proper—the desire and quest for wisdom leads to the fear and knowledge of God (vv. 1b-5), wisdom as the gift of God (vv. 6–8), the benefits of wisdom (vv.

9–11), wisdom's protection of the sage from speakers and doers of evil (vv. 12–15), wisdom's redemption from the strange woman (vv. 16–19)—and the conclusion (vv. 20–22). While following the standard pattern of the instruction genre, this text serves more as a speech of persuasion than a typical instruction that lists admonitions and prohibitions about one or more common sapiential topics.

The instruction begins with a brief introduction, addressing the listener in typical fashion ("My son," v. 1a). But the text then moves quickly into a lengthy, five-part teaching proper that provides not a list of prohibitions and admonitions and their various attached clauses but rather a series of advantages and blessings that accrue from obedience and study that lead to the possession of wisdom. These are followed by the pitfalls that result from rejecting the teaching to follow the path of wickedness. This type of argumentation shapes the instruction into more of a speech of persuasion that attempts to induce the hearer to take up the path to wisdom than a paraenetic teaching listing admonishments, prohibitions, and their results and rationales (Malherbe, *Moral Exhortation*, 122–24).

In the first two parts of the teaching proper, the teacher uses conditional clauses followed by the resulting consequences that should motivate the student to action: "if . . . , then" (vv. 1, 3, 4, 5, 9). This type of argumentation is reminiscent of case law in the Israelite and Jewish legal codes and has suggested to some scholars that among the sages were lawyers and judges engaged in the formulation of judicial law (e.g., the Covenant Code, Exod. 20:22–23:33; see Preuss, *Old Testament Theology*, 1:80–95). In the legal codes, "if" or "when" (*kî*) normally introduces the main conditional clause that precedes the description of a particular legal offense or case, while "if" (*'im*) introduces any subordinate conditional clauses (see Prov. 2:1, 3, 4). In this instruction, *'im* ("if") introduces the three main conditional clauses. In legal codes, the apodosis (introduced usually by "then" = *wāw* or sometimes *'āz*) after the conditional clause or clauses registers the legal consequences, as also is true of this instruction (*'āz;* see Prov. 2:5, 9). This formal similarity is one of the bases for arguing that the teachings of the sages are far more than simply good advice. The instruction bears the impress of authority based on the gift of divine wisdom and the wise observation of the righteous order of creation.

In the last two parts of this instruction (vv. 12–15, 16–19), as well as in the conclusion (20–22), each opening line begins in Hebrew with an infinitive (vv. 12, 16) or a comparable grammatical construction. These are used to introduce the results of following the sage's teaching. In the last two sections of the instruction proper, the student who takes up the course of wisdom will avoid the pathway of the wicked and will be saved from the strange woman, both of whom lead the unlearned to destruction. In the conclusion, the results present a contrast between the upright who inherit the land and the wicked who are uprooted.

In the initial part of the teaching proper (vv. 1b–5), the teacher, using three instances of the conditional (casuistic or case) argument of "if" (vv. 1, 3, 4) . . . "then" (v. 5), constructs the first inducement to listen and be obedient to wisdom. The argument runs accordingly. If youths will listen to the teachings of the wise and search diligently for wisdom as a valued treasure, then they will come to possess the foundational piety that becomes the essential basis for all other sapiential virtues: namely, the fear of the Lord, which allows the possibility of the most coveted of all knowledge, the understanding of the character and activity of God. The fear of the Lord is the reverent confession and reverential acknowledgment that Yahweh is the creator and sustainer of all life and the true giver of wisdom. This fundamental confession anchors the possibility of coming to understand all other elements of wisdom and to enjoy the blessings that accrue from its possession.

It is important to note the literary linkages of this first part of the instruction with the opening didactic poem in 1:20–33, which also contains elements of a speech of persuasion. As is true of the preceding poem, wisdom is compared to treasures of great worth that are highly coveted (2:4; cf. 1:9; also Prov. 3:14–15 and 8:11, 19). Like Woman Wisdom, who earlier "cries out" and "raises her voice" (1:20–21) in the public places of the city to persuade the simple to learn of her, the "son" in chapter 2 is to respond in kind by "crying out" for "insight" and by raising his voice for "understanding" (2:3). Though it is a gift that cannot be grasped, at the same time wisdom comes only to those who search for it as a greatly valued treasure (see Job 28).

The second part of the teaching proper contains the theme for the entire teaching: wisdom is the gift of God (2:6–8) and not the object of human striving. This theme makes clear that it is divine grace, not human merit whether attached to works, the intrinsic worth of personal character, or the esteem of high position, that is the source of the reception of wisdom. Like humans in Job whose rapacious appetite to discover wisdom on their own leads only to failure, for God alone knows her and her origins (Job 28), in the present instruction human striving to obtain understanding is successful only when God decides to offer wisdom freely. This gift of wisdom, however, does not come from the capricious act of an inscrutable deity. Rather, God determines those who are to enjoy the conferring of this gift of inestimable

89

value, for its reception is primarily based on their fervent desire and diligent search to obtain it. One must desire wisdom, a desire frequently couched in the language of a lover's passion, before receiving it as a prize beyond measure. This means also that God gives wisdom only to those who have developed in their character the "fear of the Lord," recognizing then that God alone is the creator of life, the sustainer of all that is, and the true source and giver of wisdom.

Assuming a hymnlike character that typically describes divine characteristics and acts of mercy and redemption (see Psalms 33 and 104; Prov. 3:19–20), this second part of the teaching proper (2:6–8) traces out the attributes of God that lead to the safeguard of cosmic and social justice and the preservation of God's "saints" or "pious ones" or "faithful ones" (cf. Ps. 34:10). The saints in this context are those who fear God, confessing him as Lord and Creator, thereby opening themselves to the possibility of the free gift of divine wisdom. This hymnlike subdivision teaches the potential student that the justice that permeates reality, holds together all creation, and sustains life in nature and in human society stands under the watchful and protective care of providence. Verse 8 returns to the common metaphor of the journey of the sage through life, comparing the sapiential life to a "path" or "road" taken by a sage who is guarded and preserved by divine oversight. The one pursuing the teachings of the wise is not left alone to grope blindly along the way in impenetrable darkness in the pursuit of life and well-being. Rather, God through the gift of wisdom pilots the sage's course of life and providentially protects him or her from misfortune and the danger of becoming lost.

Having stressed the importance of inculcating the desire and search for wisdom, all the while emphasizing that it is still a divine gift, the teacher turns to point out its benefits in the final three parts of the instruction. Verses 9–11 speak of the understanding, intelligence, prudence, and discretion that the student to whom God chooses to give wisdom will acquire. These virtues have already been listed among the goals of the study of wisdom articulated in the introduction (1:2–7). Verse 10 describes wisdom's entrance into the human heart, which, for the sages, was the organ of reason, reflection, memory (Prov. 8:5; 16:23; 18:15), and the will, where decisions were formulated and the intent to carry forth human actions was determined (Prov. 16:9; 20:4). Likewise, knowledge, a synonym for wisdom, will "delight the soul." The term for "delight" (NRSV "be pleasant to") is the human response to beauty (Song of Songs 7:7; Ezek. 32:19), while "soul" in this context most likely refers to the seat of the emotions and passions residing within human nature. Thus reason and passions are the two components of human nature necessary for the obtaining of understanding. Yet only the fear of God, the desire for wisdom, and the gift of divine insight activate them.

This entrance into the heart, which is the result of the gift of God, does not mean that the cultivation of wisdom through the discipline of study and character formation is obviated. Yet, without this divine gift, even the most industrious student will neither attain the intellectual prowess and moral virtues of sapiential teaching nor come to the knowledge of God. The gift of wisdom also provides those within whom it dwells the ability to understand and then actualize in life righteousness and justice and to practice equity or fairness in their behavior (v. 9). *Righteousness* and *justice* are often synonyms in wisdom literature and refer to the moral order of creation and society that sustains life through divine governance, as well as to the ethical character of the sage. "Equity" refers to fair treatment of others without deference to their social position and in accordance with the dictates of custom, law, and sapiential tradition. Fair treatment takes on a more specific character in the administration of justice, whether in the household by the senior male and female or in the courts by judges and governors (Pss. 9:8 = Heb. 9:8; 58:2; 75:2 = Heb. 75:3; 99:4; 96:10 and Prov. 1:3). "Discretion" or "prudence" is the ability to judge in a reasoned fashion both the facts and the situation to reach a fair and just decision (Prov. 1:4; 3:21; 5:2; 8:12).

In the fourth part of the teaching proper (2:12–15), the sage indicates to the prospective student that wisdom and its various virtues enable one to be saved from the path of the evil. Here one finds the contrast between the righteous and the wicked, a common topos throughout Proverbs (e.g., 15:8–9). The term *path* or *road* is used metaphorically to express not only the course of the life of the wise person but also that of the evil person. The evil one refers to the one whose speech is deceitful and thus cannot be trusted, and whose entire manner of life destroys the bonds of relationships and the solidarity of human community. Indeed, deceitful speech, left unchecked, perverts the moral order of the cosmos and damages the structures of life for all creation. Those who are evil are not forced to be so by Yahweh. Rather, the teacher stresses, turning toward the lifestyle of the evil ones is a matter of choosing to turn from the "paths of uprightness" to follow the "ways of darkness." Unlike the recipient of wisdom, who delights in knowledge, the wicked take their pleasure in doing evil.

The fifth part of the teaching proper occurs in verses 16–19. Paralleling the evil one in the preceding part is the strange woman. Those who heed the invitation of the sage to study wisdom will also be

91

delivered from this multifaceted figure in Proverbs 1—9, who is the metaphorical depiction of sexual promiscuity, foolish behavior, and cultural seduction. Like the wicked, she, too, misuses speech, only in this case she utters "smooth" words, that is, seductive or flattering language to entrap the unlearned (v. 16; cf. Prov. 5:3; 26:28). In this version of the strange woman, she appears in the guise of the adulteress, for she is the one "who forsakes the partner of her youth and forgets her sacred covenant" (2:17). "Covenant" refers to the marriage contract, perhaps written down (Mal. 2:14; Tobit 7:13–15; see Collins, "Marriage, Divorce, and Family," 104–62). Although love and affection are occasionally mentioned between a husband and wife (Gen. 34:3–4; 1 Sam. 18:20), marriages in Israel and Judah were essentially an economic arrangement between two family households and had as their primary purpose survival through reproduction, the securing of the husband's household's property rights, and laws of inheritance. The wife's household received from the husband's family a *mōhar* or "marriage gift" (Gen. 34:12) to compensate for the loss of her labor. She also may have had a dowry on which to draw in case she was widowed or her husband divorced her. She had no right to divorce her husband.

Large families were usually needed to enable households to sustain even a marginal existence. By means of marriage, children, most usually the males, were the heirs of the household's property, with the lion's share going to the firstborn son. The bride left her family to reside with her husband and his extended household, though she could return home if she were divorced or her husband predeceased her. Normally, however, she remained with her dead husband's extended family, particularly if the husband had a next of kin who could take her as a wife to raise up children to the deceased family member. Adultery by either partner was to be punished by death (Lev. 20:10; Deut. 22:22–24), though it is clear that prostitution was widespread (e.g., Genesis 38), and there is no evidence that the penalty was ever carried out. In verses 18–19 in Proverbs 2, this punishment seems to be reflected in the poetic language of her path leading to death and to the "shades" (the dead who are the shadowy inhabitants of the underworld; see Prov. 9:18). Death is the place from which there is no return.

Adultery in Proverbs is many things, including an ethical misdeed, faithlessness to the marriage partner, a violation of a divine norm, and a sin (or an abomination) against God. While adultery may be each of these, it is more especially an act that violates the social order that is to reflect the righteous and life sustaining order of creation. The sages shared the Yahwist's view that marriage was an institution grounded in the origin and order of creation (Gen. 2:4b–25). Adultery diminished the solidarity of the family, which was the core value among the understandings of the family in ancient Israel and early Judaism. Solidarity involved the recognition of the worth and needs of the household above those of the individual (Meyers, "Family in Early Israel," 1–47). In addition, adultery threatened the viability of the extended household, both in economic terms and in regard to the family's existence into the future. The family's labor force required numerous offspring in order to exist, as children often were subject to deadly childhood diseases and malnutrition. Children were also needed to secure the extended household's existence into the future as offspring who would possess the family's inheritance. These things were true even for the affluent families to which many sages appear to have belonged.

The third and concluding section of this instruction occurs in verses 20–22. This climactic ending is designed to appeal to the prospective student's desire to take up the course of study. In following the course of life of the good and the just, who are guided by wisdom, the upright will inhabit the land, and not the wicked, who will be removed. Frequently occurring in Proverbs are the contrasting behaviors and fates of the righteous and wicked (see especially Proverbs 10—15).

The specific content of this contrast is rather striking, for here the wisdom of the teachers enters one of the most serious economic debates in Israelite history. Most Israelite and Jewish land traditionally was owned by individual family households who transmitted this precious commodity through laws of heredity, though poverty could force the family to sell its property, including its freehold. Viewed purely in economic terms, a household's land provided the basis for its survival. This necessity led to the creation of a legal tradition about the land that had the objective of keeping this patrimony within the ownership of the individual family.

This debate grew in intensity in the early part of the Persian period, when the returning exiles laid claim to the land their ancestors had owned prior to being taken into Babylonian captivity. Were the claims of returning families to take precedence over those of households, Israelite as well as foreign, who now occupied some of these holdings? The legal tradition, which came into the control of the hierocratic party, favored the exiles. This included the legislation about the year of jubilee that resulted in the returning of patrimonial lands to their rightful households in the fiftieth year at the end of seven cycles of seven years (Lev. 25:8–17, 23–55; 27:15–25; Num. 36:4).

The family household provided the paradigm for a good deal of

93

Old Testament theology, for God, Israel, the nations, and the land were often presented in household categories easily understood by a predominantly agrarian society of family farms. Thus, for example, God was the parent of Israel; Israel was the child; the non-Israelites were resident aliens; and the land was the property of Israel, distributed to its families by divine decree (Perdue, *Families in Ancient Israel*, 223–57). Theologically speaking, each of Israel's households came to believe that its patrimony originated in the distribution of land by God to its family (Josh. 13:1—19:51), and thus they established legal and social means that would restrict in perpetuity the land being sold outside the extended family (Lev. 25:23–24).

This theological understanding of patrimonial land as a divine gift to the household provided the basis for the more comprehensive theological affirmation of the land of Israel as a divine gift to Israel's ancestors (Gen. 17:1–8) and to Israel (Deut. 1:8; 26:5–9; Josh. 1:2). Particularly important to Deuteronomy and the Deuteronomistic editors was the association of Yahweh's granting the land to Israel with obedience to the covenant. Israel would possess and continue to inhabit this land as long as its people were faithful to the covenant with Yahweh (Deut. 1:8; 8:1; 11:8–9). Should Israel violate the covenant, it faced the threat of being removed through conquest and exile (Deut. 28:36, 63–68; Jer. 7:15; see Brueggemann, *The Land*).

For the sages, the ownership and continuing inhabitation of the land, more likely the land of the individual family household than the land of Israel, was based not on the theological tradition of the land as a divine gift to Israel, its ancestors, or its households but rather on the sages' ethical understanding of justice. The gift of wisdom enabled the sage to understand and incorporate sapiential teachings in daily existence. Thus the conclusion to this instruction (Prov. 2:20–22), like Psalm 37 (especially vv. 3, 9, 10–11, 22, 28–29, 34, and 38), emphasizes that the "upright" will inhabit and continue to dwell in the land, while the wicked will be cut off and removed from the land. Removal from the household land would result in the dispersion of the family. If no related family could absorb the dispersed members, slavery, day labor, concubinage, prostitution, and even starvation and death awaited.

This reference to household land and the socioeconomic context of the family as one of the primary settings for ethical behavior corresponds to the final part of the teaching proper (Prov. 2:16–19). The strophe preceding verses 20–22 emphasizes that adultery is destructive to the two who are engaged in this deception but also to the covenant of marriage that is at the core of the family household. This instruction, at least in part, points to the household as one of the pri-

94

mary contexts for actualizing the teachings of wisdom in the moral life. In this teaching, the social and economic sphere of blessing is the family household. The violation of the marriage covenant and expulsion from the household land will result in catastrophe for the family.

Conclusion

This teaching (2:1–22) is a persuasive instruction delivered by a sage in a wisdom school to the youths of Judah ("son"), probably in the early Persian period. These youths are exhorted to take up the course of study in one of the wisdom schools that likely existed at the time. In this speech of persuasion, the teacher explains that wisdom is a divine gift that, taken into the heart, enables the youth to come to a knowledge of God, to live the moral life, and to experience divine protection and blessings. It is especially the household that is the social setting for the moral life, and this instruction seems particularly concerned to maintain the viability of the extended family. Adultery that violates the marriage covenant and wicked behavior that results in the loss of household land lead to the destruction not only of the individual evildoer but also of the family to which he or she belongs.

Theology

It is not coincidental that the emphasis on "inhabiting the land" occurs immediately after the first discourse on the "strange woman." An intended linkage between avoiding the strange woman and inhabiting the land would indicate that the sages who fashioned this instruction meant to say that land ownership and the inheritance of the land, so valued and so much at issue in early postexilic Judah, are contingent on the embodiment of the virtues of wisdom and righteousness.

3:1–12

Third Instruction:
The Blessings of Wisdom and Piety

Date and Provenance

The third instruction in Proverbs 1—9 occurs in the first twelve verses of chapter 3. This teaching is not a speech designed to induce the youth of Judah to enter a wisdom school but rather a moral discourse, or more specifically, a speech of exhortation that issues to students both admonitions and prohibitions concerning a variety of virtues to embody in life and vices to avoid. The general and specific topics range from keeping the teacher's commandments, to loyalty and faithfulness, to trusting in Yahweh, to avoiding vain self-conceit, to the offering of gifts and the observing of other sacrificial responsibilities. Placed in the setting of the early part of the Persian period, this teaching is a prime example of a conservative tradition that seeks to maintain the new order of social, political, and religious reality emerging in the early postexilic period. This new order came to favor the hierocratic group, which was given eventual control of most local matters by the Persian authorities in exchange for their loyalty.

Literary Structure and Interpretation

The instruction follows the standard literary structure of an introduction ("My son," v. 1a; NRSV "My child"); the teaching proper, which contains both admonitions and prohibitions (vv. 1b–10); and the conclusion (vv. 11–12). This poetic text contains six couplets of two lines (save for v. 3, which may contain an addition at the end: "write them on the tablet of your heart") that cover both general and specific topics (vv. 1–2, 3–4, 5–6, 7–8, 9–10, and 11–12). The admonitions and prohibitions are not apodictic in that they issue a moral command that needs no justification. Rather, each one is followed by a clause that provides in some way the rationale for obeying the teacher's instruction. Once again the teacher is not identified while the student is called the "son." Most likely the setting for this teaching is a wisdom school where the sage is instructing students in proper behavior in Judahite society of the early part of the Persian period, a society where the hierocratic party had dominance.

The teaching proper (vv. 1b–10) emphasizes most of all what best might be called "loyalty" and "faithfulness" (v. 3a: *ḥesed* and *ʾĕmet*). Loyalty to the teacher and the wisdom tradition is demonstrated by the student's faithful obedience to what is taught. Loyalty to God is expressed by the student's recognizing divine lordship, renouncing the vanity of his (or her) own wisdom, and fearing God. Faithfulness to God is shown by following divine instruction, equated with that of the teacher, and by giving one's wealth and first fruits as offerings.

The first strophe (vv. 1b–2) of the teaching proper starts with the typical exhortation to the student to remember the teacher's "instruction" (*tôrâ*—NRSV "teaching") and to observe the "commandments" (*miṣwôt*), that is, the individual admonitions (or prohibitions) that comprise the larger teaching (see, e.g., 1:8, 23; 2:1; 3:13). The motive clauses that follow in the succeeding couplet are two of the chief values of the wisdom tradition: long life (3:16; 4:10) and well-being (3:17). Well-being (*šālôm*) refers to the state of contentment, pleasantness, health, welfare, and security in which good things are had and experienced without the stress of anxiety and fear. Long life without well-being was no blessing at all, for the extension of one's days only to experience misery was not a desirable state. The ideal was to live to a ripe old age, to see one's children's children, and to die in peace and contentment while surrounded by the extended family (see Genesis 48—49 and the *Testament of the Twelve Patriarchs*). The teacher promises the student that he or she will experience these values by being obedient to the instruction.

Loyalty and faithfulness, a commonly found hendiadys in Proverbs (14:22; 16:6; 20:28), now move to center stage in the teaching proper in the second couplet or strophe (vv. 3–4). Loyalty in this literary setting refers to the virtue of commitment and dedication that binds one's life usually to an individual or group having no rivals (Doob Sakenfeld, *Ḥesed*). In Proverbs and the other texts of the wisdom tradition, loyalty refers to devotion and unwavering commitment to God (Prov. 2:8; 16:6), to the teacher and the wisdom tradition (3:3), to the spouse and larger family (5:15–23), to the king (20:28), and to the larger community (14:22), as well as to God's commitment and devotion to the sage whom God has given life and formed in the womb (Job 10:12). Loyalty is the virtue that seals and undergirds the relationship between a sage and the object of commitment. In Old Testament covenant theology, *ḥesed* refers to the steadfast love and commitment that exist between God and Israel. In Proverbs, there is no comprehensive covenant to be found or mentioned between the chosen people and Yahweh, but many important relationships are sustained by this virtue. Faithfulness is used in this context as a synonym for loyalty (see Prov. 16:6). This virtue is the expectation that the entity to which one is loyal will prove true or will act in ways that will enhance one's well-being. In this context (Prov. 3:3), the emphasis appears to be placed on loyalty and faithfulness to the teachings of the wisdom tradition espoused by the sage. The motivation for being loyal and faithful is to find favor and to have good sense in the eyes of both God and human beings (Prov. 28:23; Jer. 31:2).

The imagery of the students binding loyalty and faithfulness around their necks and writing them on their hearts is designed to emphasize the importance of these values, their remembrance, and

97

their incarnation in human character (see Prov. 1:9). This imagery also echoes Deuteronomic language about remembering the laws and teachings of this code: "Bind them as a sign on your hand, fix them as an emblem on your forehead, and write them on the doorposts of your house and on your gates" (Deut. 6:8–9). This similarity suggests that the sages of Israel and Judah may have been involved in the writing and redaction of Deuteronomy and the Deuteronomistic corpus (Weinfeld, *Deuteronomy and the Deuteronomic School*).

In the third strophe (3:5–6), the teacher admonishes the student to trust in Yahweh, not himself, and to come to know God in the experiences along life's pathway. Trust (*bāṭaḥ*) in God, according to the wisdom teachers (Prov. 16:20; 29:25), is a virtue that is central to the practice of religious faith. To trust God means to rely on God's truthfulness and integrity and on the authenticity of divine promises. The student is to hope in confidence, knowing that the teaching that reveals the character and activity of God is true and reliable and that God will protect the one who acts accordingly. Coming to the knowledge of God derives not simply or even entirely from theoretical propositions but rather and primarily from the experiences of life and the observations of creation that one has along the pathway of wisdom. These experiences of the sage are to be tested for their veracity against the traditional teachings of the ancestral wise men and women of Israel and Judah. In most cases there is correspondence, not deviation or difference. Trusting God and knowing Yahweh, while not depending on one's own insight, are the acts of piety and the moral life that lead to divine guidance along the straight path.

The teacher in couplet four (vv. 7–8) warns the student against self-conceit. Rather, the would-be sage is to fear Yahweh, that is, to acknowledge with reverence God as creator and sustainer, and to turn from evil, that is, to practice the moral life that does not deviate into frivolity and wickedness occasioned by the vicissitudes of existence (see Job 28:28). The result is healing for one's body (Prov. 4:22; 5:11) and physical being (Prov. 14:30; 15:30; 16:24). The motivation for piety and the moral life is health, which presumably comes from the divine healer (Gen. 20:17; Job 5:18; Ps. 41:4 = Heb. 41:5).

The fifth and final strophe or couplet (Prov. 3:9–10) of the teaching proper turns to the arena of worship, more specifically, sacrifice. The teacher begins with an admonition to "honor" Yahweh with one's wealth, that is, to offer gifts presumably within the context of worship, and to offer the "first fruits" of the various harvests of the vineyards, orchards, and fields. First fruits were tendered to Yahweh during the three major agricultural festivals: the Festival of Unleavened Bread (barley), the Festival of Weeks (wheat), and the Festival of Tabernacles (vineyards and orchards). This act of worship acknowledged that Yahweh was the giver of the produce on which life was dependent. To offer the first and presumably the best of the harvest was to acknowledge Yahweh's lordship and to make appropriate the human consumption of what remained. The motivation for gifts and offerings was the expectation that the Lord of the harvests would enlarge one's yield and thus fill one's barns with produce and one's vats with wine. The priests who served in the temple ate the first fruits. Gifts and sacrifices sustained the priesthood and demonstrated the sages' support of and possible alliance with the priests, especially during the Persian period.

The conclusion (vv. 11–12) returns to the beginning (vv. 1–2) with the repetition of "My son" (v. 1a = v. 11a), only now the teacher identifies his instruction with that of Yahweh. God's instruction requires continual reproof of the student, like that of a parent to a beloved child. Reproof, which probably involved tedious and laborious study and repetition of assignments as well as verbal and physical chastisement, was a motivation for the student to strive to do well in his or her studies. Such reproof should be taken not as rebuke but as the guiding hand and caring word of a loving parent toward the child.

Conclusion

This instruction of the young in the setting of a wisdom school was designed to inculcate within them proper virtues as the basis for their existence, discourse, and behavior in Judahite society during the period of Persian rule. The teaching especially stresses the virtues of loyalty and faithfulness, for these were necessary for Jewish society to exist and function during foreign rule. Yet the object of loyalty and faithfulness, while not clearly specified, appears in the larger context to be God. By incorporating these central virtues, the youth will find favor in the eyes of God and human beings. They are to trust in and come to know Yahweh, to fear God and turn from evil, to honor God with the gifts of their wealth and the sacrifices of their first fruits, and not to despise divine reproof.

It is likely that the youth (probably an idealized reference to all young men and women addressed by the sages) to whom this and other instructions were issued came from well-to-do households that belonged to social groups holding the dominant power and positions in local matters. Religious observance and conservative values were in vogue in the wisdom tradition, and particularly in Proverbs 1—9.

While not explicitly mentioned in this instruction, the Persian rulers, as was true of those of any other kingdom or empire, required loyalty and faithfulness to their external authority and the economic requirements of their empire through taxation. These virtues, then, would have sat well with Persian authorities. Once again, the tradition here is obviously socially conservative and neither advocates revolution nor envisions a new order emerging at some point in the future.

Theology

Throughout its history, Israel was defined primarily as a community bound together by "loyalty" or "steadfast love" (*ḥesed*). This is the virtue that is often associated with the covenant between God and Israel in the Hebrew Bible. While the covenant called for this loyalty by obedience to obligations in the form of commandments, the sages called for loyalty to God through obeying their teachings, which they equated with divine instruction. The wisdom of God, often personified as Woman Wisdom in Proverbs 1—9, is the creative and life-giving force that makes possible the existence of both the cosmos and the righteous. This life-giving and sustaining force was incorporated in and identified with the teachings of the sages. Obedience for the sages is obedience to their teachings and the embodiment of the virtues of those teachings in both speech and behavior.

Faith and faithfulness (*'ĕmet*), when referring to God as its object or subject, is used in the Old Testament only in regard to Israel's God, not to any other deity. Faith has nothing to do with intellectual assent to the existence of God but rather is concerned with faithfulness, both that of God to believers—or, as the sages would say, the community of God-fearers—and the faithfulness of the God-fearers to Yahweh (Hermisson and Lohse, *Faith*). Thus faith is analogous to "trust," which often appears in the same context, as is the case here. The act of faithfulness is based on the belief in or assurance of divine trustworthiness, exhibited in protecting and caring for faithful people regardless of social standing (see Gen. 15:7–21). It is through the observation and experience of the sages leading to the knowledge of God that faithfulness and its corollary, trust, are generated. Embedded deeply in the wisdom tradition and continually verified by new experiences, faith in Yahweh and faithfulness to God formed a major cornerstone of the teachings of the conservative sages of Proverbs.

100

It is also important to note that the teaching of the sage is here identified with divine instruction or discipline. It is not enough to say that the wisdom tradition, including the teachings and poems in

Proverbs 1—9, is grounded in human observation and experience. For the sages, the observation and experience of creation and life were also the observation and experience of God. The knowledge of God came through the divine gift of wisdom, which led to teachings that were considered authoritative and true. This did not mean that the sages espoused blind credulity, but they did assert that their teachings, grounded in the character and activity of God and the righteous and life-sustaining order of creation, were equated with divine instruction.

Finally, one notes at the end of this instruction (3:12) the use of the simile of father, and more specifically, a father's love, to speak of Yahweh and his divine love toward those who are pursuing wisdom's path in their course of study. Household language is often used in the Old Testament to speak of God as parent, redeemer of family members in distress, and husband, while Israel is the child, resident alien, day laborer, slave, wife, and concubine. The father in the family household usually was the senior male, who possessed considerable authority. He was responsible for assigning economic roles to household members, determining the heir (usually male) of the major portion of the family patrimony, adjudicating family disputes, arranging marriages, and determining punishment, including even death, for violations of family laws and customs. According to the sage in this instruction, however, divine reproof is like that of a father who reproves those he loves, even the son of his delight, presumably the son who would be the major heir of the household patrimony.

3:13–20

Second Poem on Wisdom: Wisdom's Gifts and Role in Creation

Literary Structure and Interpretation

Proverbs 3:13–20 is a wisdom poem of four couplets or strophes (each of two poetic lines) that centers on the metaphor of Woman Wisdom: the first strophe (vv. 13–14) speaks of the joy of the discovery of wisdom and its value; the second (vv. 15–16) describes wisdom's incomparable precious nature and its representation as a goddess of life; the third (vv. 17–18) continues the depiction of wisdom as a goddess of life; and the last (vv. 19–20) describes her role in creation (cf. the poems in Prov. 8:1–11, 12–21; and also Psalm 19). Like two

101

wisdom psalms in the Psalter (Psalms 32 and 119), this poem in Proverbs 3 about Woman Wisdom begins with a "happy" ('ašrê) saying (v. 13) and concludes with this key term. This inclusion provides the outer demarcations of the poem and focuses attention on the key theme: the one who discovers wisdom is "happy" (or "blessed"), that is, has the means by which to enter the sphere of well-being. In the Old Testament, especially the Psalter and Second Isaiah (Isaiah 40—55), hymns praise God in two major ways: as the one who creates and continues to sustain the world and humanity (e.g., Psalms 8, 33, 104, and 139) and as the savior who delivers both his people and individuals from peril (e.g., Psalms 78, 106, 135, 136). In hymns, Israel praises the glory and might of God that are demonstrated in these great acts of creation and salvation. The sages, however, choose not to extol God directly for his acts of creation and providence. Instead, they do so indirectly by praising Woman Wisdom, the metaphorical embodiment of divine wisdom as the life-giving design and activity of God. This poem joins others in Proverbs 1—9 that portray Woman Wisdom (1:20–33; 8:1–36; and 9:1–18).

This poem of four couplets begins with two proverbs: a "happy" or "blessed" saying (v. 13) and a comparative saying (v. 14). "Happy" or "blessed" sayings are so called because they begin with 'ašrê (happy/blessed), a word that in wisdom literature describes the state of well-being and joy entered by the student who follows the teachings of the sages (Prov. 8:32, 34; 14:21; 16:20; 29:18). What causes this state of blessedness is the discovery of wisdom. The first half line thus underscores the teacher's affirmation that wisdom may be found and that it does not reside beyond human reach (contrast, e.g., Job 28). Shaped in the form of a comparative proverb that stresses something has more value than another, the result clause (v. 14) added to the happy saying points to the incomparable value of the obtaining of wisdom. The wealth she produces is better than silver and gold (see Ps. 19:10 = Heb. 19:11; Prov. 8:18–19).

The second couplet also contains a better saying, in this case at the beginning of the strophe. Now wisdom is compared favorably with jewels, which are said to contain less value. Indeed, wisdom is of greater worth than anything the human heart can desire. The second line of this couplet begins the description of wisdom as a goddess of life. Long life (Prov. 3:2; 22:4), riches (Prov. 14:24), and honor (Prov. 8:18) are among the greatest values in wisdom literature (1 Kings 3:1–15). Yet, not surprising for conservative sages who belonged to or at least served the wealthy and powerful households and people in postexilic Judaism, the teacher proclaims that these objects so greatly valued are the gift of Wisdom, a goddess who distributes them to the sages with her own hands. Thus they are not the objects of human striving. The teacher declares that those who find and "embrace" Woman Wisdom are "happy/blessed" (3:13, 18).

In the third couplet (vv. 17–18), Woman Wisdom continues in her role of the goddess of life. The search to find her is not simply a quest of the intellect but also a longing of the human heart. Like a beautiful woman, Woman Wisdom is the object of the heart's desire. Like a fertility goddess of love, Woman Wisdom gives life, honor, and wealth to those who embrace her.

Metaphorically conceived, Wisdom is also the "tree of life" (Gen. 2:9; see Prov. 11:30; 13:12; 15:4), which in ancient Near Eastern literature often serves as a symbol for fertility goddesses, due to their association with the powers of fecundity and rebirth each year (Marcus, "Tree of Life in Proverbs," 118–20). Asherah, for example, the Canaanite earth-mother goddess, is portrayed as a living tree (Deut. 16:21). The pathways of Woman Wisdom are characterized by pleasantness and peace (Prov. 3:17). These descriptive terms point to the state of well-being and delight into which the sage enters, once wisdom's teaching is followed and incorporated into life.

The final strophe in vv. 19–20 concludes this poem by describing Yahweh's creation of the cosmos by means of his "wisdom" (= "understanding," "knowledge"). The wisdom that is more valuable than anything the human heart may desire, that, like a goddess of life, dispenses the valued gifts of human existence, and that leads the sage on paths of pleasantness and peace is the same wisdom God uses in creating and ordering the world and in governing its continuing operation with justice (cf. Pss. 104:24; 136:5; Jer. 10:12; 51:15). Wisdom in this strophe is both the power and the design used by God in bringing the world into being. In verse 19, the activity of creation is characterized by two verbal synonyms: "founded" (*yāsad* = Amos 9:6; Isa. 24:18; 48:13; 51:13; Zech. 12:1; cf. Prov. 8:29) and "established" (*kûn* = Prov. 24:3, Pss. 93:1; 119:90; Job 28:25, 27; cf. Prov. 8:27). These verbs suggest that God is the divine architect and builder who designs the cosmos like a building and then lays its foundations (cf. Job 38:4–7; Ps. 104:5). The verbs suggest both the artistry of design and the strength of stability, language that suggests the world is an aesthetically pleasing, sturdy structure.

The metaphor for God changes in the final verse (3:20a). Here the verb "divide" (*bāqaʿ*) is used: "by his knowledge the deeps [*tĕhômôt*] broke open" (literally, "were divided"). Several mythological texts from the ancient Near East as well as the Hebrew Bible (Old Testament) use the imagery of dividing or cutting in half the chaos monster who opposed the creator deity in battle prior to the work of creation.

103

Těhôm in Hebrew is the deep or cosmic ocean (Gen. 1:2; 7:11; Job 38:16, 30; Prov. 8:24, 27–28) and may have some connection to the name of the Babylonian chaos monster, Tiamat, whom Marduk, the warrior and creator deity, slays and then splits open to create the world. *Těhômôt* may be a plural of majesty, suggesting the powerful deep that is representative of primeval chaos (Ps. 74:12–15; also see Gen. 49:25; Deut. 33:13; Ps. 77:16; Hab. 3:8–10). Yahweh's dividing of the sea after the exodus from Egypt (Exod. 14:16; Neh. 9:11; Ps. 78:13) alludes, however slightly, to this mythological battle (see Isa. 51:9–11). The allusion to this battle between the Creator and the chaos monster in Prov. 3:19–20 suggests that wisdom is the divine power that conquers disorder, injustice, and death.

Divine providence, or sustaining of creation, is briefly mentioned in the final verse: "the clouds drop down the dew." God provides the moisture necessary for life in the cosmos to continue, a central act of divine providence (cf. Job 28:25, 26; 36:27–28; 38:28, 37; and Ps. 78:23). The world does not continue on its own but receives the blessings from the creator that sustain its existence.

Conclusion

This text is written with three purposes in mind: to assert that wisdom is of inestimable value and worth, far more than that of any human treasure; to present wisdom as the alternative to the allure of fertility goddesses and their foreign cultures; and to note that the wisdom that dispenses life and its various blessings (life, riches, and honor) to its followers is the same wisdom used by God in the creation and providential care of the world. The identical knowledge and power that reside in God's activity of creation and world maintenance are available to those who find wisdom. This text demonstrates beyond all question that the sages considered their teachings not only as a body of knowledge but also as the potent creativity of God at work in the origination and continuation of the cosmos. Woman Wisdom, dressed in the guise of a goddess of love and life, rivals the enticement of fertility goddesses who not only attempted to induce Jews to join in their worship but also sought to bring about the assimilation of their culture's religion and worldview.

Theology

104

Several metaphors are used to describe wisdom in this poem. First, wisdom is a fertility goddess who offers to her wise worshipers the most desirable of gifts: long life, wealth, and honor (compare Isis, Asherah, Anat, and Ishtar). Fertility goddesses in the ancient Near East offered their devotees the same gifts. The reference to wisdom as a tree of life may also allude to fertility goddesses, who on occasion were symbolized in this manner. The quest to discover wisdom, then, is likened not simply to the pursuit of a beautiful woman but also to engaging the devotion of the heart. This portrayal of wisdom presents an attractive alternative to the allure of fertility religions, their alien cultures, false gods and values.

Second, wisdom is the intelligence of the divine architect to design and carry out the erection of a beautiful and stable structure. This metaphor points to God's wisdom in designing and executing his well-conceived plan for the construction of a cosmos that is both stable and secure. This metaphor allows the sage to think that the wisdom incorporated in the teachings of the wise, once obtained, enables humans to participate in the shaping and ordering of moral and social reality.

Third, wisdom (or understanding) is also the faculty of wise execution and prowess in battle with the chaos monster that lead to its defeat and splitting apart. This battle metaphor suggests that humans who obtain wisdom have the strength to subdue the chaos that afflicts human societies: dissension, hatred, and falsehood that destroy community; foolish behavior that leads to destruction; the entrapment of foreign culture and religion; and so on.

Finally, God is the creator who, by his knowledge, providentially provides for the moisture that sustains life in the world. Sages, too, guided by their wisdom, have the ability to direct their own lives and to transmit to others the life-sustaining teaching that enables human communities to endure.

3:21–35

Fourth Instruction: The Life of Wisdom Is Actualized in Charity and Uprightness

Date and Provenance

The fourth instruction in Proverbs 1—9 (3:21–35) exhorts its audience to attain "sound wisdom" and "discretion" (NRSV "prudence"), for two reasons: the comfort and security that these provide individuals

105

and the guidance they offer to the wise and their households for living in community with their neighbors. Once again, the primary social context for the moral discourse and behavior set forth in this instruction is that of the family household. The instruction itself probably was formulated in the context of a postexilic wisdom school.

Literary Structure and Interpretation

The literary structure of this moral teaching follows the standard pattern of instructions: the stereotypical introduction, which mentions only the one who is addressed (v. 21a) and is followed by the initial, general prohibition and admonition concerning the obtaining and value of wisdom (vv. 21b–24); the teaching proper, which contains six prohibitions, the first and last each shaped in the form of a couplet (vv. 25–26, 31–32) and the others consisting of four one-line sayings; and the conclusion, which comprises three proverbs that contrast the fates of the wise and foolish (vv. 33–35).

The introduction (vv. 21–24) to this instruction begins in the usual fashion of naming the one addressed, "My son" (NRSV "My child"). A general couplet consisting of a prohibition and an admonition follow, where the student is exhorted to guard with diligence the possession of sound wisdom and prudence so as not to let them escape. This suggests that, for the sages, wisdom once obtained was not guaranteed to be a permanent possession. The continuing study and application of wisdom throughout a lifetime was the normal expectation. Otherwise, even the most accomplished and wisest of sages could lose this most prized possession and stray from the path to life to meet an undesired fate. Due diligence was required to assure that wisdom would continue. Two motive clauses follow in verses 22–23 which indicate that these twin virtues of "sound wisdom" and "discretion" or "prudence," two virtues closely related to and associated with wisdom (*ḥōkmâ*), are life-giving and sustaining. Sound wisdom is both reasonable judgment (Prov. 18:1) and the success that comes through its application (Job 5:12; 6:13; Prov. 2:7). "Discretion" or "prudence" is a synonym of "sound wisdom" and refers to prudent judgment in making a decision for a course of action (Prov. 1:4; 5:2; 8:12). Through the obtaining of these virtues, the student will make wise, prudent, and successful decisions that will lead to the enjoyment of security and stability along life's journey. The expression "life for your soul" contains the word *nepheš* (soul), which probably refers to the general meaning of "a living life." The vital nature of the aspiring sage, shared with all individuals, will be enhanced by the blessing of sound wisdom and prudence so essential to making intelligent and proper decisions in life. The image of sound wisdom and prudence being an "adornment for your neck" is a metaphor for the elegance and beauty of these virtues (see Prov. 1:9; 4:9). The metaphor reminds the student that sapiential discourse and behavior are not only a process of reasoned and critical inquiry and decision making but also an aesthetic enterprise in which the wisely lived life creates in the individual and in the larger community an aesthetic of reason, proportion, beauty, elegance, and grace. The introduction concludes in verse 24 with a couplet that follows the "if . . . , then" formula. The "if" clause sets forth the general situation, while the following clause indicates the result that will ensue. This couplet stresses that sound wisdom and discretion insulate aspiring sages against fear and anxiety, for they know that prudent decisions have been wisely made and offer well-being and success to both those making the judgments and the community in which they live.

As noted above, the teaching proper consists of six prohibitions, the first and sixth of which have motive clauses attached (vv. 25–32). The two more lengthy prohibitions provide this central section of the teaching with not only a form-critical but also a thematic enclosure. These prohibitions deal with two groups who are antithetical to the wise: the wicked (v. 25) and the violent and perverse (verses 31–32). The first prohibition in verses 25–26 exhorts the student not to be afraid of sudden panic (see 1:26–27) occasioned by the storm of devastation, for example, conquest (Prov. 1:27; Isa. 10:3; 47:11; Ezek. 38:9), that rages against the wicked. The reason given in the motive clause is that Yahweh, the source of the student's confidence, protects sages and those aspiring to be such from entrapment in this evil. The motivation provides a clear argument—hard to sustain, it would seem—that the sage is protected by Yahweh from any disaster, both natural as well as human, that engulfs the wicked. Placed in the context of a colony whose ancestors only several generations before had suffered both enormous pain and many casualties in the Babylonian conquest, as well as the ensuing agony and humiliation of exile to Babylon, this instruction attempts to argue, not very convincingly, that Yahweh somehow protects the wise and righteous from the destruction that overwhelms the wicked and foolish. The concluding prohibition with a contrastive motive clause in verses 31–32 admonishes the would-be sage not to envy the "violent" person or to trust in that way of acting in life (compare 1:10–19). The term *violent* refers to destructive actions directed against other human beings, in particular assault and murder (e.g., Gen. 6:11, 13; see Job 16:17; 19:7; and Prov. 10:6, 11; 13:2; 16:29; 26:6). The term *perverse* in the next verse, which parallels *violent,*

107

refers especially to devious or perverted behavior that strays from the straight and righteous course of morality (see Prov. 2:15; 14:2; Isa. 30:12). The perverse are an "abomination to Yahweh" (3:32), a frequent description in Proverbs that means an action or speech that is abhorrent to and hated by God. These abominable actions and speeches include the sacrifice of the wicked (Prov. 21:27), their prayers (Prov. 28:9), arrogance, lying, shedding of innocent blood, devising of wicked plans, hastening to perform evil deeds, false witness, and creating discord in a family (see Prov. 6:16).

The other four prohibitions, without attached motive or result clauses and internal to the teaching proper, deal with a variety of topics, although the central theme that unites them is conduct concerning one's neighbors. In the social context of villages and clans, as well as that of larger towns and cities, neighbors consisted of those who resided within this defined and narrow social setting. Indeed, the neighbor may have even been a relative or a marginal member (e.g., slave, debt servant, or concubine) of a clan or tribal household. Village households often consisted of people related by blood who lived in dwellings that were in close proximity to each other (Perdue et al., *Families in Ancient Israel,* 166). Eventually the term "neighbor" was extended to include the larger contexts of citizens of Israel and Judah and even resident aliens or foreigners who were noncitizens, residing usually within native households.

These four prohibitions involve, first of all, the exhortation not to withhold good from those who need it when one is in the position to be benevolent. This general saying could apply to all kinds of "good," but the term probably embraces especially acts of charity to those in need. In the context of this part of the teaching, more than likely the prohibition has in mind the neighbor or the neighbor's household. This means that, while acts of benevolence are not limited to the family and immediate relations, charity is especially directed to those who are close in proximity and in kinship. Exhortations and sayings that promote the sages' engagement in acts of charity on behalf of the poor are often encountered in Proverbs (see 14:31; 17:5; 22:16, 22–23). The wisdom tradition never teaches the renunciation of possessions in order to pursue a life of poverty, but it does stress the importance of supporting those in need. In so doing, sages were emulating the compassion and charity of Yahweh. This generous behavior reflects the strong probability that the sages were well-to-do and normally possessed the means by which to be charitable. The issue was not a matter of means but rather one of generosity of spirit.

108

The next two prohibitions (3:28–29) specifically mention interaction with neighbors. The first involves avoiding a deceitful act of withholding something from them (v. 28). Is this a garment taken in pledge when the neighbor borrows something, say a plow (see Exod. 22:26–27; Amos 2:8), or victuals to ease one's hunger? As is often true in Proverbs and other sayings collections, the text offers only a general exhortation and does not specify the situation. It is the responsibility of the sage to choose an appropriate saying or teaching for a particular situation. The second prohibition is the exhortation not to devise evil against the trusting neighbor (v. 29). Wise and careful planning was an important activity of the sage, whether in giving counsel to a ruler or in charting a course of action for making one's own way. Yet planning that has a wicked purpose and takes an evil turn against neighbors is especially insidious, because they tend to trust those beside (literally, "with") whom they dwell. The "with" suggests the neighbor is a close relation, perhaps even one living in the same household compound. These two prohibitions are key examples of the fact that the sages were concerned not simply with the well-being of the individual but also with the enhancement of blessing for the family household and the larger community (normally, but not limited to, the clan; see Perdue et al., *Families in Ancient Israel*, 237–39).

The next admonition exhorts the avoiding of capricious, contentious behavior against a person who has done one no harm (v. 30). The word *contend* (NRSV "quarrel") may refer to strife that arises from a dispute or quarrel (Prov. 15:8; 17:14; 20:3; 26:17, 21; 30:33). In a legal context, the word means to engage in a lawsuit (Exod. 23:2, 3, 6; Deut. 21:5). Either of these meanings would be appropriate for situations in which this prohibition should be followed. Given the immediate literary context of this instruction, the prohibition may be directed once more toward establishing and maintaining good relations with neighbors and, in particular, relatives.

The conclusion of this instruction strings together three antithetical proverbs that contrast the inheritance and fate of the wicked with those of the wise (3:33–35). In the first proverb, the curse, not the blessing, of Yahweh is directed not only against evildoers but also against their households (v. 33). In contrast, the household of the righteous receives divine blessing. This antithetical proverb underscores the fact that the sages strongly believed in the corporate effect of human behavior and speech on the households of both the wicked and the righteous, as well as on the larger community.

The second proverb contrasts Yahweh's disdain of the "scorners" with his grace exhibited toward the "humble" (v. 34). "Scorners" are those who, because of their arrogance in attitude, behavior, and speech,

109

are incapable of receiving instruction (Prov. 1:22; 9:7–8; 13:1; 15:12; 21:24), whereas the "humble" are either those who adopt the meekness of the poor (Prov. 16:19) or the poor themselves, who are often victims of oppression (Prov. 22:22; 30:14; 31:9, 20).

Finally, the teacher concludes with an antithetical proverb that contrasts the inheritance of the wise, in this case "honor," with the "disgrace" of fools. Honor was one of the sages' most desired and cherished virtues (Prov. 15:33; 18:12; 21:21), whereas disgrace was shameful, degrading, and much to be avoided (Prov. 6:33; 9:7; 11:2; 12:16; 13:18; 18:3; 22:10).

Conclusion

This teaching has the purpose of exhorting students to inculcate the virtues of "sound wisdom" and "discretion" (or "prudence") so that they may enjoy comfort and security in their life journey by making wise and successful decisions and by receiving the protective oversight of God. In addition, these virtues enable them, along with their own households, to act justly and to live in harmony with their neighbors. The specific identity of "violent" people, if one was intended, is difficult to assess. In the early Persian period, however, they may have included brigands and revolutionaries or, in more general terms, those who violated the norms of righteous life to bring wealth and power to themselves at the expense of serious harm to the larger community. Once more the conservative nature of Proverbs 1—9 is obvious, for maintaining the well-being of the community in a stable and continuing fashion was uppermost in the mind of the teachers who composed these poems and instructions.

Theology

The sages of wisdom literature often speak of the world of blessing into which those who follow their instruction may enter (Westermann, *Blessing*). In this instruction, the young people of a wisdom school, likely located in Jerusalem, are urged to retain "sound wisdom" and "discretion" that will lead to well-being, security, and contentment. What is important is that Yahweh is the one who will ensure that the ruin or "storm" that overtakes the wicked will not devastate those who hold fast to sound wisdom and discretion. This understanding of retribution is a clear indication that, while the conservative sages believed justice would prevail and the wicked would be punished whereas the righteous would be rewarded, they did not exclude

Yahweh from an active participation in this process. In addition, they did not negate divine freedom by exuding a sure and certain confidence in divine justice.

It is also important to note that once more the behavior and discourse of the individual affects either positively or negatively the well-being of a community. In this case, Yahweh curses the household of the wicked person (singular), while the "abode" of the righteous (plural) receives his blessing. The term *curse* refers to language that goes forth to destroy, while blessing consists of spoken words that are designed to bring about the well-being of a person or group.

4:1–9

Fifth Instruction: The Prize of Wisdom Is a Beautiful Crown

Date and Provenance

Once more Woman Wisdom dominates this literary text, though here the teacher issuing the instruction describes her and her actions in the third person. She does not speak or act directly; the teacher, not she, does the talking. Here she assumes metaphorically the roles of the personal goddess of individual sages and the queen of heaven who honors her followers with security, exaltation, and a "beautiful crown." As elsewhere in speaking of Woman Wisdom, the sages use the language of adulation and worship typically directed toward a deity to speak of the attitude of reverence and devotion the would-be sage should develop toward his or her "goddess." This does not mean the sages were creating a new deity who would exist alongside Yahweh or even rival God for their devotion. Rather, Woman Wisdom is the metaphorical personification of Yahweh's insight and knowledge in creation and in ruling the cosmos and the human community. This type of personification is found in exilic and postexilic texts, suggesting that this poem also was composed in a wisdom school in the Persian period.

The theme of this instruction is developed even more fully in the poem on Woman Wisdom in Prov. 8:12–21, where she chooses the kings of the earth and confers on them the requisite gifts for rule. In the teaching here (4:1–9), the one she honors with a crown, at least metaphorically speaking, is the aspiring sage who obeys the teacher's

111

instruction and comes to love and cherish her. Woman Wisdom, who creates and governs the world, is accessible to the sages who devote their life to seeking and adoring her.

Literary Structure and Interpretation

This brief instruction consists of two major strophes, each of which has five lines: verses 1–5a and 5b–9. The unifying theme is found in the repetition of the twofold imperative in each of the two strophes: "Get wisdom; get insight" (vv. 5a and 7). Even in the teacher's first encounter with instruction, he or she was taught to search for and to obtain wisdom. The first strophe deals with the reminiscences of the sage, who speaks of being instructed by his or her father and being a tender youth in the presence of his or her mother. Even at this very early age, the teacher received instruction from parents in the household, who taught the importance of observing and keeping their instruction in order to "live." The second strophe sets forth the blessings offered by Woman Wisdom to the young people who choose to follow her teachings and honor her with devotion and dedication.

The initial strophe (vv. 1–5a) begins with the address of the students ("sons"—NRSV "children") who are called on to hear (i.e., listen to and obey) the instruction (*mûsār*) of the "father" (probably the title of a male teacher in a wisdom school). These students are exhorted to "be attentive" in order to "gain [literally, 'know'] insight." Insight or understanding is a virtue comparable to wisdom and refers to the ability to analyze even complex situations and problems and understand or know how to act in a proper and successful fashion (Prov. 3:5; 23:4; 30:2). In verse 3, the teacher remembers perhaps an early encounter with instruction, when the father (probably here his parent) first taught him when he was a mere lad, a tender youth, the darling who was the only child, in the presence of his mother (probably his parent). The teacher recalls the introduction to that first, simple instruction, which has only two imperatives: "Get wisdom; get insight." Or perhaps these two imperatives, forming the teaching proper, are the gist of what he recollects about that first instruction. The introduction contains two exhortations ("Let your heart hold fast my words; keep my commandments") followed by a brief motive clause: "and live." The brevity and simplicity of the motive clause penetrates to the essence of what is taught the sage by his or her father. Obedience to his teachings results in the greatest of all human values: life.

In the second strophe (vv. 5b–9), the sage develops more extensively this simple exhortation recalled from his or her first instruction: "Get wisdom; get insight." The sage does so in series of prohibitions and admonitions with motive and conditional clauses, all of which deal with Woman Wisdom as the protective goddess of the sages. Throughout the ancient Near East, people looked to their own particular deity, usually one from a multitude of divine beings, who was their individual god. In exchange for devotion and commitment, the deity blessed the worshiper and protected him or her from evil. Often a deity was chosen because of a person's social position or occupation. At other times one worshiped the ancestral deity of the household. Ancient Near Eastern sages, while at times speaking of "the" deity (this was true even in Egypt on occasion), also had gods and goddesses of wisdom who they worshiped. Israel's and Judah's sages appropriated this language of the personal deity, "the" deity, and the goddess of wisdom to develop discourse that would stimulate worship of and devotion to Yahweh. In the discourse of metaphor and personification, wisdom becomes a goddess whom the sages cherish and to whom they devote their lives. This is the means by which they were able to speak of wisdom without compromising their theology of monotheism.

The instruction begins with the sage's own introduction: "do not forget, nor turn away from the words of my mouth" (v. 5b). Sapiential instruction, properly instilled in the human consciousness to the point where it becomes a part of sapiential character, is stimulated by an active memory so that the sage may draw on this reservoir of knowledge to act and to speak in ways that are life-enhancing, both for the sage and for the larger community. Even so, the teachings of the wise are not forced on students. Each must make the choice to begin and then continue the journey to a more complete possession of wisdom. One always has the option of "turning away." Yet, if students do not abandon wisdom, given by Yahweh to those who fear God, then "she" (Wisdom) will "keep" (better translated "guard, protect") them; if they "love" her, she will "guard" (or "watch over") them. This protection offered by Woman Wisdom is comparable to that offered by the personal gods of individuals in the ancient Near East.

Verse 7 incorporates a key phrase in sapiential discourse: "the beginning of wisdom." As noted earlier, *rēʾšît* (beginning) means both the first and the best of what is described, and in this case it is wisdom. The foundation that anchors all the sages' teachings, the precondition to seek to embody sapiential piety and ethics, is found in the brief imperative issued by the teacher's father so long ago, "Get wisdom," followed by the parallel command, "Get insight." Whatever else the

113

students may obtain, among all the possessions they acquire, the most valuable is wisdom. They are to "prize" her (v. 8), meaning that she is to be more greatly treasured than anything else is. Woman Wisdom is to be the object of greatest devotion, a devotion that is at times nuanced with the images of love and sexuality often associated with a fertility goddess. If she is "embraced," then she will honor in turn those who enfold her in their arms. But most of all, she gives to those who possess her a "fair garland" and a "beautiful crown" (v. 9). A fair garland is most likely a wreath that points to some honorable state or achievement, while a "beautiful crown" is either figurative of honor (Prov. 12:4; 14:24; 16:31; 17:6; Isa. 62:3) or a symbol of royal status (Jer. 13:18). The aspiring sage who obtains wisdom will be held in high esteem and acquire a noble state.

Conclusion

This brief instruction has two purposes. First, the reminiscences of the teacher lead to the distillation of the essence and object of all sapiential instruction: the acquiring of wisdom. This is the "first" or "beginning," that is, the foundation for all sapiential teaching. Second, Woman Wisdom is the one who, when embraced, becomes the source of honor and status and the means to experience the well-being of life.

Theology

Wisdom in this short instruction is much like the personal goddess of the aspiring sage. The one who seeks and embraces her does so as if she were the goddess of love and life to whom one devotes one's life, resources, and worship. If obtained, she in return grants her gifts of protection, life, and honor. Wisdom never actually achieved the status of a goddess in Israel and Judah, though in the imagination of the sages she continued to increase in attributes that are normally associated with Yahweh (e.g., Wisdom of Solomon 8—9). Perhaps Woman Wisdom, while a metaphor for or a personification of the creative insight and power that brings and sustains life, became the means by which Israel and Judah, or at least the sages who resided therein, could fill in the emptiness of a religion that was largely male and patriarchal. Other cultures and their religions could offer goddesses to play such a role. But Israel and Judah normally chose another way to speak of the divine world. Yahweh was the sole God, the only Creator and Sustainer, but the metaphor of Wisdom eventually became, in the post-exilic period, the means by which this hidden God could be revealed and become active in creation and history. In her description as a fertility goddess of life, the sages were able to capture the imaginations and engage the hearts of their students and followers.

4:10–27

Sixth Instruction: The Two Ways

Literary Structure and Interpretation

The sixth instruction (4:10–27) in Proverbs 1—9 contrasts the two ways along which one may choose to travel in life: the path of wisdom and the road of the wicked. In contradistinction to the preceding instruction (4:1–9), in which the teacher recalls for the students his or her first encounter with sapiential teaching in the household, this text has the appearance of being the final instruction prior to leaving the direct oversight of the teacher in a wisdom school. Once departed, the young sage will enter a new world where this "significant other," that is, the one who has had the primary role of instructing the young person through a particular stage of life (e.g., the time of study in a wisdom school), will no longer be immediately present. The young sage then must be prepared for a new status where greater responsibility and self-sufficiency are the necessary virtues that allow for maturity and wise behavior. Thus it may be that the situation envisaged is that of students leaving their wisdom school when they as young sages, properly tutored, were about to enter the stage of life in which careers, family, and the appropriate and necessary rules of proper etiquette, decorum, and behavior were to be taken on (see Perdue, "Social Character of Paraenesis," 5–39). To be successful in finding the life offered by wisdom requires the total dedication of one's entire being.

The literary structure of this instruction is a well-balanced text that breaks down into two major parts (vv. 10–19 and vv. 20–27). In the concise introduction in verse 10, the "son" (or student—NRSV "child") is admonished to accept the teacher's words so that his years will be many (v. 10). The first part of the teaching proper follows in verses 11–19 and consists of two parallel strophes: the way of wisdom (vv. 11–13) and the path of the wicked (vv. 14–19). After a reiteration and expansion of the introduction (vv. 20–22), the second part of the teaching proper elaborates on the thesis of holding to the path of wisdom (vv. 23–27).

115

The first segment (vv. 10–19), like other instructions in this first collection (chapters 1—9) of the book of Proverbs, begins with an introduction (v. 10) in which the teacher addresses the "son" and exhorts him to accept what he has taught. Once more, long life is the promised reward for diligent obedience. It is the perfect tenses of the verbs in verse 11, however, that appear to suggest that the immediate relationship between the teacher and the student is ending. The teacher says that she or he "has taught" this student the "way of wisdom" and the "paths of uprightness," the common metaphors for the journey of the wise life upon which a youth is about to embark. This course is clearly only beginning, but perhaps this was the time when the student, properly socialized and with a character formed and fashioned by the moral instruction of sapiential teaching and the teacher's example, was ready to leave the academy and go forth to a new stage of life unaided by this "significant other." This does not mean that the new sage would be entering a world where he or she was left alone and isolated from other sages. Rather, the young person would be entering a new level of social responsibility to join other sages, who, in their various occupations, formed an elite, highly educated class (see Whybray, *Intellectual Tradition*).

The student is preparing to enter a new stage of life, comprising a career, new responsibilities in the household, marriage and children, and a position of respect in the larger society. The bond that has existed between student and teacher is loosening, for the direct guidance and example of the teacher will no longer be present for the student to follow (Turner, *Ritual Process*). The years of study are at an end, and the student is to have internalized the wisdom tradition and the patterns of behavior exemplified in the activity and discourse of the teacher. At last the student is setting out on his or her own, so to speak, and the teacher fully expects the new sage to move without stumbling along the paths of uprightness (vv. 11–12). Now the teacher offers a last exhortation to encourage the student one final time to seize and keep wisdom, for "she is your life" (v. 13).

The teacher next contrasts the paths of the upright, that is, those whose behavior actualizes in both word and deed the teachings of the wise, with the paths of the wicked, that is, those whose very nature it is to work evil and to hurt others (vv. 14–16) and who cannot sleep until they have satiated their appetite by causing harm. The teacher uses the metaphors of eating the "bread of wickedness" and drinking the "wine of violence" (see Job 15:16 and 34:7). "Violence" points to physical attack, including that which results in death (Prov. 3:31; 10:6, 11; 11:30; 13:2; 16:29; 26:6; see Gen. 6:11, 13). Verses 18–19 summarize and conclude this strophe by using the similes of the "light of dawn" and "deep darkness" to characterize the contrasting paths of the righteous and the wicked. For the sage, wisdom provides the necessary light to travel the pathway of life, whereas the wicked, without this sunlight, stumble in the dark. "Deep darkness" (Deut. 28:29; Prov. 7:9) often brings with it the connotations of supernatural blackness (Exod. 10:22), the judgment that accompanies the "day of the LORD," (Amos 5:20; Jonah 2:2; Zeph. 1:15), wickedness (Jer. 23:12), and calamity (Isa. 8:22; 58:10; 59:9).

The second strophe of this instruction (vv. 20–27) expands the topic of the path of wisdom on which the student, bringing to an end his course of study, is about to embark. Prominent are references to various parts of the body, including especially those that have to do with sense perception, thought, speech, and, in a metaphorical sense, staying on wisdom's path. Thus the ear (v. 20) is to listen to the teacher's sayings. The eyes are not to allow the sayings to escape from their view (v. 21). The heart (or mind) is to be guarded with diligence (v. 23). "Crooked speech" (literally, the "mouth") and "devious talk" (literally, the "lips") are to be placed far from the student (v. 24). The "gaze" (literally, the "eyelids") is to be "straight before" the student. The "foot" is not to deviate to the right or to the left and is to turn from evil (v. 27). Indeed, the sayings of the teacher are to bring healing to one's "flesh" or body (v. 22). The point of this body talk appears to be that the entire being of the one aspiring to sagehood must be involved in and dedicated to the task of following wisdom's path. One's life, character, speech, and behavior are to be transformed by wisdom, though the wise person, newly formed, must engage in due diligence and carefully adhere to what has been taught.

Conclusion

This instruction is a farewell discourse to the student at the point of "betwixt and between," that is, during the time when the student, having finished the course of study in a wisdom school, is about to enter a new stage of life. Now the teacher offers the departing student one last instruction, one final reminder of the two paths that lay before the young sage: the way of wisdom, which leads to life, and the way of wickedness, which leads to violence and failure (see Perdue, "Death of the Sage," 81–109). To adhere to the path of wisdom requires all of the aspiring sage's devotion, commitment, and diligence. The experience in the wisdom school is to have formed the student's character, and now, as she or he is about to enter into a new phase of existence, 117 the teacher reminds the student of the necessity of implementing wisdom in daily discourse and actions.

Theology

The metaphor of the two ways is frequently used in Israelite and Jewish literature. It is employed by the sages in their teachings, as well as by the Deuteronomic and Deuteronomistic scribes in their homilies, to contrast two courses of existence and thus the two choices of life and death, wisdom and folly, and success and failure that lie before the person (Deut. 28:29; Josh. 1:8; 1 Sam. 18:14; Prov. 2:8; 3:6, 23; 11:5; 20:24; 29:27; 31:3). Yahweh has not determined which individuals will choose one path or the other, although it is possible for the God-fearer to receive the gift of wisdom and thus to follow the way of life. The choice, however, still remains for the individual to make. Even after setting out on wisdom's path, the sage must be careful and diligent in seeing to it that he or she does not stray. To do so could result in destruction. This means that the moral life is to be pursued throughout life until its cessation in death.

The theological anthropology of the sages plainly manifests itself in the latter section of this instruction. All of one's being, from the eyes to the ears to the mind to the feet, is to be used to follow the path of wisdom. The ontological refashioning of one's character by the study of wisdom is clear in this instruction. Study and the pursuit of wisdom are not simply an intellectual effort or the gathering of knowledge. Rather, through the course of study one's entire being, including especially one's character, is formed and transformed. While still subject to the temptation to abandon wisdom, the sage is well equipped to adhere to the path of wisdom that leads to life.

5:1–23

Seventh Instruction:
Avoidance of the Strange Woman

Date and Provenance

The instruction found in chapter 5 is entirely devoted to the "strange woman," one of the subjects of the instruction in 2:1–22. As noted in the commentary on 2:16–19, this enigmatic figure appears to include a variety of identities: a prostitute, a fertility priestess, an adulteress, a worshiper of a fertility goddess, and folly. Just as sexual imagery is used to speak of the attraction of Woman Wisdom, even including her seduction of youth, so the same language is employed to describe the strange woman, whose enticing appearance, words, and actions lead the foolish and the unlearned to their destruction. Only obedience to the wisdom of the teacher may preserve the aspiring sage from the entrapment of this personification of folly, pagan religion and culture, and sexual misconduct. This personification of a vice is likely to have derived from a wisdom school in the postexilic period.

Literary Structure and Interpretation

This instruction comprises the following sections: an introduction in which an unidentified teacher addresses the "son" (NRSV "child") and exhorts him to listen to the teaching (vv. 1–2); the teaching proper, which includes an introductory strophe describing the strange woman (NRSV "loose woman") and the destruction to which she leads (vv. 3–6) and two contrasting strophes, the first exhorting the student to avoid the strange woman (vv. 7–14) and the second admonishing him to rejoice in the love and affection of his own wife (vv. 15–19); and the conclusion, which speaks of the one who, lacking the discipline taught by the sages, meets destruction (vv. 20–23).

In the introduction to this seventh instruction, once more the unnamed teacher addresses the "son" (student) and exhorts him to be "attentive" to "wisdom" and to "incline" his "ear" to "understanding." As elsewhere, *son* may be an inclusive term to refer to both genders. Certainly, the audience may be considered larger than a single person. The motive clause follows in verse 2 and stresses that observing of the teacher's instruction will enable the student to practice discretion and guard the knowledge of his or her lips. Discretion or prudence (*mĕz-immâ*, v. 2; see commentary on 1:4) is the ability to judge a situation and discern the proper course of action in a reasonable fashion in accord with the teachings of wisdom. The student's guarding or adhering (*šāmar*) to the knowledge of his or her lips is the capacity to act according to what he or she has spoken, say, the recitation of sapiential teachings.

This motive clause is extended in verses 3–6 in the initial description of the "strange woman" in the teaching proper. The strange woman is described in this strophe by reference to two images: her seductive speech (vv. 3–4) and her pathway (vv. 5–6), both of which lead to destruction. A second mentioning of "lips" occurs in verse 3 to

119

refer to the seductive mouth and enticing speech of the strange woman, which, the teacher warns, "drip honey" and are "smoother than oil" but turn out in the end to be as "bitter as wormwood." Wormwood is a plant that has a bitter taste. The term is used in the Old Testament as a metaphor to refer to sorrow and bitterness (Deut. 29:18 = Matt. 29:17; Jer. 9:14; 23:15; Amos 5:7; 6:12). The second half of verse 3 uses the image of the strange woman's "speech" (*hēk*, literally "palate"; Prov. 8:7 and 24:13) to parallel the first half. Her "speech" or "palate" is poetically described as "smoother than oil," an image that intimates deceptive words (Ps. 55:22) or flattery (Prov. 2:16; 7:5, 21; 26:28; 28:23).

The other image used to describe the strange woman is the "path" that her feet take: untutored in wisdom, she wanders from the path of life and instead takes the way to death or Sheol. Death in the Old Testament is at times personified as the ruler of the underworld (Job 18:13; Jer. 9:21). As noted earlier (see commentary on 1:12), Sheol is the underworld or the land of the dead (Prov. 9:18; Isa. 5:14).

The teaching proper divides into two contrasting strophes: the first exhorts the aspiring sage to avoid the strange woman (vv. 7–14), while the second admonishes him to rejoice in and be faithful to the wife of his youth (vv. 15–19). The first strophe begins with the repetition of the introduction, only now the teacher is addressing the "sons," whom he exhorts not to abandon the "words of my mouth." The frequent occurrence of images of speech throughout this instruction underscores the power of language to bring about well-being when it is guided by wisdom but also its capacity to destroy when wisdom is abandoned and replaced by folly.

In the first strophe (verses 7–14) the teacher warns the students not to approach the "door of her [the strange woman's] house," lest they give their "honor to others" and their "years to the merciless." The "house" of the strange woman (see Prov. 2:18 and 7:8) may be her physical dwelling, the temple of a fertility goddess, or even the metaphorical world of folly and wickedness, where death dwells. Giving one's "honor" in verse 9a may refer to one's vigor (Dan. 10:8), suggesting the wasting away of one's body and strength in licentious behavior; to one's dignity; or to one's resources. If the last meaning is intended, perhaps the sage is admonishing the students not to fritter away their resources in payment to a prostitute or in efforts to try to make amends to an outraged husband who could require payment in blood for the adultery of his wife and lover (Exod. 20:14; Deut. 5:18; 22:22–24). The latter would explain the enigmatic second part of verse 9: to give one's "years to the merciless" (see Prov. 11:17; 12:10; 17:11),

120

that is, a husband who has been betrayed and will not accept payment in lieu of death. Verse 10 continues this line of thought by indicating that a liaison with the strange woman will result in "strangers" taking their fill of the student's strength (*kōah*—NRSV "wealth"), thus paralleling the preceding notion of honor as either vigor or wealth. The woman may have been a foreigner; in this case, the as yet uninstructed student is warned against a liaison, even a marriage, to an alien woman whose household may claim the possessions of his own. In any case, at the end of life, when the student's flesh and body are consumed, either through execution or wasting away from profligate living, the would-be sage, having been heedless to sapiential teaching and entrapped by the strange woman, will confess to the forgetting of the instruction of the teacher and bemoan this terrible fate (vv. 11–13). But it will then be too late (see 1:24–31). In verse 14, however, the teacher seems to hesitate in pronouncing the end of the aspiring student when he confesses that he was "at the point of utter ruin in the public assembly." This is how close the student came to public ruin in the imagination of the teacher. The assembly or congregation best refers to the community of the student, perhaps assembled together during a trial for adultery or for fraternizing with prostitutes, either common or sacred.

In the next strophe of the teaching proper (vv. 15–19), the teacher shifts the instruction from avoiding the strange woman to faithfulness to one's own wife. Verses 15–16 utilize water metaphors to refer to sexual intimacy between a husband and wife. In verse 15 the student is exhorted to drink water from his own "cistern" and "well." This imagery refers to the satisfying of one's sexual desires by acts of love-making with one's own wife (Song of Sol. 4:15). The scattering of one's springs abroad and the streams in the street (v. 16) refer probably to the release of semen in sexual acts with prostitutes and adulteresses instead of during acts of sexual intimacy with one's spouse. Possibly, though less likely, this imagery refers to the wife's acts of adultery with others, since Song of Solomon 4:15 refers to her as "water." Thus her husband's infidelity would lead to her own unchaste activity as the means to get even with her faithless spouse. Instead of these licentious acts, the student is exhorted to allow his "fountain [to] be blessed" (v. 18), that is, to enable his wife to receive the well-being that comes from faithfulness to the marriage vow. This imagery may comprise either the blessing that comes from the enjoyment of sexual intimacy or the joy of children that the union produces. The comparison of her to a "lovely deer, a graceful doe" reflects the animal imagery used by the narrator of the Song of Solomon to portray his beloved (see 2:9; 4:2, 5; 6:6; 7:3). Finally, the sage exhorts the student to delight in his

121

wife's affection and to be "intoxicated always by her love." This contrast between one's own wife and the strange woman is similar to the contrast between Woman Wisdom and Woman Folly in 9:1–18.

Verses 20–23 are the conclusion to this lengthy instruction. Beginning with two questions asking the student why he or she should embrace the strange woman, the sage adds a motive clause that in essence states that Yahweh oversees a person's actions. Yahweh will know, even if humans do not, that the student has embraced the strange woman (vv. 20–21). Finally, a saying forming a couplet brings this instruction to its culmination (vv. 22–23). The proverb affirms, first of all, that a wicked person is requited by means of the very iniquity that she or he causes (v. 22), and second, that those who practice evil die because they lack instruction and are entrapped by folly (v. 23).

Conclusion

This instruction seeks to exhort aspiring sages to avoid the seductive advances of the "strange woman," who represents many things: a prostitute, an adulteress, a fertility priestess, a foreign goddess, and the more abstract notion of folly. The description of the student who is almost destroyed by her charms serves as a strong warning against the foolish disregard of the teaching.

Probably originating during the early part of the Persian period, this instruction emphasizes the importance of faithfulness to one's own wife and the stability of the household that results. Licentious liaisons with foreigners and the seduction of foreign culture and religion threatened the viability of Jewish identity, as well as the household (including patrimony) that formed the basis of Jewish society. The sages, including the one who uttered this instruction, sought to shape a Jewish society that would survive into the future. Central to this survival were the strength of the family household and the formation of character by Jewish wisdom, culture, and religion.

Theology

The household was the institution in which many Jewish values received their formation, were transmitted in the teachings of parents, and were implemented in daily life. School wisdom incorporated these values into the ethic of sapiential teaching. The seduction of Jewish youth by foreign religion and culture, adulterers and adulteresses, and prostitutes threatened not only the viability of Jewish households but also the religion and way of life that forged Judaism emerging in the period after the return from exile. Sapiential instruction was intended to keep young males from falling for the wiles and smooth talk of the strange woman. In this instruction Yahweh, who oversees creation, society, and even the lives of individuals, is aware of those who betray their own wives and religious heritage for illicit sexual trysts and assimilation into foreign cultures and will undoubtedly bring these faithless fools to destruction.

6:1–19

Eighth Instruction:
A Miscellany of Sapiential Teaching

Literary Structure and Interpretation

The eighth instruction contains a miscellany of subjects that are important to the sapiential tradition. The primary emphasis is placed on indolence, which is the topic of interest in the first two strophes (vv. 1–5 and vv. 6–11). The third strophe addresses the worthless person, a wicked man whose behavior is described and dreadful fate is predicted (vv. 12–15). The fourth strophe in verses 16–19 contains a numerical saying that identifies seven things that are an abomination to Yahweh, things that bring discord to the larger community. The steady duration of Jewish society and culture depended in large measure on hard work within the context of the household, the elimination of the wicked who destroyed the relationships necessary for a community to continue, and the avoidance of vices that would create communal strife. In a period of Jewish history where conditions especially challenged the viability of emerging Judaism, the sages sought to instill in the character of their students the virtues that would strengthen the community, enable it to form its identity, and assist its survival into the future.

Thus, after a brief introduction ("My son," v. 1a—NRSV "My child"), this eighth instruction in the collection of Proverbs 1—9 consists of four major strophes: an emphasis on self-reliance through hard work (vv. 1–5), the example of the industrious ant to the sluggard (vv. 6–11), the description of the wicked person whose actions sow discord among the community (vv. 12–15), and the list of seven things that Yahweh hates, things that disrupt the harmony of the larger community (vv. 16–19).

123

The introductory strophe (vv. 1–5) begins with the typical address of the student ("My son"), although, as has become expected, neither the teacher nor the one instructed is identified. Immediately after this brief address, the teacher issues an exhortation consisting of a conditional admonition using the language of "if . . . , then." Here the initial conditional clause is introduced by the particle 'im ("if," 6:1a), which describes a particular situation, while the following dependent clauses set forth the action and speech appropriate for the context. The teacher describes the hypothetical situation of a hasty promise where a person has offered him- or herself in pledge for something not identified. A pledge is a legal action in which some form of surety is offered as insurance for a debt or for something borrowed. To make a pledge to a neighbor or a stranger by offering oneself as surety may refer to taking the place of another who is in some difficulty, say, as a slave or a debtor (Gen. 43:9; 44:32–34; Job 17:3), or to become personal collateral for one's own debts or those of others, including the family household (Prov. 11:15; 22:26). Elsewhere, one may proffer one's property, for instance, one's cloak, fields, vineyards, or even children, as a guarantee for something borrowed from a neighbor or stranger to attend to a variety of matters, including the payment of debts or taxes (Exod. 22:5–6; Deut. 24:6, 10–13, 17; 1 Kings 4:1; Neh. 5:3–5; Prov. 20:16 = 27:13; Amos 2:8). The act of making a pledge involved both the giving of the hand (handshake? Job 17:3; Prov. 6:1; 17:18) and a verbal declaration. A pledge may have been a public act to reinforce its authenticity and legality.

The sages in Proverbs warn strongly against this practice, especially when it comes to offering oneself as surety (Prov. 11:15; 17:18; 22:26–27; 27:13). This foolish action, whether the offering of the self or one's possessions, potentially threatens one's well-being by coming under the power of either a neighbor or a stranger. If, however, students one day should find themselves in this predicament, then they should humble themselves before creditors, implore them for additional time and opportunity to make good their promises, and then know no rest until the debts are paid or the pledges are made sure (6:4). In so doing, the students will be rescued from potential disaster, like a gazelle from the hunter or a bird from the hand of the fowler (v. 5). Comparisons from nature are not simply colorful illustrations used by the sages to spice up their language. They are also used to point to an underlying order in reality that operates in and connects the various elements of creation in fundamental ways (von Rad, *Wisdom in Israel*, 74–96).

124

In the second strophe (vv. 6–11), the teacher resumes the subject of hard work mentioned in verse 4 and directs the exhortation to the "sluggard" (NRSV "lazybones"). To make the point, the sage once more draws on an example from nature and speaks of the industrious ant. Of amazement to the teacher is the observation that the ant, without any leader to organize and direct its work, still gathers its food during the harvest. Unstated but assumed is that the ant recognizes that this preparation will enable it to survive sustained periods of drought and bitter cold. This illustration from nature becomes for the wise a compelling example of the necessity of hard work and requisite preparation for future survival. Otherwise, indolence and even the taking of too much of a respite from one's toil will result in poverty that takes one unawares. The sages often looked to patterns of order in creation from which they could draw important lessons for human living. This included the behavior of creatures (Job 12:7; Isa. 1:3; Jer. 8:7), of which Solomon is said to have spoken (1 Kings 4:33 = Heb. 5:13), although it cannot be determined whether that instance refers to fables or various proverbs and sayings. The example of the ant is a major case of an extended saying that points to this insect as an example of industry and preparation.

The third strophe (6:12–15) points to the behavior of the "worthless one" ('ādām bĕlîya'al—NRSV "scoundrel"), that is, the wicked person (NRSV "villain") whose behavior and speech create discord in the community. Bĕlîya'al, a word generally meaning "worthlessness," refers to good-for-nothing, base people when used to modify human beings whose actions are foolish, unethical, perverse, or destructive (1 Sam. 25:25; 2 Sam. 16:7; 20:1; 1 Kings 21:13; Prov. 16:27). Their deeds and speech cause harm to others. The "villain" or wicked person (Prov. 10:29; 21:15; Isa. 55:7) refers to a troublemaker or an evildoer who brings calamity to others as well as to him- or herself. But suddenly, without warning, he will be destroyed. The suddenness of the onslaught of destruction is mentioned earlier in regard to the fools who reject Woman Wisdom's invitation to life (Prov. 1:27).

The various activities of the wicked person are briefly enumerated in 6:12–14. Crooked speech (v. 12) refers to devious or deceptive talk that misleads (Prov. 4:24; 19:1), one of the important subjects in Proverbs. Deceptive talk destroys human relationships and the bonds of trust on which community is built. Such devious speech unleashes a destructive power not only against the speaker but also against the communities in which he or she is situated.

The next three actions, however, while involving various parts of the human body, are not very apparent as to their proper meaning. "Winking eyes" (v. 13) appears to refer to some malicious movement

125

of the eyes (Prov. 10:10), though the meaning of this metaphor is not exactly clear. "Scraping" (*mōlēl*) or "shuffling" feet is also ambiguous, occurring only here with this particular meaning. Another possible meaning of *mōlēl* is the verb "to speak or say," though "speaking with his feet" is equally unclear. A pointing finger (v. 13) may refer to indicating something, identifying someone, or showing the way (Exod. 15:25; Job 6:24; Ps. 45:5). While unclear in their meaning, these three bodily movements may refer to physical means of conveying secret information to others who are allied with the evildoer.

Much clearer are the activities attributed to the one who has a "perverted heart" (NRSV "mind"): "devising evil" with a perverted heart and "continually sowing discord" (v. 14). A "perverted heart" (Prov. 16:30) refers to twisted or evil thoughts that are at the origins of planning evil and that lead to actions that cause disharmony among the human community. "Devising evil" refers to the planning and carrying out of deeds that cause harm to others (Prov. 3:29; 12:20; 14:22). "Sowing discord" includes activities such as quarreling that create strife or contention among human communities (Prov. 6:19; 15:18; 16:28; 17:14; 18:19; 22:10; 23:29; 26:20; 28:25; 29:22).

The final strophe (vv. 16–19), loosely attached to the instruction, is a numerical saying that sets forth seven things Yahweh considers to be abominable, with the customary emphasis on the last one (Roth, *Numerical Sayings*). As noted in the introduction to Proverbs, numerical sayings (e.g., Prov. 30:15–16, 18–19, 21–23, 24–28, and 29–31) normally open with a title line that indicates two or more things plus one share a common characteristic. In this case, six things plus one share the common feature of being an "abomination" (*tô'ēbâ*) to Yahweh. "Haughty eyes" (literally, "raised, uplifted") are a poetic expression for arrogance (Ps. 131:1; Prov. 30:13), while "a lying tongue" is an expression for deceitful, untruthful statements. These would include the perjury of a false witness in court (see v. 19; also cf. Exod. 20:16; Deut. 19:18; Ps. 27:12; Prov. 14:5; 25:18). "Hands that shed innocent blood" refers to murder (Deut. 21:8, 9; 1 Sam. 19:5; Isa. 59:7; Jer. 7:6; 22:3). In the case of a murderer who has not been brought to justice, Deuteronomy sets forth a ritual and confession of innocence for purifying the cities nearest the victim, so that they will not be held guilty for the crime and thus their land will not be polluted with innocent blood. The "heart" or "mind" is the seat of human thinking or reason that lays out a course of action to follow, in this case, "wicked plans" that are harmful to others as well as to the perpetrators (Isa. 59:7; Jer. 4:14; see Prov. 15:26; Wolff, *Anthropology*, 40–58). "Feet that hurry to run to evil" is hyperbole to express the notion that

126

the wicked do not need even to think before quickly pursuing actions that are harmful to themselves and to others (Prov. 1:16). The "feet" are often an image in Proverbs to refer to making the journey along life's way. A "lying witness" or "false witness" specifically refers to perjury in a courtroom that is injurious to the one against whom the lying words are directed (Exod. 20:16; Deut. 19:18; Prov. 14:5; 25:18).

The seventh thing that Yahweh hates represents the one on which the greatest emphasis is placed, and it serves to unite the others in common. This culminating evil that serves as a synthesis for the other abominations of the entire saying is the sowing of "discord among brothers" (NRSV "discord in a family"), restating the final evil deed of the wicked person of the preceding strophe (6:14b). This is the one evil that conjoins all the others: haughty eyes, a lying tongue, shedding innocent blood, and so forth produce contentiousness among a community, whether a village, city, or household. "Sowing discord," as noted in verse 14b, involves the creating of strife in human communities that can bring them to destruction (Prov. 6:19; 15:18; 16:28; 17:14; 18:19; 22:10; 23:29; 26:20; 28:25; 29:22).

Conclusion

The eighth instruction is a miscellany of topics loosely placed within an instruction issued to students by a teacher in a wisdom school. Three particular topics are addressed: indolence, the wicked person, and things that are an abomination to Yahweh. What unites these different subjects is the fact that the lazy, the wicked, and abominable acts undermine the stability of cohesiveness of the human community, whether household, city, or clan. Placed in the context of a Jewish community struggling to gain its identity and achieve the ability to cohere and move into the future, a time of challenge like that of the early Persian period, these subjects became all the more necessary to expose and attempt to eradicate.

Theology

The Jewish community was many things, but it especially was a group of people defined by tradition and brought together by their commitment to common elements of faith and morality. Without these ties that bind, the community faced certain extinction. Human actions, so the sages witnessed, contained within them the ability to form and shape identity and to undergird the viability of households, clans, and the larger Persian colony. Yet human actions, if perverse, could

127

undermine the entire social experiment, resulting in Judaism's demise before its actual formulation as a community with a clear and forceful identity. The sages believed that their teachings could transform human character that would in turn lead to behavior that would give strength to a struggling community of people.

6:20–35
Ninth Instruction: Warning against Adultery

Provenance

The ninth instruction in the first collection (Proverbs 1—9) repeats the affirmation that obedience to sapiential teaching will protect the student from the strange woman, in this case clearly an adulteress (see 2:16–19). In the Old Testament, adultery comprised a forbidden sexual relationship between a married or betrothed woman and a man who was not her husband or intended (Perdue et al., *Families in Ancient Israel*, 184–85). The offense was considered to be against the husband, not the wife. Part of the concern with this illicit act was to ensure the husband that he would have his own offspring to inherit the household's property and to carry on the family name. Proscribed in various law codes (Exod. 20:14; Lev. 18:20; Deut. 5:18), adultery was punishable by death for both parties in Deuteronomic legislation (Deut. 22:22–24). It is doubtful, however, that this penalty was strictly enforced.

Literary Structure and Interpretation

This instruction begins with an introduction exhorting the student to obey the commandment of the father and the teaching of the mother (6:20). The teaching proper then follows with a section that develops the introduction by indicating that the instruction of the wise is a "way of life" and preserves one from the "evil woman" (vv. 21–24—NRSV "wife of another"). The final, lengthy section of the teaching proper is devoted entirely to the subject of avoiding the evil woman who is identified in this setting as an adulteress wife (vv. 25–35).

The extended introduction (v. 20) mentions both the "father" and the "mother" as teachers of the student (see 1:8; 4:3). Once more, these are probably titles of teachers, though they could refer to parents who undertook to instruct their children in the context of the family household. The "father's" commandment (see Prov. 13:13; 19:16; plural: 2:1; 3:1; 4:4; 7:1–2) and the "mother's" teaching (see Prov. 1:8; 3:1; 4:2; 6:23; 7:2; 13:14; 28:4, 7, 9; 29:18) are two terms for sapiential instruction in Proverbs. Because of their frequent reference to laws and law codes elsewhere in the Old Testament, these terms may have been used to underscore the authority of sapiential instruction.

The first strophe (vv. 21–24) of the teaching proper consists of an exhortation to follow the instruction of the father and mother. The motivations for doing so are that these teachings guide one along the path of life, and they offer protection from the "evil woman," in this context an adulteress. The two terms used for the teaching of the father and mother (*miṣwâ* and *tôrâ*) suggest the equivalence of their instruction in authority to legal prescriptions. This is further emphasized by the language about the teaching in vv. 21–23. What is particularly striking about this strophe are the echoes of the Shema or confession of faith in Deut. 6:4–9 and its partial reiteration in Deut. 11:18–20.

All three texts speak of the heart as the place where the words of the law or sapiential commandments reside. These three texts also speak of binding—in two cases, the words as a sign on the hand (Deut. 6:8; 11:18); in the other, the commandment and the teaching on the heart (Prov. 6:21). In Deuteronomy the "words" of the law are to be taught to the children (Deut. 6:7; 11:19), talked about when sitting in the house, when walking by the way, when lying down, and when rising. In the instruction in Prov. 6:22, the commandment and teaching will lead the son when walking, will protect him when lying down, and will talk with him when he awakes. The similarity between the three texts is too close to be coincidental. The approximation of the language is one of many indications—ranging from the formal comparisons of case law and sapiential prohibitions and admonitions, to thematic correspondences—that the sages and the jurists of Israel and Judah were closely related. Rather than suggesting one is literarily dependent on the other, this close approximation is best explained by the view either that sages were involved in the producing of laws and law codes as jurists and scribes or that they had the same education as the jurists and scribes. It is likely sages were involved in the producing of Deuteronomy and perhaps even the Deuteronomistic History and redaction (see Weinfeld, *Deuteronomy and the Deuteronomic School;* and Gerstenberger, "Covenant and Commandment," 38–51). 129

In verse 23 the commandment is also compared to a "lamp," while the teaching is a "light." This imagery is found in other wisdom texts (Job 18:6; 29:3; Prov. 13:9) as well as one Torah psalm (Ps. 119:105) and is used to speak metaphorically of being able to find one's way along the path of life, even during periods of darkness. Finally, the teaching of the wise preserves the student from the evil woman, from the "smooth tongue of the adulteress." The image of the "smooth tongue" is common in Proverbs, for it refers to seductive speech used either by the "strange woman" or by evil people to entrap the naive student with wickedness (Prov. 2:16; 5:3; 7:5). The "adulteress" or "adventuress," as noted above (2:16), is the strange woman, who represents a variety of things, ranging from an adulteress to a prostitute to a fertility goddess to folly. Here she is obviously the adulteress, for she is married to another man.

The teaching proper continues with a lengthy list of prohibitions, admonitions, and rhetorical questions, followed in each case with a variety of clauses (6:25–35). The unifying theme is the "evil woman" or adulteress, who fits into the larger theme of the "strange woman." Thus the majority of this instruction is directed to teaching the student to avoid the destructive course of adulterous liaisons.

This part of the teaching begins with a prohibition to the student against allowing the beauty of the adulteress to entrap him (vv. 25–26). The attached motive clause contrasts the payment to a prostitute, a loaf of bread, with that of an adulteress ("the wife of another"), namely, one's life. The adulteress "stalks" a man's life much as a hunter pursues wild game, a graphic metaphor to speak of the price one pays for adultery. Prostitutes, women who accepted payment for sexual favors, were common in Israel and Judah. Not all were stigmatized, as is evident from the stories of Rahab in Jericho (Joshua 2) and Tamar (Gen. 38:14–18). In general, however, they were regarded as shameful women engaged in wanton activity (Gen. 34:31; Lev. 19:29; 21:7, 9; Deut. 23:18; Jer. 5:7; Hos. 1:2). Adultery, however, was a greater abhorrence. Deuteronomy 22:22–24 legislates death for both parties who engage in adultery, but there is no example in the Old Testament of this penalty ever being carried out (however, see John 7:53—8:11).

The teaching proper in this ninth instruction then continues with two rhetorical questions, that is, questions that have an obvious answer (6:27–28). Rhetorical questions are found only here among the ten instructions in chapters 1—9. These questions are poetic descriptions of sexual desire that leads to harm, as the comparative clauses make clear in verse 29. The adulterer will not go unpunished (literally, "will not be held innocent"; see 11:21; 16:5; 17:5; 19:5, 9; 28:20), though it is not clear here what the punishment is. Later, the punishment is specified: wounds, dishonor, and the revenge of a husband who refuses any compensation for the wrong done him. Another rhetorical question occurs in verse 30, best understood as people not despising a hungry person for stealing bread. Even so, the crime of stealing is still repaid sevenfold and with all of one's household goods (v. 31). Elsewhere the payment is two-, four-, or fivefold (Exod. 22:1–4, 7 = Heb. 21:37, 22:1–3, 6). But by contrast, the one who commits adultery destroys himself (Prov. 6:32). He will be beaten, regarded with disgrace, and face the wrath of a husband who will not be appeased even with gifts (vv. 33–35).

Conclusion

This instruction emphasizes that obedience to the teaching of the sages enables the student to adhere to the path of life and to be preserved from the "strange woman," who in this literary context is the adulteress. Wisdom as guidance for the way of life and as protection from the strange woman is a common metaphor in Proverbs 1—9. The identification of the strange woman as an adulteress, however, is far clearer and more detailed in this teaching than elsewhere in the collection. As noted earlier, the household is not simply the place for the formulation and transmission of sapiential values but also a major social setting in which the moral teachings of the sages are actualized. Through this actualization, the stability of the family household and larger Jewish society is created.

Theology

In a fragile social and political world, when Judah was a weak and struggling Persian colony in a large and powerful empire, Judaism was in the incipient stage of formation and faced serious challenges to its survival as a culture and a religion. The conservative sages participated in the social world of the hierocratic party and helped shape a conservative tradition designed to ensure the stability of the fragile social institutions during this period of rebuilding Jewish culture and religion. These institutions included the temple and priesthood, the wisdom schools in their various forms, the local political institutions of governance and administration, and the household. While the sages did not set forth an explicit exhortation to support the Persian rulers and their empire, their moral teachings, on the whole, were conservative, not skeptical, and certainly not revolutionary. If the restoration of kingship was a goal, it was largely hidden in the superscription that mentioned Solomon as the patron of the tradition.

131

The sages operated out of a social paradigm of order, meaning that the primary elements of Jewish culture and identity were already largely in place. There were, of course, numerous threats to the achievement of Jewish stability in these early generations after the return from Babylonian captivity. The abandonment of major features of Jewish life coming into formulation could destabilize Judaism and lead to its dissolution and disappearance. This meant, for example, that the sages believed the endurance of the family household was absolutely essential to assure continuation of the Jewish community into the future. Adultery was a major danger to the viability of early Judaism. This act of betrayal threatened the household not only by undermining the marriage relationship but also by jeopardizing the cohesion of the family in the fundamental matters of household patrimony, custom and values, and even what was often a minimal economic existence. Sexual indiscretion in Judah was not simply an immoral act viewed with Victorian prudery in an ancient society that was not characterized by that nineteenth-century ethos. Rather, adultery violated the covenant bond of marriage; fragmented the solidarity of the family that emphasized the needs and well-being of the larger group; and, most of all, was a destructive act that could undermine the economic subsistence of the household, endanger the lives of its family members, and destroy the ethos where values of heredity, religion, and moral instruction were largely implemented in social life. Even more, adultery threatened Jewish society, culture, and religion, for the household was the key, central institution for shaping the identity and ensuring the survival of emerging Judaism.

7:1–27

Tenth Instruction:
Seduction by the Strange Woman

Date and Provenance

The tenth and final instruction in Proverbs 1—9 is the lengthy discourse in chapter 7 that is devoted entirely to the theme of the strange woman. Following similar instructions that treat this figure in 2:16–19; 5:1–23; and 6:20–35, this text identifies the strange woman as an adulteress. What is new in chapter 7, however, is the strong possibility that she is also a devotee of a fertility god or goddess. Moreover, residing behind this figure may be a poetic, metaphorical description of something even more fundamentally dangerous to Judaism: the allure of foreign religion and culture and their threat to the religion and culture of Jews residing in the colony of Judah in the early postexilic period. While most of this instruction consists of a warning to students against a sexual dalliance with this enigmatic figure, it should be noted that sexual seduction also is used metaphorically elsewhere in the Old Testament to illustrate in graphic terms religious apostasy and cultural assimilation (Jer. 3:2–4, 12–13, 20; 4:30–31; Ezekiel 16; and Hosea 1—3).

In contrast to this seductive and alluring woman, the first strophe (7:1b–5) personifies wisdom as the one whom the aspiring sages are encouraged to seek out as their lover. It is no question that Woman Wisdom is not a literal person but rather serves as a metaphor to represent the wisdom tradition and the instruction of the wise. Now wisdom, metaphorically at least, begins to take on dimensions of the goddess of love, who counters the seduction of the strange woman in her various guises. This poetic device encounters the aspiring sages and seeks to shape for them a worldview that rivals those of fertility goddesses, foreign cultures, and ways of living that are contradictory to the teachings of the sages. While not a goddess in literal terms, Woman Wisdom serves as a personification of sapiential teaching, and in a monotheistic religion, she takes on the character of a divine being without being more than a metaphor. Like their counterparts in other cultures who worshiped the gods and goddesses of wisdom and life, so the sages of Israel, in their imagination, devoted their lives and service to not a goddess but rather a tradition that shaped their character and governed their existence. Also new in this text is the appearance of a first-person style assumed by the teacher. In a lengthy discourse that assumes an autobiographical narrative style, the sage describes the eventual seduction and destruction of the simpleton who has not embraced Woman Wisdom.

Literary Structure and Interpretation

Following the typical teacher's exhortation to "keep" his or her words (v. 1), the instruction moves progressively through five strophes: the emphasis on the observance of sapiential teaching and the introduction of Woman Wisdom as a goddess of love whom aspiring sages are now to embrace (vv. 2–5); a first-person discourse about the strange woman's seduction of a young fool (vv. 6–9, 10–20, 21–23); and a conclusion in which the teacher returns to the beginning by exhorting the students (now "sons," plural—NRSV "children") to listen to his

133

or her instruction and to avoid the wiles of the strange woman, whose many victims have been led unwittingly to their destruction.

The instruction draws on the stock language for teachings found in Proverbs 1—9, suggesting that a reservoir of common terms and expressions existed that the sages used in their exhortations to students to pay heed to what they are taught. The introduction (v. 1) opens with the traditional address of "My son" or "My child," who is exhorted to "keep" (or "guard, watch"; see 4:21; 7:2) the "words" (2:1; 4:20) of the unnamed teacher and to "treasure" or "store up" his or her teachings (cf. 2:1b). This introduction is expanded in the first strophe (vv. 2–5), in which the teacher admonishes the student to "keep my commandments" (miṣwâ; cf. 2:1; 6:20) in order to "live" and to "keep my teachings" (tôrâ; cf. 1:8; 4:2; 6:20) like the "apple of the eye" (Deut. 32:10; Ps. 17:8), a metaphor that denotes something valuable and precious. Language echoing earlier descriptions in Proverbs and in Deuteronomy is now used once more by the sage to emphasize that the teachings of the wise are to be kept uppermost in the mind and heart of the young students: the sages' instructions are to be "bound on the fingers" and "written on the tablet of the heart" (see Deut. 6:4–9; 11:18–20; Prov. 1:9; 3:3; 6:20–24; Jer. 31:33). As noted earlier, these common images suggest that the compilers and writers of Deuteronomy likely belonged to the class of the "wise scribes" who also produced the conservative wisdom tradition of Proverbs and Ben Sira (see Weinfeld, *Deuteronomy and the Deuteronomic School;* and Gerstenberger, "Covenant and Commandment," 38–51).

Like the exhortation in 6:20–24, this instruction in Proverbs 7 emphasizes that obedience to the teacher's commandments will preserve the student from the "strange woman" or "adventuress" (NRSV "adulteress"), whose words are seductive (2:16; 5:3–4; 7:21). It is her language more than her actions or appearance that has the power to entrap and destroy. It is the speech of this woman that brings the unsuspecting fool within her orbit of destruction. Added in the present text (7:4), however, is the promise that obedience will lead to the gaining of Wisdom as one's lover. The terms for lover are *sister* and *intimate friend*. In the ancient Near East, *sister* is often a term for a lover or a bride (see Song of Sol. 4:9, 10, 12; 5:1) while *intimate friend* is a reference to either a relative (Ruth 2:1) or, more likely, a confidant and lover with whom one shares secrets and is intimate (Gen. 19:8; Judg. 11:39; 21:11). This language of love and intimacy is once more indicative of the effort of the sages to combat the attraction of prostitutes, adulteresses, and fertility goddesses by portraying in alluring terms the beauty and enticement of Woman Wisdom, the metaphorical incarnation of sapiential teaching.

The instruction takes a dramatic stylistic turn in verse 6, continuing on through verse 23, as the direct address of the sage changes to first-person narrative style. Assuming the autobiographical style of firsthand observance, the teacher now speaks of secretly watching the seduction of a young man by the strange woman, who uses her alluring enticements to lead him not simply to the promised gifts of forbidden love but also to the pain of unsuspected death.

This discourse (vv. 6–23) continues through three strophes: verses 6–9, 10–20, and 21–23. As a sapiential form, the autobiographical discourse is a frequent mode of literary discourse in wisdom literature, not only in Israel and Judah but also in the other regions of the ancient Near East (Perdue, *Wisdom and Creation,* 198–202). The book of Ecclesiastes is the best example of this autobiographical style assumed by a narrator who relates to students what are presented as observations and reflections based on his or her own experience. Other examples include Job's soliloquy in Job 3, his contrasting of his present misfortune with his blessed past (Job 29—30), and his oath of innocence (Job 31). One wisdom psalm also has a strophe in which the teacher assumes this literary mode of narration (Ps. 37:35–36).

The Greek Septuagint and Syriac texts have the third-person form of the verbs in this discourse at Prov. 7:6–9, suggesting that the strange woman is the observer. By contrast, the Masoretic Text has the first-person form of the verbs, and this is likely an indication that it is either the teacher or Woman Wisdom who is speaking. The language that introduces the autobiographical mode of narration may indicate that it is neither the teacher nor the strange woman who is setting forth observations of the seduction and death of the fool, but rather Woman Wisdom herself. The expression "looking out through the lattice of [my] window" is language associated with the artistic representations of fertility goddesses (Anat, Asherah) in Canaanite religion. Phoenician ivory plaques found in Samaria, Arslan Tash, Nimrud, and Khorsabad artistically depict this particular pose of a goddess. Instead of coming to Woman Wisdom's house for the love feast of study and insight, the simpleton makes his way to the house of the strange woman to take his fill of carnal love, in this case, with an adulteress and perhaps a devotee of a fertility goddess (Asherah? see Albertz, *History of Israelite Religion,* 1:85–87, 193–94).

There is ample evidence to suggest that this adulteress is also a worshiper of a fertility goddess. The seductress indicates to the young

135

fool that she is in the process of offering her communion sacrifices, a type of offering that had as its objective the binding together through ritual of a deity and his or her worshipers (v. 14; see Lev. 17:11–21; 1 Sam. 9:11–13). After the deity consumed the divine portion of fat and viscera, cultic officials received their meaty portions, as did the one who made the offering. The last of these would take the portions home, invite guests to the meal, and then celebrate a sacred festive occasion. A type of communion sacrifice was the votive offering, in which the worshiper fulfilled a vow after the deity's granting of the worshiper's petition. Dressed like a harlot (1:10), the strange woman here seizes the young man, speaks of fulfilling her vows, and invites him to join her at home in bed while her husband is away on a journey on business and will not return until the full moon, a time believed in the ancient near East to be opportune and propitious for travel. More than likely, the woman issues the simpleton an invitation to a sexual rendezvous that includes the sharing of a sacred meal and engaging in fertility rites that will allow her to fulfill her vow to her deity. This representation of Woman Wisdom as a fertility goddess and the strange woman as an adulteress and a devotee of a fertility goddess prepares for the literary transition to the following and concluding poem on Woman Wisdom and the strange woman as goddesses of love, each attempting to lure the unlearned to their embrace (9:1–18).

The grisly description of the death of the simpleton follows in verses 21–23. Woman Wisdom warns again of seductive speech that induces one to experience destruction. The destruction is described in rather graphic and repulsive images of butchering and the hunt: the "ox" that goes "to the slaughter," the "stag" that is caught fast "until an arrow pierces its entrails," and a "bird rushing into a snare." Like these dumb animals, the untutored one does not know that his folly will cost him his life.

In the concluding strophe of this lengthy instruction (vv. 24–27), the sage speaks again and returns to the initial exhortation to encourage once more obedience to the teaching. Calling on his or her "sons" or "children" to obey his or her instruction, the teacher issues one final direct exhortation for them to avoid joining the hordes of the victims of the "strange woman," whose slain are a "mighty host" (v. 26). Her house of seduction is on the way to the underworld and serves as the gateway to the chamber or rooms of its house (Ezek. 32:20–32). Here one finds mythological echoes of the goddess of war and love (e.g., Anat) who brought countless warriors to their death and of Prince Mot, the god of the underworld. The conclusion ends with the sage's

136

exhortation to the student not to be seduced by the strange woman, whose house leads to death for her victims.

Conclusion

The tenth and final instruction is devoted entirely to the subject of the "strange woman." Here one finds not only the contrast between Woman Wisdom and the strange woman but also the heightened use of the language of sexual intimacy. While the sages personified their tradition as a beautiful and alluring woman, this instruction speaks of her as an intimate lover. In so doing, they drew from the reservoir of mythological imagery of fertility goddesses of the ancient Near East who granted to their lovers the favors of life, wealth, and insight. Wisdom, the personification of the teachings of the sages, is to replace greatly adored goddesses who were believed, in the world of fertility religion, to possess the same powers, which they could bestow on their followers. The sages in this instruction warn, however, that the gifts of the strange woman are death, not life; destruction, not salvation.

After the imagery of Wisdom as a goddess of love (7:4), the teacher has her observe the not-so-subtle seduction of a fool who falls prey to the alluring words and sweet embrace of the strange woman. Slowly the latter entices him to her bed and ultimately to his destruction. Here the strange woman is not only an adulteress who betrays her husband but also the devotee of a fertility goddess who, with an insatiable appetite like the gaping jaws of Prince Mot (Death) in Canaanite religion, lays low her countless victims and leads them to their death. At stake in this instruction are not only the avoidance of adultery but also the rejection of fertility religion and its threat to emerging Judaism in the early Persian period.

Theology

Two religions vied for the allegiance of the youth of the colony of Judah in the years after the return from Babylonian captivity. The reformulation of Jewish religion that came to focus on the priestly religion of the Torah and the temple in Jerusalem was threatened by the allure of enduring fertility religion that had taken root centuries before in Israel and continued well into the Persian, Greek, and Roman periods, though in different forms. The weapons to combat this pagan religion included the teachings of the sages who believed that through the formation of sapiential character and the actualization of proven virtues Yahwistic religion and sapiential morality could be maintained.

137

Woman Wisdom gave herself and her accoutrements of well-being to those whom she favored. Yet the "strange woman" and her entourage of the adulteress, the prostitute, and folly lay in wait to lay low the simpleton who was seduced by her charms. Not only the simpleton was endangered by an unwitting flirtation with the strange woman; Judaism itself, as it was coming into form during the early Persian period, was at risk. The ally who could allay this devastation of early Judaism was Woman Wisdom, the incarnation of the teachings of the sages that promoted and extended life to the wise and existence to a developing Jewish way of existence.

8:1–36
Woman Wisdom: Wisdom as Teacher, Queen of Heaven, Child of God

Literary Structure and Interpretation

Proverbs 8 is an artistically shaped poem on Woman Wisdom that consists of four sections:the teacher's introduction of Woman Wisdom (8:1–3); Woman Wisdom's invitation to the simple (8:4–11); Woman Wisdom's rule as the queen of heaven (8:12–21); Woman Wisdom's role in the creation of the cosmos (8:22–31); and Woman Wisdom's instruction for life (8:32–36).

The teacher begins the poem with two rhetorical questions that ask if Woman Wisdom is not a peripatetic teacher who invites people to come and learn of her. Naturally, the answer is that she is. The teacher then describes the places, in this case likely all urban, where she issues the invitation to take up her course of study: the heights beside the way (or road), the gates of the city, and the entrance of the portals of the gate. In the next section, Woman Wisdom speaks of herself as a teacher issuing her invitation to come and learn of her (8:4–11). The concluding voice in the final section is likely that of Woman Wisdom again, who, now identified as a teacher, the queen of heaven, and the offspring of God and instrument of creation, opens her mouth to issue an instruction (8:32–36). Thus wisdom as teacher is the fundamental emphasis made by this inclusion. Captured in between are two strophes on Woman Wisdom's roles in providence (8:12–21) and creation (8:22–31). The striking effect of this literary structure is to show that the divine wisdom that shaped the cosmos

138

and rules providentially over creation and history is both the instructor of the unlearned and the embodiment of sapiential teaching in the form of a well-crafted poem.

In similar fashion to 1:20–33, Woman Wisdom becomes a peripatetic teacher who searches out the unlearned and issues to them her invitation to study her teaching (8:1–3). The context for this invitation is the city and various important locales where it is probable that teachers sought and persuaded the unlearned to take up the study of wisdom. It is also in these locales that sapiential schools were likely conducted, and not in houses or in other structures associated with modern education (see Lang, *Wisdom and the Book of Proverbs*). We are moderately well informed about schools in the ancient Hellenistic world, and in this later culture also the peripatetic teacher is well known. Teachers and philosophers traveled throughout cities and towns to induce students to undertake their courses of knowledge. Perhaps students or their families would pay some form of tuition to teachers to study under them. The speech of persuasion was the type of exhortation designed to invite and persuade students to enter a course of study, while paraenesis was both "exhortation" and "affirmation," that is, teaching that shaped the moral life of the unlearned and proved the validity of the instruction. It is not altogether clear whether Israelite and Jewish teachers also traveled to find students, although Woman Wisdom's travels in 1:20–33 and 8:2–3 suggest that this was a common practice. Furthermore, Ben Sira notes that the wise person travels to foreign countries to study wisdom (Sir. 39:4).

In addition to the city as the social location for the issuance of sapiential teaching, creation is presented in the poem's opening verses as an urban reality to which Woman Wisdom as peripatetic teacher travels in order to offer her instruction. Thus Woman Wisdom makes her way to the heights, presumably the acropolis of the urban center (cf. Prov. 9:3, 14), where she offers her invitation; utters her call at the entrance (i.e., the "gate") to a city; and is beside the road that leads to the urban center. In this world of human commerce, dwelling, and social organization, Wisdom takes her place and seeks out those who would learn of her. In the use of this imagery, the immanence of God in the form of divine Wisdom is made real and effective. In the world of Israel's and Judah's dwelling, mythological texts often portray the cosmos, that is, the world of human habitation, as a city. Key cities such as those that were political or religious capitals were seen as the center of reality, where the major deity or deities dwelt. Here the deity or deities of creation and providence maintained the order of creation through divine rule, temple cultus, and human ritual. Here the powers of chaos, both mythic and historical, were kept from consuming the life-giving order of creation (see Psalms 46, 48, and 76). Sacred cities such as Jerusalem contained the divinely chosen monarchy and the temple or sacred dwelling place of the great deity or deities that served as the linkage between heaven and earth.

The heights (8:2; see 1 Sam. 9:12–25; 10:5, 13; 1 Kings 3:2–4; Jer. 19:5; 32:35) more than likely refer to the geographical location of the temple of a city in the ancient Near East. Normally situated on the highest point of a city, the temple represented the imagery of divine transcendence and the entrance into the dwelling place of the gods. Perhaps this is why sanctuaries in ancient Israel were commonly called "high places." In addition to temples, royal palaces were found on the heights, in part for defensive reasons and in part to symbolize visually the august authority of the monarchy. Indeed, royal palaces and urban temples were often built in close proximity, at times even within the same compound, allowing the monarchy to draw on the legitimation of the major cultus for authority in ruling the country (see 1 Kings 5—9). The temple in Jerusalem was situated on the heights (see Jer. 17:12; 31:12; Ezek. 20:40), as was the likely location of Solomon's palace. Thus the teacher in 8:1–3 draws on mythological imagery of the city as cosmos to speak of Woman Wisdom uttering her invitation to come and learn of her. And those who take up this course of study are those who share in the life-giving power of divine wisdom and the order of creation that it creates and maintains. Wisdom, not simply the monarchy or the temple, serves as the link between heaven and earth.

The presence of Woman Wisdom at the gates of the city (8:3; see 1:21) also presents a significant image of the city, for it was in these locales that traffic, commerce, and legal proceedings occurred. The major gate was a large structure containing rooms for a variety of public functions, from commerce to judicial hearings (e.g., see 2 Sam. 18:24, 33). Prophets came to the gates to proclaim oracles of judgment and salvation (Amos 5:12, 15), while courts convened to settle legal disputes (2 Sam. 15:2; Job 29:7). It also may have been the case that merchants plied their wares in the gates to travelers entering and leaving the city, while teachers gathered and instructed their students in these structures. Woman Wisdom's issuance of her invitation and her teaching at the gate draws on the images of human activity, commerce, justice, and teaching so central to human social organization and existence. Wisdom becomes the medium of social order and the basis for life-sustaining teaching that maintains creation.

140

The reality of Woman Wisdom is not simply an urban center that draws within its boundaries multitudes of human inhabitants and visitors seeking to carry out their daily lives. Her reality is also a cosmos for human dwelling. In a period when the transcendence of God brought into question divine participation in human life, Woman Wisdom represented neither the silent meditation of human spirituality nor mystical encounters with God through pious repose or cultic ritual. Rather, Woman Wisdom went into the highways and byways of human life and sought to instruct those who would willingly accept her call. She presented to them an instruction for life that provided them means by which to live in harmony with the world and to experience success in all their daily pursuits, from business to family to politics. Wisdom here is not an escape from the world but rather is a complete and full participation in the human reality of God's own making. Woman Wisdom becomes the mediator between heaven and earth, between God and human creatures.

The narrator's voice changes in the second strophe (8:4–11) from that of an implied sage speaking in the third person to the first-person narration of Woman Wisdom, who issues her speech of persuasion to humanity (see 1:21, 24, 28; 9:3). Now Woman Wisdom extends her personal invitation to the simple, who are untaught, to come and learn of her. Ostensibly this invitation is universal and is not limited only to Israelites, Jews, the wealthy, the powerful, or males. Rather, all are included, for wisdom is open to anyone who accepts the offer to enter into its study. More practically, however, it may have been the case that the sages and their patrons (e.g., the court, the colonial government, and constituencies of the hierocratic party) appealed in particular to more well-to-do clients, whose families could afford to pay for the students' education and who could expect their children to enter into careers and sociopolitical circles of some substance and importance. As we have seen before, however, Woman Wisdom is not only the embodiment of the wisdom tradition. She is also the "voice" of God (see Isa. 40:3, 9), who is revealed by the teachings of the sages, the order of creation, and the prudent behavior of those who are guided by sapiential instruction.

The second strophe (8:4–11) presents Woman Wisdom's assertion of the integrity of her words and the truthfulness of what she teaches. Speaking as a teacher, she places emphasis on the authenticity of the verbal content of the teaching that she utters. She speaks "noble things," "what is right," the "truth," words that are "righteous" and "straight." She denies that what she utters contains "wickedness," which is "an abomination to [her] lips," and that the speech she delivers is "twisted or crooked." This contrast of the character of language is central to the sages' understanding of the word, which may possess

141

not only the power of truth to create and undergird life and well-being, but, if deceptive and corrupt, the ability to devastate and destroy both the speaker and those who are taken in by the deception of what is said. Indeed, the sages thought that the character of the spoken word had the power to shape the moral character of people, the wise and the foolish, the righteous and the wicked. The word became the formative force in human life and directed the actions of both sages and fools. Thus, in verses 10–11, Woman Wisdom as teacher once more compares favorably what she offers to her students to jewels and all that one desires. Indeed, wisdom is incomparable (see especially Prov. 3:13–18).

In the third strophe of the poem (8:12–21), Woman Wisdom assumes the guise of the queen of heaven, that is, a fertility goddess who is the metaphorical representation of divine governance of the world and the giver of life, wealth, honor, and prosperity (v. 18; *ṣĕdāqâ*, translated "prosperity" by the NRSV, is better understood as "righteousness," that is, the just order that pervades the cosmos, regulates and sustains human society, and enables its kings and governors to rule wisely). Drawing on mythical images of goddesses of war, wisdom, and fertility from the ancient Near East, Wisdom speaks as a royal goddess, the queen of heaven, who possesses not only the dispensable gifts of fertility and wisdom but also the power and right to rule over the earth and appoint as rulers "kings" who "decree what is just" and "nobles" who govern the earth (8:15–16). She dispenses to kings the life-creating and prudent counsel needed to plan successfully and to rule wisely. The social and political structure of nations is to emulate the larger cosmic order, so that they might experience stability, success, and well-being (see Job 12:18; 36:7).

Yet even this divine appointment of rulers through Woman Wisdom is conditioned on the reception given her by those who love her and seek her as their own. This language, laced with images of love, continues to give expression to the passionate quest for understanding undertaken by those who would be wise. This type of language would be familiar to an audience who knew the mythological stories of the ancient Near East that spoke of fertility goddesses who dispensed their rewards to human beings who were their offspring or even, at least for a time, their lovers. The rewards of Woman Wisdom given to those who succeed in their quest to embrace her are those values most highly esteemed by the traditional sages: "riches and honor," "enduring wealth and prosperity" (Murphy, "Wisdom and Eros in Prov. 1–9," 600–603). Finally, in this discourse Woman Wisdom once more asserts that her gifts are better than the other treasures often held in high esteem and sought out by human beings: "gold," "fine gold," and "choice silver" (v. 19; see 3:13–18; 8:11). Since Woman Wisdom herself walks in the paths of "righteousness" and "justice," the rewards of material gifts are offered to the sages who seek to emulate her behavior and to follow her instruction (8:20–21). This is similar to the gifts bestowed on Solomon because of his quest for an "understanding mind to govern [God's] people" (1 Kings 3:9–14). The "wise scribes" who integrate wisdom with the Deuteronomic law couch this language in 1 Kings in the Deuteronomistic rendering of sapiential language.

The poem concerning Woman Wisdom continues in Proverbs 8:22–31, where Wisdom, continuing to speak in the first person, sings a song of self-praise in which she tells of her primeval origins, when, as the offspring of the creator, she became the beloved child who soon was the mediator between heaven and earth. One of the striking images of Yahweh in this sapiential hymn is that of the divine parent. Wisdom is first "created" (8:22; literally, "fathered," *qānâ*) and "brought forth" (8:24–25; literally, "was given birth," *hûl*). The verb *qānâ* may mean "to acquire or obtain," in the sense either of acquiring wisdom (Prov 1:5; 4:5, 7) or of buying something (Exod. 21:2, a Hebrew slave). The verb also carries the meaning "to create." Thus God "creates" the heavens and the earth (Gen. 14:19, 22) or God "creates" human beings (Ps. 139:13). In the case of creating, the more specific nuance of the term is that of procreating, as in Deut. 32:6 where God created (fathered) Israel. The verb *hûl* (brought forth) means more specifically the act of writhing in birth pains (Deut. 32:18; Job 39:1; Pss. 51:5 = Heb. 51:7; 90:2). While the verb is passive, it seems clear that Wisdom is saying that Yahweh is the one who gave her birth. In this metaphorical image of procreation, Yahweh is presented as both the father and the mother of wisdom, who "created" her as the first born of creation (see Perdue, *Wisdom and Creation,* 89–91).

The NRSV's translation of *rē'šît darkô* in 8:22 is "at the beginning of his work." This translation perhaps is an echo of Gen. 1:1 (*běrēšît,* "in the beginning," or "when [God] began"). More likely the expression in Prov. 8:22 means the "first of his [creative] activity" or the "firstborn of his creation" (see Job 40:19; Pss. 78:51; 105:36). The word *first* suggests that Wisdom was the initial product of divine creation. This also may indicate the sense of being the best and most valued of all the things that God created (see, e.g., the "first fruits" of the harvest, Amos 6:1, 6). The firstborn son in Israelite and Jewish society held a privileged rank (Gen. 43:33) and received a double portion of the family estate (Deut. 21:17). He was expected to become the head of the

143

family eventually, after the death of his father (see Perdue et al., *Families in Ancient Israel,* 191). In the poem in 8:22–31, however, Wisdom is a female offspring. The poem breaks with social convention that often placed greater value on the male. While the word *work* (*derek;* 8:22) elsewhere in Proverbs usually refers to the "path" to wisdom, moral action, or the course of life (Prov. 2:8; 3:6, 23; 4:26; 5:8, 21; 10:29; 11:5; 20:24; 29:27; and 31:3), "his work" (*darkô*) likely refers to creation or the activity of creation (Job 26:14; 40:19).

The verb in verse 23 translated by the NRSV as "I was set up" (*nissaktî*) suggests one of two actions: "poured out" (Gen. 35:14; Exod. 25:29), perhaps reflecting the birth process, when the womb's water breaks; or "installed," that is, as a ruler at the beginning of one's reign (Ps. 2:6). The first meaning is compatible with the imagery creation as the engendering and birthing of life, while the second points to Woman Wisdom's royal status in the cosmos. Both are metaphors suggestive of divine creation and providence.

What follows in verses 23b–26 is a formula readily present in numerous creation texts of the ancient Near East. The introduction to each line (save for v. 26b) is "when there were no" or "before." In the imagination of the sages, as well as that of the mythmakers, reality prior to creation was seen as a lifeless chaos that had no form or shape. Creation thus was not *creatio ex nihilo,* that is, creation out of nothing. Rather, prior to the life-giving, transforming, and shaping action of God, only darkness, the force of mighty waters, and nonlife existed (see Gen. 1:1–2). God's shaping of creation out of chaos portrays reality as consisting of three parts: earth, the deep, and the heavens (skies). The cosmos is made stable by the great mountains that serve as the pillars of reality (Prov. 8:27), by the "circle on the face of the deep" (that is, chaos; Prov. 8:27), and by making "firm the skies above" (8:28). Thus creation is the well-crafted and securely founded reality of a divine architect whose careful work ensures that the cosmos will not collapse (see Job 38:4–6).

In verse 29, Yahweh issues two legal decrees. The first restrains the "sea," a reference to Prince Yam, the lord of the seas in Canaanite mythology, who battles Baal, the god of fertility, for rule over the earth. Prince Yam was the incarnation of chaos, the sea that threatened the order of creation. This first decree, an example of the creative power of the word (see Psalm 33), establishes boundaries that Prince Yam cannot pass beyond in order to destroy the fertile earth. The other decree "legislates" (*ḥûq*—NRSV "marked out") into existence the "foundations of the earth." These decrees, reflecting the judgments of the court, give stability to the new creation and enable it to continue (see Job 38:8–11).

Verses 30–31 present the most perplexing section of this lengthy poem on Woman Wisdom. In particular, Woman Wisdom describes herself as an *'āmôn,* translated by the NRSV as a "master worker" (Jer. 52:15; see *'ammām,* in Song of Sol. 7:1 = Matt. 7:2 = 7:1, which possibly means "master workman"). This translation intimates that Wisdom is an architect who designs and builds, in this case, the cosmos. This translation does correlate well with the context, for verses 27–29 depict Yahweh as the divine architect. Wisdom of Solomon 7:22 supports this view with the description of Woman Wisdom as the divine *technitis* (artisan). It may be, however, that a more accurate translation is "little child" (see *'āman,* "to nourish, nurse, nurture" an infant or small child; Num. 11:12; Ruth 4:16; 2 Sam. 4:4; Esth. 2:7; Isa. 49:23; Lam. 4:5). Earlier in this poem, Woman Wisdom states that she is both "fathered" and "begotten." If this latter translation is the correct meaning, then Wisdom is the "nursling" or "little child" in whom Yahweh continually ("daily") delights (Isa. 66:12; Jer. 31:20). Wisdom, in turn, like a small child, "rejoices" or plays before her divine parent. She "rejoices" (*śāḥaq,* "makes merry" over, v. 31; see Jer. 30:19; 31:4; Zech. 8:5) in Yahweh's "inhabited world." This "play" of Child Wisdom and the "delight" of the parent in the child is an imaginative way of speaking of Wisdom as the linkage between the heavens and the inhabited earth or the Creator and the created world. Wisdom serves as the divine attribute that overcomes the distance between the transcendent creator and the world of human dwelling. Yahweh's delight in the character and activity of divine wisdom is the power that enables the creation to endure.

The concluding strophe of the poem (8:32–36) presents Wisdom once more as the teacher, completing the circle that began in the introduction and first strophe (8:1–3, 4–11). On the basis of her roles as the queen of heaven and divine child, she now invites once more her "sons" to listen to her teaching and to keep to her ways. The divine wisdom that was used by God in creating and sustaining the world is now offered to human beings. Through their embodiment of the teachings of the wise, human beings have the opportunity to experience the life-sustaining power of creation. And through their own behavior they contribute to maintaining the order of the cosmos and human society.

Twice in this concluding invitation, teacher Wisdom uses the word *happy* (*'ašrê,* vv. 32, 34). As noted earlier (3:13–20), "happy" refers

145

to the state of well-being that the sage enters by means of the incorporation of wisdom. Through the study and practice of wisdom, the student "became wise" or entered the state of being best described as sagehood, that is, the mode of being where one's character was shaped by the virtues of the sapiential (v. 33).

Conclusion

This extended poem on Woman Wisdom intends to present the wisdom tradition as a metaphorical personification of a divine attribute, perhaps the key attribute from the viewpoint of the sages. This is the attribute that God uses in creating and providentially directing the world and its inhabitants. This divine Wisdom thus becomes the teacher who instructs the unlearned so that they may participate in the divine, life-giving power of creation. But she is also the queen of heaven who chooses and then gives life and counsel to kings of the earth so that they may rule wisely and well. This role of wisdom teaches that kings and governors rule by divine right, a conservative teaching intended to undergird the emerging sociopolitical and religious order of the early Persian period.

Wisdom also becomes the divine child, present at and active in creation. The most valued of all things created, Wisdom becomes the mediator between the Creator and the created world. In an age when Yahweh was increasingly understood as transcendent, that is, far removed from the world of human dwelling and thus from the ken of human knowledge and experience, personified Wisdom and the tradition she embodied became the means by which to come to the knowledge of God. More and more, the wisdom tradition became a major source of divine revelation that taught directly about God and the divine will for human behavior and enabled the wise to observe correctly the nature and operation of the cosmos, which in turn would allow some insight into the Creator.

Theology

In Proverbs 8, Woman Wisdom takes on the guise of a sage who invites students to take up her course of study. She also serves as the queen of heaven who chooses kings to reign and provides them with the gifts of wealth and insight in order that they may rule wisely and well. This understanding of wisdom enables the sages to speak of the providence of God, who continues to guide creation, and at the same time to invoke the theological argument that reigning kings receive

146

legitimation for their rule from divine wisdom, in other words, the Creator.

At the same time, the poem conceives of the cosmos as a well-ordered dwelling, a structure planned by the divine architect, who uses wisdom to shape an artistic, well-integrated building. In addition, Yahweh restrains the waters of the deep by constructing a heavenly vault to protect the earth and orders Prince Yam to respect the boundaries of the living creation. Here is no hint of cosmic struggle between the Creator and a monster of chaos (see Job 40:1—42:6; Isa. 51:9–11). Rather, through the ordering and sustaining power of divine command and Woman Wisdom, creation continues without threat to its existence—save one. Only the fools who reject the teachings of the sages, that is, the invitation of Woman Wisdom to pursue the proper course of study and to learn to behave in prudent and life-sustaining ways, may injure the good creation and disrupt the order of life established in primordial times. By contrast, the student who says yes to Woman Wisdom's invitation, who seeks to embrace her as a lover does the beloved, will discover and experience life in all its beneficent qualities. And in at least a small way, the sage contributes to the order of creation and its continuation into the future.

9:1–18
Poem on Wisdom and Folly: Contending for the Heart

Date and Provenance

The conflict between Jewish tradition and foreign cultures in the early Persian period presents itself once more in the final chapter of the opening collection. Most likely this chapter also belongs to a wisdom school that spoke of the "two ways" that presented themselves to Israelite and Jewish youth. To this point in the collection, wisdom has been personified as the wise teacher who invites the unlearned to follow her pathway to life; the firstborn, beloved child of God in whom the Creator takes delight; the witness of and participant in the creation of reality; the mediator between heaven and earth; the queen of heaven who providentially rules over the world of human habitation; and the divine goddess who offers wealth and honor in one hand and long life in the other. Now she is portrayed as the goddess of life who

147

builds her palace, inaugurates her worship, and sends forth her maidens to invite the simple to her banquet of life (9:1–6). In the setting of this great banquet, Woman Wisdom resumes her role of teacher, offering her final instruction to those who desire to learn of her (9:7–12).

Residing behind these poetic metaphors of Woman Wisdom is the sapiential tradition that was shaped by the sages in the schools of the court, the temple, and the cities of ancient Israel and early Judaism. This tradition came to incorporate what the sages saw as the essential virtues of Jewish life that were to be transmitted, taught, and incorporated in individual and social existence. The values of education, honor, wealth, long life, and family were placed within the contours of a social and religious conservatism that counseled against both the extremes of revolutionary activity and outlawry and the more ordinary pitfalls and entrapments of imprudent and foolish behavior that undercut the stability of colony, national religion, and traditional family life.

These extremes and entrapments were also personified in the form of a frequently encountered figure in the first collection, commonly known as the "strange woman," a polyglot of many images, all sharing the integral characteristic of "folly." She is by turns the adulteress who abandons the marriage covenant of her youth to seduce the unwitting fool (2:16–19; 6:24–35), a prostitute (6:26) or foreign wife who leads the fool to his destruction and robs the traditional household of its wealth and honor (5:1–23), and an adulteress who worships a fertility deity and entraps the fool in a vow of illicit sex (7:5–27). In each case, a dalliance with the strange woman leads to destruction and death for the fool.

Now she is presented as Woman Folly, who, as a noisy and wanton prostitute, sits by her house on the "high places" of the town and invites the foolish to enter and eat of her poor victuals. The simpleton accepts her invitation and goes blindly into her house, only to discover that he has entered the realm of the dead. This frequently encountered figure is also representative of something larger than foolishness and sexual misconduct. She represents the seduction of alien religion and culture that threatened to lead to the undoing of Jewish tradition and its virtues and values, by outright apostasy or by slow assimilation or by unwise, even nihilistic behavior that could contribute to the disassembling of the conservative Judaism that was seeking to take shape and survive in the early Persian period. Family, religion, and some measure of Jewish identity within the larger Persian Empire were the real stakes in the conflict between Woman Wisdom and her nemesis Woman Folly.

148

Literary Structure and Interpretation

Proverbs 9:1–18 consists of an elegant poem of two strophes (9:1–6, 13–18) that envelop a brief instruction where, once again, the voice of Woman Wisdom is distinctly heard ("by me" in v. 11 refers to wisdom and knowledge in v. 10). The two strophes of the poem contrast Woman Wisdom's invitation to the simple to participate in her banquet of life with that of Woman Folly, who attempts to seduce the unlearned to partake of her feast that leads to death. This either-or of sapiential teaching is reminiscent of the paraenetic exhortations in Deuteronomic and Deuteronomistic preaching that speak of choosing life and death in reference to obedience to or disregard of the Torah (Deut. 6:1–3; 8:11–20; 11:13–17; 28:1–68; Josh. 24:2–28; and Jer. 7:1–15). When Woman Wisdom opens her lips for the last time in the collection, she uses once more the key refrain of "the fear of the LORD is the beginning of wisdom" that opened the collection, thus providing a striking *inclusio* (1:7). Only Wisdom offers long life to those who learn of her.

The grammatical arrangement and thematic texture of the poem's opening (vv. 1–6) and closing (vv. 13–18) are much the same. Both subjects (Wisdom and Folly) are spoken of in the third person. Both invite and attempt to persuade the unlearned to partake of their victuals. The strophe about Woman Folly, however, adds an element not present in the initial strophe: the fate of the fools who are tempted by Folly's invitation is vividly described in terms of death. The fool joins the dead as guests at Folly's banquet.

Seen in a less metaphorical way, the poem speaks of the invitation of sages to the unlearned to take up their course of study, in order that they may find life and avoid the destructive entrapments of foolishness, prostitution, adultery, fertility religion, cultural and religious apostasy, and assimilation into a foreign culture. This struggle between Wisdom and Folly is real. It is an intense counterpoising of two very different ways of life and, from the sages' way of thinking, two very different outcomes: life and death.

In the initial strophe of this poem (vv. 1–6), Wisdom is clearly represented as a fertility goddess who builds her house (palace or temple) of seven pillars and then sends forth her maidens to issue her invitation to celebrate its dedication in a grand banquet. The meaning of the building of the house has been understood in a variety of ways, ranging from the creation of the cosmos, much as an architect would design and then build the world, to the construction of a palace or

149

temple, to the formation of the wisdom tradition, to the literary construction of a poem (the one in chapter 9) or the larger collection of ten instructions and several wisdom poems (in chapters 1—9), to an aristocratic house, to a place of study in which students also resided. If the earlier images of Woman Wisdom in the striking poem of chapter 8 are kept in mind, it would seem that her building likely represents several levels of meaning: the one who designs and builds the cosmos (Prov. 8:30 = *'āmôn* as "builder"; Wisd. Sol. 7:22), the queen of heaven who inaugurates her reign with the construction of her palace and its dedication with a great banquet (Prov. 8:12–21), and a house of study for those who take up her course of study (Prov. 8:32–36). In merging these images with the "building" of a magnificent poem, Wisdom is the divine creative and sustaining power that originates and maintains the cosmos, teeming with life, and who, incarnate in both the wisdom tradition and its teachers, offers life and well-being to all who choose to learn of her.

Wisdom's act of "setting up" (the Hebrew more likely reads "hewing out") her seven pillars suggests the image of the stonecutter who dresses newly cut columns that have been removed from a stone quarry (see 1 Chron. 22:2). The pillars were likely used in a large public building to support the structure's roof, though the temple of Solomon had two free-standing pillars outside the porch (1 Kings 7:15–22, 41–42) that may have had a symbolic, not a functional, purpose. Suggestions for these Solomonic pillars have included stelae (= Hebrew *maṣṣēbôt* that represented deities in Canaanite temples) and the pillars of the earth that support the stability of the cosmos (Job 9:6; 26:10–11; Ps. 75:3 = Heb. 75:4). The number seven for Wisdom's pillars has also elicited numerous explanations, including the spacious size of the structure (thus a palace or temple) or the planets.

Perhaps the most compelling argument for understanding Wisdom's activity in verse 1 is to identify the building of the house and the setting up (hewing) of its seven pillars with the construction of a divine dwelling that, in turn, has theological and cosmological symbolism. The mythic symbolism of Yahweh's dwelling in the temple in Jerusalem (see esp. Psalms 46, 48, and 76) and of the Canaanite god Baal's construction of his palace to represent his assuming his rightful place among the gods in the Baal Cycle are two parallel examples. The construction of Yahweh's temple is described in 1 Kings 5—8, while that of Baal is present in the Baal Cycle of texts from Ugarit. These acts of temple building point to the lordship of their respective deities as those who providentially sustain the world, and in Yahweh's case, as the one who has called and continues to rule over Israel, punishing the nation when sinful but rewarding it when faithful. In the case of Baal, he is the conqueror of Lotan, the monster of chaos, and later, through the assistance of his consort Anat, is able to win partial control of the cosmos, the reign over which he shares with Prince Mot, the lord of the underworld. In both accounts, details of the construction of the temple are presented, followed by a great feast celebrating the acknowledgment of their divine status and lordship—over creation and national history in Yahweh's case and over creation and, implicitly, human life in the case of Baal.

If construed by looking through these lenses, it seems quite possible that Wisdom's activity of building her house and hewing her seven pillars symbolically refers to her taking her place as queen of heaven and earth, the one who was present at creation and perhaps was the divine architect by whom Yahweh created a well-constructed cosmos. She also becomes the one who continues to maintain reality and the structures of life. Through acknowledgment of her rule, the unlearned come to at least a partial knowledge of God and have the instruction necessary to secure life for themselves and to contribute to the stability and continuation of society and the larger world.

At the completion of her building activity, Wisdom slaughters (likely "sacrifices") her beasts, mixes her wine, and sets her table. She then sends out her maids from the highest places of the town to invite the simple to come and partake of her sumptuous banquet. Because of their enormous cost, meat and wine were rarely consumed by common people and usually were the delicacies associated with cultic festivals. The feast to which Wisdom's maidens issue invitations parallels the type of celebration that inaugurated officially the reigns of Yahweh and Baal (Prov. 9:2–6). Wisdom's rightful place in the heavens and her rule over the cosmos, at least as the divine virtue of Yahweh, is acknowledged now by the celebrants partaking of the feast that initiates the beginning of her reign; only Wisdom invites not cultic devotees but rather the unlearned to partake of her victuals that lead to life.

Wisdom's maidens, suggestive of her royal retinue or perhaps the sacred votaries of a fertility goddess, sing their alluring, siren song from the highest places of the town to invite the simple to participate in her meal. The highest places also integrate well with a larger royal or cultic collage of images, since temples and palaces were usually placed on the highest points of a city, to symbolize power and majesty as well as to offer the best protection against attack. The feast to which the maids of Wisdom invite the simple is a banquet of life. By leaving behind their folly and simple-minded behavior, the unlearned come to enjoy not a literal meal of meat and spiced wine but rather a festival of

151

life. The maidens invite the unlearned not to sexual intimacy but to a banquet of life and an embrace of Woman Wisdom, whose gifts of insight and life are far greater than those offered by any fertility goddess. Wisdom, the goddess of creation and life, has assumed her place in her temple and invites all to come and worship her.

With the completion of her temple and the issuance of her invitation to the simple to join in her banquet of bread and wine, Woman Wisdom assumes once more the voice of the teacher who utters her instruction of life (9:7–12). She begins with a warning against offering correction (or "discipline") and reproof to a "scoffer" and a "wicked" person. The participle for "correction" (*yôsēr*) derives from the same root as "discipline" (*mûsār*). This root is commonly used in Proverbs to refer to the discipline of study, reflection, and piety; the form as well as the content of sapiential teaching; and the guidance of correction (Job 4:3; 5:17; Prov. 1:2, 3, 7; 19:18; 23:23; 29:17). The student is admonished not to waste the effort to instruct "scoffers" (9:8), for they are incapable of discipline (Prov. 13:1; 15:22) due to their quarrelsome and proud nature (Prov. 21:24; 22:10). The scoffer is paralleled to the wicked who, due to immorality and frivolity, cannot learn wisdom and thereby embody the righteousness that the sage teaches. To invite scoffers and the wicked to take up wisdom's course of study is an inefficacious effort, for they have neither the desire nor the tractable character that allows formation by instruction. By contrast, even the wise and righteous, offered additional teaching, will gain in wisdom and righteousness (9:9). The embodiment of wisdom and righteousness is a pursuit that endures for a lifetime, for no one reaches the final culmination of complete and perfect knowledge and character.

Woman Wisdom as teacher now moves to the basis for accepting her invitation to pursue wisdom by returning to the oft-repeated affirmation: "The fear of the LORD is the beginning of wisdom" (v. 10; see 1:7). This repetition provides a striking inclusion for the entire collection of chapters 1—9. It is through the fear of the Lord, that is, the pious affirmation that Yahweh is not only the creator but also the sustainer of life and the giver of wisdom, that wisdom can come to its seekers. For the sages who composed this collection, wisdom that provides insight into God and existence and that becomes embodied in human character does not derive from native intelligence but rather is a divine gift to those who fear God. The acceptance of Wisdom's invitation and the quest for knowledge and insight must begin with faithful confession. The promise of Wisdom does not rest content with the offer of insight but, once accepted, yields the increase of years

152

(v. 11). Verse 12 contrasts those who seek wisdom and become wise with those who "scoff" and bring on themselves the consequences of their contentious and arrogant behavior.

The third and concluding strophe of this final poem in the first collection is located in 9:13–18. This strophe, which contrasts with the first one in 9:1–6, presents the calamity that awaits those who accept not the invitation of Woman Wisdom but rather that of her opponent, Woman Folly. Woman Folly, in contrast to Woman Wisdom, who offers life and the increase of years to those who accept the invitation to her banquet, is a shameless and wanton prostitute who seduces her followers and leads them into the "depths of Sheol" (v. 18).

Folly, the opposite of Wisdom (see Prov. 14:1), may be understood in a variety of ways. First, her description compares to those of the "strange woman" in earlier sections of this collection (see 2:1–22; 5:1–23; 6:24–35; and 7:1–27) and thus seems to offer continuity with this multifarious figure. Earlier the strange woman was an adulteress, prostitute, and devotee of a fertility goddess. Here she, like her opposite, Woman Wisdom, is an incarnation, in this case of folly, reckless and thoughtless behavior that not only rejects the sages' quest for the knowledge of God but also undercuts the order of cosmos and society with stupidity, contentiousness, licentiousness, boisterousness, shamefulness, lawlessness, and dishonor. As in her earlier portrayals, she entices the unlearned and the fools to destruction. Yet fools do not simply enjoy the fruits of their own disastrous behavior. They also create havoc and disorder in both the life-giving order of creation and the righteous pattern of society. Thus individual frivolity, wickedness, and foolishness lead to disastrous consequences for creation and community.

It appears that the imagery that characterizes the strange woman and, here, Woman Folly, suggests the allure of fertility religion and goddesses for the devotion of Jewish patrons. The absence of a divine consort for Yahweh in Jewish religion left open an opportunity for enticement by fertility religion and its offers of life, pubescence, and promiscuity to potential followers. Woman Wisdom, then, became the agency for securing the devotion of Jews to the reformulation of religion in the postexilic period and to the study of Jewish tradition that would bring continuity and vitality to a community threatened by dissolution.

Folly (v. 13—NRSV "foolish woman") is a feminine noun meaning "foolishness" and "stubbornness." In wisdom literature, the "fool" is one who is lacking in sense, is incapable of taking instruction, behaves and speaks in a stupid manner, and transgresses the divine order of creation and society that brings about and sustains life (Prov. 1:22; 10:23; 12:23; 15:2, 14; 18:2). The end for the fool is destruction (Ps. 49:10–11; Prov. 1:26).

Who is Woman Folly? In many ways, her behavior reminds one of the fool. She is "wanton," that is, lacking in control; she is shameless; and she sits instead of stands by the entranceway to her house. Yet she also sits at the seat of the "high places of the town" (v. 14, for her house, see 5:8; 7:8), suggesting the location of power, either that of a god or a royal figure. This image intimates that she possessed a position, status, and esteem, either religiously or politically, in the social and religious structure of postexilic Judah. Like her opposite, Woman Wisdom, she invites the unlearned to enter her dwelling. Her seductive speech, like that of the common whore, titillates those who passed by: "Stolen water is sweet, and bread eaten in secret is pleasant." Her banquet is not that shared in public by those who choose to worship Woman Wisdom but instead a sorry meal eaten in secret. Intercourse with Woman Folly, while carried out in the secrecy of her bordello, leads the fool to the underworld, where only the dead have their abode.

Folly is thus portrayed as a fertility goddess who offers life to her followers. She summons the fool to lie with her and to obtain the life and well-being so eagerly sought by all. The carnal embrace of Folly leads not to life, however, but rather to the underworld, where the "shades" dwell (v. 18). Entrance into her house is passage through the gateway to death. Foolishness, the opposite of wise behavior, produces only destruction for those who embody its constituent features.

Conclusion

This concluding poem, in which is inserted a final instruction, contrasts wisdom and folly, both personified as goddesses seeking to recruit followers from among Jewish youth to pursue two opposing views of the world. Woman Wisdom, the incarnation of the teachings of sages during the Persian period, invited Jewish youth to take up her course of study and to discover life and well-being. Woman Folly, the opposite of Wisdom, represented not simply frivolity and foolishness but also the vices that would undermine a Jewish community struggling to form itself into a society that would survive into the future. The virtues of wisdom incarnate in the young people of Judah, a colony of the Persian Empire, would enable incipient Judaism to take root and survive as a religious community. The vices and indiscretions of folly would ensure that formative Judaism would fail.

154

Theology

The opposition of two deities vying for lordship over the cosmos and its human occupants is a common theme in ancient Near Eastern literature. In Canaan, Baal and Mot as well as Baal and Lotan were mortal enemies bent on ruling creation. In Israel, Baal and Yahweh were the major antagonists seeking to gain the allegiance of the masses. Drawing on the images of divine conflict, the sages of the early Persian period depict Wisdom and Folly as divine rivals who seek to rule the human heart and the larger creation.

Thus, Wisdom is the queen of heaven who, having constructed her temple, offers her banquet of life to those young Jewish people who will partake of her bounty. Likewise Folly, while offering a far less sumptuous fare, sits on the heights of the city and tempts the young people of Judah to taste of her meal. The choice between the two is that between life and death; ultimately, this is what separates wisdom and folly. The fate of Judaism in the early Persian period depended on the choices its youth would make in this most precarious of times.

The Second Collection

"The Proverbs of Solomon"

PROVERBS 10:1—22:16

Date and Provenance

The dating and provenance of this lengthy collection of the book of Proverbs are difficult to establish. Contemporary interpreters who have hazarded hypotheses about this collection of brief sayings have dated these predominantly two-line proverbs anywhere from the pre-exilic period to late postexilic times. The social locations have been identified as the court, school, and family household. The superscription, which attributes the collection to Solomon, is probably of little use in determining any concrete answers to these questions, other than to indicate that the house of David was a patron of the activity of royal sages in the courts and schools of Jerusalem before the demise of the kingdom of Judah and its monarchy in the Babylonian conquest of 586 B.C.E. As noted earlier, Solomon became a symbol of the ethos and social world of the sages. This suggests that wisdom was at least in part a royal enterprise for many centuries (see Kalugila, *Wise King*). Finally, the link to Solomon may well have been an implicit and thus politically construed affirmation of postexilic sages living in the colony of Judah who looked to the monarchy for legitimation and perhaps even anticipated, for a brief time, the reinstitution of this royal dynasty.

One may begin to answer the questions of the date and provenance of this collection first of all by reference to the Persian period, when the canonical (excluding the deuterocanonical books of Sirach and the Wisdom of Solomon) books of wisdom received their final shape. The final editors more than likely belonged to the conservative sages of colonial Judah, who eventually joined with the hierocratic party and its Zadokite priest leaders to set forth an agenda that placed these two groups in control of internal Jewish affairs while the Persians ruled their country (see Hanson, *Dawn of Apocalyptic*). The goal of

157

the hierocratic party was to set forth a social world that ostensibly supported both the existing political arrangements with the Persians and the local institutions of temple, priesthood, and traditional household, though there may have been a slight implicit and initial hope that the house of David would one day be restored and Jewish independence thereby achieved. This incipient messianism, if present, quickly died as the allegiance of sages and priests became attached without major qualification to the Persian, Greek, and finally Roman empires. Thus the dream of a restored monarchy finally dissipated among these two social groups.

The individual sayings, however, likely covered a wide span of time, encompassing the early monarchy through the initial generations of the postexilic period. What unites their sapiential creators is the likelihood that the school in its various forms was the center of sapiential intellectual, moral, theological, and literary reflections and activities, and that the household as both a subject of ethical reflection and a context for the moral life continued unabated, though at times threatened, throughout this lengthy time period.

Suffice it to say, then, it seems probable that much of the wisdom in this collection, as was the case in other sapiential books, grew out of various types of schools, from those of the royal court, to those of the temple, to civil academies during the colonial period, to scribal families (see Crenshaw, *Education*). Some of the sayings may well have been produced originally in the family household and entered the literary tradition of royal, temple, and civil scribes through the lenses of their reflection and activity. In most cases, references to the household probably indicate that this was one of the key institutions of Israelite and Jewish social life and an important setting for existing sayings dealing with this topic, especially the scribal households that served as guilds. In addition, as a theme, the sayings that approach the subject of the household set forth traditional and conservative observations for guidance in the moral life that often require insight about conducting one's life within the social structure of the family and its variety of social roles, customs, and laws.

Literary Structure and Interpretation

The second collection in the book of Proverbs is largely a list of sayings (375, which equals the numerical value of the name Solomon) of various types and many topics that provided moral instruction for the young among the conservative sages and nobility in the early postexilic period (see Murphy, *Wisdom Literature,* 63–74). Language is an overarching theme in this second collection of sayings, which breaks down thematically and formally into two major subdivisions: 10:1—15:33 and 16:1—22:16. Although no superscription opens the second subdivision, it should be noted that the last saying of the first subdivision provides a clear ending and a smooth transition to the second:

> The fear of the LORD is instruction in wisdom,
> and humility goes before honor.
> (Prov. 15:33)

The contrast between the righteous sage and the wicked fool is the key theme in chapters 10—15, with the prominent presence of the antithetical saying contrasting these two categories of people. The righteous sage in this first subdivision more than likely refers to the conservative class of teachers and scribes attached to the court and temple of the preexilic period. The transition to the postexilic period witnessed the eventual displacement of the royal court by local governments who owed their position and gave their allegiance to a successive series of foreign empires. In this latter time frame, the temple emerged as a major institution in Jewish social and religious life and united with Jewish governments on the local scene in legitimating foreign rule. The wicked fool on occasion could be more than simply the one who avoided sapiential instruction. This figure symbolized those who sought to negate the conservative social and religious life of postexilic Judaism.

The second subdivision (16:1—22:16) consists of 190 sayings. "Yahweh sayings" (10:3; 12:2, 15:11, 25, 29; 16:1–4, 7, 9, 11, 20, 33; 17:3; 18:22; 19:3, 14; 20:12, 22, 24; 21:2–3, 30, 31; 22:2) and proverbs dealing with kingship and the court (16:10, 12, 13–15; 19:12; 20:2, 8, 26; and 21:1) figure especially prominently as major themes. The latter theme suggests a preexilic dating for many of these sayings, since Davidic kingship was not restored after the Babylonian conquest in the early sixth century B.C.E.

Literary evidence suggests that the two subdivisions were joined together at a later time: a decline in the use of the antithetical saying, the number of duplications in the second subdivision of sayings found in the first, and the prevailing use of the Yahweh saying in the second subdivision (Crenshaw, *Old Testament Wisdom,* 61–62). Both subdivisions of the larger collection (10:1—22:16) are particularly interested in wise and foolish speech, thus demonstrating that the sages throughout their history believed in both the creative and the destructive power of human language and taught their students about its elegance and creative effect. This overarching theme brings together the two subdivisions in the larger collection.

10:1a

The Superscription: "The Proverbs of Solomon"

Date and Provenance

The second major collection of Proverbs is found in 10:1 through 22:16. While edited as one section comprised largely of individual sayings, this collection of Proverbs is often broken down into two major subdivisions: 10:1—15:33 and 16:1—22:16. The entire collection of 10:1—22:16 is introduced in 10:1a by the superscription "The proverbs of Solomon." These sayings probably came into existence over several centuries, prior to their collection into one piece by wisdom editors in a sapiential school. They may have originated in many social locations, including the family, the court, guilds, royal and temple schools, and wisdom schools.

The attempt to trace this collection in some fashion to Solomon appears to be more traditional than historical. If historical, the sayings could point to either the authorship or more probably the patronage of this king of Israel (1 Kings 3—11), considered in the Deuteronomistic History as the wisest ruler not simply in Israel but in the entire ancient Near East during the period of Israel's united monarchy (tenth century B.C.E.). More likely, however, the sapiential redactors followed the literary fiction in which much of Israelite and early Jewish wisdom literature was associated with this ruler (in addition to the "books" or collections of Proverbs, cf. the implicit autobiographical section in Ecclesiastes 1—2, the Hellenistic text called the Wisdom of Solomon, and the later *Psalms of Solomon*). This tradition grew out of the largely legendary composition of Solomon as the wealthy, wise king in 1 Kings 3—11. In the development of the Israelite and Jewish wisdom tradition, Solomon became the literary symbol and paragon of the tradition.

The redaction of this collection of sayings, many of which probably derived from royal and temple schools as well as familial guilds during the monarchy (tenth to sixth centuries B.C.E.), probably occurred during the Persian period. Placed in this context, it would have been a traditional though late practice to associate royal sayings with the patronage of the house of David in general and Solomon in particular.

Conclusion

Some of the sayings from the first subdivision of 10:1—15:33 probably originated in various social settings during the preexilic period. The sages who edited this collection in the early period of Persian rule, however, were likely aligned with the hierocratic party of the Zadokites, whose political liaison with the Persian-appointed governors provided them considerable wealth and influence during this period of postexilic Jewish history. They gave themselves the title of *ṣaddîq*, or "the righteous," whose speech and behavior undergirded and sustained the existing social world dominated by priestly and sapiential families (Prov. 10:2–3, 6–7, 11, 24, 28; 11:4–6, 8–10, 18–20, 21, 23, 28, 30–31; 12:3, 5, 7, 10, 12–13, 17, 26, 28; 13:5–6, 9, 21, 23; 14:19, 32, 34; 15:6, 9, 28, 29; 16:8–13, 31; 17:15, 26; 18:5, 17; 20:7; 21:3, 12, 15, 18, 21, 25, 30–32), and "the wise" (10:1, 8, 14; 11:29; 12:15, 18; 13:1, 14, 20; 14:1, 3, 16, 24; 15:2, 7, 12, 20, 31; 16:14, 21, 23; 17:28; 19:26; 21:11, 20, 22).

Given this historical and political setting, the wise-righteous of Proverbs 10:1—15:33 would have included those who supported Persian rulers and their appointed governors by creating a conservative social world that was viewed to be constructed and maintained by God. As dreams of a restored monarchy quickly died, conservatives, including the hierocratic party, would have opposed any opposition to this social world, not only overt revolution but also other foolish acts that would have led to the deterioration of the fragile socioreligious and political composition of Jewish life under Persian rule. The opposition of civil and temple scribes to those who exhibited foolish behavior, including both social marginals who ignored the sages' teachings and revolutionaries overtly seeking the overthrow of the religious and political social structures of the time, would have made sense at a time when the hierocratic party gained power and wealth because of its association with the Persian rulers and sought to sustain the existing society through conservative religious and political teachings.

The foolish-wicked would have included several varieties of marginals who did not enjoy the power and wealth of the centrist scribes, priests, and Jewish political figures. The wicked were called the *rāšāʿ*, "evil ones," who distorted and disrupted social order (10:3, 6, 11, 16–17, 20, 24–25, 27, 28, 30, 32; 11:5, 7, 8, 10, 11, 18, 23, 31; 12:5, 6–7, 10, 12, 21, 26; 13:6, 9, 15, 17, 25; 14:11, 19, 32; 15:6, 8–9, 28–29; 16:4;

161

17:15, 23; 18:3, 5; 19:28; 20:26; 21:4, 7, 10, 12, 18, 27, 29), and "fools" (*kĕsîl:* 10:1, 18; 12:23; 13:19; 14:7, 8, 24, 33; 15:2, 7, 14; 17:10, 12–13, 16, 21, 24–25; 18:2, 6, 7; 19:1, 10, 13, 29; and *'ĕvîl:* 10:8, 10, 14, 21; 11:29; 12:15–16; 14:3, 9; 15:5; 17:28; 20:3). A concrete example would have been those of the visionary party who opposed the social world of the sages and priests. As noted earlier, the visionaries were the charismatic leaders of the postexilic populace who were largely marginalized in regard to power and wealth in the new Persian order. These leaders envisioned the cataclysmic overturn of Persian as well as all other foreign rule and the emergence of a new heaven and new earth in which a Jewish state, led by a messiah who was a descendant of the house of David, would emerge, free from outside entanglements with other governments. Their "foolish and wicked behavior," to use the language of the sages, along with that of others who spurned the conservatives' teachings, would have undermined the new order and threatened the preeminence of the Zadokites and their Jewish supporters. What better way for the hierocratic party and their sapiential supporters to claim the authenticity of the reconstituted Jewish homeland under Persian rule than to capture for themselves the patronage of wisdom and the legendary accomplishments of King Solomon? This royal legitimation would have given greater credence to the hierocratic efforts.

Theology

In the wisdom tradition's moral literature, it is not unusual to find the sages contrasting the wise righteous with the foolish wicked. These observations could easily fit many social and historical settings. Most sages were invariably conservatives who constructed a social world that supported the status quo of power and status. The foolish wicked were those who ignored the teachings of the sages and either inadvertently or purposefully undermined the social order by their speech and behavior.

If the final editing of this collection did take place during the Persian period, however, then the contrast would have included both centrists, that is, social conservatives who supported the status quo of the new theocracy recognized and authenticated by the Persians, and marginals, that is, radicalized apocalypticists and revolutionaries who would use the past glories of an Israelite state to speak of a reconstituted Jewish governance devoid of foreign intrusions. This literature casts the latter as simpletons or the unlearned (Prov. 14:15, 18; 19:25; 21:11; 22:3) who spurned wisdom's teachers and thus undermined the legitimacy of the Jewish state. These two social groups both worked out of a theology of cosmic and social order. The hierocratic party articulated a "realized eschatology," whereas the visionaries presented a "future eschatology" to be realized in God's new creation. This new heaven and new earth, so graphically depicted by Second Isaiah and other peripheral prophets (e.g., Haggai and First Zechariah), would require an overturning of the current order by divine intervention and faithful human effort, both social and individual. This second collection of sayings, at the level of redactional interpretation, would likely have sought to give royal and divine legitimation to the present order. Thereby Solomon, who in Israelite sapiential legend prays for and receives divine wisdom, creates and governs a wealthy and powerful Israelite state, and serves as the patron of much of Israelite and Jewish wisdom, gave his imprimatur to the new order of Persian and local hierocratic rule. Yahweh was the one who created and then maintained this social world. The second collection (10:1—22:16), then, is one that contrasts behavior that leads to order and stability with misbehavior that undermines the current religious, social, and political structure.

10:1b—15:33
First Subdivision

Date and Provenance

The sayings of the first subdivision may have originated in the royal and temple schools, family guilds of sages who served at various levels the government, and possibly even Israelite and Jewish households. At least the households of scribal families that formed guilds would have been a conceivable setting for some of the sayings. The literary polish of the sayings clearly suggests, however, that those possessing the gift of language shaped the sayings in an aesthetic manner that represents both the artistry and the creative power of human speech. This theme is the one that unifies both subdivisions. While the individual sayings originated over several centuries and in different social locations, it is probable that the final editors of the first subdivision belonged to the conservative scribes who supported the hierocratic party in the early Persian Empire.

Literary Structure and Interpretation

163

No perceivable structure may be found in this subdivision (Murphy, *Wisdom Literature,* 63). Instead, this is a sayings collection with a largely disparate literary structure. This subdivision on the whole is a collection of individual sayings dominated by antithetical proverbs (163 out of 183) that contrast thematically the conduct of the righteous wise and its outcome with those of wicked fools. The inherent moral philosophy is retribution, captured, for example, in the following:

> If the righteous are repaid on earth,
>   how much more the wicked and the sinner!
>   (11:31)

Retribution does not negate the free will of the Creator, who chooses if and when to bring just deserts to both the righteous wise and the wicked fool. The Creator, however, works through this process of justice to exact both rewards and punishments for human behavior. Righteous human acts and proper speech at an appropriate time and place bring rewards, whereas foolish and wicked behavior and language are requited by divine punishment. Thus knowing the time and place for just behavior results in well-being and stability, while even righteous speech and acts are doomed to fail when undertaken at an inopportune time and incorrect place (see Boström, *God of the Sages*, 90–140).

Human acts and language, just and unjust, wise and foolish, have a direct impact not only on the perpetrator but also on the created order and the social structure. The righteous create and extend cosmic, social, and individual order, whereas the wicked subvert order in creation, society, and individual life. This view, particularly in regard to the use of human language, provides the foundation for the moral teachings of Israel's sages in Proverbs 10:1—22:16.

Chapter 10. The wise righteous are characterized by the following virtues and benefits: righteousness that preserves from death, Yahweh's provision of food to the hungry, diligence that produces wealth, prudence to harvest in the summer, memory that is a blessing, obedience to life-giving and sustaining commandments, integrity that brings security, speech that brings about and sustains life, love that covers all offenses, a storehouse of knowledge that guides and provides insight into life, wealth that serves as a fortress to the rich, wages that lead to life, the ability to heed life-giving instruction, wealth in the form of a gift from Yahweh, wise conduct that is compatible with and pleasant to human understanding, the granting of one's desires, the establishment of the wise-righteous throughout the ages, a religious piety ("the fear of the LORD") that prolongs life, hope that ends in gladness, adherence to the way (i. e., the teachings of Yahweh that sustain life), and lips that know what is acceptable.

164

In the first subdivision, the antithesis of the righteous wise and the wicked fool begins in chapter 10. The chapter notes that, in contrast to the righteous and their virtues, the foolish-wicked embody and practice a variety of vices and receive various misfortunes: ill-gotten gain that does not profit, Yahweh's causing them to go hungry, poverty resulting from laziness, shame resulting from sleeping in harvest time, speech that conceals violence, a name that will rot, babblings that result in ruin, perversions that are revealed, hatred that produces strife, a beating that results from a lack of sense, poverty that brings ruin, gain that leads to sin, being led astray through rejection of rebuke, lying lips that conceal hatred, the utterance of slander, transgression resulting from loquacious speech, a mind that is of little worth, death resulting from a lack of sense, the doing of wrong that is like sport, dread of what will come, laziness that is painful to employers, lives of short duration, expectation that comes to nothing, destruction according to Yahweh's way, the cutting off of a perverse tongue, removal from the land, and a mouth that knows from experience what is perverse.

In addition to the contrast between the wise righteous and the wicked fool, two other themes dominate this chapter: (1) Yahweh is the one who maintains the social order through the just distribution of rewards and punishments, and (2) the proper use of language creates life, both for the community and the speaker. Yahweh is the one who creates and sustains the world and the social reality. Divine control of retribution as the means for rewarding the righteous and punishing the wicked resides at the heart of this theology (Boström, *God of the Sages,* 90–140). Thus, Yahweh ensures that the righteous do not go hungry, while he punishes the wicked by denying to them food (10:3). Human strivings, especially diligence toward the task at hand, are not the ultimate cause of wealth. It is Yahweh alone, not human toil, who dispenses blessings that enrich. The beginning of wisdom and the foundation for its moral teachings is the fear of Yahweh (10:22; see 10:27; 14:26, 27; 15:16, 33; 16:6, 10; 19:23). It should be recognized that religious piety is not a late development in sapiential teaching but rather is present from its inception. Thus there is no development from an originally secular worldview to religious piety. In 10:27 it is the "fear" of Yahweh that prolongs life, not simply the adherence to moral instruction, while the wicked, who do not engage life through the avenue of religious piety, will experience lives that are shortened. Finally, it is the way of the Lord, that is, the moral teachings of the wise founded on religious piety, that becomes a fortress for the sages, while the same instruction brings about destruction for those who practice evil (10:9, 29; see 11:5, 20; 12:15, 26, 28; 13:6, 15; 14:2, 8, 12, 14; 15:9,

165

19; 16:2, 7, 9, 17, 25, 29, 31; 19:3, 16; 20:24; 21:2, 8, 16, 29; 22:5, 6; see the synonym *path:* 10:17; 12:28; 15:10, 19, 24; 17:23).

The proper use of language, which embodies the power to create life or to destroy, is also a major theme in this chapter and continues to shape the content of the entire collection. Important metaphors for speech include "mouth" (10:11, 14, 32; 11:9, 11; 12:6, 8; 13:3; 15:2, 14, 28; 19:28); "tongue" (15:4; 16:1; 17:4, 20; 18:21; 21:6); "lips" (10:8, 10, 13, 18; 12:13; 14:23; 16:10, 21, 23, 27; 17:4; 18:20; 19:1; 22:11); "word" (11:13; 12:6, 26; 13:5; 14:23; 15:1; 18:4, 8, 13; 22:12); "commandment" (10:8; 19:16); and "discipline" or "instruction" (10:17; 12:1; 13:1, 18, 24; 15:5, 10, 32–33; 19:20, 27).

In chapter 10, "the babbling fool will come to ruin" (10:8, see v. 14), while the wise give heed to the commandments. These commandments likely are the exhortations of the teachers, though they may also include the legal decrees of the court and the cult. The sage knows that to rebuke the wicked and foolish creates peace (10:10). The "mouth of the righteous" is a "fountain of life," whereas the "mouth of the wicked conceals violence" (v. 11). Life-giving wisdom is found in the mouth of the one who possesses understanding; the wicked shall receive a beating for their folly (v. 13). The one who heeds instruction has guidance for the path of life, while those who reject a rebuke lose their way (v. 17). The fool is one who possesses "lying lips" that conceal hatred and who utters slander, both abuses of language that bring devastation (v. 18). The sage is one whose words are few, whereas the fool is known by his or her loquacious speech, which brings about transgression (v. 19). The "tongue of the righteous" is valued like choice silver, the most precious metal in ancient Israel (v. 20). Through the lips of the righteous many are fed (v. 21). The mouth of the righteous produces wisdom that guides one on the path to life, whereas the crooked tongue is cut off (v. 31). The lips of the righteous know what is acceptable behavior, whereas the mouth of the wicked knows only perversity (v. 32).

Chapter 11. The thematic contrast between the righteous wise and the wicked fool continues in this chapter, also in largely antithetical sayings. The wise-righteous practice virtues that lead to well-being for themselves and their social order. These include an accurate weight that is Yahweh's delight; wisdom that emerges from humility; integrity that guides the upright; righteous behavior that delivers from death, that keeps their path straight and leads to their salvation; righteousness that delivers from trouble; the rejoicing and exaltation of a city when it goes well with the righteous; a silence that ensues from wisdom; trustworthiness that leads to confidence; an abundance of counselors that produces safety; security that results from refusing to guarantee loans to a stranger; feminine graciousness that obtains honor; kindness that is the reward of the wise; life resulting from steadfast righteousness; blameless ways that are the delight of Yahweh; escape from punishment; desire that ends in good; generosity that enriches; blessings that return to those who extend them to others; seeking of favor; flourishing like green leaves; and fruit of behavior that is a "tree of life."

By contrast, the wicked-foolish practice vices that lead to destruction: the use of a false balance, which is an abomination to Yahweh; pride that is followed by disgrace; treachery that destroys; riches that do not profit on the day of wrath; wickedness that causes the evil to fall; scheming that leads to one's own capture; behavior that results in the perishing of the hope of the wicked when they die and in expectations that come to nothing; destructive speech that undoes the neighbor and overthrows a city, resulting in jubilation when the wicked are destroyed; belittling that derives from the lack of sense; gossip that reveals secrets; a lack of guidance, leading to the fall of a nation; guaranteeing loans for a stranger, which results in trouble; hatred of virtue that covers with shame; timidity that results in destitution; cruelty that results in self-inflicted harm; behavior that produces the absence of real gain; wickedness that causes those who pursue it to perish; crooked minds that are an abomination to Yahweh; behavior that will not fail to escape punishment; lack of sense; expectation that culminates in wrath; failure to render what is due, bringing about the suffering of want and a curse on the evildoers; false trust in wealth that leads to destruction; troubling of the household that inherits the wind; acts that lead to falling into servitude to the wise; violence; and behavior that provokes chastisement for wicked and foolish acts.

In addition to the contrast between the wise-righteous and the wicked fool, major themes in chapter 11 include a clear emphasis on retribution and the importance of language. Proverbs 11:31 summarizes well the theme of retribution:

> If the righteous are repaid on earth,
> how much more the wicked and the sinner!

Righteousness, a character trait that involves orderly and moral behavior, secures the lives of the wise-righteous, provides guidance in ways that are straight, delivers them from death, exalts a city, enables one to keep a confidence, provides safety to a nation, obtains honor for those who embody it, allows the generous to be enriched by their own generosity, enables one to escape punishment, seeks favor, and

167

appears as a tree of life. The wickedness of the foolish-wicked leads to their destruction, results in disgrace, causes the wicked to be captured by their own schemes, dashes the hope of the wicked, leads to trouble for those who practice it, is used to destroy the neighbor with improper speech, overthrows a city, results in shame, brings harm to the cruel, punishes wicked fools and causes them to suffer want, makes them wither, and takes away lives.

Language is also an important theme in this chapter, for its power to create and destroy is at the center of much of the wisdom tradition. The mouth of the godless destroys their neighbors, and one who belittles another lacks sense, while the trustworthy person preserves a confidence.

Chapter 12. The contrast between the wise righteous and wicked fools continues. The wise love discipline or instruction because they love knowledge; the good receive favor from Yahweh; the root of the righteous will never be moved; they obtain a good wife, possess thoughts that are just, engage in behavior that delivers them from danger, build a house that will continue to stand, are commended for good sense, recognize the importance of rejecting self-importance, do not lack for food, know the needs of their animals, till their land in order to have plenty of food, produce a root that bears fruit, escape from trouble, are filled with good things from the fruit of their mouths, recognize that manual labor has its reward, listen to advice, ignore an insult, speak truth that is based on honest evidence, possess a tongue that heals and truthful lips that enable them to endure forever, counsel peace, experience joy and avoid harm, act faithfully and consequently are Yahweh's delight, avoid the ostentatious display of knowledge, know that their diligence will enable them to rule, utter a good word that cheers up the human heart, give good advice to friends, recognize that diligence leads to the obtaining of wealth, and are aware that the path of righteousness leads to life, not death.

In antithesis to the above, chapter 12 contrasts the vices and consequences of wicked fools and their behavior. The teachers note that one who hates rebuke is stupid; Yahweh condemns those who devise evil; wickedness does not discover security; and the wicked man has a wife who brings him shame. Wicked fools give treacherous advice, utter words that are a deadly ambush, are overthrown and exist no more, possess a perverse mind that is despised, are cruel to animals, are ensnared by the transgression of their own lips, wrongly think that their own way is right, show their anger, are false witnesses who speak deceitfully, utter rash words, possess a lying tongue, engage in planning evil, are filled with trouble, possess lying lips that are an abomination to Yahweh, broadcast folly, are put to forced labor due to their laziness, are afflicted with anxiety that weighs down the human heart, follow a path that leads astray, and, due to laziness, do not take the time to roast their game.

In addition to the contrast between the righteous wise and the wicked fool, two other themes figure prominently in this chapter: the social setting of the household and the proper use of language. The household (11:29; 14:1; 15:6, 25, 27; 17:1, 13; 19:14; 21:9, 12) was a common setting for the issuance of wisdom in the form of the teachings of the parents to their children. In addition, the moral life often dealt with issues common to the household. The household in ancient Israel and later Judaism was an extended social unit that lineally included multiple generations (i.e., grandparents, parents, and children) and laterally extended to include aunts, uncles, and cousins. In addition to those related by blood, the wealthy household could include slaves, concubines, day laborers, and strangers (either foreigners or individuals from different tribes or villages). In addition to people, the household included the estate of land that was used for farming and grazing, the house and its contents, and the domestic animals that provided labor, food, and various materials for family use.

Especially important was the land that was handed down through the male children, with the firstborn receiving the largest share. The land provided the means for household life in the farming villages. Thus security and the continuing ownership of the land, which was not to be sold or traded, were central values to this way of life (12:3, 7). Being aware of and then tending to the needs of the household animals was a part of moral life in this social setting (v. 10), and hard work and manual labor were continuously required (vv. 10–11, 14; contrast v. 24). Marriage was a central feature of this social institution, for it produced not simply companionship but also children, who became laborers and the heirs of the household's estate and social roles. Thus the finding of and marriage to a good wife was of paramount importance in this social world (v. 4).

Proper language is once again a prominent theme in this chapter (see 12:14). Correct language by the righteous leads to their salvation, whereas the words of the wicked result in their destruction (v. 6). The acceptance of rebuke during the occasion of moral instruction characterizes the wise student (v. 1), and the ignoring of an insult is prudent (v. 16). The giving and receiving of advice or counsel that has the ability to direct one's actions to a successful conclusion is also underscored in

169

the teachings of this chapter (12:5, 15, 20, 26). Telling the truth and avoiding lips that lie are central to the proper use of language (12:17, 19, 22).

Chapter 13. The contrast between the righteous wise and the wicked fools continues in chapter 13. The wise righteous even as children love discipline that derives from obedience to instruction. They eat good things from the fruit of their words; guard their mouths to preserve their lives; find their appetite satiated due to their diligence; hate falsehood, guard one whose way is upright; may pretend to be poor and yet possess great wealth; recognize that wealth ransoms a person's life; realize that wisdom comes to those who take advice; gather wealth little by little and increase it; know that a desire fulfilled is a tree of life; respect the commandment and are rewarded; engage in teaching that is a fountain of life, allowing one to avoid the snares of death; know that their good sense wins favor; do all things intelligently; know that the faithful envoy brings healing; receive honor by heeding reproof; realize desires that are sweet to the soul; walk with the wise in order to become wise themselves; experience prosperity; leave an inheritance to their children's children; discipline their children because they love them; and have enough to satisfy their appetite.

Wicked fools, by contrast, are scoffers who do not listen to rebuke and are treacherous people who desire wrongdoing. They open wide their lips and thus come to ruin; act shamefully and disgracefully; allow their sin to overthrow them; include among them those who pretend to be rich yet have nothing; engage in insolent behavior that causes strife; possess hastily gotten wealth, which eventually is lost; possess sick hearts due to hope that is deferred; despise the word and bring destruction; follow a path that leads to their ruin; display folly; receive a bad messenger, whose words bring trouble; ignore instruction and thus experience poverty and disgrace; are an abomination because they do not turn away from evil; cause their companions to suffer harm; are ever pursued by misfortune; obtain wealth that is laid up for the righteous; are unjust to the poor, who lose even a fruitful field; spare the rod and thus spoil their children; and go hungry because their belly is empty.

Two additional themes figure prominently in chapter 13: proper language and prosperity. The sages, by the very nature of their activity as teachers who transmitted a tradition through instruction and exhortation of the young, placed great emphasis on the proper use of spoken language. Sayings were meant not to be read but to be spoken and heard. The articulate use of language was not simply the embellishment of content but also gave shape and veracity to the meaning of a saying through the spoken and written word. Thus the discipline that the student gladly receives, though it contains rebuke, is rejected by the scoffer, who negates any rebuke of his behavior and speech (13:1). Proper language leads to good results (13:2), though it is to be carefully guarded so that the life of the speaker is preserved (13:3). The sage is one who respects the commandment (13:13), and the teaching of the wise is embodied in language and life (13:14). This teaching is a "fountain of life," a common metaphor for sapiential teaching in Proverbs (see 10:11; 14:27; 16:22). The wise are those who receive and dispense counsel that leads to success (13:10).

Prosperity (wealth) is another common theme in this chapter (see also 15:16; 21:6). The sages regarded wealth, properly acquired, as an inherent good, whereas poverty normally was viewed as the punishment of the fool (13:21; "poverty" = 6:11; 10:15; 13:18; 24:34; 28:19; 30:8; 31:7; see Crenshaw, "Poverty and Punishment in the Book of Proverbs," 396–405). Wealth and poverty nevertheless are dependent on who possesses them: the wise or the fool. The life of the wise, even if a poor one, is superior in value to wealth of the wicked that is wrongfully obtained (see 15:16–17). It is still the case, however, that wealth is normally a value in sapiential literature, suggesting that the wise righteous belong to or at least serve the elite of Israelite and later Jewish society. Wealth may only be a pretense by the fool, who in reality is poor. In lacking the ostentatious character of the wicked, and the righteous may only appear to be poor and yet own great possessions (13:7). The pragmatic value of wealth over poverty is sometimes stressed (13:8). Wealth slowly obtained is superior to that which is hastily obtained and quickly lost (13:11). In an ironic twist, the sages teach that the righteous are those for whom the sinner lays up his wealth (13:22; see Washington, *Wealth and Poverty;* and Whybray, *Wealth and Poverty*).

Chapter 14. Besides the antithesis between the righteous wise and the wicked fool, no other theme is prevalent in chapter 14, though the issue of proper use of language occurs several times (14:3, 5, 7, 25). The wise righteous are represented with the following virtues and rewarded accordingly: the wise woman builds her household; the upright fear Yahweh; the lips of the wise preserve them; abundant crops come from the strength of an ox; a faithful witness does not lie; knowledge is easy for one who understands; the wise leave the presence of a fool, since there they do not find words of knowledge; the clever understand where they go; the upright enjoy God's favor; the tent of the upright flourishes; the good get what their deeds deserve; the clever consider their steps; the wise are cautious and turn away

171

from evil; the clever are adorned with knowledge; the rich have many friends; happiness belongs to those who are kind to the poor; those who plan good find loyalty and faithfulness; in toil there is profit; the crown of the wise is their wisdom; a truthful witness saves lives; one has confidence in the fear of Yahweh; one's children have refuge in the fear of the Lord; the fear of Yahweh is a fountain of life to avoid the snares of death; the glory of a king is a multitude of people; one who is slow to anger has great understanding; a tranquil mind gives life to the flesh; those who are kind to the poor honor their Maker; the righteous find a refuge in their integrity; wisdom is at home in the mind of those who have understanding; righteousness exalts a nation; and a servant who deals wisely has the king's favor.

By contrast, the wicked fools are known by their vices and receive punishment: the foolish woman tears down her household with her own hand; one who is devious in conduct despises Yahweh; the talk of fools is a rod for their backs; there is no grain where there are no oxen; a false witness extinguishes lives; a scoffer seeks wisdom in vain; in the presence of a fool, one does not find words of wisdom; fools mislead; fools mock at the guilt offering; the foolish heart knows its own bitterness, and no stranger shares its joy; the house of the wicked is destroyed; there is a way that seems right to a person, but its end is the way to death; even in laughter the heart is sad, while the end of joy is grief; the perverse get what they deserve; the simple believe everything; the fool throws off restraint and is careless; one who is quick-tempered acts foolishly, and the schemer is hated; the simple are adorned with folly; the evil bow down before the good, and the wicked bow at the gates of the righteous; the poor are disliked even by their neighbors; those who despise neighbors are sinners; those who err plan evil; mere talk leads only to poverty; folly is the garland of fools; one who utters lies is a betrayer; a prince without people is ruined; one who possesses a hasty temper exalts folly; passion makes the bones rot; those who oppress the poor insult their Maker; the wicked are overthrown by their evildoing; wisdom is not known in the heart of fools; sin is a reproach to any people; and the king's wrath falls on one who acts shamefully.

Language as a theme plays a minor role in chapter 14. Carefully guarded lips preserve lives, whereas those who are quick to speak receive punishment (14:3). In the law court, a faithful witness does not lie, whereas a false witness "breathes out lies" (14:5). Knowledgeable words are not to be found in the presence of fools (14:7).

Chapter 15. The wise righteous are taught to exude in their character virtues that lead to well-being and sustain the social order. A

soft answer turns away wrath; the tone of the wise dispenses knowledge; a gentle tongue is a tree of life; one who heeds admonition is
prudent; in the house of the righteous there is much treasure; the lips
of the wise spread knowledge; the prayer of the upright is Yahweh's
delight; Yahweh loves the one who pursues righteousness; as Sheol and
Abaddon lie open before Yahweh, how much more human hearts; a
glad heart makes a cheerful countenance; the mind of one with understanding seeks knowledge; a cheerful heart has a continual feast; better is a little with the fear of Yahweh than great treasure and trouble
with it; better is a dinner of vegetables where love is than a fatted ox
accompanied by hatred; those who are slow to anger calm contention;
the path of the upright is a level highway; a wise child makes a glad
father; a person of understanding walks straight ahead; with many
advisers, plans succeed; an apt answer is a joy to anyone; a word in season is good; the path of life leads upward, to avoid Sheol below; the
Lord maintains the widow's boundaries; those who hate bribes will
live; the mind of the righteous ponders how to answer; Yahweh hears
the prayer of the righteous; the light of eyes rejoices the heart; good
news refreshes the body; the ear that heeds wholesome admonition
lodges among the wise; those who heed admonition gain understanding; the fear of Yahweh is instruction in wisdom; and humility goes
before honor.

Chapter 15 also contrasts the behavior and punishments of the
wicked fool. A harsh word stirs up anger; the mouths of fools pour out
folly; perverseness in the tongue breaks the spirit; a fool despises a parent's instruction; trouble befalls the income of the wicked; the minds
of fools do not spread knowledge; the sacrifice of the wicked is an
abomination to Yahweh; the way of the wicked is an abomination to
the Lord; one who forsakes the way of Yahweh will die, as will one who
hates a rebuke; scoffers do not like to be rebuked; by sorrow of the
heart the spirit is broken; the mouth of fools feeds on folly; all the days
of the poor are hard; the hot-tempered stir up strife; the way of the
lazy is overgrown with thorns; the foolish despise their mothers; folly
is not a joy to one who has no sense; without counsel, plans go wrong;
Yahweh tears down the house of the proud; evil plans are an abomination to Yahweh; those greedy for unjust gain make trouble for their
households; the mouth of the wicked pours out evil; Yahweh is far
from the wicked; and those who ignore instruction despise themselves.

As is the case in the entire second collection of sayings, language
figures prominently in chapter 15 and provides the overarching theme
for the entire collection. The sages teach their students to use elegant
or gracious language (v. 26), that a "soft answer" turns away wrath

173

whereas harsh words lead to its creation (v. 1), thus pointing to one aspect of the power of the spoken word. The students of the sages are taught to use language to dispense knowledge (vv. 2, 7), which derives from the tradition they receive through instruction (vv. 5, 31–33), whereas fools utter folly that ignores tradition and overturns the social order. The youthful sages also learn the importance of proper counsel (v. 22), that language is appropriate for a particular time and place (v. 23), that the rebuke of the sage is to be accepted (v. 10), and that words uttered in prayer are received by Yahweh (v. 26), whereas evil plans are an abomination to God. Language possesses the power to create or to destroy. Even proper language, however, is qualified by time and place. To speak successfully and truly depends on time and circumstances (von Rad, *Wisdom in Israel*, 138–43).

Conclusion

The major themes of the subdivision of chapters 10—15 consist of antitheses between the righteous wise and the wicked fool. Wisdom and its synonyms (*understanding, knowledge, insight,* and *prudence*) are rational, empirical, and imaginative knowledge that derives from understanding and then is incorporated into human behavior in the moral instruction of teachers who pass on their conservative tradition. This tradition is critically engaged and then reformulated by those who receive it and learn to embody its teachings. The literary polish of these sayings suggests that more than moral content is presented. Elegant language, spoken as well as written, stimulates the imagination and allows an encounter with the content of the teaching. Content and its literary dress become the means for moral reflection, conviction of the authenticity of what is taught, and the ability to embody the teaching in daily behavior and discourse. This wisdom guides one on the course to sagehood and, eventually, life in all of its fullness.

Folly, by contrast, is foolish behavior and perverted language that result from the rejection of the teachings of the sages. Folly diverts one from the pathway to sagehood and life and leads instead to misfortune and death. The students of the sages not only are to reflect on the proper virtues and rewards that derive from wisdom but also are to be aware of and avoid the vices and subsequent punishments that come from foolish behavior and speech. The embodiment of folly in human character comes from the ignoring of sapiential teaching and a misguided life.

174

As noted earlier, the moral philosophy of Proverbs 10—15 is retribution. God rewards the wise righteous for their order creating behavior and language while punishing the wicked for disrupting cosmic, social, and individual order. The path to life is found in obedience to and then embodiment of the teachings of the sages, while the way of death is followed by those who reject or ignore what the teachers instruct.

A number of Yahweh sayings are present in this initial subdivision of the second collection. Two frequently encountered Yahweh sayings are, first, "abomination" (11:1, 20; 12:22; 15:8, 9, 26; 16:5, 12; 17:15; 20:10, 23; 21:27) as contrasted to what is "pleasing" to or "delights" Yahweh (11:1, 20: 12:22; 15:8) and, second, the "fear of Yahweh" (1:29; 2:5; 8:13; 9:10; 10:27; 14:2, 27; 15:16, 33; 16:6; 19:23; 23:17; 24:21). Behavior and language said to be an abomination to Yahweh include a false balance, crooked minds, lying lips, the sacrifice of the wicked, the way of the wicked, evil plans, the arrogant, kings who do evil, justifying the wicked and condemning the righteous, diverse weights and measures, differing weights, and the wicked's sacrifice compounded by an evil intent.

Just action and proper speech said to "please" or "delight" Yahweh are an accurate weight, those of blameless ways, those who act faithfully, and the prayer of the upright. These Yahweh sayings are especially important in stressing the authoritative character of what is taught. Ultimately, it is Yahweh who is the teacher of the sages and, through them, of the students who seek to follow wisdom's path.

"The fear of Yahweh" is an expression for religious piety combined with the moral life. For the sages, proper conduct and wise speech were grounded in their religious faith. The sages in this collection, and one, might add, in all the sapiential books, were not secular humanists who ignored the teachings, admonitions, and constraints of religious life. Rather, the moral life was to be based on religious faith. What the sages teach here is founded ultimately on their religious worldview, centered in the Creator and Sustainer of cosmic, social, and individual order.

Language, as noted above, is the key theme for the second collection. Speech for the sages was more than the verbal articulation of moral instruction. Indeed, speech conveyed the content of moral instruction and foolish behavior alike. Speech for the sages, however, had the additional functions of combining with content to capture moral reflection, to induce righteous living, to describe and negate foolish behavior, and to enhance the power of what was taught to shape cosmic, social, and individual order. Speech was more than aesthetic embellishment of content, though indeed it served this function. More important is the view that language has the power to shape

175

behavior that will create the moral order that resides within and sustains the cosmos, a stable society, and righteous living. Sapiential language also has the power to undermine the chaos that dwells ever present on the edge of, if not also within, creation, society, and human existence.

Counsel is also a prominent theme in this first subdivision (chapters 10—15). "Counsel" or "advice" (12:15; 19:20–21; 20:18) would be the guidance especially of the teachers at court and in the family to shape a course of action that leads to success (de Boer, "The Counsellor," 42–71). This success may have emerged in the sphere of the court, in ordering society or in gaining military victory. Thus counselors were considered of significant importance in advising kings and other governmental leaders. In the family, the teachers, primarily parents, uttered counsel that, once followed, would allow the children to learn to engage successfully in actions that would sustain the household, from harvesting crops, to marriage to a wise woman, to raising a family.

"Discipline" or "instruction" (10:17; 12:1; 13:18; 15:5, 32; 19:20, 27) also figures prominently in Proverbs 10—15. For the sages of this collection, piety and ethics converged into a flowing stream of faithful knowing that shaped the moral life. Discipline was the formation of character that resulted from obedience to the instruction of the teachers. It led not only to the moral transformation of human character but also to a result. The obedient student would enter a state of well-being and engage in successful actions (Perdue, "Wisdom in the Book of Job," 73–98). Comparable to the meaning of *mûsār* as "instruction" is *tôrâ* ("teaching": 13:14; see 1:8; 3:1; 4:2; 6:20, 23; 7:2; 28:4, 7, 9; 29:18; 31:26), a term more frequently encountered in the first and fifth collections. The eventual identification of priestly Torah and sapiential teaching was made by Ben Sira in the second century B.C.E. (Marböck, *Weisheit im Wandel*).

The sages of Proverbs 10—15 contrast the righteous wise with the wicked fool in regard to temper. The righteous wise are slow to anger, that is, they control their passions so as not to engage in behavior and speech that undermines proper decorum. By contrast, the wicked fool is hot of temper and unable to control his or her passions. Anger is a destructive force that undermines the foolish-wicked and distorts the harmony of social life. Unchecked anger destroys those who lack self-control.

The diligence of the wise righteous is contrasted with the sloth of the fool. Sloth leads to hunger, failure, and death, whereas diligence in labor and in following the teachers' instruction produces bellies that are full, success, and life. This work ethic of the sages became the practical foundation for the moral life that sought success and well-being. Sloth, embodied in human behavior, was sure to lead to failure and misfortune.

Wealth for these sages was a positive feature. Indeed, presented as one of the results of obedience to moral instruction is the obtaining of a good livelihood, even riches. Poverty, by contrast, is at times a negative consequence of failure to obey the teachings of the wise. There is no piety or righteous quality that is associated with poverty in and of itself, though poverty and justice are preferred over wealth wrongfully obtained (Whybray, *Wealth and Poverty*).

The sages of Proverbs 10—15 set forth their teachings as commandments or torah and thus participated in an ethos of religious and legal life. The teachings of the wise may have been the object of disputation when not confirmed in the arena of human experience, but this section of Proverbs shows movement to the point where sapiential teachings bore the impress of divine sanction and were likened at times to apodictic law. While some teachings may have been open to question, those uttered by sages on behalf of Yahweh regarding God's will and that compare to the religious and civil commandments of cultic and legal life would have been beyond dispute.

A final major contrast in Proverbs 10—15 between the righteous wise and the wicked fool resides in the emotions of joy and sorrow. The righteous wise experience a joyful existence even in the worst of circumstances, whereas the wicked fools are those who, even in possessing great wealth, are afflicted by anxiety and sorrow.

In conclusion, Proverbs 10:1—15:33 is largely a conservative ethical collection that encourages the sages to incorporate and live out virtues that will enable them to enter and sustain the world of order and life. This subdivision is a collection of sayings that sets forth the major virtues of the moral life. Virtues of the righteous wise will be rewarded. The wicked fools, by contrast, engage in behavior that leads to their destruction.

If this subdivision is placed in the redactional setting of the early Persian Empire, the sages may be identified as those whose behavior enabled the social order to become stable and life enhancing, at least for conservatives considered to be righteous and wise. Those who would fall among the "wicked fools" would not have to have been active revolutionaries who sought to bring down the new political reality through acts of destruction, but they would have undermined the created and social order through misbehavior, including sloth, lying, ignoring the commandments, and other acts that were by their nature subversive for the social world as well as for themselves.

177

Theology

As is the case for most sapiential texts, creation theology and providence reside at the center of moral reflection in this subdivision. Creation theology for the wise involves not only cosmic origins but also world maintenance (= providence). While few sayings directly speak of world origins or the creation of humanity, these common Old Testament traditions nevertheless reside at the heart of sapiential theology. More often, however, Yahweh is seen as the one who maintains the righteous social order through guidance and judgment. Indeed, the "fear of the LORD," a common theme in this second collection as well as elsewhere in wisdom literature, expresses the sages' faith in a God of creation and maintenance who works through retributive justice to uphold the social world he has established.

This understanding of creation and providence is emphasized by several sayings in this first subdivision of the second collection. For example, a number of sayings approach the issue of rich and poor/wealth and poverty from the theological perspective of creation and providence. In 14:31, one reads:

> Those who oppress the poor insult their Maker,
> but those who are kind to the needy honor him.

As noted above, the topic of rich and poor/wealth and poverty receives significant attention in Proverbs 10—15. Especially important to the sages was the principle of familial and other forms of societal solidarity (kinship or loyalty and faithfulness) that led to the sharing of provisions for the poor. The poor formed a social class created by Yahweh. Nevertheless, as individuals they were often held accountable for their own poverty, as this collection and other wisdom sayings reflect. Whether directly responsible for their own poverty because of such flaws as sloth, or indirectly as the victims of circumstances beyond their control (say, famine, war, or disease), the poor were to receive the goods necessary for existence from those who were well-to-do. This understanding was especially grounded in the institution of the family, which was bound together by means of loyalty and kinship.

The intimacy of family life from the beginnings of tribal life well into early Judaism was expressed in the principle of kinship. This social principle allowed intimacy as the basis for communal relationships to make its way into the teachings of the postexilic theocracy, whose local center was the temple and its priesthood. Family solidarity (= kinship) placed the care of unfortunates in the family and larger society within

178

the responsibility of the extended household, the larger communities of clans, the court, and eventually the temple. The well-off were to care for the fundamental needs of those members who experienced want.

In the wisdom tradition, the responsibility for caring for the poor was grounded not in exodus liberation, as was true in many other texts (e.g., Exod. 15:13; Pss. 74:2; 78:5), but rather in creation theology. The theological grounding of social responsibility for the poor is the recognition that the rich and the poor possess common origins: God is the creator of life, the Lord of the womb, who is responsible for conception, nurturing the fetus, giving birth to or attending to the birth of the newborn child, and, like a parent, sustaining the life of the individual. The imperative for the sage is to care for the poor, for they have the same origins and share a common humanity. The oppression of the poor in 14:31 "insults" or "mocks" the Creator (Prov. 17:5; see Judg. 8:15; 1 Sam. 17:10, 25, 26, 36, 45; 2 Kings 19:4, 16, 22, 23; Isa. 65:7). Thus, in the act of failing to care for the poor, the wealthy are in effect reproaching and mocking their common Creator.

By contrast in 14:31, to be "kind" to the poor includes generous support. This word often is understood as grace because the recipient does not merit the generosity and support shown him or her. Thus kindness in this saying is an act of mercy extended to the poor that involves a gift that enables the helpless to sustain their lives. This act of charity therefore "honors" the Creator. For the sages, acts of kindness and mercy extended to the poor honored God as much as, if not more than, sacrifices (cf. Micah 6:1–8).

16:1—22:16
Second Subdivision

Date and Provenance

This subdivision is principally a "royal" collection that consists largely of synonymous sayings, as contrasted to the predominance of the antithetical proverbs in the first subdivision of 10:1—15:33. The primary emphasis is placed on behavior and speech at the royal court (see the "words of King Lemuel" in 31:1–11). The location is probably the royal school. This setting would have been more appropriate for preexilic kingship, though the adaptation to Persian rule was likely

179

undertaken by scribes in the early postexilic period. In addition, emphasis is placed not only on primarily wise behavior and speech but also on the theological character of the sapiential tradition. The latter is especially noted by the prominence of "Yahweh sayings" in the second subdivision.

Literary Structure and Interpretation

Chapter 16. The heavily theological character of this subdivision is especially prevalent in 16:1–11. The sage at court is particularly interested in setting forth plans but all the while recognizes that Yahweh is the one who enables this planning to be accepted and carried through to successful conclusion (16:1, 9, 25). By committing their labors to Yahweh, their plans will be established (16:3).

The sages of the royal court recognized the limits of their own ability to gain the state of purity and an upright moral nature, for it is ultimately Yahweh who weighs the human spirit (16:2) and recognizes the frailty of human limitations. In addition, Yahweh is not only the judge of human character but also the creator who brings into existence all things for a purpose, including even the wicked to experience the "day of trouble" (16:4).

The royal sages also valued loyalty to and trust in Yahweh, and not simply to or in their fellow citizens and lords, for these two religious virtues comprised the means by which they received atonement for iniquity (16:6; see 16:20). Likewise religious piety, that is, "the fear of the LORD," would enable one to avoid evil (16:6). This piety was the foundation for the moral life of the sage. The way of life of royal sages here pleases Yahweh so that even their enemies are at peace with them. In this way, conflict and hostilities may be avoided by divinely determined peace that results from God's pleasure in righteous and just behavior (16:7).

Yahweh requires a just social order, according to these teachers. For example, royal judgment is inspired by Yahweh leading the king to avoid issuing wrongful verdicts in this important setting. Bribery and other forms of injustice are not present in the royal legal proceedings, for Yahweh directs the kings' legal decrees (16:10). In addition, honest business practices are grounded theologically in the justice of Yahweh (16:11). Likewise, in temple proceedings, the casting of the lots by the priest to determine guilt or innocence, acceptance or rejection, would result in justice not because of the magical powers of the priests who used these lots but because Yahweh alone was making the decision (16:33).

180

The royal sages valued righteousness over injustice even if the former path provided few possessions, whereas the latter might include great wealth (16:8). This indicates that Yahweh oversees and directs a just social reality, including in particular the actions and decrees of the royal monarchy (16:10–15). The foundational saying for the royal institution is found in 16:12:

> It is an abomination to kings to do evil,
> for the throne is established by righteousness.

The monarchy was to value the just speech of the righteous, since a just society was the goal of royal rule (16:13, 23, 24). In addition, the sages at court recognized the danger of royal anger that destroys. Thus the prudent attempted to placate the king with just behavior and correct speech, so as to avoid royal punishment (16:14). By contrast, the sages knew that gaining royal favor led to life (16:15). This is one reason they valued wisdom more than gold and understanding more than precious silver (16:16).

The value of justice and other virtues is the subject of the remaining sayings of chapter 16. In general, the royal sages argued that the "highway of the upright" avoided evil, while the careful guarding of their way would preserve their lives (16:17). The old age of the sage was particularly valued: gray hair was a crown of glory, resulting from living righteously (16:31). The royal sages also taught that control of human anger was better than great acts of power and glory (16:32).

Vices to be rejected included, above all, pride. The arrogance of human pride led to one's downfall and was to be avoided at all costs (16:18). Thus the humility even of the poor was preferred to "dividing the spoil" with the proud (16:19). Wicked planning (16:27), destructive speech (16:27, 30), the spreading of strife (16:28), seduction of others into ways of wickedness (16:29), and violence (16:29) also were to be avoided by the royal sages. These vices led to failure and destruction.

Chapter 17. The royal sages in chapter 17 speak not only of divine judgment and behavior in the court but also of the moral life and proper social roles in the family household. In reflecting on the moral life, especially in the household, the sages made various observations in largely synonymous proverbs. Even poverty and low status in the household were to be preferred in certain circumstances over wealth and high station: "Better is a dry morsel with quiet than a house full of feasting with strife" (17:1). In speaking of marginals who were members of the household, they noted that "a slave who deals wisely rules over a child who acts shamefully, and will share the inheritance as one of the family" (17:2). Thus even marginals in the family, when

181

righteous, could supplant the shameful family member in gaining an inheritance.

The value of parents, children, and grandchildren in the linear descent of the household is noted by the saying "Grandchildren are the crown of the aged, and the glory of children is their parents" (17:6). The principle of kinship that binds together the family even in periods of diversity is present in the saying "A friend loves at all times, and kinsfolk are born to share adversity" (17:17).

Wicked behavior and fools in the household would tend to taint and disrupt family existence: "Evil will not depart from the house of one who returns evil for good" (17:13). The foolish child brings trouble to the household: "The one who begets a fool gets trouble; the parent of a fool has no joy" (17:21). Likewise, "foolish children are a grief to their father and bitterness to her who bore them" (17:25).

The sages return to the theme of divine creation, providence, and judgment in several sayings in chapter 17. "The crucible is for silver, and the furnace is for gold, but [Yahweh] tests the heart" (17:3). Thus it is Yahweh who assays the virtues of the righteous. Furthermore, Yahweh is the protector and guide even of the poor: "Those who mock the poor insult their Maker; those who are glad at calamity will not go unpunished" (17:5).

Life in the community of households, including both the city and the village, is also frequently mentioned in this chapter. Friendship, for example, is of significant value to the royal sages: "One who forgives an affront fosters friendship, but one who dwells on disputes will alienate a friend" (17:9) and "A friend loves at all times" (17:17a). Yet one is warned against giving a pledge for a neighbor: "It is senseless to give a pledge, to become surety for a neighbor" (17:18). The sages here ignore the bond of neighborly existence and replace it with a more business-like mode of transaction that, in this case, points to the possible entanglements and loss of guaranteeing surety for even those who are neighbors and thus well known.

Legal issues also weighed heavily on the mind of the royal sages, who addressed the roles of jurists, the accused, and plaintiffs. It is clear from this chapter that corruption in the legal sphere was a serious problem. Bribery in the legal court, while disdained, was often practiced to the benefit of the one who offered the bribe: "A bribe is like a magic stone in the eyes of those who give it; wherever they turn they prosper" (17:8; see 17:23). The sages noted that corruption often existed in the sphere of judgment, where a judge might make unjust pronouncements in rendering his verdicts of innocence and guilt: "One who justifies the wicked and one who condemns the righteous are both alike an abomination to the LORD" (17:15; see 17:26). This affront to justice is repugnant to Yahweh, who seeks to establish and then oversee a just social order, especially through just jurisprudence.

The common theme of language is addressed repeatedly by the royal sages in chapter 17. The wicked misuse language and thus harm themselves as well as the larger social order of nation, court, and household. In place of giving heed to righteous and wise instruction, "an evildoer listens to wicked lips; and a liar gives heed to a mischievous tongue" (17:4). Elegant language is inappropriate for the fool, and lying talk is not fitting for a ruler: "Fine speech is not becoming to a fool; still less is false speech to a ruler" (17:7). In their philosophical understanding of retributive justice, the royal sages spoke of the punishment due the fool who abused language: "The crooked of mind do not prosper, and the perverse of tongue fall into calamity" (17:20).

By contrast, the wise righteous are those who give heed to proper instruction and take rebuke from their teachers when appropriate: "A rebuke strikes deeper into a discerning person than a hundred blows into a fool" (17:10). The true sage also is one who uses words sparingly and controls his or her passions: "One who spares words is knowledgeable; one who is cool in spirit has understanding" (17:27; see 17:28).

The strife caused by the fool, along with his or her arrogance, is destructive to the social order: "One who loves transgression loves strife; one who builds a high threshold invites broken bones" (17:19; see 17:14). Rebellion against the social order received the warning of the sages: "Evil people seek only rebellion, but a cruel messenger will be sent against them" (17:11). This intimates that in Israelite and then Jewish society those who did not belong to the centrist party of rulers, priests, and sages sought to overthrow its conservative social world.

Finally, the behavior of the fool falls under the scrutiny of the teachings of the royal sages: "Better to meet a she-bear robbed of its cubs than to confront a fool immersed in folly" (17:12). Fools do not have the mind to learn wisdom: "Why should fools have a price in hand to buy wisdom, when they have no mind to learn?" (17:16). Likewise, the fool, in contrast to the sage, does not look to wisdom to guide him or her along the way (17:24).

Chapter 18. Language is once again a common theme in this chapter of the second subdivision. The recognition of the power of speech that both creates and destroys life is reaffirmed: "Death and life are in the power of the tongue, and those who love it will eat its fruits" (18:21). A proper answer following careful hearing and moral reflection is emphasized by the sages: "The poor use entreaties, but

183

the rich answer roughly" (18:23, see 18:13, 15, 20). The depth of human speech that often escapes simple understanding is underscored in the saying "The words of the mouth are deep waters; the fountain of wisdom is a gushing stream" (18:4). It is only through wisdom, as moral reflection and careful thought, that understanding is obtained. By contrast, fools misuse language to their and others' detriment: "A fool's lips bring strife, and a fool's mouth invites a flogging" (18:6, see 18:7, 13). The abuse of language in the words of a whisperer misshapes his or her character (18:8).

Legal judgment is also a frequent theme in Proverbs, including this chapter. Partiality to the guilty in judgment is repudiated (18:5), as is a hasty judgment that does not hear both sides (18:17). Casting lots was often used to settle disputes and is affirmed as a proper legal procedure (18:18).

The family is once more an important topic, since the household was a common setting for the moral life. Marriage is a valued gift from Yahweh (18:22), while living alone leads to self-indulgence and foolishness (18:1). True friendship is even more valued than the household's next of kin, who was responsible for delivering the family member from dire straits and for taking as wife the spouse of a deceased husband in the household (18:24).

Other themes surrounding values and vices involve diligence and hard work in contrast to sloth, which is destructive (18:9); the importance and power of wealth (18:11; see 18:16); humility that precedes honor and contrasts with the vice of arrogance (18:12); the value of wisdom as opposed to folly, which brings disgrace (18:2–3); the negation of strife (18:19); the sadness resulting from a broken spirit (18:14); and the power of the name of Yahweh, whose divine presence in cult and community provide a refuge for the righteous (18:10).

Chapter 19. Similar themes in the second subdivision of the second collection in Proverbs continue in chapter 19. The importance of rhetoric once again appears as a strong theme, demonstrating that royal sages recognized that when the garments of aesthetic language clothed the content of their life-giving and valued tradition of guidance in human living, human character could better be shaped and the moral life guided. The tradition of the wise is compared to the commandments that guide human interaction and provide the knowledge of the divine will (19:16), while obedience to instruction gives guidance for the moral life into the future (19:20; see 19:27). Fools are those who are weighed down by frivolous or perverse talk (19:1).

The royal sages warn against the destructiveness of anger and uncontrolled passions (19:2–3, 11–12, 19). Indeed, the various elements of foolish behavior and social standing are to be avoided, including the inappropriate natures of the fool who lives in luxury and the slave who rules over princes (19:10), as well as laziness in general (19:15). The latter part of verse 10 testifies to a proper social order that, once disturbed, brings social upheaval and unbearable chaos. Laziness (19:15, 24) and scoffing (19:25, 29) are justly requited.

The contrast of corruption to justice in the courts is also a common theme in this chapter. The false witness is punished (19:5, 9), while the worthless witness mocks at justice (19:28). Providence is also a common theme in world maintenance. Divine providence overrides any human planning and decision making (19:21), and only the fear of Yahweh offers safe refuge (19:23).

The household provides a frequent setting and theme for the moral life in this chapter as throughout the book of Proverbs. Thus a stupid child ruins a father, and a quarreling wife is likened to dripping rain (19:13). The household and its wealth are inherited, but it is Yahweh who provides one a prudent wife (19:14). The discipline the parent gives to the children allows them to escape destruction (19:18). This last verse emphasizes the importance of instruction within the household. Children who are violent to their parents bring shame to the household and suffer reproach (19:26). Loyalty to others, especially within the household, is also stressed (19:22). Solidarity provides the bond that holds together life in the household.

The value of wealth, coupled with generosity to the poor, indicates that many sages belonged to or at least served the social elite in Israelite and Jewish society (19:4, 6, 7, 17). However, the true source of prosperity is understanding that derives from obedience to sapiential instruction (19:8).

Chapter 20. The royal sages in this chapter address similar topics to those found earlier in the second subdivision of 16:1—22:16. Divine providence and judgment that maintain the social order are the theological foundations of chapter 20. Yahweh orders all human life in ways that escape human awareness (20:24). Yahweh is the divine judge who examines the innermost parts of human character (20:27) and assists the one wronged in the repayment of evil (20:22). As creator of humanity, Yahweh is the one who has created the organs of perception that enable people to gain wisdom (20:12).

The royal court and kingship are part of the ethos of the royal sages in this chapter. Thus they argue that the throne of the king is established on righteousness, the principle that is at the foundation of cosmic and social order, and that his rule is sustained by the loyalty of his subjects (20:28). The wise king destroys the wicked (20:26), and

185

military advantage comes to the court through the presence of wise counselors and by accepting their advice (20:18). Furthermore, the king is the just judge who destroys wickedness (20:8), and his anger is dreaded and not to be provoked (20:2; see Preuss, "Old Testament Theology," 2:19–38).

A just society is characterized by an ethical barter economy. Thus to be avoided are "diverse" or "differing" weights and measures, because they are an abomination to Yahweh (20:10, 23), while bread gained by deceit will turn to gravel in the mouth (20:17). Boasting over the purchase of an item wrongly identified as of little value is to be avoided (20:14).

The household is again a common setting for the moral life and receives the scrutiny of the royal sages. An estate quickly gained will not bring about blessing (20:21). And, similar to the fifth commandment (Exod. 20:12; see Exod. 21:17), parents are not to be cursed (Prov. 20:20), for the power of the curse to destroy was well known in Israelite and Jewish society. A pledge was to be taken as surety for what a stranger borrowed (20:16; see Amos 2:8), though it was to be returned when the stranger gave back what he or she had borrowed.

Quarreling and other expressions of strife disrupt social harmony and lead to destruction (20:1, 3). Even physical punishments, however, are acceptable in teaching the simple (20:30). Other values include the strength of youth and the gray hair of the aged (20:29); a careful intention to fulfill vows, which nevertheless, are not to be rashly made (20:25); the avoidance of associating with a babbler who reveals secrets (20:19); the acquiring of "informed lips" (20:15); loyalty and trust (20:6); the sapiential ability to search out the deep waters of the human mind (20:5); integrity (20:7); hard work and the avoidance of sloth (20:4, 13); and the recognition of the purity of actions (20:11), which cannot be completely embodied in human nature and practiced in daily life (20:9). Indeed, the sages recognized that all human nature was beset by evil, to the point that perfection was beyond reach.

Chapter 21. Providence is once again a common topos and is coupled with retribution as the moral foundation of the sayings. Even the monarch is one whose mind is directed by Yahweh, who "turns it wherever he will" (21:1). Yahweh continues in this chapter to be the one who judges human action and thoughts. While human beings judge their deeds as right, it is Yahweh who "weighs the heart" (21:2). The metaphor of "weighing the heart" is a common one in ancient Near Eastern literature, where scales weigh the heart in order to determine the righteousness of the individual in judgment.

Likewise, no human counsel, usually thought to provide guidance that leads to success, can prevail against Yahweh (21:30). Normally, rulers depended on the sages to provide plans in peacetime and in war that would lead to success (see 21:22). In this chapter, however, the sages recognize that no human wisdom and planning can prevail against the providential guidance of Yahweh, who determines the outcome. Planning and military prowess were especially desirable in wartime, but only Yahweh would give the victory (21:31).

Righteousness (= justice) is a common theme in this second subdivision. In this chapter, it is judged to be superior to sacrifice (see Proverbs 15:8). The term for sacrifice (*zebah*) may refer to "sacrifice" in general, that is, any type of sacrifice practiced in Israelite religion. It may also refer to a specific type of sacrifice, the "communion" or "peace" offering. This specific kind of sacrifice (= *šālēm*) was given in order to establish communion between Yahweh and the worshiper, cultic personnel, and any guests invited to share in a sacrificial meal. Whether the sages had in mind a general term for sacrifice or the more specific "communion" offering, they still stressed that righteous behavior transcended the value of sacrifice. This is not an anticultic statement but rather a saying that stresses that righteousness (= justice) is superior to sacrifice. The establishment of order in the cosmos, society, and the individual by righteousness is superior to similar effects sought in the offering of sacrifice. A similar saying is found in verse 27, when the sages observe that the sacrifice of the wicked is an abomination (understood as "to Yahweh") that is made worse by the "evil intent" of the worshipers. They hope by their offerings to gain the favor of Yahweh but instead only worsen the destruction they will receive.

Pride is ever an evil emotion that leads to destruction. In chapter 21 the royal sages warn against the inculcation of this vice in several sayings. "Haughty eyes" and a "proud heart" are cultivated by the wicked (21:4). The "scoffer" is one whose behavior is characterized by "arrogant pride" (21:24).

The household is also a setting where wisdom is practiced. A common saying, sexist in nature, points to marriage as a possibly conflictive relationship between a man and a woman. A house shared with a contentious wife is to be avoided (21:9, 19). The household of the wicked is cast down by the righteous (21:12). The righteous preserve the wealth of their household, whereas the fools devour their estate (21:20).

Other virtues to be cultivated include diligence that leads to success (21:5); generosity (21:26); pure conduct (21:8); careful thought (21:29); the practice of righteousness, which leads to cosmic, social,

187

and individual order and harmony (21:15); instruction of the wise, which involves both observing the punishment of scoffers (21:11) and careful thought (21:29); and the proper use of language (21:23). Vices (= the "way of the guilty," v. 8), which figure more prominently in this chapter than do virtues, include lying (21:6), violence (21:7), the absence of mercy toward the neighbor and the poor (21:10, 13), false witness at court (21:28), bribery (21:14), love of pleasure (21:17), and laziness (21:25). The end of the wicked and the fool includes serving as a ransom for the righteous (21:18), the reaping of calamity (see 22:8), and resting in the "assembly of the dead" (21:16).

Chapter 22. The second subdivision concludes with the first sixteen verses of chapter 22. In this final list of sayings, the royal sages speak of a theology of creation and providence grounded in a philosophy of retribution. Thus, Yahweh is the creator of both the rich and the poor (22:2), while riches, honor, and life are the reward for two virtues, humility and the "fear of the LORD" (= piety; 22:4). Yahweh is the one who oversees knowledge and "overthrows the words of the faithless" (22:12), and he throws into the deep pit of the strange woman those who receive his anger (22:14). The social order is structured so that the rich and powerful rule over the poor and commonplace (22:7).

The righteous teach their children virtues so that they will continue, when old, to live a life that endeavors to realize sagehood (22:6). This saying points to the importance of the teacher of the household, who educates children in the moral life through instruction and physical punishment (= "rod of discipline," v. 15). Even when the household is left or the teacher passes away, the children who mature in life embody what they have learned so that they may successfully pass through the various stages of life until old age.

Virtues and rewards include a good name (= honor) as having more value than great wealth (22:1), the hiding from danger (22:3), a cautiousness that avoids the pitfalls of life (22:5), generosity (22:9), the elimination of scoffers and quarreling from the social order (22:10), and gracious speech that leads to the friendship of the king (22:11). Vices and punishments include laziness (22:13), folly (22:15), and oppressing the poor (22:16).

Conclusion

Royal scribes prior to the Babylonian exile composed the second subdivision of the second collection. The purpose of 16:1—22:16 was to instruct young students on proper behavior, not only in the ways of the larger society they were preparing to enter at a new stage of human

188

existence but also for life in the household, which would accompany this status elevation, and, at least for some, in proper behavior in the royal court as court scribes and governmental sages who served the monarchy. Thus young people needed to be prepared by their teachers for the moral life in general, in the household, and, for some, in the royal court. The teachings issued by royal sages embody their tradition of shaping the character of the students, both while the students were undergoing moral instruction and then in the new life for which they were being prepared. Even when the royal teachers were no longer present, separated as they would be from their students by space, time, and eventually death, their teachings might be incorporated into the moral life undertaken by their students. Students were thus educated to embody the tradition of the royal wise, by which they were to live and from which they were to draw their direction for life at court, in the household, and in general societal existence.

Important themes in this second subdivision include Yahweh sayings (creation and providence), the royal court, the household, the law court, language, the contrast between the wicked fool and the righteous wise, and wealth and poverty.

The Yahweh sayings, particularly important in the second subdivision (16:1—22:16), speak of creation and especially divine providence. Yahweh has created everything to have a purpose, even the wicked for the "day of trouble" (16:4). Those who mock the poor insult Yahweh, who is the creator of all humans and their social classes (17:5). Yahweh is the one who creates the organs of perception, the "hearing ear" and the "seeing eye," with the result that humans have the capacity for the reception of wise instruction that will guide them successfully through life (20:12). The sage incorporates in his religious orientation the fear of Yahweh (16:6; 19:23). This expression for piety points to the foundation of wisdom from its inception as a tradition. Fearing Yahweh means that Yahweh is worshiped as the Creator and Sustainer of life, whose gifts of success, well-being, and life come to the God-fearer (16:20).

Most important for the sages, however, was divine providence. Humans, including even sages and counselors, may plan a course of action, but it is Yahweh who determines its outcome. Thus humans plan, but the answer comes from Yahweh (16:1). It is Yahweh who establishes the plan of one who commits his or her work to God (16:3). Yahweh directs the steps of human beings whose minds plan their way (16:9). The human mind plans, but it is Yahweh's purpose that will be established (19:21). The contingencies of life are recognized by the sages, who note that Yahweh directs the steps of human beings, who

189

are unable to know God's actions (20:24). Even kings, who are the instruments of divine will, discover that their heart is turned wherever Yahweh chooses (21:1). No human counsel can prevail against Yahweh's will (21:30). While humans see counselors and military might as ensuring success in war, it is Yahweh who gives the victory (21:31).

Yahweh as judge is frequently found in this teaching about divine providence. In a general sense, it is Yahweh who assesses the human heart (16:2; 20:27). Yahweh is the one who brings vengeance against the wicked (20:22). Human beings often engage in self-justification, but it is Yawheh who weighs the heart (21:2). Honest business dealings are Yahweh's will, for he rejects false weights and balances (16:11; 20:23). Yahweh insists that the wealthy provide for the poor and will see to it that the generous are consequently rewarded (19:17). The sages who please Yahweh by means of their moral life are rewarded in a variety of ways (16:7). For example, Yahweh's gifts to the righteous wise include not only wealth, success, and well-being in life (22:4) but also a prudent wife (18:22; 19:14). Moral behavior is more valued than sacrifice, especially when the latter is offered with an evil intent (21:3, 27). By contrast, the wicked fools are eventually punished by Yahweh (22:12). Their heart rages against Yahweh (19:3), and their arrogance is an abomination that will not go unpunished (16:5).

Judgment in the legal settings of court and temple are specific cases of divine decrees to be enacted in the distribution of human justice. Thus the priestly prerogative of casting lots to decide cases of dispute has its true origins in divine judgment (16:33). Wicked verdicts that declare the innocent guilty and the guilty innocent are viewed as an "abomination to Yahweh" (17:15), for Yahweh is the one who oversees legal proceedings and ensures that justice ultimately will prevail.

Kingship and the royal court are another theme in this second subdivision (16:1—22:16). Yahweh is seen as the one who works through the actions and decrees of kings, who establish and maintain a conservative social order through their rule in both their general decrees and in the rendering of legal verdicts (20:26, 28). Thus inspired decisions are on the mouths of kings who do not sin in judgment (16:10; see 21:1). The monarchy is established on justice (16:12), borrowing from Egypt a metaphor that "order" (*ma'at*) was the foundation for cosmic creation where the Creator stood in originating the world. It was then the Creator's responsibility for maintaining cosmic and social order through the dictates of *ma'at*. Righteous lips in general and in legal proceedings especially are a delight to kings (16:13), since the sages aid the monarchy in sustaining a just social order (see 17:7; 20:28). By contrast, false speech is not becoming to monarchs

190

(17:7). The rewards for proper service to the kings include life, favor, blessings, and royal friendship (16:15; 22:11). By contrast, the wicked fools who enrage the king suffer the brunt of his anger (16:14; 20:2).

The household is both a theme and a setting for the moral teachings of the sages. They urged the discipline of children by parents (19:18), the result of which would be happiness and well-being when their teachings were observed (20:7). When they grew old, children would still be guided by the instruction of their household teachers (22:6). This discipline included not only teaching but also the instruction of the rod on the back of the recalcitrant (22:15). The cursing of parents was strictly forbidden, since they not only were the heads of the household but also the teachers of their young (20:20).

The sages recognized that inheritance was the major means of obtaining an estate (19:14; though see 20:21), which by frivolous living could be forfeited to even marginals, including slaves, who were righteous (17:1–2). Laziness was one means of losing an estate, since hard work maintained its value and existence (21:25; see 22:13). While valued, a household, including its estate, could be tainted and even gladly forfeited if shared with a contentious wife (21:9, 19). Still, the wealth of the sage's household remained while that of the fool dissipated (21:20; see 21:12).

The law court in both the royal and priestly systems is a frequent topic in the second subdivision (16:1—22:16). As noted above, Yahweh was the one who established and worked through legal proceedings to see to it that justice was done. Injustice in the law courts was an abomination to Yahweh, who oversaw legal proceedings (17:15). Likewise, the king, whose reign was established and supported by Yahweh, was to maintain justice in the royal courts, including in his position as high judge (16:10; 20:28). Bribery of judges and witnesses is specifically condemned in these verses for perverting legal justice (17:8, 23), as is the imposition of punishment on the righteous innocent (17:26), and partiality at court is not considered right (18:5). Scoffers and fools were to be condemned and flogged (19:29). It was Yahweh who was behind the decision rendered through the casting of lots by the priests in their legal proceedings (18:18).

Especially condemned is the bearing of false witness at court, since testimony was the key instrument to obtaining truth and thus to the proper rendering of justice. Consequently, a false witness who mocked at justice (19:28) would not go unpunished (19:5, 9), whereas a good listener would testify successfully (21:28).

191

As is the case in the first subdivision (10:1—15:33), this second subdivision (16:1—22:16) contrasts the behavior, language, and retribution of the righteous wise and the wicked fool. The sages recognized the sinful nature of all human beings, yet they maintained the general categories of the wicked fool and the righteous wise, placing most people into these according to their behavior and language. In this collection, the wicked fool is portrayed as the one whose behavior and language distort the social order and lead to chaos (17:2, 11). What is particularly striking is the teaching that Yahweh is the one who created the category of the wicked, who will experience the "day of trouble" (16:4). Indeed, Yahweh established and oversaw the conservative social order. Thus, it was not considered appropriate for a fool to live in luxury or the slave to rule over princes (19:10). Inevitably, the wicked fool would experience destruction (17:13). This was one way of addressing the problem of theodicy, even if it proved not entirely satisfactory; the suffering of the righteous, a question posed by Job, countermanded or at least qualified this teaching. Even so, the wicked, known by their arrogance, are an affront (abomination) to Yahweh (16:5; see 21:24). Pride and arrogance are especially identified with the wicked fool and are sinful and lead to contempt (18:3; 21:4) that eventuates in destruction (16:18; 18:12; 19:3; 21:16).

The wicked are known by their laziness, which leads to their eventual ruin (19:15, 24; 20:4, 13; 21:25; 22:13), as well as by their violence and ill temper (16:29; 19:19; 21:7), deceit in obtaining victuals for life (20:17), showing no mercy or hospitality (21:10), boldness and thoughtlessness (21:29), accepting of bribes to pervert justice (17:23), overindulgence of wine (20:21), adherence to the teaching of the wicked (17:4), quarrelsome nature (20:3), and love of the fine things of life (21:7). Their sacrifice is considered an abomination (21:27), even as their behavior and corrupt speech are an affront to kings (16:12). The end of the wicked fool is condemnation, ruin, and destruction (19:29; 22:25; 22:8), for they do not possess wisdom even for a price (17:16). The begetting of a fool is dangerous both to parents and to the larger household (17:21).

The righteous wise, by contrast, are those who experience well-being and life for seeking goodness and obeying the teachings of the sages (16:22). They appease the king's wrath (16:14), are judged perceptive by their peers (16:21), suffer rebuke for misdeeds willingly (17:10), possess wisdom that is more valuable than precious jewels and metals (20:15), travel in the right way because they are guided by the wisdom of the ancestors (21:8), maintain the wealth of the estate (21:20), through wisdom can defeat a city of warriors (21:22), are generous (21:26), possess humility and the fear of Yahweh (22:4), have the wicked as ransoms (21:18), rejoice over the doing of justice (21:15), are

192

generous to the poor (22:9), and hide when they see danger (22:3). The sages possess the mind as well as the desire to obtain and then practice life-giving wisdom (16:17, 23; 20:18). They are generally rewarded with life, honor, and good things (21:21), though it was deemed better to be poor and righteous than wealthy and wicked (16:8). The sages also recognized the limits of their wisdom, which could not prevail against the will of Yahweh (21:30).

Language is a theme that connects the second subdivision in this collection with the first. The power of speech and the literary artistry of the wisdom sayings combined to formulate elegant language that possessed the power of life and death (18:21). This aesthetic was especially viewed as possessing the power to create and sustain the cosmos and the social order which was to embody righteousness. Thus informed lips were valued as a precious jewel (20:15), though they were to be used carefully (17:27). The sage was conceived as the "cool," dispassionate person who would use words sparingly (17:27). Yahweh remained the one whose "tongue" gave the proper answer that would guide the plans of mortals and bring about their success, if rightly ordered (16:1). At court, sapiential language proved invaluable. Kings were trained to speak wisely and well, for they possessed the power to issue "inspired" verdicts and degrees that championed justice in the court and in the larger society (16:10). Thus kings desired to have in their presence those possessing "righteous lips" that would provide justice and order in the social world of wise rulers (16:13). Courtiers possessing this gift of language were able to articulate speech that gained in its persuasive powers (16:21), brought them well-being (16:24), and made them the friends of kings (22:11). The "friend" of the king may be a term of endearment and trust or even an office in the royal cabinet ("adviser"; see 1 Kings 4:5). In the school, a rebuke taken to the heart would increase the wisdom of the discerning person (17:10). The recognition of the power of the tongue caused the wise to guard this gift well (21:23). Nevertheless, the depth of mystery that at times surrounded speech made it complex and difficult to know (= "deep waters," 18:4).

By contrast in the area of language, the wicked fool looked all the more foolish when attempting to speak rightly, elegantly, and well (17:7). From listening to "wicked lips" and giving heed to a "mischievous tongue" (17:4), the fool's perversity of language entered deep into the recesses of his or her character and became a part of who he or she is (18:8). Still, left to utter foolishness without consequence, those foolish of speech could cause social havoc for others and would reap a reward of punishment (16:27–28; 17:20; 18:7, 16). The fool was the

193

one who would reveal secrets, babble, and mock at justice (19:28; 20:19). Even so, he or she might appear wise when silent (17:28). Yahweh was the one who would overthrow the words of those who were faithless (22:12), seeing to it that their destructive powers did no harm. It was better, in the assessment of the sage, to be poor with integrity than a fool who possessed perverse speech (19:1).

Foolish language that harms both the one who utters it as well as others is recognized by the sages. One who curses a parent will perish (20:20), while a vow frivolously taken unleashes the power to destroy its speaker when not fulfilled (20:25). Even the liar who gains great treasure by misspoken words will find that the profit is quickly lost and death is the true reward (21:6). Unlike the righteous person, who heeds the cry of the poor and then is heard when he or she cries out in need, the fool will not be heard (21:13). When a "scoffer" is punished or removed from society, quarreling ceases and wisdom is learned (19:29; 22:10–11).

Finally, the topic of poverty and wealth appears frequently in this second subdivision. Wealth was a valued commodity that brought its owners strength (18:11), social prestige (18:23), power (22:7), and many friends (19:4), and no one wished association with the poor (19:7). Nevertheless, it was better to be poor with integrity than rich with injustice (16:8, 19; 19:1). The rich and the poor both could claim the same Creator (22:2). Wisdom was thus judged to have greater value than great riches (16:16; 20:15), and a good name was preferable to great wealth (22:1).

Yet the sages determined that wealth would come to the righteous wise who followed the teachings of the ancestors, possessed humility and piety (19:8; 22:4), and generously shared their goods with the poor (22:9). Still, the teachers concluded that it was unfitting for the wicked fool to live in luxury (19:10). Although valuing the existing social order, the sages nevertheless taught that when the child acts shamefully even a marginalized member of the household, for example, a wise slave, could inherit part of the estate as though he were a descendant (17:2). Even slaves could point to the Creator as the one who made them as well as the more well-to-do (17:5).

While wealth was generally inherited through the bequest of the parents (19:14), it remained to be kept by diligence and wisdom or lost due to sloth and indolence (20:4; 21:20). The wicked fool was one who could obtain wealth through deceit and oppression of the poor, yet he or she found his or her possessions were quickly lost and became a snare of death (21:6; 22:16). The seeking of hedonistic pleasures ensured that wealth would escape its possessors (21:17; see Hausmann, *Studien*, 77–93).

Theology

The world as seen through the eyes of the sages, including human existence in general as well as the specific roles of household, royal court, and law court, is shaped and directed by the Creator and Sustainer of cosmic, social, and individual life. Divine direction and retribution reside at the foundation of the sapiential tradition. Retribution is neither an automatic system by which invariably the wicked are punished and the righteous are rewarded nor a system that eliminates divine will and decision making. Rather, retribution is grounded in divine justice, which, for the sages, is a principle of order through which Yahweh creates and sustains cosmic, social, and individual existence (Boström, *God of the Sages*). Sages participate in this ordering of the cosmos and society and in the righteousness of human life by embodying in their existence the teachings of the royal sages that present Yahweh as the creator and sustainer. They seek to become those who, through their behavior, help sustain all of life. Thus it is righteousness, the major characteristic of the divine sage, that creates and maintains existence. The righteous behavior of the sages participates in this life-originating and sustaining activity of Yahweh.

The royal sages draw on the common tradition of Yahweh as the creator of humanity in 20:12:

> The hearing ear and the seeing eye—
> the LORD has made them both.

This saying tailors the tradition of the creation of humanity by specific reference to the sapiential teaching that Yahweh is the one who creates in humanity not only the ear and the eye but all organs of perception that are open to divine and human moral instruction. This saying is another way of articulating the teaching that Yahweh is the creator of wisdom (see Proverbs 8—9).

In the second subdivision of this collection, however, Yahweh's creation is primarily found in the theological understanding of providence. Yahweh has established social institutions that are to reflect cosmic justice. It is the monarchy that principally is given the responsibility to maintain this divinely established social order. General social life, including the legal sphere, the family, and the court, is shaped and sustained by Yahweh, who is the Creator and just Judge. The behavior

195

and language of the sages aid in sustaining and directing this social world. In drawing the major categories of the wise and the foolish, the righteous and the wicked, and the rich and the poor, the sages see Yahweh as the one who establishes and maintains these categories (16:4; 17:3; 22:2). Implicit is the teaching that wisdom presents a conservative social order that is to be perpetuated and not overthrown by activities of revolution or disorder, which would result in upheaval of the social life (22:7). Thus the monarchy is directed by Yahweh (16:1, 10; 21:1), and the household, both the estate and its inhabitants, is established by divine creation and perpetuated through God's guidance (21:20). Through the kings, justice is secured both in peacetime and in war (20:8; 21:30–31). Kings are to repudiate injustice and maintain their institution, for their throne is the foundation of divine activity (16:12; 20:26, 28).

Marriage, in particular the gift of a good wife, is one of Yahweh's blessings to the wise for maintaining the household (18:22; 19:14). Yet a contentious wife is a divine punishment (21:9, 19), for she disrupts familial life. Wise and righteous offspring also have their origins in divine action that oversees and sustains the social institution of the family (19:18; contrast 17:21, 25; 19:13; see Perdue et al., *Families in Ancient Israel*).

Yahweh as the judge of human life and the knower even of the innermost thoughts is a frequently found theme in this subdivision (17:3; 20:27; 22:12). All righteous decisions in the royal court and in the legal sphere have their origins in divine justice, for it is ultimately Yahweh who is the foundation of these human institutions and who sees to it that justice is carried out. Yahweh is the one who establishes legal decrees and is the source of justice at the court (17:26). The wicked and foolish are to be found guilty and punished (19:29). Even the cultic sphere yields to the justice of Yahweh (21:3). The abuse of legal power, that is, the practices of bribery (17:8, 23), lying (19:5) and false witness (19:28, 21:28), and excessive deference toward the rich as well as the wicked (18:16) are not appropriate for this human sphere of divine decision making and activity (18:5). Even the casting of lots, often considered in the Old Testament to be a priestly prerogative to determine guilt or innocence, is said to have its origins in divine decision making (16:33; 18:18). The topos of weighing the heart is used to speak of arriving at and then meting out divine justice (16:2; 21:2).

196   Frequently found is the notion that certain types of behavior and language are repugnant to God, or an "abomination" to Yahweh. This includes the sacrifice of the wicked, that is, of those who pervert the

social order (21:27); the abuse of justice in the legal sphere (17:15); and a corrupt business economy (20:23).

While wisdom and sapiential guidance are to rest at the core of human planning and behavior (20:18), divine mystery and the contingencies in life are ever present in sapiential literature, including in this subdivision (20:24; see von Rad, *Wisdom in Israel,* 292–96). Human plans may be pursued, but it is only the will of Yahweh that will prevail and lead to a sure outcome (16:9; 19:21; 21:30). A person may assess his or her own behavior as right and pure, but only Yahweh assays the justice of such actions and thoughts (16:2).

Thus royal sages are to transmit their understandings of human behavior by beginning with the "fear of Yahweh," that is, piety that directs and guides the moral life of the wise (16:6; 19:23). As noted earlier, this expression is frequently encountered throughout the book of Proverbs. This religious piety and the faith that Yahweh creates and sustains the structures of human life are not only the final outcome of sapiential religion but also its beginning.

The Third Collection

"The Sayings of the Wise"

PROVERBS 22:17—24:22

Date and Provenance

The third collection of Proverbs is found in 22:17—24:22. The redacted form of the entire collection is a "teaching" that, in its reference to "thirty sayings" (22:20) and its content, appears to be based to some extent on the Egyptian *Instruction of Amen-em-Opet*, the teaching of a high official in the administration of royal estates (Murphy, *Tree of Life*, 23–25; Murphy, *Wisdom Literature*, 74). The Egyptian collection dates as early as the nineteenth dynasty in the thirteenth century B.C.E., when Egypt was well into the period known as the New Kingdom (1558–1085 B.C.E.). This Egyptian collection was written to the son of Amen-em-Opet, Hor-em-maa-kheru, a young priestly scribe functioning in the temple of Min. The official, Amen-em-Opet, instructs his son in the areas of scribal functionaries who served in the vast Egyptian bureaucracy. What ties together the Egyptian teaching is the theme of the "silent man," who is to incorporate discretion and submissive faith in the moral life conducted by the Egyptian scribal official. This sapiential ideal contrasts with the passionate man, who engages in impulsive behavior and lacks self-control. The basis in the Egyptian collection means that at least the major part of the collection in Proverbs 22:17—24:35 could date from the royal monarchy, perhaps as early as the tenth century B.C.E. Likely, the social setting for this collection came from scribal servants of the king who taught in a court school or ran the administrative bureaucracy of the house of David. The instruction was intended to teach young courtiers behavior at court and the moral life in serving in the royal bureaucracy.

Literary Structure and Interpretation

The collection in 22:17—24:22 is a teaching that consists of seven instructions of various lengths—22:17—23:11; 23:12–18; 23:19–21; 23:22–25; 23:26—24:12; 24:13–20; and 24:21–22—with sayings predominantly in the form of synonymous parallelism. The number seven is of particular symbolic value in the Old Testament in general and in Proverbs in particular. The number stands for "wholeness," "completion," "perfection," and "order." The general superscription of the entire collection is embedded in 22:17a: "The words of the wise." Following the literary structure of instructions, this collection consists of an introduction that addresses the youths who are being instructed and exhorts them to listen to and obey their "teachers" (parents). The introduction of an instruction is typically followed by a series of admonitions and prohibitions that are coupled with a variety of clauses, in particular result and circumstantial ones. Occasionally, ensconced within instructions are sayings and rhetorical questions that add to the veracity of what is being taught. Instructions may end with a conclusion that either returns to the beginning or sets forth sayings that emphasize the truth of what has been taught.

22:17—23:11

First Instruction

Date and Provenance

The first instruction probably originated in a wisdom school during the period of the monarchy and was directed to youth who were preparing to become courtiers and bureaucrats to serve the royal house. These would have included high-placed scribes, judges, teachers, architects, and government officials. The moral discourse passed on to these young students was essentially instruction in how to think and behave ethically in the new level of existence for which they were preparing.

Literary Structure and Interpretation

The first instruction is the lengthiest in this collection and is the part most dependent on Amen-em-Opet. This instruction includes a superscription that, during the course of scribal transmission of the text, was inserted in 22:17 ("The words of the wise"). The introduction proper (22:17–21) includes an exhortation to the youthful audience to listen to and apply the following teaching (22:17), a result clause (22:18a), a conditional clause (22:18b), a result clause (22:19a), a declarative affirmation (22:19b), and a rhetorical saying (22:20–21).

The instruction consists primarily of nine prohibitions (22:22–23, 24–25, 26–27, 28; 23:3, 4–5, 6–8, 9, and 10–11), along with two rhetorical questions (22:27, 29) and an admonition (23:1–2). Each is normally connected with a variety of clauses, in particular result and circumstantial ones.

The various topics addressed by this instruction include matters of interest to courtiers, judges, scribes, and the well-to-do. Among the subjects are just treatment of the poor, avoidance of those who are governed by their anger, not engaging in giving pledges or becoming in any manner surety for debts, honoring the ancient landmarks, skillful workers who serve kings, proper etiquette at the ruler's table, rejecting the pursuit of wealth, not partaking of the victuals of the stingy, not uttering one's words in the presence of the fool.

Moral behavior for those who find themselves in the presence of kings and rulers is of particular interest in this instruction (22:29—23:3), a point that suggests the royal school may have been the life setting for the instruction. In 22:29 the person who is "skillful" in his labor "will take his place" or "serve" before kings and "will not [take his place] before those who are obscure" (NRSV "common people"). "Skillful" may refer to the general talent of polished, fine work, a talent that is especially valuable in any profession. "To stand before" or "to take one's place before" rulers likely refers to those who present themselves to royalty as courtiers or servants (Josh. 24:1; 1 Sam. 10:19; Job 1:6; 2:1; Zech. 6:5). Ben Sira mentions this social function of highly placed sages in Sir. 39:4. Proper etiquette in eating at the table of "rulers" is also a topic for moral instruction for those who will dine with royalty (Prov. 23:1–3), a subject especially important for highly placed sages, courtiers, and diplomats. Ben Sira also speaks of table etiquette (Sir. 31:12–24) to be followed when eating before the great.

The high social standing to which the youth receiving this instruction aspire is also reflected in their future treatment of the poor. The "poor" (see Exod. 23:3; 30:15; Lev. 14:21) and "afflicted" (see Isa. 3:14; Ezek. 18:16–18; Amos 2:7) are not to be robbed or denied justice at the gate (Prov. 22:22–23; 23:10–11). The poor are the destitute who lack not merely wealth but even the material goods necessary for existence. They also may include those who have lost their social status

201

and have become physically and mentally impaired, while the "afflicted" are often those who have been maltreated by the wicked powerful and rich (Whybray, *Wealth and Poverty*). The poor and afflicted have no personal means by which to receive justice, nor the means to survive. The oppression of the poor is specifically condemned (Exod. 23:3; Lev. 19:15; Isa. 1:23; Ezek. 22:6; Micah 2:2), and their support through justice and charity is enjoined upon all Israelites and Jews (Ps. 41:1; Prov. 14:21; 29:7).

The theological reason given in this admonition for administering justice to the poor is that Yahweh is the one who is their defender. The "poor" in the Old Testament receive special protection from Yahweh (Job 5:15; Pss. 9:12; 10:12; 107:41). God's legislation was designed to establish and maintain social justice on their behalf (Deut. 10:17–18; 2 Sam. 22:28; Isa. 25:4; Amos 2:6 and 4:1). The theological rationale for the just treatment of the poor at times includes the fact that the people of Israel saw themselves as slaves in Egypt who were redeemed from their pitiful plight by a merciful and just deity (see Deut. 15:11; 16:12; 26:5–9). Yahweh is the "redeemer," that is, the "next of kin" (Lev. 25:25, 47–49), responsible for defending the rights and securing from bondage not only the goods and people of Israel (Exod. 6:6; 15:13; Deut. 7:8; Ps. 106:10) but also the poor (Job 19:25; Pss. 26:11; 49:15; 69:18; 103:4; Prov. 23:11). Yahweh does so in part by maintaining their just cause at court, arguing (Job 13:8; Ps. 103:9; Isa. 3:13; 57:16) on their behalf against the oppressor and the thief who would take what they owned and place them in bondage (Perdue et al., *Families in Ancient Israel*, 229–30).

This admonition concerning the just treatment of the poor (Prov. 22:22–23) is placed in the context of the legal courts. The reference to the "gate" in verse 22 points to the common place where legal proceedings were often held (Amos 5:12, 15). This intimates that the rich may be not only those who have the wealth to pervert the justice due to the poor in judicial proceedings but also that some sages were lawyers and judges who were to see to it that even the poor received proper treatment.

Two theological rationales are given in Proverbs to support the just treatment and support of the poor: creation theology (14:31) and divine justice, practiced especially in the courts (22:23). In this context, Yahweh is understood as establishing the law of the "redeemer," the one who pleads the case of the poor at court, meaning that Yahweh is the one who ensures that justice is to prevail in legal proceedings and that even the poor, who have no means of financial support, can assume that their next of kin will be their defender and will "plead

202

their cause." Retributive justice, overseen by Yahweh, is exacted of those who exploit the poor at court.

At the same time, the youth aspiring to be sages were warned not to give pledges or to become surety for debts. The common practice of the poor in Israel was to pledge one or more of their possessions, and even themselves, when borrowing something from a well-to-do neighbor. Failure to return the borrowed item could lead to the forfeiture of their possession or even of the freedom of the debtor. Debt that required interest was originally disallowed (Lev. 22:25) but came to be practiced at a later time (Lev. 25:26–27; Deut. 23:19–20). The borrowers joined the social outcasts. A system of providing the lenders surety against what was borrowed developed, although an item deemed to be necessary for life was generally not offered. Instead, a pledge was usually given that was a symbol of the guarantee of returning what was borrowed (Exod. 22:26–27; Deut. 24:10–13). On occasion a poor person could persuade a wealthy neighbor or relative to provide the surety (Prov. 6:1; 11:15; 17:18; 20:16; 22:26; 27:13). This type of security system not only represents engagement in foolish behavior but also points to the impoverished state of those finding themselves having to borrow what they do not own. Charity toward the poor should not lead the prosperous sage into providing them surety.

Maintaining the ancient landmarks that demarcated a household's estate is also a legal concern in this text (Prov. 22:28; 23:10–11). It is a law found elsewhere in the legal corpora and in other literary contexts (Deut. 19:14; 27:17; Prov. 22:28; Isa. 5:8–10). Households in ancient Israel and early Judaism owed their existence to the farmland and pastures that were the economic basis for members' life, and they were part of the estate that was handed down through the generations. Familial land ownership was the economic basis for households in Israel and Judah. Traditions and laws developed pertaining to land distribution (Lev. 25:10–12, 24–55; Deut. 25:5–10; Joshua 13—22; Ruth 4:10). Land was passed from generation to generation as a part of the household's estate, normally through inheritance at the father's death. Household land was not an economic commodity to be bartered in ancient Israel and early Judaism, since the viability of the family depended on its resources. Without land, it was impossible for the family to continue to exist as a social entity. Without land, household members dispersed to join related families, to reside as resident aliens (Lev. 25:35–38), to become marginal members of unrelated households in work as debt servants, to become migrants who would work as day laborers, or to join the underclass of the poor who were

203

forced to live off the charity of the well-to-do (Perdue et al., *Families in Ancient Israel*, 179–203). The references to the ancient landmark in Prov. 22:28 and 23:10–11 may suggest not only the proper and just treatment of the poor but also that some of the sages might aspire to careers in the courts as judges and lawyers.

The second reference to maintaining the integrity of the family lands, occurring in 23:10–11, suggests that greedy nobles often sought to incorporate within their own holdings the family farms of others, especially when landowners became impoverished and had no means by which to survive, save in using their lands as security for debts or even in selling them. At times the lands of the poor were even stolen in order for the wicked to increase their holdings. Especially vulnerable were orphans, who had no father to protect their economic rights (see Exod. 22:22–24; Deut. 10:18; 24:17–18; 26:12–13; 27:19; Jer. 7:6; 22:3). The legal corpora, prophets, and sapiential literature spoke against mistreatment of the poor, and this would have included the appropriation of the households of other families (2 Kings 8:1–6). In this context in 23:10–11, the poor, including orphans, are not to be abused by the misappropriation of their lands. Indeed, their "redeemer," or next of kin, will rise up to defend them in the courts and will "plead their cause," that is, present a proper legal case, to ensure that their land is not taken unjustly (Lev. 25:25–33, 48–49; 27:13, 15, 19–20, 31).

This instruction also warns against associations with those prone to anger (22:24–25) and speaking in the presence of the fools (23:9). Angry people are guided not by reasoned wisdom and quiet reflection but rather by uncontrolled passion, which often drives them to make foolish decisions that lead to destruction. Indeed, to associate with such fools may lead the youthful sage into embodying within his or her own character the same type of destructive behavior. Speaking in the presence of the fool is also warned against, since discourse with such a person leads to the rejection of the sage's teaching and is wasted speech. It is far better to utter one's wise teachings in the presence of those willing to learn and to incorporate within their character what is taught.

Youthful sages, who usually came from well-to-do families or who aspired to be wealthy, are here warned not to engage in the quest for wealth (23:4–5). Such wealth, hastily obtained, quickly dissipates. Certainly, the sages valued wealth, but should it come, it should derive from wise behavior, not from greed (Prov. 3:16; 10:4, 22; 14:24; see van Leeuwen, "Wealth and Poverty," 25–36).

Finally, in Prov. 23:6–8 the sages are warned to be circumspect in regard to those with whom they eat. The stingy who offer the delicacies of food and drink are to be avoided, since they are not sincere in the offering of their hospitality. Table conversation in this context is wasted, since the stingy are not truly interested in sharing their bounty or in listening to the wisdom of their guests, which ultimately falls on deaf ears.

Conclusion

This instruction is likely the product of royal sages who were teachers and courtiers. In a royal school, they sought to teach youth who aspired to become servants of the king in a variety of professions: courtiers, government officials, scribes, judges, and lawyers. Proper behavior before the king and the value of their skilled work to the court would ensure that they would have successful careers. In addition, these youth would be expected to be aware of legal and social responsibilities that would ensure they would function well both in their careers of royal service and in Israelite and Jewish society in general. Caring for the rights of the poor, avoiding the presence of the fool and the stingy, and not wasting words in the presence of hotheads who will not listen to wisdom are common teachings in the sapiential literature. The frequent emphasis on legal statutes may suggest, however, that the teachers had in mind those who might pursue legal careers once their education was complete.

Theology

This instruction emphasizes that Yahweh is the just deity who demands that the sages incorporate in their behavior legal justice and social responsibility, especially toward the poor. Yahweh defends the poor and expects the sages to do the same. Implicit in the command to observe the ancient landmarks and the social responsibility of the "redeemer" is the view that Yahweh has established legal restraints that forbid the misappropriation of the land of the poor and the orphans. Even they have legal rights at court, and the abuse of these rights will lead to the deprivation of the wicked person's life. Retribution is exacted against those who rob or crush the poor, and the effort to encroach on the fields of the orphans will be met with swift justice at court.

205

23:12–18

Second Instruction

Provenance

The instruction found in 23:12–18 emphasizes the importance of "discipline." It is clear from the content of this text that the setting is one of education, in which teaching that is reinforced by physical punishment is underscored. This setting is probably that of a royal school that is preparing youth for careers in various professions of the king's bureaucracy.

Literary Structure and Interpretation

The second instruction (23:12–18) consists of an admonitory introduction (23:12), two prohibitions (23:13–14, 17–18), and an admonition (23:15–16). The admonition and the two prohibitions are connected to a circumstantial or result clause that intensifies the truth of what is taught.

The admonition to learn the wisdom (23:12), "discipline," or "instruction" (*mûsār*) that is taught by the teacher (or parent) is common in wisdom literature (e.g., Prov. 2:1–5; 3:1–2, 21–24; 4:1–9, 10–27; 5:1–2; 6:20–23; 7:1–4; 22:17–21). Discipline refers both to the content of what is taught and a way of behaving that is based on the incorporation of the teaching. In this setting, the parent or teacher transmits to his or her children or students the discipline that is to be learned. Corporal punishment at times accompanies the oral instruction in order to reinforce the truthfulness of what is taught and to gain the attention of the youth who is being instructed (23:13–14; see Prov. 13:24; 17:10; 19:18; 29:15, 17; Sir. 30:1–2, 1–13). Corporal punishment was seen as a valid instrument to save the aspiring sages from Sheol (23:14). Those who respond favorably to what is taught and accept its validity bring joy to the teacher (23:15–16).

Finally, those who do not envy sinners but rather "fear Yahweh" (23:17; cf. 1:7) will have a future. They will not die prematurely, as do fools and the wicked, whose behavior leads to their downfall. The Israelite and early Jewish belief in corporate identity meant that the future of the wise included not only their own, private existence but also that of their descendants, through whom they would live into the future.

Conclusion

This instruction focuses primarily on the educational setting of Israelite and early Jewish wisdom. While the family could be the context for the teaching, it is more likely that the royal school provided the setting for the issuance of this short instruction. Parents and children were not only familial terms but also served as titles for those engaged as teachers and students, respectively, in the education of various types of schools. Those who obeyed the instruction of their teachers could rest assured that they would have a future, both as individuals and as heads of families, through whom they would continue to live. This emphasis on life was the greatest reward guaranteed to obedient youths.

Theology

The single reference to Yahweh has to do with the frequently repeated admonition to "fear Yahweh." This refers to obedience to the teachings of the sages, whose wisdom was believed to derive from God, and to the faith that Yahweh was the one who created and continued to maintain the righteous order of the cosmos and the society that was modeled after it. Yahweh is honored and worshiped by those who embody wise teachings and who affirm that wisdom has its grounding in the divine nature and character.

23:19–21
Third Instruction

Date and Provenance

Located within the larger third collection (22:17—24:22), it makes sense to date this instruction (23:19–21) to the premonarchical period and to place it in the context of the court. Those aspiring to be sages here would have become servants of the king and were taught proper behavior at court and in the larger social context of monarchical Israel. Drunkenness and gluttony would have been a hazard, especially of the

207

well-to-do who had significant access to wine and food. The prohibition against excess in drinking and eating would fit the context of the wealthy and those who enjoyed the bounty provided them by important stations in life in the administration and noble hierarchy of royal Israel.

Literary Structure and Interpretation

The third instruction in the third collection is an abbreviated one found in 23:19–21. It consists of an introduction in verse 19 and a prohibition against drunkenness and gluttony in verses 20–21 that is resumed in greater detail in 23:29–35. The prohibition is strengthened by two result clauses (v. 21) that conclude that poverty is the consequence of excess in drinking wine and eating food.

Wine in ancient Israel and early Judaism was a valued commodity, easily produced by an agricultural society in which vineyards thrived. Though grapes easily perished, their transformation into wine made it possible to produce a commodity that was easily preserved, traded in commerce, and consumed. In addition, drinking wine was a considerably pleasurable activity (Judg. 9:13; Ps. 104:15; Prov. 23:29–35; 31:6–7). Excess in the consumption of wine, leading to intoxication, was warned against, however, (Gen. 9:20–27; 19:31–38; Jer. 13:13; Ezek. 23:33). The sages were particularly opposed to drunkenness (Prov. 20:1; 21:17; 23:29–35), as were the prophets (Isa. 5:11–12; 28:7–8; 56:11–12; Amos 6:6). The legal tradition prohibited priests from the consumption of wine while serving in the sanctuary (Lev. 10:8–9: Ezek. 44:21). Drunkenness and gluttony were expressly condemned (Deut. 21:20). Excessive eating was also condemned by the sages as behavior inappropriate for the wise (Prov. 28:7).

Conclusion

Sages were expected to show moderation in their entire behavior, including eating and drinking. Drinking to excess and gluttony were foolish activities for those who sought to inculcate in their character wise behavior. The temptation to drunkenness and to overindulgence in eating, however, was especially present for those who were well-to-do and had ready access to wine and food. The leaders of Israel were expressly condemned for intoxication, which was seen as a dimension of immoral behavior (Isa. 56:11–12; Hos. 7:5). Those who sought to walk wisdom's path avoided excess in drinking and eating.

Theology

There is no explicit theological rationale for the avoidance of drunkenness and gluttony. Moderation, however, was a common virtue for the sages, who grounded their wisdom in the nature and character of God. Wine offerings were made to Yahweh, but Israel and early Judaism expressly forbid bacchanalian behavior, associated with gods of wine and gluttony who were worshiped by the Canaanites. Yahweh was not considered to be the deity of wine, though vineyards and this commodity were a gift, as were other blessings, to the faithful (Gen. 27:28; Joel 2:24; Amos 9:13; Zech. 10:7; Sir. 39:25–26).

23:22–25
Fourth Instruction

Provenance

The fourth instruction deals primarily with the household. This suggests that the household is either the setting or the subject of an instruction presented to youth aspiring to be royal servants in the king's bureaucracy. It may be that the household is the life setting, since the father of the child is the teacher in this context. In either case, the topic is the same: the joy of parents who produce a wise child.

Literary Structure and Interpretation

The fourth instruction in 23:22–25 is comprised of an introduction in verse 22 and an admonition in verse 23 that is strengthened by a result clause in verse 24 and an exhortation in verse 25. The subject is that of the joy of parents (father and mother) who beget a wise child.

The teacher is father, in this case the one who produces the child. The father and, at times, mother as teacher form a common motif in Proverbs (4:1; 10:1; 15:20; 17:21; 17:25; 19:26; 27:10; 30:11, 17). At times, the titles of father and mother may refer to the teacher (possibly 1:8; 6:20; 13:1, 12; 15:5), while the "child" is often the student (1:8; 2:1; 3:1, 11, 21; 6:20; 15:5), but not in this case.

The begetting of children, both a wise child and a foolish offspring,

209

is a common theme in Proverbs. The producing of a wise child makes a father glad (3:12; 10:1; 15:20; 29:3). By contrast, a stupid child brings ruin to the father (19:13); the foolish despise the mother (15:20); a foolish child is a parent's grief (10:1 and 17:25); the lamp of one who curses the father or mother will go out (20:20; see 30:11); the foolish child keeps company with prostitutes (29:3); and those who do violence to their father and chase away their mother cause shame and reproach (19:26). In essence, wise children bring joy to their parents, whereas foolish ones cause destruction.

In this context, the child who listens to the instruction and becomes righteous becomes a joy to the father who begot him and the mother who bore him. Despising the mother when she is old (23:22) is a violation of the fifth commandment (Exod. 20:12; Deut. 5:16; Sir. 3:1–16). Death was enjoined on those who cursed their father (and mother? Exod. 21:15, 17). "To despise" is a frequent theme in Proverbs (Prov. 1:7; 6:30; 11:12; 13:13; 14:21, 30:17; Song of Sol. 8:1, 7; Zech. 4:10) and refers to holding a person in contempt. The aged were to be honored and were regarded with special esteem, especially when they were one's parents (Prov. 17:6; 20:29).

Conclusion

The parents, especially when advanced in years, were to receive special respect. It is clear in this context that at least the father is the teacher of children. When children obey the instruction of the parent, they become righteous and thus bring joy and gladness to their father and mother. The child obedient to the teaching honors the parents, in particular the mother, and holds her in great esteem.

Theology

There is no particular reference to Yahweh in this brief instruction, but Yahweh was viewed as the one who established and maintained the household. As the fundamental bond of society, the household was held together by obedient children who adhered to the instruction of their parents. Mothers were in particular the teachers of youngsters until they reached a certain age, when the sons came under the tutelage of the father. The father took special responsibility for instructing the sons in the social decorum and economic details of the household, while the mother continued to teach the daughters proper behavior in the household and in raising a family. Through the instruction of parents, households were nurtured in the social traditions, manner of

210

behavior, and socioreligious traditions that held the family together and made it possible for the household to continue throughout the generations.

23:26—24:12

Fifth Instruction

Provenance

On the basis of content, it appears likely that the fifth instruction originated in a royal school. While avoiding prostitutes and strong drink are common themes in Proverbs, the teaching on war and military strategy suggests a connection to kingship.

Literary Structure and Interpretation

The fifth instruction occurs in 23:26—24:12. The general introduction is comprised of an exhortation to obedience to the parent's teaching (23:26) that is followed by two sayings that, as result clauses, contrast obedience to the sage's teaching with following to destruction the seduction of a prostitute (vv. 27–28). The earlier teaching on alcoholism in 23:19–21 is resumed here. The instruction proper in 23:29–35 is introduced by six rhetorical questions (23:29) that pertain to the evil results of drunkenness. The questions are answered in verse 30, which in turn is followed by a prohibition, the truth of which is enhanced by a series of result clauses in verses 31–35.

After the teaching on drunkenness in 23:29–35 are a series of sayings (24:5–9), a prohibition (24:1–2), and a twofold rhetorical question (24:12c–12d) introduced by three circumstantial clauses.

Following the general call to youth to observe the ways of the teacher, this instruction begins by warning against two pitfalls: dallying with prostitutes and intoxication by the imbibing of too much wine. Avoiding prostitution is a common theme in Proverbs. Harlotry, while expressly forbidden on pain of death (Gen. 38:24; Deut. 22:21), appears to have been a common practice in ancient Israel (Gen. 34:31; 38; Deut. 23:18; Prov. 7; 9:13–18; Jer. 3:3; Ezek. 16:16; Amos 7:17). In Prov. 23:27–28, the youth is warned against engaging a prostitute, who lies in wait like a robber and increases the number of the faithless. Those who had contact with prostitutes were likely to join the wayward who abandoned the worship of Yahweh.

211

The lengthy discourse on excessive drinking of wine (23:29–35) picks up the theme that was initiated in 23:20–21. In this larger context, the terrible effects of intoxication are described in detail. These effects include the producing of strife, complaints, wounds, redness of eyes, seeing of strange things, muttering of perverse things, and being immune to pain. The allure of wine is described in terms of its red color and sparkling nature and its smooth taste.

War is another topic in this instruction, suggesting perhaps that those taught it were among the counselors and highly ranked soldiers who served the king. Wisdom, in particular counsel that guided a king's strategy in war, was valued more than strong soldiers. Counselors provided generals and kings with direction in carrying out a successful battle, and soldiers trained in wisdom were even more important than strong ones. Training in war, particularly military strategy, was probably taught to youth in royal schools who would then enter the army as officers and strategists. This topic likely would have originated in the context of royal schools, since it was appropriate for elite youth to learn the ways of military engagement. On the "day of adversity," including most likely warfare, the fool holds back from rescuing those who are faced with slaughter (24:10–12).

In addition to being heavily fortified, since it served as an entrance to the city, the gate was a center for commerce and news (2 Samuel 18—19). It was also the place of judgment, where court was held (Amos 5:12, 15). It is likely in Prov. 24:7 that the reference to the gate is suggestive of legal proceedings that on occasion were held in this location in the city. Fools, not being skilled in jurisprudence and wise speech, keep their mouths shut in this context. This suggests that some sages became lawyers and judges, who knew the law and how to make convincing legal arguments at court.

The wise youth are warned against envying the lives of the wicked (24:1–2) and to avoid their company (see 24:8–9). The behavior of the wicked easily rubs off on unwitting youth, and thus they are best avoided. Unlike the sages, whose lips speak life-creating wisdom, fools are those who devise violence and speak mischief that causes harm to others. Wicked speech and scoffing unravel the social fabric of Israelite and Jewish society. By contrast, wisdom builds a "house," a metaphor for wise language and behavior that creates and sustains a family household. Wisdom results in the filling of a house with great treasures, a much desired objective among sages who sought through their learning to acquire wealth.

Conclusion

This instruction probably originated in the context of the royal school and deals with a variety of topics: despising one's mother, the avoidance of prostitution, intoxication, contact with the wicked, and failing to save those in peril. On the positive side, the wise youth brings gladness to the parent, avoids prostitutes and drunkenness, builds by wisdom the household, obtains wealth, and plans and carries out successfully the conduct of war.

Theology

In 24:10–12, Yahweh is the one who keeps watch over human beings, weighs their hearts, and exacts retribution against them for their fear in times of adversity, which keeps them from saving the lives of those who are threatened by death. Even the excuse of being unaware of the life-threatening danger that their fellows face cannot save them from divine judgment. Yahweh acts through the process of retribution in bringing judgment against these fearful and recalcitrant ones. This providential oversight of human behavior is perhaps the key feature of divine activity in Proverbs.

24:13–20
Sixth Instruction

Date and Provenance

Located within the larger teaching of 22:17—24:22, this instruction probably originated in the context of a royal school during the monarchical period. The one who issues the instruction is more than likely a royal teacher, who addresses the youth as "My child" (24:13). The students likely aspired to enter the royal service of the king in a variety of different occupations as servants to the monarchy.

Literary Structure and Interpretation

The sixth instruction is found in 24:13–20. It consists of a standard introduction, bolstered by result clauses and a circumstantial clause

213

that exhort the child to follow wisdom (24:13–14), and three prohibitions that are strengthened by result clauses (24:15–20).

The introduction to the instruction issues the standard call to learn from the teacher, only in this case, wisdom is compared to "honey" and "drippings of the honeycomb." The taste of wisdom is like the sweetness of honey. If the youth find wisdom, they will have a future grounded in hope. This promise of hope for a future for the wise youth is found elsewhere in Proverbs (23:18). By contrast, implicit to this promise is the recognition that the fools and sinners have no future (Job 27:8; Ps. 34:16; Prov. 24:20). The future has to do with a variety of things, but especially with longevity and well-being.

The first prohibition occurs in verses 15–16. The youth are admonished not to engage in violence against those who are righteous. Inevitably, the perpetrators of violence will fail and be overthrown by their own wickedness, but the righteous will prevail; even though they fall seven times, they will rise again. This emphasis on retribution is common to the moral teachings of the sages. In this case, the violent will suffer the very calamity they seek to exact against the righteous, that is, those who live in concert with the cosmic and social order established by Yahweh at creation. The righteous eventually will prevail, even if they are the victims of violence seven times (Boström, *God of the Sages,* 90–140).

The second prohibition occurs in verses 17–18 and continues the thesis of violence. In this case, the wise youth are taught not to rejoice at the downfall of their enemies. If they do, Yahweh, who oversees and maintains the moral teachings grounded in the righteous order of the cosmos and society, will be displeased and will exact the punishment that is the enemies' due.

The third and final prohibition of this instruction continues the line of thought evoked in the preceding prohibition. The wise youth should not be anxious about the well-being of the wicked, because they have no future (see Job 27:8; Ps. 34:16; Prov. 24:14). Implicit is the teaching that Yahweh will eventually cut off the future of the wicked. Consequently, the wise youth should rest content with the realization that the evildoers will eventually receive their just deserts.

Theology

214

The explicit theology of this instruction occurs in the second prohibition: Yahweh is displeased when one rejoices over the fall of one's enemies (24:17–18). It is Yahweh who oversees the just order of society, which has its grounding in the righteousness of the cosmos.

Yahweh is the one who will see to it that the enemies of the righteous receive their punishment. Consequently, it is wrong for the wise youth to rejoice over the fall of their enemies. Gloating is a vice that is to be avoided even when one's enemies suffer.

24:21–22

Seventh Instruction

Provenance

The concluding instruction contains only the introduction of an instruction. Its admonition to fear Yahweh and the king suggests that the entire teaching of 22:17—24:22 occurs in a royal school. In this context, a royal teacher provides to youth who seek to enter the royal bureaucracy in a variety of occupations moral guidance on how to behave at court, in their occupations as servants of the king, and in the larger society. By following the teacher's instruction, wise youth live in concert with the righteous order of the cosmos and society.

Literary Structure and Interpretation

The final instruction in 24:21–22 concludes the third collection. It returns to the beginning of the collection with an introduction and includes the two major topics for the entire teaching of 22:17—24:22: the fear of the Lord and the fear of the king.

The fear of Yahweh is placed in the form of an admonition, "fear Yahweh" (NRSV "fear the LORD"), and serves as one of the major themes in Proverbs (1:7, 29; 2:9; 8:13; 9:10; 10:27; 14:2, 27; 15:16, 33; 16:6; 19:23; 23:17; 24:4). To fear Yahweh means to believe in him as the Creator and Sustainer of the cosmic and social order that is grounded in the righteousness of God. Yahweh is the one who created the cosmos and permeated it with righteousness, which serves as the bond of creation. At the same time, Yahweh is the creator of the social order, whose righteousness holds together the constituent elements of human society. Yahweh is the one who maintains the cosmic and social order through the principle of retribution: the righteous wise are rewarded and wicked fools are punished. By becoming wise, the youth have the means by which to participate in establishing and maintaining a righteous society. Their behavior becomes, in effect, a key way in

215

which the social order is maintained. At the basis of all wisdom, then, is the fear of the Lord (Prov. 1:7).

The fear of the king is also important for wise youth to embody in their character. In the theology of kingship, Yahweh is the one who established the Davidic monarchy (2 Samuel 7; Psalms 2, 45, 72, 89, 110) and requires the king to be obedient to Yahweh's commandments. While this royal covenant is not explicitly mentioned, several of its features are implied. Kingship is grounded in the cosmic and social order and is the institution responsible for maintaining justice in society. When it does so, the cosmic and social order is sustained. The king is also responsible for seeing to it that, through just laws and edicts, righteousness and the righteous prevail while wickedness and the wicked are exterminated from society. Fearing the king, then, means that the wise youth recognize that this institution was established by Yahweh and is the major means through which justice is administered.

It is through the principle of retribution that wise behavior receives its just reward, while wickedness leads to destruction. Obedience to God and king is important, for they are powerful rulers who bring disaster to those who fail to fear them.

The Fourth Collection

"These Also Are Sayings of the Wise"

PROVERBS 24:23–34

Date and Provenance

The references in this brief instruction to judgment and to a field suggest it was produced in the court or scribal school any time from the monarchy to the postexilic period. The literary polish of the sayings suggests that learned scribes produced the instruction in one or the other context.

Literary Structure and Interpretation

The literary structure of the instruction consists of a superscription in 24:23a ("These also are sayings of the wise"), a discourse on judgment (24:23b–26, 28–29), and an autobiographical discourse on household labor (24:27, 30–34).

The superscription would appear to be a redactional insertion that connects this instruction with the teaching in 22:17—24:22 (Skehan, *Studies in Israelite Poetry and Wisdom,* 21). If so, then it is possible that, at least in the eyes of the redactor, this instruction has the same setting as the teaching in 22:27—24:22. The discourse on judging is introduced by a brief "not good" saying (24:23b) that is followed by two antithetical sayings, with the contrast between "whoever . . . , but" (vv. 24–25), and concludes with a saying on honest speech (v. 26). The discourse on judgment ends with two prohibitions in verse 28 and verse 29.

Judgment is a frequent theme in Proverbs (8:16; 16:10; 18:18; 19:5, 28–29; 20:8; 21:14, 28; 22:22–23; 29:9, 14). In the context of 24:23–34, judgment has to do with the legal setting of jurisprudence. The "not good" saying on partiality in 24:23b sets the tone for the

217

discourse on legal judgment in this instruction (24:23b–26, 28–29): "Partiality in judging is not good." As judges, the sages were to refrain from showing favoritism, especially to the rich and powerful to the detriment of the poor, who lacked influence and resources.

There were three settings for the administration of legal judgment in ancient Israel: the court, with the king as the high judge and royal appointed judges (Exod. 2:14; 2 Sam. 15:1–6; 1 Kings 3:16–28; Prov. 8:16; Isa. 1:26; 16:5; Jer. 7:1–15; 26:16–17; Amos 2:3; Zeph. 3:3); the temple, which had priestly judges who dealt not only with matters of cultic and moral purity but also with legal jurisprudence (2 Kings 17:27; 2 Chron. 18:8–11; Jer. 18:18; Ezekiel 18); and the clan and tribe, where judgment was administered by elders (Exod. 18:22, 26; Num. 22:16–30; Deut. 19:12; 21:2–4, 19–20; 22:15–18; 25:7–9; Ruth 4:2, 4, 9, 11; Ps. 107:32). It is likely that the setting for jurisprudence in this instruction (24:23–34) is the system of royal courts. Some youth would eventually become judges and lawyers active in the legal system, while all aspiring sages were admonished to testify truthfully in order that justice might be maintained.

Thus to pronounce the wicked one "righteous" means to pronounce him or her innocent. The result of this type of legal injustice is to be "cursed" by the people and "abhorred" (literally, "cursed") by the nations (Prov. 24:24). To "rebuke" (or "convict"; see Job 6:25; 32:12; Ps. 50:21; Prov. 25:12; 30:6; Hos. 4:4; Ezek. 3:26) the wicked, however, that is, to pronounce him or her guilty, results in "delight" and a "good blessing" (Prov. 24:24). "Cursing" in the Old Testament refers to pronouncing evil against someone, usually an enemy. The Israelites and Jews believed that the curse was laden with divine power that would subject the object to harm, even destruction. Curses were used in a variety of contexts in ancient Israel. Self-cursing was uttered in order to assure that one's testimony was true (Num. 5:19–22; Job 31:7–10, 19–22, 38–40; Ps. 7:4–6) and to emphasize that promises regarding the future would be carried out (Ps. 137:5–6). Curses were also spoken against those who broke treaties and covenants (Deut. 27:15–26; 28:15–19, 20–36; Judg. 9:15; 21:18; Ezra 6:12), those who were or would or might become enemies of the nation or of the person uttering the curse (2 Sam. 18:32; Job 27:7; Pss. 35:4–8, 26; 40:14–15 = Heb. 40:15–16; 79:6–12; Jer. 10:25; 11:20; Dan. 4:16), those who desecrated tombs, and the one who rebuilt Jericho (Josh. 6:26). In the context of this instruction (Prov. 24:23–34), however, "peoples" and "nations" will curse and "hold in abomination" those who pronounce the guilty righteous. This general cursing by other countries suggests that the one who was sitting in judgment was the king who failed to establish justice (see Jer. 21:12). In each case, the curse was uttered to harm or destroy one's enemies, real or potential. It partook in the belief in the power and the efficacy of the spoken word attributed to all aspects of language, but in a destructive manner. The curse contained the power to bring about its desired effect, regardless of the name of the deity being invoked (see Brichto, *The Problem of "Curse"*).

Blessing is the opposite of cursing (see Preuss, *Old Testament Theology*, 1:179–83; and Westermann, *Blessing*). Blessing shares the understanding of efficacious speech that establishes a state of well-being for its recipient, whether or not God's name is invoked. The recipient may be an individual, a group, or a nation. The blessing was found in a variety of contexts: the covenant renewal ceremony (Deut. 28:3–6), the old age and approaching death of the father and his pronouncement to his children (Genesis 27, 48), worship where God is thanked for God's grace and mercy (Gen. 9:6; 24:27; Exod. 18:10; Judg. 5:1; Ruth 4:14), the performing of a righteous deed (Judg. 24:1; Ruth 2:19–20; 1 Sam. 25:23), the royal court (1 Kings 15:13), the arrival or departure of a person (Gen. 24:60; 47:7, 10; 48:20), the greeting issued by a messenger (1 Sam. 25:14), acts of homage (2 Sam. 14:22; Ps. 72:15), and the making of peace treaties (2 Kings 18:31). In the setting of Prov. 24:23b–26, the blessing is uttered over the wise judge who pronounces that the wicked are guilty.

The first part of the discourse on judgment (24:23b–26) concludes with a saying about giving an honest answer. This likely refers in this context either to testifying honestly or to pronouncing a correct verdict. Giving "a kiss on the lips" when testifying or judging rightly was a ceremonial action, not an erotic one. For instance, a kiss often accompanied a solemn blessing (Gen. 27:26–27; 31:55; 2 Sam. 19:39). In the legal setting presupposed by this discourse, it appears that the judge or witness who judges rightly kisses the one who is found innocent or guilty in a ceremonial action to show that the verdict or testimony is true.

The second part of the discourse on judgment (24:28–29) pertains to false witness, also a common topic in Proverbs (6:19; 14:5, 25; 16:13; 19:5, 9). Wisdom was based on the affirmation of righteousness permeating the cosmos and all phases of social life, especially jurisprudence (15:3, 25; 16:33; 21:2; 22:22–24) and the royal responsibility for righteous verdicts (16:10; 20:8; 29:14; 31:8–9). The entire social structure was based on this belief in justice. If unrighteous verdicts and false testimony were made in this context, then the entire fabric of the social and cosmic order would disintegrate. False witness is not to be

219

uttered in court against the neighbor even when he or she is considered to have participated in wrongdoing against the one tempted to lie at court. False testimony has no place in Israelite society, especially at court when life, punishment, and possessions hang in the balance and depend on the truth coming out.

The discourse on working a field occurs in work in verses 27 and 30–34. This discourse contains an admonition that is comprised of three imperatives (v. 27) and an autobiographical speech or example story (vv. 30–34; see Ps. 37:25–26, 35–36; Prov. 4:3–9; 7:6–23; Sir. 1:12). In the Old Testament, human work is done for the well-being of humanity and not for the benefit of God. Indeed, humans are created for the purpose of labor (Gen. 1:26–31; 2:5, 15–17). Work is not a simple, easy task but rather can be arduous and difficult, due to the curse of humanity (Gen. 3:17–19). The result of human labor may at times be in vain and not carried out in a successful way (Eccl. 3:9; Ps. 127:1). Thus labor is not mentioned as something positive in and of itself but must be done well as part of human activities in order to meet the requirements for life (Gen. 1:29; 2:15; Ps. 104:23; Prov. 14:23; 31:15, 18).

Of all human endeavors, labor especially drew the attention of Israel's sages. Hard work was encouraged and placed humans within the righteous social order established by God. The scribes established a natural law grounded in retribution which suggests that hard work guarantees and brings success, whereas laziness results in poverty and want (Prov. 10:4; 13:4; 14:23). The sluggard who shirks his or her work is foolish and is often mentioned in Proverbs as one who suffers as a result of laziness (6:6–11; 10:4–5; 20:4; 24:30–34; 26:13–16; Eccl. 10:18). Sloth is characterized by excessive sleep (Prov. 6:9–11), excuses to avoid labor (22:13), and much talk (14:23). The sages especially emphasize labor associated with tending to a household's field (3:9–10; 6:6–11; 10:5; 18:21; 20:4; 31:16).

While hard labor was much encouraged, the sages recognized that certain caveats accompanied this value. It is Yahweh's blessing that brings about wealth, whereas human toil adds nothing to one's riches (Prov. 10:22). To possess a little along with the fear of Yahweh is more valuable than great treasure that is accompanied by trouble (Prov. 15:16). Righteousness, not treasure, saves one on the day of wrath (Prov. 11:4).

Conclusion

220

The fourth instruction originated in the royal school and sought to instruct youth who aspired to enter the various occupations of royal service in two areas: righteous judgment and hard work in making one's field productive. Certainly, some of the sages would become judges and lawyers, and thus they were admonished to ensure that justice would prevail at court. Most sages would own households, and as landowners they were encouraged to work their fields and to avoid the poverty that besets the sluggard.

Theology

While there is no direct reference to God in this instruction, it seems plausible that creation theology in regard to both world origins and world maintenance is presupposed. Yahweh is the one who established cosmic justice in the creating of the world and works to ensure that it continues. Social structures, including in this case jurisprudence and growing crops, are a part of the order that Yahweh created and maintains. Those who do not maintain justice at court, especially kings, and who do not work their fields will experience, in the first case, the cursing of peoples and nations and, in the second case, poverty that results from ignoring the natural law and failing to produce crops.

221

The Fifth Collection

"These Are Other Proverbs of Solomon That the Officials of King Hezekiah of Judah Copied"
PROVERBS 25—29

Date and Provenance

The fifth collection is a medley of sayings dealing with a variety of topics. This collection, attributed to the literary activity of the "Officials of King Hezekiah," who are said to have copied Solomonic proverbs, points to sapiential activity at the court of this Judahite king, who ruled from 715 to 687/6 B.C.E. (see Murphy, *Wisdom Literature*, 77–80). If the superscription is given credibility, it may be that the collection was put together for the education of courtiers or youths who were being educated for a variety of positions in the royal state. The references to kingship (see especially 25:2–7, 15) and the concern for justice found in this collection support the argument for the court and possibly the royal school as the social location (see van Leeuwen, *Context and Meaning in Proverbs*, 25–27).

Literary Structure and Interpretation

In regard to structure, it may be that this collection has two parts, because of different literary features and topics. Chapters 25—27 are dominated by comparative sayings and metaphors that make frequent use of images from the natural world, while chapters 28—29 consist principally of antithetical sayings, with a significant emphasis once again on the contrast between the just and the wicked (see chapters 10—15); references to the Torah, an infrequent topic in Proverbs; and the treatment of social problems. Especially important subjects in the instruction as a whole include sayings that deal with God (Yahweh; 25:2, 22; 28:5, 25; 29:13, 25, 26); kingship and the royal entourage (25:2, 3, 5–7, 15; 27:24; 28:2, 3, 15, 16; 29:2, 4, 12, 14, 16, 26); the

223

unusual occurrence of the law in chapters 28—29 (28:4, 7, 9; 29:18); the numerous references to the cosmic and animal world, especially in chapters 25—27 (e.g., 25:13, 14, 16, 20, 23, 25, 26, 27; 26:1, 2, 3, 8, 9, 11, 13, 17, 20, 21, 27; 27:3, 7, 8, 9, 15–27; 28:1, 3, 15, 18, 19); the righteous/righteousness (25:5, 26, 28:10, 12, 29:2, 6, 7, 16, 27); the wise/wisdom (25:2–3, 12; 27:11; 28:7, 11, 26; 29:3, 8, 9, 11, 15), the fool/folly (26:1–12; 27:3, 22; 28:26), the wicked/wickedness (25:5; 26:3, 26; 28:4, 5, 6, 10, 12, 15, 28; 29:2, 6, 7, 12, 16, 27); the lazy/laziness (26:13–16, 20); the use of spoken language (25:9–10, 11, 12, 15; 26:4–5, 7, 18–19, 20–21, 22, 23, 24, 28; 27:1, 2, 11, 14; 28:23; 29:5, 8, 9, 19, 20); jurisprudence (25:7c–10, 18; 28:21; 29:9); and wealth/poverty, especially in chapters 28—29 (27:7; 28:3, 6, 8, 11, 15, 19, 20, 22, 25, 27; 29:7, 13, 14). In addition to repeated topics that occur in both sections (especially the king, Yahweh, the righteous, the wicked, and spoken language), the instruction is held together by a predilection for antithetical and comparative sayings (most often containing the word *like*).

While the general overarching structure points in general to two major sections in the collection (chapters 25—27 and 28—29), the more detailed literary and topical composition of the entire instruction includes the following.

Chapter 25. This chapter has four distinguishable subsections. The first subsection consists of 25:2–7, which handles primarily the topic of kingship in ancient Israel (see Kalugila, *Wise King*). This section consists of five sayings: an antithetical proverb in verse 2 that contrasts the glory of God with the glory of kings; a comparative saying that likens the unsearchable mind of kings to the height of the heavens (v. 3); a synonymous saying that deals with the removal of dross from metal in order to have material fit for a silversmith (v. 4); a synonymous saying which notes that the removal of the wicked from the king's presence leads to the establishment of his throne in righteousness (v. 5); and a prohibition that admonishes young aspiring scribes to wait on the king's summons to come into his presence (vv. 6–7b).

The second major subsection in the first part of the collection presents an admonition on bringing a dispute against the neighbor to court (25:7c–10). The saying consists of a conditional clause (v. 7c), a prohibition (v. 8a), a rhetorical question (v. 8b–c), an admonition that contrasts the prohibition in v. 8a with the advice that disputes should be handled directly with the neighbor (v. 9), and a motive clause that concludes the admonition (v. 10).

224

The third major subsection (vv. 11–14) deals with various aspects of language: a word fitly spoken (phrased in a comparative saying, v.

11); a listening ear (also phrased in a comparative saying, v. 12); faithful messengers (placed in a comparative saying, v. 13); and boasting about a gift not given (v. 14).

A medley of topics continue in the fourth subsection in chapter 25 (vv. 16–28). These are presented in several different forms, though predominantly in the shape of comparative sayings. They include a saying that compares the patience of a ruler to a soft tongue that breaks bones (v. 15); an admonition concerning eating only enough honey to satisfy the hunger (v. 16); an admonition concerning not wearing out one's welcome at a neighbor's home (v. 17); a false witness compared to club, sword, or arrow (v. 18); trust in a faithless person compared to a bad tooth or a lame foot (v. 19); the singing of songs to a heavy heart compared to vinegar on a wound (v. 20a); sorrow in the human heart likened to a moth in clothing or a worm in wood (v. 20b); an admonition on giving one's enemy food to eat and water to drink (vv. 21–22); a backbiting tongue that produces angry looks compared to the north wind that produces rain (v. 23); a better saying that prefers living in the corner of the housetop to a house shared with a contentious woman (v. 24); good news from a far country likened to cold water to the thirsty (v. 25); the righteous giving way to the wicked likened to a muddied stream or a polluted fountain (v. 26); a comparative saying that compares eating much honey to seeking honors (v. 27); and the lack of self-control likened to a city breached, without walls.

Chapter 26. The first subsection of this chapter is found in the first twelve verses and focuses its attention on the fool. Various forms are found in this section, though the comparative proverb is the most frequently encountered. Nine sayings compare the fool or the fool's behavior with something else: snow in summer or rain in harvest, with honor given to a fool (v. 1); a sparrow's flying about, with an undeserved curse (v. 2; spoken by a fool is understood in this context); a whip for the horse and a bridle for the donkey, with a rod for the back of fools (v. 3); cutting off one's foot and drinking down violence, with sending a message by a fool (v. 6); the legs of a disabled person, with a proverb in a fool's mouth (v. 7); binding a stone in a sling, with giving honor to a fool (v. 8); a thornbush in the hand of a drunkard, with a proverb in the mouth of a fool (v. 9); an archer who wounds everyone, with a passing fool or drunkard (v. 10); and a dog returning to its vomit, with a fool reverting to his or her folly (v. 11). An antithetical admonition occurs in verses 4–5: not answering a fool according to his folly and answering him according to his folly. Finally, a rhetorical question addresses the persons wise in their own eyes and the exaggeration that there is more hope for fools than for them.

225

The second subsection of chapter 26 occurs in verses 13–16 and addresses the subject of the lazy: a synonymous saying in which the lazy uses the excuse that a lion in the street prevents him or her from working (v. 13); a comparative saying that compares a door turning on its hinges to a lazy person in bed (v. 14); a synonymous saying that the lazy person is too tired to bring his or her hand from a dish to the mouth (v. 15); and a comparative saying, functioning as hyperbole, that indicates a sluggard is wiser in his or her self-esteem than seven people who know how to answer discretely (v. 16).

Chapter 26's third subsection occurs in verses 17–28. The thematic unity is derived from the topic of speech (speaking, intruding in a quarrel, deceiving, whispering, quarreling, smooth lips, and a lying tongue). The section is also knit together by means of comparative sayings: taking a passing dog by the ears is likened to meddling in another's quarrel (v. 17); a maniac shooting deadly firebrands and arrows is compared to the one who "jokingly" deceives a neighbor (vv. 18–19); a fire going out from lack of wood is likened to quarreling ceasing when there is no whisperer (v. 20); charcoal to hot embers and wood to fire are compared to a quarrelsome person, for kindling strife (v. 21); the words of a whisperer are likened to delicious morsels that penetrate deep within the body (v. 22); and the glaze covering earthenware is compared to smooth lips with an evil heart. While continuing the subject of speaking, verses 24–26 deal specifically with the enemy (see 25:21): the enemy dissembles in speaking while harboring deceit (v. 24); the gracious speech of the enemy contains seven abominations (v. 25); and the enemy's wickedness will be exposed in the assembly. Verse 27 offers a general comparative saying that likens digging and falling into a pit to a stone that comes back on the one who pushed it. Finally, the topic of speech returns in the concluding verse in a synthetic saying that deals with a lying tongue hating its victims and a flattering mouth working ruin.

Chapter 27. The antithetic proverb is the preeminent literary form in this part. There are two identifiable subsections: 27:1–22 and 27:23–27.

The first subsection contains the following topics and forms. Verses 1–2 are an admonition that deals with boasting and praise. It begins with a prohibition not to boast (v. 1a), followed by a motivation clause (v. 1b) that indicates it is impossible to know what a day may bring. The admonition continues in verse 2 with a synthetic admonition to allow another one, a stranger, to praise one, rather than praise oneself.

Verses 3 and 4 are topically unrelated antithetical sayings. Verse 3 notes that while a stone and sand are heavy, the provocation of a fool is heavier than both. In a similar way, in verse 4, jealousy is said to be greater in its effect as an unlicensed passion than wrath and anger.

Verse 5 is a "better saying" indicating that open rebuke is preferable to hidden love. Verses 6–7 contain two antithetical sayings. Verse 6 contrasts the excessive character of the kisses of an enemy with the good intention of the wounds (probably verbal) inflicted by a friend. Verse 7 contrasts the satisfied appetite that spurns honey with hunger that finds sweet even what is bitter.

Verse 8 contains a comparative ("like") saying in which a person who strays from home is like a bird that strays from its nest. Verse 9 is an antithetical saying that contrasts a soul torn by trouble with perfume and incense that make glad the heart.

Verse 10a–c contains two prohibitions: the first not to forsake either one's own friend or the friend of one's parents, the second to avoid going to a relative's house during a time of calamity. Verse 10d contains a "better saying" related topically to the second prohibition in v. 10:b: to have a neighbor who is nearby is better than to have relatives who are distant.

Verse 11 contains an admonition introduced by the naming of the recipient of the teaching, "my son" (NRSV "my child"), an address that refers either to an offspring or, more likely in this setting, to a student aspiring to be a sage. The admonition stresses that the "son" should be wise in order that his teacher's heart be glad and thus be able to respond to the one who reproaches the teacher.

Verse 12 is an antithetical saying that contrasts the clever who see danger and hide with the simpleton who does not and thus suffers for it.

Verse 13 contains two admonitions that are paralleled: the garment of the stranger should be taken as surety, and any pledge offered by a foreigner should be received. This practice was a part of the borrowing-and-lending system in ancient Israel and early Judaism, when, in this case, the pledge of an unknown person, a stranger or foreigner, that is given in exchange for borrowing something is to be accepted. The pledge is a guaranty that the loan is to be repaid (see Exod. 22:26–27; Deuteronomy 24; Prov. 6:1; 11:15; 17:18; 20:16; 22:26).

Verse 14 is a synonymous saying that indicates one who utters loudly the blessing of a neighbor early in the morning will have his blessing counted as a curse.

227

Verses 15–16 contain an extensive comparative saying that

concludes with two impossible result clauses. A contentious wife is like the steady dripping of rain; to restrain her is impossible. It would be like restraining the wind or grasping oil.

Verses 17–21 consist of five synthetic, comparative sayings. Verse 17 compares the sharpening of iron with iron to a person sharpening the "face" (metaphor for "wits") of another. Verse 18 compares the eating of the fruit of a fig tree that one has grown with a person who is honored for caring for his or her master. Verse 19 compares the reflection of the face in water to a human heart that reflects another. Verse 20 is a comparative saying that likens the ravenous hunger of Sheol and Abaddon to human eyes that are never satisfied. Sheol in the Old Testament refers to the netherworld; it most often points to the underworld in which the spirits (often the Rephaim) of the deceased dwell (Prov. 9:18). The term, along with its synonym *death,* is used occasionally in mythological texts to refer metaphorically to a devouring god (Isa. 5:14). Abaddon is an important synonym for Sheol (Job 26:6; 28:22; 31:12; Ps. 88:11; Prov. 15:11). Verse 21 is a synthetic, comparative proverb that compares the testing of a person by being praised with the crucible for silver and the furnace for gold. The smelting process removes many of the impurities from and strengthens precious metals even as praise is said to test the mettle of a person.

Verse 22 is an antithetic, comparative proverb that is topically similar to verse 21. The proverb contrasts the inability to remove the folly of a fool who is crushed in a mortar with grain.

The second subsection of chapter 27 is an instruction to a farmer to care for his herd of sheep (vv. 23–27). The instruction begins in typical fashion with a synthetic admonition (v. 23): "Know well the condition of your flocks, and give attention to your herds." This admonition is supported by two synthetic motivation clauses: "riches do not last forever, nor a crown for all generations." The term *crown* suggests that among the recipients of the teaching are royal children or at least youths preparing to serve in a royal court. Sages were often among the wealthy nobles, and included among their possessions were households with herds. They would have been, as it were, gentlemen farmers whose wealth included especially landed estates, farmlands and crops, and herds (see, e.g., Job 1:1–5).

The instruction continues with two synthetic sayings (vv. 26–27): lambs will provide clothing and goats the price of a field; goat's milk will be sufficient to provide its owner, his household, and his servant-girls with food. The sayings are introduced by three conditional, parallel clauses in verse 25: when the grass is gone, new growth appears, and the herbage of the mountains is gathered. Servant-girls were part

228

of the entourage of marginal members of large and wealthy estates, pointing again to the wealth of the landowner.

Chapter 28. The second part of the collection occurs in chapters 28—29. After three disparate sayings in the first three verses (vv. 1–3), there are two subsections in chapter 28 that may be generally distinguished: one that deals mainly with the Torah (vv. 4–9) and a more lengthy one that largely contrasts the rich and the poor (vv. 10–28).

The chapter opens with a general antithetical comparison in verse 1 that contrasts the bravery of the righteous with the cowardice of the wicked: wicked ones flee when no one pursues, whereas the righteous are bold as a lion (v. 1). A major topic in this chapter and in chapter 29 is the contrast between the righteous (28:10, 12; 29:2, 6, 7, 16, 27) and the wicked (28:4, 5, 6, 10, 12, 15, 28; 29:2, 6, 7, 12, 16, 27). Verse 2 speaks of the rebellion of the land when it has many rulers, but when there is an intelligent man ruling, there is a lasting order. This saying contrasts the rule of a wise man (= king?) that produces a lasting social order with the chaos that results from having many officers ruling the land. It emphasizes the importance of a wise ruler in establishing and maintaining a just order in society, contrasted with the rebellion that results from having many (rival?) officials attempt to carry out the dictates of a righteous order. This saying introduces another frequent topic in the second part (chapters 28—29) of the fifth collection: kingship and the importance of just rule (28:15, 16; 29:2, 4, 12, 14, 26). The third introductory saying compares the poor person oppressing the poor to a beating rain that leaves no food. Poverty is a major theme in the second subsection of chapter 28 (28:10–28; also see 29:7, 13, 14).

The first major subsection occurs in 28:4–9 and deals with an unusual topic for Proverbs: the Law (*tôrâ*). The formation of the Torah as a law to rule the land in both cultic and civil matters was an extended process covering many centuries. It was during the eighth and seventh centuries B.C.E., however, that the scribes who fashioned the Deuteronomic tradition began the formulation of a comprehensive theological rendition of the Law. If the superscription that traces the origins of this collection to the eighth century B.C.E. is largely correct, then "the law" would likely refer to this early work of the Deuteronomic scribes who shaped the book of Deuteronomy and the other elements of the Deuteronomic tradition between the eighth century and the fifth century B.C.E.

Verses 4, 5, 7, and 9 deal directly with the Torah. Verse 4 is an antithetical saying that contrasts those who forsake the Law and praise the wicked with those who observe the Law and struggle against the wicked (see Psalm 1). Verse 5 is a more general reference to justice, but in this context the text likely refers to the justice of the Torah. This antithetical saying contrasts the evil who do not understand justice, presumably because they do not read and study the Torah, with those who seek Yahweh and thus understand justice (= the Law?) completely. Knowing and not knowing justice is the major difference between the righteous and the wicked in Proverbs. It is not until Ben Sira (ca. 190 B.C.E.) that wisdom and the Law are finally equated, though this section in Proverbs provides an important step in that direction.

Verses 6 and 8 broach the subject of poverty and wealth, the major topic of the second subsection in 28:11–28. Verse 6 is a "better saying" that contrasts a poor person who has integrity with a rich person whose ways are perverse. Verse 8 is a synonymous saying which notes that one who increases his or her wealth by means of excessive interest obtains it for another person who is kind to the poor. Charging a fellow Israelite interest for a debt is condemned by the early legal codes; fellow Israelites should receive a loan interest free (Exod. 22:25). The Law condemned those who received interest when making loans (Lev. 25:36–37; Deut. 23:19–20). This legal stipulation was often ignored, however, with the result that many Israelites experienced significant poverty due to incurring substantial debt. The practice of charging interest was condemned not only by the Law and the sages but also by the prophets (Ezek. 18:8, 13, 17; 22:12) and Governor Nehemiah (Neh. 5:6–13).

The remainder of the first subsection of chapter 28 deals with the Torah. Verse 7 presents an antithetical saying that contrasts wise children who keep the Law with gluttons who bring shame to their children. This saying is only a step or two away from Ben Sira's identification of the Law with wisdom. Gluttony normally refers to one who has a voracious appetite, a vice that is condemned by the Law (Deut. 21:20) and said by the sages to lead to poverty (Prov. 23:21). Gluttony is a serious offense in Deuteronomy. In Deuteronomy, the stubborn son who rebels against the authority of his parents and is a glutton and a drunkard is to be taken before the elders of the town at the gate for trial and then, if found guilty, is executed by the men of the town.

The last saying in this subsection (v. 9) notes that even the prayer of those who do not listen to the Torah is an abomination. "Abomination" refers to whatever is considered either ritually or morally repugnant either to Yahweh, as the case is here, or to human beings. Said to be abominations to Yahweh in Proverbs are sacrifices and prayers by the wicked (Prov. 15:8; 21:27) and immoral people and their behavior (Prov. 3:32; 6:16–19; 8:7; 11:1, 20; 12:22; 13:19; 15:9, 26;

16:5, 12; 20:10, 23; 24:9; 26:25; 29:27). Failure to obey the Torah would likely include both the moral and the cultic commandments it contains.

The second subsection in chapter 28 (vv. 10–28) deals primarily with poverty and wealth, although other topics are mentioned as well. The subject of wealth and poverty is ambiguous in Proverbs. Part of the difficulty resides in the fact that the sages did not give a clear definition of wealth and poverty, nor did they indicate who they considered to belong to the categories of the rich and poor. Deuteronomy defines the poor as those who include the widow, orphan, Levite, and stranger (resident alien). Proverbs, however, provides no clear-cut definition. It may be argued that, for the sages, the poor are specifically those who lack the means to sustain their existence (food, drink, clothing, and shelter), whereas the wealthy are those who have far more than they need for survival and, if righteous, share some of their surplus with the poor.

Wealth and poverty, however they are specifically understood, are simply a part of the social reality in Proverbs (see Whybray, *Wealth and Poverty*). Wealth is greatly valued and much to be desired, for its possession provides its owners not only necessities for sustaining life but also a surplus of commodities and even various luxuries that offer some security against the contingencies of life. By contrast, poverty in Proverbs is a state of existence where the necessities of life are not owned. The poor therefore would have probably included marginal family members (slaves, servants, concubines, and resident sojourners), day laborers, and the underclass of poor who did not possess the means to survive, save by charity from the rich.

Yet wealth and poverty are not seen in such black-and-white terms. In the list of sapiential values, righteous character and wise behavior are more valued and desirable than wealth. Also, the foolish or wicked rich are likely to lose their resources; but even if they do not, it is better in the eyes of the sages to be poor and wise or righteous than rich and foolish or wicked. It is the responsibility of the wealthy to share their excess resources with the poor. The sages do not specify a certain amount be given to the poor, for example, some of the gleanings of the field at harvest, though it is clear that generosity is an important virtue in Proverbs. The wealthy who do not share their excess goods with the poor or who gain their wealth by oppression or other dishonest means fall under the condemnation of the sages, who argue that these wicked people are subject to divine punishment. Retribution is believed to include the means by which the wicked or foolish rich receive their just punishment, whereas the righteous or

231

wise poor will be sustained. It is important to remember that the sages of Proverbs never value poverty in and of itself. The sages do not teach that those who seek wisdom and justice are to divest themselves of their possessions in order to proceed progressively along the path to sagehood. Poverty is never a state of existence that is thought to enhance one's wisdom and piety. The terrible results of being poor are many and much to be avoided, if possible. The poor are due justice and hospitality, however, and enjoy divine protection to see to it that they survive.

The sages of Proverbs indicate at times that wealth is a reward for following the moral life, for private initiative, and for hard work. At times, too, they regard poverty as a punishment for the wicked or lazy. Yet the sages also realized that wealth and poverty might come to those who have no personal responsibility for either. War, drought, unjust actions by the powerful, and the death of a provider might rob people of their resources and livelihoods. By contrast, wealth might be inherited or even result from an unexpected stroke of good fortune. The sages do not suggest that God has predestined certain ones to wealth and others to poverty, regardless of their merits and failures. Indeed, Yahweh is the one who gives, either directly or through the system of retribution, wealth as a reward and poverty as a punishment. Even so, God is the defender of the poor who requires that the powerful and wealthy meet their needs for justice and for sustenance.

Verse 10 opens this subsection in the form of an antithetical saying, with the emphasis placed on a substantial inheritance. Those who lead the upright into evil ways are contrasted with the blameless, who will have a "goodly inheritance." The major source of wealth in the Old Testament is the household's estate, which was inherited by children when the head of the family household passed away (see Wright, *God's People in God's Land*). The family household was a pragmatic requirement for survival in a largely rural environment. Social cooperation among members of the household, including marginals who were slaves, servants, concubines, or sojourners, was necessary for the continued existence of households. The major sources of food included crops and fruits as well as herds of sheep, goats, and small cattle. Farming in ancient Israel, due to the lack of soil conducive to the growing of crops in the highlands where most Israelites dwelt, was labor intensive and required the work of not only household members and marginals but even children prior to the establishment of their own households through marriage and the attainment of property (Meyers, "The Family in Early Israel," 1–47). Land was passed to succeeding generations through the inheritance (*nāḥal,* Prov. 28:10) of patrimony when the father died, with the eldest child receiving the largest share (see Num. 27:7; Deut. 21:16; Josh. 19:49b–50; 24:30; Judg. 2:9, 21:23–24; Ruth 4:5–6, 10; 1 Kings 21:3–4; 1 Chron. 16:15–18; Ps. 105:8–11; Ezek. 47:14). The household estate was not a commodity to be bought and sold, since land ownership was necessary for the viability of the family. When the selling of land became necessary due to misfortune, families fragmented and members dispersed and became marginal members of other households, to work as debt servants or day laborers, or joined the underclass of the poor who were sustained by the charity of intact households (Exod. 21:2–11; Lev. 25:35–55; 2 Kings 4:1; Neh. 5:1–5).

Social cooperation among families, including marginals, was needed to build and maintain terraces on the slopes of the hill country in order to conserve soil and reduce water runoff, to share water sources, to construct cisterns that retained water from the rainy season, to establish boundaries of fields, to harvest crops, to settle judicial matters, and to establish a common defense against invading armies and marauders. A network of care was established among related households in villages and clans in order to help with survival during crop failures and disease. This network of care extended beyond the households to include taking responsibility for the survival of the poor, who included widows, fatherless children, resident aliens, debt servants, slaves, sojourners, and Levites (see Perdue et al., *Families in Ancient Israel*, 192–203). The family household had to be largely self-sufficient in the manufacture of raw materials into clothing and other textiles, in building structures, and in the making of pottery. "Cottage industries" that included households specializing in the manufacture of pottery and textiles did develop among clans, and trade among clans, especially under royal supervision, added to the material culture of ancient Israel. Even among the sages who served in the royal bureaucracy, the household was the major resource for economic well-being. Thus, according to Prov. 28:10 those who are "blameless" will receive a goodly inheritance, whether they are the firstborn or among those who are born later. This suggests that the father had some discretion in the distribution of goods that would occur at his death.

Verse 11 of chapter 28 touches on the subject of the wealthy. Although the sages valued wealth over poverty, they viewed a virtuous life even with poverty to be more important than being wealthy and foolish or wicked. Thus, in this saying, placed in the form of an antithetical proverb, the rich are wise in their own self-esteem, but an intelligent poor person sees through the guise. This is another example of the wise poor having more insight into justice and proper behav-

233

ior than the rich, who in this case are arrogant due to their own self-importance.

Leaving aside for a time the subject of wealth and poverty, verse 12 of chapter 28 deals with the righteous and the wicked. Verse 12 is placed in the form of an antithetical proverb and contrasts the triumph of the righteous producing great glory with the hiding of people when the wicked prevail. "Glory," literally "weight, importance, consideration" in the Old Testament, refers both to God and to human beings. When it refers to human beings, glory points to such matters as wealth (Ps. 49:16; Isa. 61:6), a great army (Isa. 8:7; 17:3–4), royalty (Esth. 1:4; Ps. 45:3; Isa. 14:18), a reputation (Job 29:20; Ps. 49:17), piety (Ps. 8:5), priestly apparel (Exod. 28:2, 40), the king of Israel (Micah 1:15), and the ark (1 Sam. 4:22). While glory may refer to physical attributes that can be seen, it also, as is the case with this proverb, has to do with virtue and piety. It is possible that the proverb is alluding concretely to the ascendance to the throne of a virtuous king that leads to great glory, contrasted with the ascendance to power of the wicked, which leads people into hiding.

Verse 13 of chapter 28 returns to the topic of poverty and wealth when it contrasts hiding transgression, causing one not to prosper, with confession, which leads to receiving mercy. The sages often associate the gaining of prosperity with proper, virtuous behavior, as they do here. In this saying, the one who conceals his or her transgression will not prosper. By contrast, the one who confesses his or her transgression receives not wealth but mercy. Confession in the Old Testament refers to the open acknowledgment to God and to the human community of sin; the proclamation of God as the redeemer, both of Israel and of the confessor; and the praise of Yahweh for salvation (Pss. 22; 30; 34; 40:1–2; 51:4). The result of open confession is that God will rescue the suppliant from distress and he or she will return to the assembly, usually the temple worship, and give thanks to the Almighty for salvation (see Pss. 7:17; 9:1; 26:7; 28:7; 50:14; 100:4). In the saying in Prov. 28:13, the confessor acknowledges to the assembly that he or she has sinned but that God is the redeemer. As a result, the confessor is delivered from difficulties and returns to the assembly to praise God as the merciful redeemer. The one who does not confess will not experience prosperity.

In 28:14, the sages issue a "happy" (*'ašrê*) saying in which a person who recognizes the authenticity of fear in certain instances is said to be "happy," whereas the person whose braggadocio disallows him or her to recognize fear will experience calamity. "Happy" in the Old Testament refers to divine blessing that comes to a person for engaging in wise and righteous behavior. "Happy" refers to a state of existence in which well-being is experienced, whereas its absence is a state of misfortune. A complete and happy existence is the goal of the sages, and happiness refers to this state of well-being (Prov. 8:32–36).

The sages return to the topic of wealth and poverty in 28:15–16. Both verses deal with a ruler who has shortcomings. In verse 15, a comparative saying, a wicked ruler is likened to a roaring lion or charging bear. Rulers were expected to occupy the throne of justice and to distribute righteousness in their reign that would bring well-being to the nation. This well-being would cover a variety of areas, including a just society that was in tune with cosmic justice; a righteous legal system that would ensure that the wicked would be punished and the righteous rewarded and that even the poor would receive justice; bounty in the form of plentiful crops, rich harvests of fields and vineyards, productive herds; and victory in warfare. The comparison of a wicked ruler, in this case oppressing his own nation and impoverishing it, with destructive beasts is made to point to the devastation that confronts a people. This comparison with nature, with wild and fearsome beasts, continues the effort by the sages not only to enhance the literary quality of a saying, but also to note likenesses between human society and the world of nature.

The second saying dealing with a ruler occurs in verse 16, when an uneducated king, not schooled in the wisdom of rulers, becomes a cruel oppressor of his own people. In the form of an antithetical saying, this proverb contrasts the wicked ruler who mistreats his own people with the person who hates unjust gain. The latter will enjoy the much-sought-after blessing of long life, whereas, by implication, the wicked ruler and those oppressed by his rule will not. The fate of a people is often entwined in the Old Testament with the rule of kings. A people wisely and justly led will experience well-being, whereas those who are victims of misrule, say, in the exacting of harsh taxes or in the conducting of a foolish war, will suffer calamity, much as their ruler will, eventually. The reigns of the Israelite and Judahite kings in 2 Samuel through 2 Kings illustrates in concrete terms the veracity of this saying (see Kalugila, *Wise King*).

Verses 17–18 leave aside the topic of wealth and poverty and touch on murder (v. 17) and the safety provided by integrity (v. 18). In the Old Testament, murder was a heinous crime to be punished by death. Bloodshed could be brought about by murder, justifiable homicide, accidental spilling of blood, and execution. The act incurred defilement that threatened the perpetrator, his or her family, and the larger society (Num. 35:33–34; Deut. 19:10; Jer. 26:15). In the case of

235

murder and unintentional killing, blood vengeance could be extracted by the avenger, that is, a family member who was authorized to spill the blood of the perpetrator, whether or not the act was intentional (Num. 35:27; Deut. 19:10; 22:8; Josh. 2:19; Judg. 9:24; 1 Sam. 25:26, 33; 2 Kings 9:26). Those committing accidental homicide had the right to seek asylum (Exod. 21:12–14; Num. 35:9–34; Deut. 19:1–13; Joshua 20) at the altar of Yahweh and in a designated city of refuge (Num. 35:6, 13–14; Deut. 4:41–43; 1 Kings 1:50–53; 2:28–34). The land could be held guilty if it did not offer asylum to the one who kills accidentally (Deut. 19:10). Murderers found guilty, however, by a tribunal of the city of refuge were to be handed over to the avenger for execution. Those found guilty of accidental manslaughter were sentenced to live their days in the city of refuge. Should they leave, they were subject to execution by the avenger. Asylums were likely priestly cities where important shrines existed.

Proverbs 28:17 probably refers to the person who intentionally murders another person. This person will be a fugitive until death and will receive no assistance from anyone, including those living in a city of refuge who may safely reside there until death.

Verse 18 refers to the belief that one's integrity will secure one's safety, whereas the wicked will meet calamity. This saying, placed in the form of an antithetical proverb, is yet another example of the principle of retribution at work in the book of Proverbs.

The subject of wealth and poverty is taken up again in verses 19–22. In verse 19, in the form of an antithetical saying, the sages teach that the one who fills the soil will produce plenty of bread, whereas the one who engages in worthless pursuits will have only plenty of poverty. Worthless pursuits refer to people, things, or activities that are empty, without value (Gen. 41:27; Deut. 32:47; Judg. 9:4; 11:3; Prov. 12:11). In this context, the expression probably refers to activities without value that lead to poverty. This contrasts to the activity of the tilling of the soil, which produces plenty of bread.

The antithetical saying in verse 20 also deals with the topic of wealth and poverty. It asserts that the faithful have a bounty of blessings, whereas the ones who hasten to become wealthy will be punished. The "faithful" in the Old Testament refers mainly to those who believe in the God who has revealed himself to Israel in mighty acts of redemption and continues to deliver the nation from destruction. God is an object of trust who has a personal relationship with the nation and with the individual (Ps. 78:32). This means that Israel views God as trustworthy and reliable. Faith in God means that God is the one upon whom all living things in general, and Israel in particular, depend for their existence and well-being (Genesis 1—2; Exod. 3; 20:2–3; Deut. 4:39; Isa. 43:10–11). In wisdom literature prior to Ben Sira, God is the creator before whom a human being stands as a creature and whom the person is to obey, love, remember, fear, and turn (Gen. 22:1–18; Deut. 6:5, 13; 7:18–19; 8:2–3; 9:7; 10:20; Josh. 1:7–8; 24:22–31; 1 Sam. 15:17–33). Faith is not an assent to the veracity of certain doctrines. Rather, it is a moral response to the goodness and trustworthiness of God. In Prov. 28:20, the faithful likely are identified with those who fear God (Ps. 111:10; Prov. 1:7; Isa. 11:2). Thus, like the fear of the Lord, faithfulness is the foundation of wisdom. To fear God means to rest secure in the trustworthiness of God (see Job 4:6). Thus, according to the proverb in 28:20, the faithful will abound in blessings, that is, in the accoutrements of well-being that the sages sought—joy, happiness, wealth, and longevity—whereas to hasten to become wealthy leads to reckless, wicked pursuits that are sure to lead to divine punishment.

Verse 21 also is presented in the form of an antithetical saying in which the showing of partiality is condemned, even though this sin is committed for the small price of a piece of bread, perhaps a bit of hyperbole in this expression. Partiality (literally, "recognizing the face"; cf. Deut. 1:17; 16:19; Prov. 24:23) has to do with showing favoritism at court, especially to the rich and powerful or to one who has offered the judge a bribe. Yet the sages teach in this saying that for as little as a piece of bread people will show partiality in judgment. Youth aspiring to be judges are taught to avoid this type of sinful behavior when they sit on the bench.

In verse 22, a synonymous saying indicates that a miserly person hastens to obtain wealth and does not know that his or her actions will lead to loss. The sages disdain hasty action, knowing that actions that do not receive careful reflection and consideration as to their nature and outcome are likely to fail. The miser (literally, the "evil of eye" = *ra' 'ayin*) points to the figurative use of the word *eye*. In numerous places in the Old Testament, the eye refers to a mental or spiritual faculty or state (Gen. 3:5, 7; Num. 24:4, 16; Isa. 42:7). In Prov. 4:25, the "good of the eye" is a metaphor for "bountiful." The word *eye* also refers to the avenue of temptation (Job 31:1, 7) and design (Ps. 17:11).

In verse 23, the sages move momentarily from the topic of wealth and poverty to that of rebuke and flattery. In a "whoever" saying, the contrast is that the one who rebukes finds "more favor than one who flatters with the tongue." "One who rebukes" refers to a variety of spoken statements, including judging (Gen. 31:42; 1 Chron. 12:17; Ps. 94:10; Isa. 11:3), proving to be right (Job 19:5), convincing (Job 32:12;

237

Pss. 50:21; Prov. 30:6), reproving (Job 6:25; 22:4; Pss. 50:8; 105:14; Prov. 24:25; 25:12), and correcting (2 Sam. 7:14; Job 5:17; 13:10; Pss. 6:1 = Heb. 6:2; 38:1 = Heb. 38:2; 141:5; Prov. 3:12; Hab. 1:12). In this setting, the phrase best refers to verbally reproving, rebuking, or chastising one's behavior. "One who flatters with the tongue" refers to one who is a "smooth" talker and easily offers praise, whether it is deserved or not (Pss. 5:9 = Heb. 5:10: 36:3; Prov. 2:16; 7:5; 29:5; see Prov. 5:3; 26:8). Finding "favor" refers to finding grace or acceptance (Prov. 3:4; 5:19; Jer. 31:2). In this setting, the phrase appears to refer to one's rebuke finding more acceptance, especially from a sage, than does flattery that has no basis in fact.

Verse 24, in a synonymous saying, returns to the topic of wealth and poverty by speaking of the robbery of parents. The person who robs his parents, denying it is a crime, is a partner to a "thug." *Mašḥît* may refer to "one who brings ruin or destruction" (Jer. 5:26; Ezek. 5:16; 9:6; 21:36; 25:13) or may mean to "pervert, corrupt" morally (Gen. 6:12; Prov. 6:32; Ezek. 23:11). The harshness of the first alternative of the two meanings appears to be the meaning in this setting. Robbing parents, particularly in their old age, would leave them destitute and eventually bring about their ruin, especially if their means of livelihood were stolen. Children were expected to respect parental authority (Exod. 21:15, 17; Deut. 21:18–21; 27:16), care for their parents until the latter's death, and then to see to it that the parents had a proper burial (Sir. 3:1–16). This was one way of "honoring" the father and the mother (Exod. 20:12; see Lev. 19:3; Deut. 5:16; 28:24; Prov. 19:26).

The topic of wealth and poverty continues in verse 25 where, in an antithetical saying, the contrast between a greedy person and who one trusts in the Lord is made. "Greedy" (see Prov. 21:4) refers to one who is beset with selfish desire. This person stirs up strife among people, whereas one who "trusts" in Yahweh will "grow fat," that is, gain in prosperity (Prov. 11:25; 13:4; Isa. 34:7). Trusting in Yahweh is a common trait of the pious in the Old Testament (2 Kings 18:5; 19:10; Pss. 9:10 = Heb. 9:11; 21:7 = Heb. 21:8; 22:4–5 = Heb. 22:5–6; Prov. 16:20; 29:25).

Verse 26 develops more thoroughly the theme of trust by means of an antithetical saying that contrasts fools who trust in their own wits with those who walk in safety. The object of trust should be Yahweh (2 Kings 18:5; 19:10; Pss. 40:4; 55:23 = Heb. 55:24), wisdom, or other people who are wise or righteous (Prov. 31:11), but not mere mortals or human flesh (Jer. 17:5). Certainly, trust in oneself is misplaced, for one assumes that his or her abilities, in this case, intelligence, are

238

dependable in situations of threat or difficulty. The teacher directs the students to trust in the tradition of the sages that has proven by experience to be true and reliable over the generations.

Verse 27 is an antithetical proverb that contrasts those who give to the poor with those who ignore them. The one who is generous to those in poverty will lack nothing, whereas the one who turns a blind eye to their condition will receive many curses. "Curses" refers to a devastating ruin that brings destruction to those who are its recipients (Deut. 28:20; Prov. 3:32; Mal. 2:2; 3:9). Hospitality toward the poor was an important teaching of the sages, prophets, and priests and was often grounded in an ethic of love and compassion (Exod. 23:3; Lev. 19:18; Deut. 19:19; Ps. 82:3). The poor were to receive alms (Deut. 15:7–11), not to be charged interest (Exod. 22:25), and were to eat grain from their neighbors' fields both before and after the harvests (Lev. 19:9–10; Deut. 23:24–25; 24:19–21; and Ruth; cf. Prov. 14:31; 17:5; 22:2, 22–23; 29:13; Isa. 14:30; 25:4; Jer. 2:34–35; 5:28; 20:13; Amos 2:6; 4:1; 5:12; 8:4, 6). According to the sages, whatever the cause of one's poverty, he or she was to receive charity from the well-to-do.

The second subsection concludes with a saying that contrasts the unjust with the upright. The unjust are an abomination to the righteous, that is, something foul or odorous, whereas the righteous are an abomination to the wicked.

Chapter 29. This chapter has no obvious literary structure that may be delineated on the basis of either topics or themes. The antithetical proverb dominates its form-critical character. The chapter appears to be best understood as a summary of the earlier topics treated in chapters 25—28. Three topics, interspersed among a variety of others, are the most frequently encountered in chapter 29: rule or kingship, the antithesis between the righteous and the wicked, and the contrast between the wise (wisdom) and the fool (folly).

Four of the six sayings dealing with rule are placed in the form of an antithetical proverb (vv. 2, 4, 16, 26), while two are synonymous sayings initiated by circumstantial clauses (vv. 12, 14). In verse 2, the contrast is drawn between the righteous who are in authority (probably read *rĕdôt*, "to rule"; see Gen. 1:26, 28; 1 Kings 5:4, 30; Neh. 9:28; Ps. 110:2; Isa. 14:2; Ezek. 29:15; 34:4), that is, who have authority over creation and others, and the wicked who rule over others or over creation (Gen. 3:16; 4:7; Prov. 6:7; 12:24; 16:32; 17:2; 19:10; 22:7; 29:12, 26). Thus, for this saying in verse 2, when the righteous have dominion, the people rejoice, for these rulers are the ones who establish and maintain justice in the cosmos and in society. When the wicked have dominion, the people groan, because these rulers disrupt the cosmic

239

and social order and bring suffering and distress to the nation. Verse 4 continues the topic of kingship. In this context, a king brings stability to the land in the creation and maintenance of a just social order, whereas the ruler who places the heavy burden of increased taxes and labor for royal projects on the nation (1 Kings 4:7; 5:13; 2 Kings 18:13–16; 23:35; 2 Chron. 17:5) eventually brings ruin to the nation.

Two circumstantial clauses initiate the next two royal sayings in verses 12 and 14. In verse 12, the circumstance described has to do with when a king listens to falsehood. "Falsehood" may simply mean deception; however, it also refers to false testimony (Deut. 19:18) and false prophets (Jer. 14:14; 23:25–26). Kings were responsible for seeing to it that justice was meted out in the royal courts, and they had among their advisers prophets (see 1 Kings 22:13–28; Jeremiah 28; 34:6–7). When the ruler listens to falsehood, the officers who serve the king will be wicked, that is, they will participate in perverting the social order the ruler is responsible for establishing and maintaining. A circumstantial clause also opens the saying on kingship in verse 14: "If a king judges the poor with equity. . . ." This synonymous saying continues with a result clause: "his throne will be established forever." Justice at the royal courts, especially in defending the rights of the poor, was a royal prerogative (see 2 Sam. 15:1–6; 1 Kings 3:16–28; Psalm 72). The establishment (Prov. 16:12; 25:5) of the royal throne may refer to the establishment and maintenance of kingship in the social order as an act of God in creation and providence, or even more specifically, to the continuation of a dynasty or an individual king's rule.

The final two sayings on kingship occur in verses 16 and 26. In verse 16, the contrast is drawn between the wicked in power (probably *rādâ;* see comments on v. 2) and the righteous. The sage recognizes that there are times when the wicked assume the reins of power and increase transgression, but he or she teaches the students to rest secure in the recognition that the righteous will look upon their downfall. Inevitably, unjust reigns will lead to the overthrow of their perpetrators, as the books of Kings and Chronicles often note. While the dynasty of David continued, many of its rulers were unjust and met terrible fates. In the Northern Kingdom, no dynasty succeeded in taking root, and thus the history of its kingship was one of constant turmoil. The wise teacher wishes to assure the students that the wicked rulers will one day meet their downfall and that the righteous will be there to witness the ruin of wicked rulers. The final saying, verse 26, also crafts a contrast, in this case between the favor of a king and the justice of Yahweh, who is its true distributor. Kings were often solicited in the courts and in their rule to grant favors ("to seek the face"). If the

ruler was just and the request had merit, the king would grant the petition. On the contrary, an unjust ruler or an illicit request could lead to
the failure of the petition to be recognized and accepted as valid. It is
Yahweh, however, who in the final analysis grants justice to petitioners.
Yahweh is the one who creates and preserves cosmic and social order
and is behind the justice that is meted out at court. The implication is
that the petitioner should acknowledge not only God as the distributor
of justice through the king but also that it is divine righteousness that
permeates the cosmic and social order. To be in tune with order means
that one recognizes and confesses that Yahweh is the one responsible
for establishing and maintaining justice in creation and in providential
actions.

The second important theme that reiterates earlier sayings in this
fifth collection is the contrast between the righteous and the wicked
(29:2, 6, 7, 10, 12, 16, 27). In verse 2 (see above), people rejoice when
the righteous have dominion, but groan when the wicked rule. In verse
6, the righteous are contrasted in an antithetical saying with the
wicked. The former sing and rejoice, in contrast to the evil, who are
ensnared by their own transgression (*pešaʿ;* see Gen. 31:36; 50:17;
Prov. 10:19; 17:19; 28:24; 29:16, 22). At times, God is the one who
explicitly is said to deal with transgressors (Job 13:23; 39:8; Ps. 89:23;
Isa. 50:1; Amos 3:14). In Proverbs, Yahweh is understood as the one
who works through the system of retribution to bring punishment
upon those who are guilty of wickedness or transgression. This appears
to be the implication in the saying in verse 6. The contrast between the
righteous and the wicked continues in verse 7, which indicates that
the righteous know, and thus, implicitly, advocate for the rights of the
poor, whereas the wicked have no such understanding. Like Yahweh,
the righteous are those who are the defenders of the poor and lowly,
especially in the courts. Verse 10 speaks of the "bloodthirsty" (literally,
"men of blood"; see 2 Sam. 16:7, 8; Pss. 5:6; 26:9; 55:23; 59:2; 139:19),
those who are guilty of murder or killing in battle. In this synthetic saying, the sage speaks of "men of blood" who hate the blameless and
seek the life of the upright. Apparently, these "bloodthirsty" are murderers who desire to extinguish the lives of the righteous either
because of their blameless living or because their possessions are
sought as spoil. As noted earlier, verse 12 indicates that the king who
is deceived in issuing his verdicts or in rendering judgment is responsible for his servants becoming wicked and violating the boundaries of
order. Verse 16, as noted above, refers to the wicked in authority, who
therefore are responsible for the increase in transgressions of the social
order, and contrasts them with the righteous, who will eventually

241

see the downfall of kings and their dynasties that are behind the social disorder in the nation. Finally, in verse 27, the contrast is drawn in an antithetical saying between the unjust as an abomination to the righteous and the upright as an abomination to the wicked. Each group, the wicked and the righteous, considers the other to be odorous and foul.

A third important topic in chapter 29 is the contrast between the wise (wisdom) and the foolish (folly): vv. 3, 9, 11, and 15. In verse 3, an antithetical saying contrasts the wise son who loves wisdom with one who wastes his wealth on prostitutes. The Old Testament includes both secular prostitution, where a person earns her living by selling sex, and religious prostitution, where a priestess or worshiper of a fertility deity engages in sexual intercourse as an act of worship (Proverbs 7). Well-known examples of "righteous" harlots are Rahab of Jericho (Josh. 2:4–16) and Tamar, the daughter-in-law of Judah (Genesis 38). In most cases, however, prostitutes both secular and religious were the object of condemnation in the Old Testament (Lev. 19:29; 21:9; Deut. 22:21). While a woman guilty of harlotry was to be executed by stoning (Deut. 22:21), it is clear from many references to the practice that prostitution was widespread in ancient Israel. The prostitute usually frequented public places to find her customers, wore attractive and revealing clothing, and used seductive language. Cultic prostitution involved both sacred harlots and female worshipers who participated in fertility rites designed to imitate the gods and to bring about productivity of the members of the household, its fields, and its flocks (1 Sam. 2:22; 2 Kings 23:7; 2 Chron. 15:16; Ezek. 8:14; Hos. 4:13–14). There were also male sacred prostitutes who plied their trade in ancient Israel (1 Kings 14:23–24 and 15:12). Whether involving women or men, cult prostitution is condemned in the Old Testament (Deut. 23:17; 2 Kings 23). Israel's worship of other gods is often characterized as spiritual harlotry (Num. 25:1–2; Judg. 2:13, 17; 8:27, 33; Jer. 3:6; Ezek. 6:9; Hos. 4:12). Thus, in Prov. 29:3, the true love of wisdom that causes a parent to rejoice is contrasted to wasting one's resources on prostitutes to engage in lustful intercourse.

In verse 9, a synonymous saying is initiated by a circumstantial clause: if the wise go to court with the fool, the result is "ranting and raving [NRSV 'ridicule'] without relief." While the courts were to serve in arbitrating legal disputes, the sages were reluctant to go to court. Matters were to be settled when possible on a face-to-face basis (Prov. 25:7d–10). If a sage were to go to court with a fool, however, the ranting of the latter would make it difficult to reach a just solution to the dispute. A contrast between the fool and the wise is also drawn in verse

11. The fool who lacks control of his or her passions, in this case anger, is contrasted to the sage who holds back his or her emotions. In the wisdom literature, the fool is the heated person, the one who cannot contain his or her passions, whereas the sage is the silent person, the one who controls his or her passions through reasoned reflection and disciplined restraint that derive from the pursuit of wisdom and adherence to the sapiential teachings.

The topic of folly or falsehood continues in verse 15. In this antithetical saying, license is given to rebuke and the physical discipline of children or students by the parent or teacher, whereas the child or student who is neglected, who does not receive either rebuke or physical punishment, becomes a disgrace to his or her mother or woman teacher. Physical punishment was a part of the discipline of students who sought to learn the wisdom of the ancestors (Prov. 13:1; 23:13; cf. Sir. 22:3–6; 30:1–13). Failure to rebuke or to punish physically the student or child resulted in the student's failure to develop the discipline that characterized the life of the sage.

Poverty and wealth also become an important topic in this summary chapter (see 29:13, 14). In verse 13, a synonymous saying compares the poor and their oppressors by pointing to their common origins as objects of divine creation. In verse 14, a conditional clause opens a synonymous saying that indicates the king who judges the poor fairly will find that his throne is established forever. The "oppressor" refers to the person who causes harm to others, in this particular case to the poor (see Pss. 10:9 = Heb. 10:7; 55:11 = Heb. 55:12; 72:14). The second part of the saying of 29:13 points to creation as the theological tradition that binds together the common nature of both the poor and their oppressors: Yahweh "gives light to the eyes of both." "To give light" refers to "enlighten" in the sense of imparting understanding that especially comes through study of the law (Pss. 19:8 = Heb. 19:9; 119:130), "to cause the face to shine" in describing divine blessing (Num. 6:25), and the meaning in this setting of the gift of life (Ezra 9:8; Ps. 13:3). Yahweh gives life to both the poor and their oppressors. Thus the wise teacher underscores the commonality of the origins of both groups, and both are to recall that Yahweh is the special defender of the poor who are treated unjustly or without the sustenance of hospitality from the wealthy. Yahweh is the Creator and Sustainer, the one who gives life and continues to revive the deserving from death.

As noted above, Proverbs presents the theme of wealth and poverty, rich and poor, in ambiguous terms. Wealth and poverty, as well as the wealthy and the poor, are never clearly defined and delineated. For the sages, however, the poor are specifically those who lack

243

the means to sustain their existence (food, drink, clothing, and shelter). Deuteronomy offers the social categories of widow, orphan, Levite, and stranger (resident alien) as a way of defining the poor. Similarly, the wealthy not only are those with substantial riches but may include those who have not only the basic necessities and means by which to support themselves and their dependents but a surplus of goods that may be shared with the destitute.

Usually the sages present only a descriptive observation of the social reality of rich and poor, wealth and poverty, and thus provide no explanation for why people belong to either group. Wealth and poverty, rich and poor, are simply a part of the social reality that confronts the sages in everyday life. In addition, wealth is normally valued and to be sought. Its possession provides one with not only necessities but surplus commodities that offer some security against the contingencies of life, as well as some luxuries in life. On the scale of values, however, certain things are a part of the character and behavior of the righteous, wise person that are more desirable than wealth (e.g., "a good name"). In addition, the wealthy have responsibilities to share their excess resources with the poor. The sages articulate no specific limits or amounts, though generosity is an important virtue in wisdom texts. The wealthy who do not share their goods with the poor or who gain their wealth by oppression or other dishonest means are condemned by the sages and by God and ultimately face ruin.

The sages never consider poverty in itself to be a virtue. Indeed, they appear to be themselves either wealthy or in the service of those who are. Poverty does not enhance one's wisdom and piety, though the poor are often presented as enjoying divine protection. The ill effects of poverty are outlined, and it is a state of existence to be avoided. God not only requires the wealthy to share their excess goods with the destitute but also will rise up in judgment against those who oppress or ignore the poor.

The sages do note at times that wealth is a reward both for righteous, ethical behavior and for initiative and hard work. By contrast, they sometimes consider poverty to be a punishment for the wicked and slothful. Yet the sages also realize that wealth and poverty might come to those who have no personal responsibility for either. The sages never teach that God has predestined certain people to be wealthy and others to embrace poverty. God is the one who rewards and punishes, at times with the conditions of wealth and poverty. Yet God also is the defender of the destitute who rises up as their advocate and the judge who punishes those who oppress the poor or ignore their plight.

The king, as the ruler and chief judge of the land, is promised that his throne will be established forever if he treats the poor with justice (see Psalm 72). As noted above, the ruler is to ensure that justice permeates his realm, thus placing it in harmony with the order of creation. In so doing, the king's throne and possibly his dynasty will endure forever, that is, for many years.

Language is also mentioned in this final summary chapter, in verses 19 and 20. First, servants or slaves are not disciplined simply with words, "for though they understand, they will not give heed" (v. 19). This saying suggests that a harsh rebuke and even corporal punishment are necessary to motivate servants or slaves to carry out their tasks (see Exod. 21:20). Second, the one who speaks without thinking clearly about what he or she will say or without considering the outcome has less hope than a fool (Prov. 29:20). Sages, of course, prided themselves on the ability to control their speech and to choose their words carefully, recognizing the appropriateness of a particular time and place for what was to be said. If they spoke, they also contemplated the possible outcomes of what they said. Language was considered to have a potency that could shape the social reality and its events. Foolish speech could bring about disruption of the social order and cause harm both for the speaker and for the social world in which the words were uttered. By contrast, appropriate language could bring about well-being for the speaker and the social world, as long as the right words were uttered at the correct time and in the proper place.

Three Yahweh sayings are found in chapter 29: verses 13, 25, and 26. As noted above, Yahweh is the creator in verse 13 who gives life to both the poor and their oppressors. The creation-of-humanity tradition (see, e.g., Gen. 2:4b–25) is a major one in the Old Testament and perhaps is a tradition older than that of cosmic origins. Creation, both of humanity and the cosmos, was not a once-and-for-all event locked in the past but an ongoing process that continued throughout the ages (Westermann, *Creation*).

Verse 25 contrasts in an antithetical saying human fear that lays a snare with the security that comes to one who trusts in Yahweh. In Israelite religion, faith was not belief in the existence of God or giving assent to certain dogmas but rather trust in God's promises, words, and acts of salvation. Trust is not an intellectual exercise involving judgment or even knowledge but rather refers to a relationship between the believer and God (Pss. 9:10= Heb. 9:11; 21:7 = Heb. 22:8; 22:4–5 = Heb. 22:5–6; 25:2; 26:1; 28:7; and Prov. 16:20).

The third Yahweh saying occurs in verse 26, in which an antithetical saying emphasizes that Yahweh is the one who gives justice. As noted above, people often seek the favor of a ruler in order to gain justice and blessing, but ultimately it is Yahweh, working through the principle of retribution, whose decrees are just and who sees to it that justice is given to the well deserving.

Finally, verse 18 returns to the topic of the Torah (see 28:4, 7, and 9). In a "blessed" or "happy" saying, those said to be happy, that is, to live in a sphere of well-being, are those who keep the teachings of the Torah, in contrast to those who cast off restraint when there is no prophecy (literally, "vision"). "Vision" refers to one of the means of prophetic revelation, when the prophet or seer enters into a state of ecstasy and "sees" what Yahweh is going to do (2 Sam. 7:17; Job 4:13; 7:14; 20:8). While prophecy in its ecstatic form is given credence for the moral guidance of people, the saying may intimate that the revelation of the Torah is superior to that of the "vision."

Conclusion

The fifth collection sought to educate youths who were seeking to enter various positions in the royal state. The many references to kingship (25:2, 3, 5–7, 15; 27:24; 28:2, 3, 15, 16; 29:2, 4, 12, 14, 16, and 26) and the frequent references to justice in this collection suggest that the royal school was the setting for the origins and transmission of this collection.

The collection has two somewhat distinct parts, due to the predominance of different literary forms and themes in each. Comparative sayings occur most frequently in chapters 25—27 and often refer to images that are taken from the world of nature, thus perhaps reflecting the fact that the sages often spoke of the creation of the cosmos (e.g., 25:13, 14, 16, 20, 23, 25, 26, 27; 26:1, 2, 3, 8, 9, 11, 13, 17, 20, 21, 27; 27:3, 7, 8, 9, 15–27; 28:1, 3, 15, 18, 19). Antithetical proverbs are the dominant form in chapters 28—29 and draw a contrast between the just and the wicked (25:5, 26; 28:10, 12; 29:2, 6, 7, 16, 27; see chapters 10—15), contain the unusual references to the Torah (*tôrâ*; 28:4, 7, 9; 29:18), and often deal with problems in the social reality.

Theology

The fifth collection (chapters 25—29) contains seven references to Yahweh or God: 25:2, 22; 28:5, 25; 29:13, 25, and 26. In 25:2, God's glory is related to his concealing of divine actions in providence. "Glory" refers to a variety of features of God in the Old Testament. Its fundamental meaning has to do with weightiness or significance. The term refers not only to the reality of God's importance but also to the feeling of awe and respect in the worshiper. The term is closely connected to the divine character of holiness or "otherness." When associated with the cult, the term refers to divine presence in the form of light or fire (Exod. 14:4, 17–18; 24:16–18) and especially to the priestly tabernacle or temple (Exod. 16:7, 10; 29:43; 40:34–35; Lev. 9:6, 23; Num. 14:10; 16:19, 42; 20:6). Sometimes the glory of God refers to the manifestation of favor, and at other times, wrath. Especially important is the notion of glory as divine revelation in the cosmos and in acts of history (Pss. 29; 148:13). During acts of worship, the glory of God is said to be revealed to the worshipers who seek divine presence and knowledge of God's will. In the eschatological realization of the kingdom of God, the divine glory will be manifest to all (Ps. 57:5–11 = Heb. 57:6–12; Isa. 58:8; 59:19; 60:1). By contrast, Prov. 25:2 speaks not of revelation but of divine concealment of acts of providence, which the king is to discover. In Proverbs, the Deity is more secretive. Yahweh's nature and divine activity are capable of being known by the cultivation of wisdom and the teachings of the sapiential tradition, but God is not one who is known directly through revelation. Rather, God is known through the wisdom tradition in an indirect manner.

In 25:22, Yahweh is the one who rewards the sage who gives food and water even to his enemies (see the admonition in vv. 21–22). The enemies would experience shame and guilt in a society in which shame was a major element of punishment, both self-inflicted and recognized by others in the community. The sages taught that Yahweh expected them to show hospitality to and provide for the needs of the poor. Here the sages go a step further and teach that even an enemy in need is to be provided with victuals necessary for life. The enemy is the one who hates the person who turns around and provides him or her with food and drink. The principle at work in this admonition is retribution. While the enemy will experience shame for receiving charity from the one he or she hates, the sage, in giving food and water even to the enemy, will be rewarded by Yahweh.

The third reference to God in this collection is not found until 28:5. In this antithetical saying, the evil do not understand justice, but those who seek Yahweh have a complete understanding of it. Seeking God (the fuller expression is "to seek the face of") is a common expression in the Old Testament (Pss. 24:6; 27:8; Hos. 3:5; 5:6, 15; Zeph. 1:6, 2:3; Zech. 8:21–22). In a cultic setting, the expression refers to the attempt to draw near to the presence of God in order to worship, to experience the glory of, or to receive the revelation of God. In the

247

setting of Prov. 28:5, the expression refers to seeking the knowledge of justice, which has its location and activation in divine behavior and character, through understanding the wisdom tradition. It is by means of the teachings of the sages that the wise come to an understanding of God and divine justice. This awareness comes only to the sages seeking to understand God, and not to the evil who ignore or reject the teachings of the wise.

Proverbs 28:25 contains the fourth reference to God in the fifth collection (chapters 25—29). This antithetical saying contrasts the person who is greedy with the one who is enriched by Yahweh. The greedy person creates strife as a result of his or her appetite for gain. Order in society was understood as having its origins in creation. God permeated the cosmos with a righteous order, and human communities were to emulate that order in the social reality they constructed. The contentious person who, due to greed for food and possessions, disrupts the social order, brings about chaos, making it impossible for a human community to live to concert with world order. The one who trusts in Yahweh, however, while not seeking to satiate his appetite for food and perhaps possessions, will be the one enriched by Yahweh. "Enriched" may be a reference either to material blessings that allow one to have bodily fat or to intangibles such as joy (Ps. 23:5; Prov. 15:30) and prosperity (Prov. 11:25; 13:4).

Proverbs 29:13 contains the fifth reference to Yahweh, who in this case is presented as the one who creates all humanity. There are two creation traditions in the Old Testament: the creation of the world (Gen. 1:1—2:4a; Job 38—39; Psalm 104) and the making of humanity (Gen. 2:4b; Job 10; Pss. 8; 139:13–18). Both traditions are present in Proverbs (Proverbs 8—9; 17:5). The creation-of-humanity tradition, which may be the older of the two, is referenced in this saying in 29:13 to emphasize that God gives "light," meaning either life or enlightenment, to both the poor and their oppressors. There is no indication that Yahweh has predetermined those who belong to either category, though certainly "oppressors" could choose to abuse their power in their mistreatment of the poor. The sages teach that while Yahweh is the one who has created both categories of people, the oppressors and the oppressed, he will rise up in defense of the poor, especially in defending their rights in the courts (Prov. 22:22–23). Those who abuse the poor by misusing their power should be aware that Yahweh is the creator of all humanity, including the oppressed, and they should know that God defends the rights of the poor to ensure that they receive justice. In addition, creation is not a once-and-for-all primordial act or merely the birth of a newborn. The sages believed that even as God continued to sustain the cosmos through acts of providence, so they shaped their character according to divine teaching in the sapiential corpus through studied reflection and righteous behavior on the way to sagehood.

The sixth reference to God (29:25) in the fifth collection contrasts human fear that lays a snare with trust in Yahweh that brings one security. Based on the experience of the sages, God is trustworthy (Ps. 37:5, a wisdom psalm; and Prov. 16:20), for he acts to establish justice and life for those who fear and honor him. "To bring security" (*yĕśûggāb*) literally means to "set on high" or "be exalted" (Job 36:22; Ps. 139:6; Prov. 18:10). The expression is used metaphorically to refer to the security that comes from being on a high place, easily protected (Ps. 9:9 = Heb. 9:10; Isa. 25:12; 33:16). On occasion, the nominal form of the word refers to God as a refuge (Pss. 9:9 = Heb. 9:10; 18:2 = Heb. 18:3; 46:7 = Heb. 46:8, 11 = Heb. 12; 59:9 = Heb. 59:10, 16–17 = Heb. 17–18; 62:2 = Heb. 62:3, Pss. 62:6; 94:22; 144:2). Thus security rests in God, whereas human fear is a snare that entraps those overcome with terror. Human fear offers no security or protection; only God does so.

The seventh and final reference to God or Yahweh in this fifth collection occurs in 29:26. Here, seeking the face (NRSV "favor") of the king refers to making an entreaty to or gaining an audience with the ruler, in order to obtain from him wisdom and justice (1 Kings 10:24). The sages, however, teach that the true giver of justice is Yahweh. Yahweh is the one who ensures that justice prevails for the righteous in their social reality.

Thus the fifth collection (chapters 25—29) speaks of God as one whose presence and wisdom are concealed yet known by the discerning ruler, who provides the reward of blessings to those who extend food and drink to the ones who hate them; who gives the understanding of justice to those who seek divine presence through meditating on the teachings of the sages; who bestows prosperity and "fatness" on those who trust; who gives life to both the oppressor and the recipients of their abuse, that is, the poor; who provides a refuge to those who trust; and who is the true reservoir of imparted justice to the wise-righteous. God in this collection is the one who creates humanity, who establishes a social order in which the sages, especially wise kings, may know who God is and enact the dictates of justice in their behavior, and who is the source of security to those who trust. Through divine providence, justice is actualized in human society, and sagehood is achieved through reflection on and the enactment of wisdom in human behavior.

249

The Sixth Collection

"The Words of Agur"

PROVERBS 30

Date and Provenance

The first four verses of this chapter are among the most difficult to translate not only in the book of Proverbs but, indeed, in the entire Old Testament (van Leeuwen, "The Book of Proverbs," 250–55). This difficulty is due to the problems of textual corruption and the meaning of obscure words. For instance, the term *maśśā'* may be either a term for "oracle" or "word" or the name of an Arabian tribe of Massa located to the east. If the term refers to the Arabian tribe of Massa, then some light is shone on the provenance and date of the early layer of the sixth collection. This tribe appears in Assyrian sources as Mas'aia in the late eighth century B.C.E. Massa (see Prov. 31:1) was most likely a wandering Arabian tribe whose major areas of migratory movement were somewhere to the east of Israel, in Arabia, Edom, the Transjordan, or beyond Seir (see Gen. 25:14; 1 Chron. 1:30). If this is the case, then Agur is presented as a non-Israelite, non-Jewish sage from the East whose wisdom has been preserved by the wise teachers of Israel (see 1 Kings 4:29–34 = Heb. 5:9–14; the friends of Job in Job 3—27, Eliphaz, Bildad, and Zophar). If this is the meaning of the term, then *hammaśśā'* means that Agur was a Massa'ite who was a member of this particular tribe (see Prov. 31:1, where Lemuel is called the king of Massa). That Agur was a foreign sage from the East may be argued, since the term is not a typical Hebrew name, and Jakeh, the name of his ancestor, is otherwise unknown in Hebrew.

The date for this text is hard to pinpoint, as is the time of its inclusion in the book of Proverbs by Israelite sages who transmitted and redacted the finished product. It would seem from the precious little evidence we have within the written Assyrian and biblical sources,

251

however, that the earliest date for composition would be the later part of the eighth century B.C.E., and the latest period for inclusion in the book of Proverbs would be the early Persian period (late sixth century to fifth century B.C.E.).

Literary Structure and Interpretation

This collection has for a superscription the following: "The words of Agur, son of Jakeh, a revelation [*maśśā'*]/the Mass'aite: The oracle of the man" (30:1a; see Crenshaw, "Clanging Symbols," 371–82). As indicated, the term *maśśā'* may be translated in this superscription as an "oracle," "revelation," "burden," or "utterance," a term that refers to prophetic, ecstatic speech that is issued in or as a result of the state of revelation (2 Kings 9:25; 2 Chron. 24:27; Isa. 14:28; Jer. 23:33–38; Zech. 9:1; 12:1). The content of the first four verses would appear to negate this possibility, since the teacher appears to question the special, revealed knowledge of God, something that the prophets and particularly those who entered into an ecstatic state of revelation claimed to possess. Agur even disputes the contention of the traditional sages, who not only believed that their teachings were not simply the result of astute observation of their experiences but also claimed to possess in their traditions enthroned wisdom, the handmaiden of God through whom God created and continues to sustain the cosmos and society (see Proverbs 8—9; Job 28; Sirah 24). Thus their teachings incorporated this same heavenly wisdom that stood by and knew intimately the Creator and was revealed, if only indirectly, to them by the God of wisdom (see 1 Kings 3:3–15).

The extent of the collection attributed to Agur and its literary structure is a matter that has consumed much scholarly debate, which has produced two major views. One view is that only 30:1–4 are the words of a non-Israelite cynic, Agur, who denies that humans know or even have the possibility of directly knowing God. A more extreme extension of this view is that Agur is a non-Israelite atheist who denies the existence of God. Thus, verses 5–6, 7–9, and 10 are the responses of pious Israelite sages who, as later redactors, tend to dispute directly the teachings of this impious agnostic or atheist. This response is continued in the remainder of the collection, verses 11–33. The second view, similar to the first, is that the entirety of chapter 30 is collectively known as "The words of Agur," though the cynical wisdom in the first four verses serves as the springboard to later sapiential response by those generations of sages who developed and preserved this collection. It is highly doubtful that Agur spoke the words in verses 5–33,

252

since they are best understood as originating from the hand of later redactors responding to what they consider to be too cynical a view of the nature and character of wisdom.

The literary structure of the collection may be summarized as follows: a superscription (30:1a); a first-person internal dialogue by a cynic in the first three verses (30:1b–3), followed by his six questions and concluding taunt (30:4); a later pious response by a traditional sage, consisting of a synonymous saying (v. 5) and a prohibition (v. 6), that seeks to correct with traditional theology the skepticism of Agur; a later prayer of a pious sage (vv. 7–9); a redactional insertion of a prohibition (v. 10); four sayings of various kinds that describe four categories of wicked people (vv. 11–14); five numerical sayings (vv. 15–16, 18–19, 21–23, 24–28, and 29–31); a redactional insertion of a synonymous saying dealing with retribution against those who do not honor their parents (v. 17); a redactional addition of a synonymous saying about an adulteress (v. 20); and a partial instruction opening with two conditional clauses, continuing with an admonition, and concluding with a comparative saying (vv. 32–33). The partial instruction in verses 32–33 provides a summarizing teaching that embraces the central teaching of the traditional response to the skeptic Agur regarding the sin of arrogance or hubris. This redactor teaches that the student is to cease having pride over what he or she claims to know or not know, to avoid the planning of evil actions that result from a lack of knowledge of God, and to bring to an end the communal strife to which hubris leads.

There is little question that the first four verses, at the very least, were believed by the teachers of Israel to have originated with Agur, the non-Israelite sage to whom the entire somewhat disparate collection of chapter 30 eventually is attributed or that at least is occasioned by his cynicism. The superscription (30:1a) is best read as follows: "The words of Agur, son of Jakeh, the Massa'ite: The oracle of the man." This means that it is more likely that *maśśā'* refers to the name of an Arabian tribe to the east of Israel than to a prophetic speech based on divine revelation. For parallel introductions to oracles or teachings, see the introductions to the oracles of Balaam in Numbers 24 (vv. 3–4 and vv. 15–17) and the "Last Words of David" in 2 Sam. 23:1–7.

The second part of verse 1 is particularly difficult to translate and understand. The "saying of the man" contains a noun, *nĕ'ūm*, that is often associated with ecstatic prophetic speech given as a divine revelation (see Num. 24:3–4, 15–16; 2 Sam. 23:1; and the *nĕ'ūm* of Yahweh in Gen. 22:16; Num. 14:28; Isa. 14:22; 30:1, 31:9; and Ezek. 13:6, 7).

The term is found in the superscription of Habakkuk to refer to the entire vision that he saw concerning the destruction wrought by the Babylonians (Heb. 1:1). Thus, the entire book of Habakkuk is designated by this term. Subsequently, the term *něʾūm* suggests more than a mere observation. It refers to the insight of a "man," who is the source of his own wisdom—not God, not the prophets, and not the wisdom schools. Agur makes no claim for divine revelation as the location of any true wisdom. Some have seen in the parallel introduction to Balaam's oracles in Numbers 24 an indication of some connection between Agur and this seer of the East, in that they both came from the same general geographical region and are understood to have uttered ecstatic speech. This connection, if it may be made at all, is too general to prove any direct association. The term *man* (*geber*) is a general expression for male human being. Thus Agur is introducing his teaching as the word of a mere mortal that has no grounding in divine revelation or in the schools of prophecy and wisdom.

The Hebrew terms *lěʾîtîʾēl* and *ʾūkāl* are understood in different ways. *Lěʾîtîʾēl* and *ʾūkāl*, first of all, could refer to proper names, thus reading "to/for *ʾîtîʾēl*" (see Neh. 11:7), "to/for *ʾîtîʾēl* and *ʾūkāl*." The Targum, or Aramaic translation of this text, and the Syriac in part support this reading. Second, these two terms could be translated as pointing to the futility of trying to use human resources to come to a knowledge of God: "I am weary, O God, I am weary O God. How can I prevail/I am exhausted?" Third, these two terms could be understood as expressing a skeptical, even atheistic view: "There is no God, there is no God. How can I prevail/I am exhausted?" Fourth, the terms could be translated as pointing out the frailty and severe limitations of human knowledge in contrast to divine power and knowledge: "I am not God, I am not God, how can I prevail/I am exhausted?" (see van Leeuwen, *Proverbs,* 250–51). It is highly unlikely that the two Hebrew terms refer to personal names. And it is not at all congruent with the remainder of the collection, and indeed, the entire book of Proverbs, to suggest that the words refer to an atheistic worldview. But it is quite plausible to suggest that with these two expressions, coupled with the expression "the word [*něʾūm*] of a man," Agur is pointing to the limits of human wisdom and humankind's knowledge about God and to his utter exhaustion with attempting to find God through human wisdom or to believe the authenticity of the portrayal of God in prophetic ecstatic speech. It is the word (*něʾūm*) of a man, not God as claimed by the prophets, that Agur concludes is the one and true source of his insight. This would be an ironic use of a prophetic term for ecstatic revelation and its content. For Agur, only God may provide the divine

254

knowledge that would come through prophetic inspiration. Agur makes no claim to such knowledge. Human wisdom cannot come to a knowledge of God (see Job 28, especially v. 28). In so arguing, Agur sets himself in opposition to much of the pious wisdom tradition, which taught that the sages came to a knowledge of God through study, reflection, and obedience to the teachings, later on understood as incorporated in the Torah (Clifford, *Proverbs*, 260–63).

In verses 2–3, Agur then confesses, in a type of internal dialogue or autobiographical narrative (see Ps. 37:35–36 and Prov. 24:30–34) of four parts, that he is "too stupid to be human," that he does not "have human understanding," that he has "not learned wisdom," and that he does not have "knowledge of the holy ones [or One]." The first self-deprecation, that he is "too stupid to be human," is an example of hyperbole similar to other texts where human speakers state that either they or categories of human beings are like brute beasts, too dumb to know the limits of their own knowledge (Pss. 49:11–13; 17–20; 73:21–22; see van Leeuwen, "The Book of Proverbs," 252). The second self-deprecation, that he does not "have human understanding," is in synthetic parallelism with the first. With the third self-deprecation, Agur notes that he has not learned wisdom, in contrast to Israel's sages, whose task it is to create, to learn, to teach, and to transmit wisdom through oral and written sources. Finally, in the fourth self-deprecation, which exists in synthetic parallelism with the third one, Agur says he has no knowledge of either the "holy ones" (i.e., semidivine beings who make up the divine council; see Ps. 89:5 = Heb. 89:6, 7 = Heb. 6; Job 5:1; 15:15; Dan. 8:13; Zech. 14:5; Mullen, *Assembly of the Gods*) or, preferably, the "Holy One," a plural of majesty used to refer to God (see Prov. 9:10). Thus, Agur denies that he has any knowledge of God issued to him by the wisdom teachers or by the prophets in a state of ecstatic revelation (contrast the claim of Eliphaz in Job 4:12–21). His knowledge is that of a mere man, but this does not lessen its veracity. To underline the authenticity of what he says, Agur couches his teaching in the form of rhetorical questions and a concluding taunt.

Verse 4 contains six rhetorical questions about creation:

> Who has ascended to heaven and come down?
> Who has gathered the wind in the hollow of the hand?
> Who has wrapped up the waters in a garment?
> Who has established all the ends of the earth?
> What is the [person's] name?
> And what is [his son's name]?
> Surely you know!

255

If the entire collection (chapter 30) of the "words of Agur" is concerned largely with the sin of exalted self-pride or arrogance, then it may well be that this first section presents in the form of rhetorical questions the theme of rebellion against creation, a mythic theme that, in the ancient Near East, is grounded in hubris (the arrogant pride that leads human beings to reject the rule of heaven). If so, this means that the questions of Agur probably are not asking for information that is beyond human knowledge, that is, are not impossible questions, but more likely are rhetorical questions with obvious answers. The teacher, Agur, would be saying: God, not human beings, has the wisdom and power to rule the cosmos. While the wise redactors would agree with this theme, they deny that sapiential discourse cannot discover something of the nature of God and that Yahweh does not provide the sages insight into the divine character.

The first rhetorical question contains the antithesis of ascending and descending. One may recall Jacob's dream in Gen. 28:10–22, when he sees "angels . . . ascending and descending" a ladder that reaches to heaven. Rousing from his sleep, he names the place of his dream revelation Bethel, or "house of God." The antithesis of "ascending" and "descending" has to do in part with the obtaining of divine knowledge (see the Tower of Babel narrative in Gen. 11:1–9). Thus, Jacob establishes at the site of his dream revelation a sanctuary, Bethel, where divine revelation may occur. In Isa. 14:12–21, the fall of the king of Babylon is described in the language of the myth of "Day Star," a minor Canaanite deity whose hubris leads him to attempt to ascend to the heavens in order to sit on the throne of the high god. His arrogant pride, however, results in his being "brought down" to Sheol when the sun rises and obliterates the fragile light of the ascending star. Ezekiel (chap. 28) uses similar mythical language to describe the fall of the king of Tyre, whose hubris led him to sit on the throne of gods, claiming to be divine. There is no reference to ascending in Ezekiel's account, though it is implied by the description of the king's arrogance leading him to sit on the throne of the gods. Hubris is on occasion described in terms of ascending to heaven. It is that arrogant pride that causes people to believe they can reject divine rule to follow their own selfish ambitions. By contrast, "to go down" (or "being cast down," *yārad*) is sometimes used to describe the fall of the arrogant (Job 20:6; Psalm 73; Isa. 14:14–15; Amos 9:2).

The first question, "Who has ascended to heaven and come down?" is found in a variant form in Mesopotamian texts that have a cynical character. One case in point is the *Dialogue of Pessimism* (circa

1200 B.C.E; see *ANET,* 600–604). In this wisdom text, the master is a rich nobleman who despairs of life and meaningful human activities. Lacking the wisdom to gain release from his despair, he asks his wise slave: "What, then, is good?" The slave, obviously a sage, responds: "To have my neck and your neck broken and to be thrown into the river is good." In undergirding this rather shocking counsel, the wise slave appends two questions:

> Who is so tall as to ascend to the heavens?
> Who is so broad as to compass the underworld?

These related questions in their present context suggest that human wisdom is incapable of discerning the "good in human existence," since the sources of the comprehensive knowledge needed to determine the answer to the nobleman's quest for the good, that is, the gods, are in heaven and beyond human reach. The limitations of mortal existence preclude obtaining such comprehensive knowledge. A similar question occurs in the Gilgamesh epic, in which the semidivine hero eagerly pursues his quest for immortality. Gilgamesh says to Enkidu, prior to their battle with Huwawa, the monster guarding the cedar forest: "Who, my friend, can scale heaven?" (*ANET,* 79). The question is a rhetorical one, expecting at this point in the story "No one" for an answer. The context is that of the gods' decision to reserve immortality for themselves while ordaining death for humanity. Humans may not ascend to the heavens and live forever as gods, but they may obtain a "name" for themselves and live through their fame. These texts, including Agur's first rhetorical question, recognize that human beings lack the capacity to obtain divine wisdom or immortality. Try though some will, they will inevitably fail and fall to their destruction.

In Proverbs 30, Agur emphasizes that he has not been schooled in the wisdom schools of the Near East and that he does not possess the ecstatic divine knowledge claimed by the prophets. Using the mythic language of ascent and descent, Agur points to those lower gods, kings, and semidivine heroes who, filled with hubris, attempted unsuccessfully to scale the heavens to obtain divine knowledge, power, and immortality. But the final result is their failure. They were cast down. The answer to the question "Who has ascended to heaven and come down?" is the group of mythic and legendary beings who attempted to usurp the rule of heaven or to obtain a divine attribute (wisdom or immortality) but in the end failed miserably and fell to their destruction. Heaven will tolerate no rebellion among mortal or even semidivine beings.

257

The next three questions in verse 4 point to divine activities associated with the creative power of God, which God and God alone possesses:

> Who has gathered the wind in the hollow of the hand?
> Who has wrapped up the waters in a garment?
> Who has established all the ends of the earth?

The expression "gathering the wind" occurs twice more in the Old Testament: Job 34:14–15 and Ps. 104:29. Each of these texts points to God's power to take back ("gather") his divine, life-giving spirit. This action leads to the death of all living creatures. In Prov. 30:4 the image is similar. Here, however, the metaphor moves from that of breathing out and breathing in the life-giving spirit to folding it up in the hands. Only the Creator has the power to give life by means of releasing the divine spirit or wind and to remove it by taking it back.

The next rhetorical question centers on the activity of wrapping the waters in a garment, a creation image that appears in Job 26:8: "He [God] binds up the waters in his thick clouds." God is the one who places rain in the clouds and commands it to pour forth on the earth to bring and sustain life. No human being has that power (see Job 38:25–27).

The "ends of the earth" in the next rhetorical question refers to the outermost boundaries of the cosmos (Deut. 33:17; Ps. 59:13 = Heb. 59:14), including even those regions that stand in opposition to divine rule (1 Sam. 2:10; Ps. 2:8–9). God "establishes" with these boundaries the orderly limits of creation, differentiating between chaos and cosmos. In Job, Yahweh speaks of helping the birthing of chaos and then establishes bars and doors and commands, "Thus far shall you come, and no farther, and here shall your proud waves be stopped" (Job 38:8–11).

The fifth and sixth rhetorical questions, "What is [his] name? And what is [his son's name]?" drive home the point: only God—not humans, not even semidivine heroes or lower gods, and not their offspring—has the strength and wisdom to create and sustain the cosmos. Agur has learned this from his own understanding and not from the wisdom of the schools or the ecstatic revelation of the prophets and seers. When humans assume for themselves the ability to obtain divine wisdom and power, along with other characteristics, such as immortality, reserved for God alone, and the ability to rule as God, their arrogance leads to rebellion against the Creator and Ruler of the universe and threatens the divine order of cosmos and history. Agur's concluding taunt, "Surely you know!" underscores his point: no human or human child has the divine wisdom and power to scale the heavens and to rule the cosmos as God.

In verses 5–6, a pious sage, probably a later redactor, changed the text into a dialogue between a cynical sage (Agur) and a religious one (unnamed). The redaction of cynical wisdom is found elsewhere in Job (see Job 28:28) and Qoheleth (Eccl. 12:9–14). The pious sage responds to Agur with his affirmation that "every word of God proves true." In this way, the sage affirms the traditional belief of the wise that their wisdom ultimately rests in the fear of God and faith in God's power to serve as a refuge. Agur is rebuked for creating this cynical portrait of wisdom's limitations and thus risks God's rebuke and discovery as a liar.

Verses 7–9 incorporate the one sapiential prayer found in the book of Proverbs. This prayer follows, appropriately, the response of the pious sage in verses 5–6. The prayer consists of four parts: the divine petition (v. 7), the first request (v. 8a), the second request (v. 8b–c), and the evil results that will occur if the petition is not granted (v. 9). In the divine petition (v. 7), God is asked to give to the pious sage two requests. These are removal of falsehood and lying (v. 8a), and the giving, not of wealth or of poverty, but only of sufficient victuals that the petitioner needs to survive. Falsehood and lying may be general character flaws that could disrupt the effort to live in concert with divine justice or, more specifically, evils in the court of law that could lead to the abuse of justice. The desire to have only what is necessary to live provides a medium ground between poverty—a situation usually detested by the sages, who saw in it neither a desired virtue nor a necessary context for developing a life of self-denial—and wealth—a normally desirable possession if obtained and maintained by righteous, not wicked, means. The concluding potential results, if the petitioner's two requests of God are not granted, are satisfaction that leads to the denial of God or poverty that results in theft and the profanation of the name of God. "Satisfaction" may refer to one's appetite or hunger being sated (Isa. 19:19; 44:16; Hos. 4:10). This type of satiation may lead to human arrogance and a forgetting or denial of God as the giver of sustenance, a dominant theme in Proverbs 30 (see Deut. 6:10–15; 8:11–20; 31:20; Hos. 13:6). A more general sense of satiation refers to having abundance and desiring even more, a sin that exposes one to the danger of arrogance (see Prov. 27:20; 30:15). To "profane" (literally, "to grasp") the name of God refers to the character of humans who engage in unlawful acts, in this case stealing, that allows them to think they are God, for they own and rule everything. "Name" is often a divine title to refer either to God or to the reality of God, who is present through the name, including when it is invoked, and yet remains

259

transcendent (see Deut. 12:5; 2 Sam. 7:13; 1 Kings 9:3; 11:36; Isa. 30:27). Thus the name of God is a theological effort to speak of divine presence and revelation while still holding onto the concept of other-worldliness. To steal not only may involve taking what is not one's own but also may refer to the hubris of thinking that all that is belongs to the thief. In granting the petition, God allows the petitioner to recognize that it is God who is the owner and giver of every good gift and not human beings.

The prohibition in verse 10 is a later redactional insertion that continues the theme of arrogance. Reflecting the context of the household, the sage is not to slander or talk about a servant to his or her master. The verb *lāšan,* meaning "slander," is found only here and in Ps. 101:5. In the latter text, slandering of the neighbor results in the destruction of the slanderer by God. This expression also has to do with arrogance, something that God will not tolerate. In Prov. 30:10, the slave who is slandered will utter a power-laden curse designed to call upon divine power to destroy the perpetrator of the slander. To be found "guilty" possibly alludes to God's retributive justice that will not tolerate such injustice.

Verses 11–14 consist of four descriptive sayings that set forth four categories of wicked people: those who curse their fathers and do not bless their mothers (v. 11), those who are pure in their own eyes and yet are not cleansed of their filth (v. 12), the haughty ones (v. 13), and those whose teeth shall devour the poor. While the condemnation of these four categories is not stated, it is obvious that they and their acts are rebuked.

Cursing and blessing parents is an important theme in Israelite law and derives from the context of the household traditions. Much of the authority of the Israelite and Jewish family was vested in the father or head of the household. In this life situation, the authority of the senior male manifested itself in every area of family life, including economics, teaching of the ancestral traditions and the practical matters of daily existence, judging family disputes, arranging marriages with other households, and deciding which male heir would assume the head's role when he became incapacitated or died. Even the power of life and death resided at times in the hands of the household's father (see Gen. 19:8; 38:24; and Exod. 21:7–11). Married sons remained under the authority of the head of the household until the father died or became incapable of fulfilling his role. In the household, women, including the mother, were legally subordinate to men, first their husbands and then their household head. The mother provided the household progeny and cared for her children; performed important economic tasks that included weaving, making wool, cooking, and sewing; and experienced an authority in the immediate family that was second only to that of her husband. Legislation and tradition demanded that she be respected and obeyed (Exod. 20:12; Lev. 19:3; Prov. 19:26; 20:20; 23:22; 30:17; Sir. 3:1–16). Disrespect and disobedience were prohibited (Exod. 21:15, 17; Lev. 20:9; Deut. 21:18; 27:16). Children who were rebellious in their actions could be executed (Deut. 21:18–21). As noted earlier, cursing invoked the divine name to unleash a destructive force that would harm, even destroy its object. Blessing, by contrast, drew on the power of the divine name to create a sphere of well-being and good fortune for its recipient. Those who did not bless their parents were condemned, as were those who cursed them. Indeed, whoever cursed his or her parents was to be executed (Exod. 21:15; see Deut. 27:16).

The second category of wicked people consists of the self-righteous, those who are "pure in their own eyes," who do not recognize their own filthiness. Self-righteousness is a detested vice in Proverbs and is condemned (see Prov. 20:9).

The third category consists of the arrogant, those who have haughty eyes. This fits well the dominant theme of chapter 30 and especially the sin that Agur unveils in speaking of those who attempt to reign in the place of God. "Haughty eyes" (NRSV "lofty eyes") are a symbol for arrogance elsewhere in the Old Testament (2 Sam. 22:28; Ps. 18:27; Prov. 6:17).

The fourth and final category of wicked and evil persons consists of those whose sharp teeth devour the poor and needy. This sin may involve not only the refusal of hospitality to charity cases because of greed but also the avarice that leads to the desire to have even what little the poor possess to sustain themselves (see Amos 2:6–8).

Verses 15–31 chiefly consist of five numerical sayings: four appetites that are never satiated (vv. 15–16), four things that leave no trace (vv. 18–19), four circumstances that disturb the social and cosmic order (vv. 21–23), four things that are small yet wise (vv. 24–28), and four things that are stately in their gait (vv. 29–31). Inserted by a later redactor are two synonymous sayings about the dishonoring of parents (v. 17; see v. 11) and the adulteress who denies her guilt (v. 20; see v. 19).

A title line normally initiates a numerical saying, which then lists two or more things that hold some feature or features in common with the beginning. The list contains at least two and often more things that share something in common. In Amos 1—2, the prophet uses this traditional wisdom form to speak of transgressions committed by the

261

neighbors of Israel: "For three transgressions of X, and for four, I will not revoke the punishment." This list serves as the prophetic indictment in a judgment speech that then leads to the sentence of punishment against the perpetrator of evil. In Prov. 6:16–19, the title line refers to seven things that Yahweh hates and that are an abomination: haughty eyes, a lying tongue, hands that shed innocent blood, a heart that devises wicked plans, feet that hurry to commit evil, a false witness, and one who sows discord in the family. The first five are parts of the human anatomy that are used in the committing of evil, while the last two refer to behavior that disrupts the social order.

Verses 15–16 contain the first numerical saying in the collection of Agur. It speaks of four appetites that are never satiated. The title line in verse 15 has been expanded by the partial presence of a synonymous saying in verse 15a: the leech that has two daughters who continue to cry for blood to feed their unquenchable appetites. Who the two daughters are is not continued in the tradition, since only the first part of the saying was preserved when attached to the initial numerical saying found in verses 15b–16.

This numerical saying has in common with the synonymous proverb the theme of three, even four things that are never satisfied: "Sheol, the barren womb, the earth ever thirsty for water, and the fire that never says, 'Enough.'" Sheol in the Old Testament is the land of the underworld where the dead dwell. In mythic terms, Sheol is often personified as a hungry deity or demonic power, ever devouring the living with its gaping jaws and open mouth (Prov. 1:12; Isa. 5:14; Hab. 2:5). Sheol's appetite knows no limits.

The barren womb refers to the social view in ancient Israel and early Judaism that the primary worth of a married women lay in her ability to produce many children. In the Old Testament, one finds numerous texts that illustrate the desire of households to have many children (Gen. 15:5; 22:7; 24:60; 26:4; Ruth 4:11–12). Barrenness, attributed to the inability of the wife to conceive and bear offspring, was considered to be a divine test or punishment and a cause of great disgrace (Gen. 16:2; 30:2; 1 Sam. 1:3–11). The household's desire for many progeny was due to such considerations as the economic impact that children would have as laborers on the household estate and the preservation of patrimony, for it was by offspring that the household estate would be inherited and thus continued. It was usually the case that the firstborn male would inherit the largest part of the estate and would replace the father as the head of the household. In this way, the name of the family would continue through the ages, allowing for a type of corporate immortality. Finally, faithful children were necessary in providing a system of care for aged parents and in seeing to it that they received a proper burial in the family tomb. Failure to produce offspring caused the wife to desire continuing acts of intercourse in order to conceive, and she would never be satisfied until her barren womb was opened to conception and the bearing of children (see Hannah in 1 Samuel 1–2).

The third insatiable appetite, that of the earth for water, clearly derives from Israel's climatic features. The climate of Israel, located in the northern margin of the subtropical zone, shifts slightly to the south during the winter. Summer in Israel went almost without rain, and almost all the moisture came during the winter season, which still is mild but from time to time experiences storms and significant rain. To the east, southwest, and south Israel had deserts of the subtropical zone. Rainfall slowly decreased from the coastal plain region inland and from north to south. Since Israelites and Jews lived in a region that bordered the desert, existence in this marginal space was precarious. Without rainfall in the valleys and western hill country during the winter, droughts would ensue, leading to famine and starvation. The dryness of the summer period began from May or June and lasted until September. Rain was rare except in the northernmost area in June and was almost totally absent in July and August. The winter season, running from late September or early October to May, was the period for most of the rainfall, an essential meteorological feature that, if absent, spelled disaster for the population and the animals and crops on which it depended for its survival. Given this climate, the earth would appear to the sage ever to be thirsty, even in the wetter portions of Israel to the east and north, and in constant need of rain in order to make life possible. Though wells and cisterns could sustain a population for a time by capturing the excess rain and reaching underground to draw from subterranean springs, rainfall was essential for human survival in this climate. Precipitation was barely sufficient and could be interrupted, as is suggested by the droughts and famines mentioned in the Old Testament (see Gen. 41:54; 1 Kings 17:1; 2 Kings 8:1).

The fourth insatiable appetite belongs to fire. While fire often was a symbol for theophany or judgment, the sage here speaks of fire that in its burning consumes all combustibles with which it comes into contact. Fire has no appetite that is finally satiated, for it burns continuously as long as there is fuel available for consumption.

The second numerical saying appears in verses 18–19. This saying refers to four wonderful things that even the sage cannot understand: the way of an eagle in the sky, the way of a snake on a rock, the way of a ship on the high seas, and the way of a man with a girl. What all four

263

have in common is movement that leaves no trace to suggest any motion or its cause has been present. The last example, the way of a man with a maid, refers to sexual intercourse that leaves no external trace to prove the act has occurred.

Verses 21–23, the third numerical saying, speak of four circumstances that disturb the social and cosmic order, or that cause the earth "to quake/tremble." These are a slave who becomes a king, a fool who is full, an unloved woman who gets a husband, and a maid when she succeeds her mistress (see van Leeuwen, "Proverbs 30:21–23," 599–610). The element held in common by these four examples is that people of low standing, should they reach a higher or more desirable position or when they are content with food, become arrogant and destructive to social and thus to cosmic order. For the sages, the social and cosmic worlds were inextricably linked. Hence, when disorder existed in society, it had a deleterious effect on the community and caused the world "to quake/tremble." The sages could not imagine that slaves, usually either foreigners taken in war or hopelessly indebted Hebrews, could ever become kings. If such were to happen, the entire social order would collapse.

The second case for causing the cosmos to quake or tremble is the fool whose stomach is full. The fool in wisdom literature usually did not have enough to satiate his appetite because of his sloth and his lack of planning when it came to farming (Prov. 6:6–11; 24:30–34), for he failed to respond positively to the teachings of the sages to work hard and to be prepared for the times beyond the harvest. A fool who ignores the teachings of the wise yet achieves a full stomach, however, would pose a threat to the integrity of sapiential discourse and instruction. This, too, considered almost impossible to the wise, would result in the "quaking of the earth."

The third example of social disruption and cosmic disorder is that a woman unloved, despised, or perhaps "spurned" by suitors for unstated reasons, which could include many possibilities (divorce, sexual defilement, abuse, or homeliness; see Deut. 22:13–14; 24:3; 2 Sam. 13:15), becomes wed and ultimately leads to ruin the man who married her. This marriage would inevitably result in discord and cause the social order of the community, grounded in the union of male and female, to be upset.

The fourth and final example of an unacceptable social outcome that causes the earth "to quake/tremble" is that of a maiden, usually a lowly servant who performs only menial tasks (Exod. 11:5; 1 Sam. 25:41; 2 Sam. 17:17), who supplants her mistress, say, by catching the eye of her lady's husband, only to cause him great duress even as she

264

makes life difficult for the one whom formerly she had served (see the rivalry between Sarah and Hagar in Genesis 16 and 21). The maid normally would not possess the social graces and training to lead the household's internal workings to the profit of her husband and family; and, to her disadvantage, she would rival the mistress in seeking the favor of her lord.

The important feature of this numerical saying is the view that the upheaval of the social order leads to the "quaking" or "trembling" of the earth. In theophanic texts this refers to earthquakes that mythology describes as the reaction of the created order to the Divine Warrior, who comes to do battle against chaos, in either mythic or historical form (Job 9:6; Ps. 77:16–20; Isa. 13:13; Joel 2:10; Amos 8:8–10). Social upheaval, warns this saying, leads to cosmic disorder. What happens in Israelite society affects creation, for both are grounded in a just and proper order.

In this redactional setting, then, Agur is not reinterpreted as a skeptic who denies either the existence of God or the possibility of discovering at least a limited wisdom, though he boasts he has achieved its insight as a mere mortal untrained in the wisdom schools. As a common man, he comes to the striking realization that it is God alone who is the Creator and Sustainer of the earth. Hubris, or arrogant pride, is the one sin that stimulates the human quest to obtain sovereignty over creation and the unwillingness of humans to accept their place in the cosmic and social order. Once unleashed, hubris has the capacity to disturb in serious ways the cosmic and social order.

The fourth numerical saying in verses 24–28 describes four things that are small and weak yet wise: ants, badgers, locusts, and lizards. Their wisdom is due to their ability to provide food when it is summer by storing it during the harvest (ants), to have a home in the rocks that gives them security from harm even though they are small (badgers), to march in rank even without a king (locusts), or to live in royal palaces even though they may be grasped in the hand (lizards). These references to nature, as a part of natural theology and the cosmic order, indicate to humans that even though these creatures are small and without strength, they, too, may possess the wisdom that leads to their survival by means of food, homes, and order. By extension, humans, not through arrogant pride but through wisdom that is God-given, have the capacity to survive and dwell secure.

The fifth and final numerical saying occurs in verses 29–31 and refers to four things that are stately in their gait: the lion, which is the mightiest of all wild creatures; the rooster; the he-goat; and the king riding before his people. What these have in common is power,

265

strength, and orderly rule over their various communities: a pride of lions and lionesses, a he-goat who leads other goats and sheep, the rooster who is master of his hens, and the ruler who reigns over his people. The strutting by all four groups is not necessarily a negative element, though it can be when pride enters the heart and these creatures begin to think that they alone rule over their respective groups. In the context of the collection of Agur, where hubris is a dominant theme, the redactor who adds this numerical saying probably has in mind this misbegotten sense of self-importance. Only God is the creator and ruler of the cosmos and nature, and those who lead in nature and in human society are but chosen vessels through whom divine rule is to be recognized and expressed.

There are inserted within the list of these five sayings two synonymous sayings that are not directly related to the content and structure of the collection of Agur in chapter 30. Retributive theology is found in verse 17 and centers on the punishment that comes to those whose eye mocks their fathers and disobeys their mothers. Those who show this unacceptable dishonoring of their parents are metaphorically described as those condemned to be blinded by ravens that peck out the eye, which is devoured by vultures. As noted above, parents were to be honored by their children through obedience, care in old age, and a proper burial at death. Rebellious and insolent children could expect to receive the wrath of their parents and even execution by the community. The family system of order could not be disturbed if stability and well-being for the household, the larger community, and the cosmos were to be maintained. The synonymous saying in verse 20 returns to the common theme of adultery in the book of Proverbs (see 2:16–19; 5:15–23; 7:1–27; 9:13–18) and perhaps was placed here by a wise redactor because of the image of undetectable sexual activity in the last line of the preceding numerical saying in verses 18–19. Adultery was to be punished, normally by execution of the guilty partners (Deut. 22:22–24; Ezek. 18:11–13; 22:11; Mal. 3:5), since this act of immorality violated the right of the husband to have sole sexual possession of his wife (Exod. 20:14; Lev. 18:20; Deut. 5:18). In his oath of innocence in chapter 31, Job refers to this immoral act as a terrible crime worthy of the enslavement of his wife and the possession of her body by others (Job 31:9–12). In this saying in Prov. 30:20; it is little wonder that an adulteress would declare her innocence after wiping from her mouth the spittle or semen of her lover.

266

The collection of Agur in its final redaction concludes with verses 32–33. A redactor belonging to the wisdom school that added to and then handed down this collection brought it to an end with a partial instruction that begins with two conditional clauses (v. 32a–b), continues with an admonition that forms the center of the teaching (v. 33c), and concludes with a comparative saying. The admonition underscores the meaning of not only this partial instruction but, indeed, the entire collection attributed to Agur. Putting the hand to the mouth was a sign of reverence when one approached God or a human superior (see Job 40:3–5). In the context of this collection, the admonition stresses that one should stand in reverence before the awesome Creator, who originates and sustains the cosmic order. This reverence, acknowledged by silence and the symbolic gesture of placing the hand on the mouth, should replace any human hubris that conceives of a person as ruling the world. The preceding two conditional clauses support this interpretation. If one has been foolish through the act of self-exaltation or through the devising of evil that assumes one can engage in acts that subvert heaven's rule, then that person is entirely misguided. Finally, the admonition to be silent and to show reverence before the Creator of the cosmos and the divine Ruler of justice concludes with the analogy that even as pressing the nose causes bleeding, so pressing anger causes strife. Arrogance and anger disrupt the social order and set the cosmos on its end. Silent respect in the face of the awesome and fearful Creator and Sustainer is the proper attitude that should characterize the true sage. Thus the sages would have agreed with Agur about the danger of pride and its associated vices, but they disagreed that they could not come to a divine revelation, at least indirectly, through their traditions that incorporated the wisdom of God.

Conclusion

This collection was built up over several centuries, beginning with the assertion of an Eastern man who, while not schooled in wisdom, claimed to possess a limited knowledge based on his own observations and conclusions. He rejected the affirmation of schooled sages that they had access to divine wisdom and thus a full revelation of God. Agur regarded these audacious claims to be grounded in a sapiential arrogance and not in the reality of authentic epistemology. For him, only God had the wisdom and power to rule the cosmos, and God chose to do so ensconced in mystery. Not content to allow this criticism to remain unchallenged, traditional Israelite sages responded that every divine word, including those that they had received, proves true. Thus, true wisdom, to which they had access, rested in the fear of God and faith in divine power to serve as their refuge. A pious prayer then follows, seeking of God only what is necessary to live and the removal

267

of falsehood from the petitioner. If the petition is not granted, then satisfaction leading to arrogance and a denial of God, poverty resulting in theft, and profaning the divine name are the possible consequences.

Arrogance continues as a major theme in verses 10–14, leading to a rejection of God, slander, self-righteousness, and the devouring of the poor. Five numerical sayings compare unsatisfied appetites, things that leave no trace, circumstances that disrupt the social and cosmic order, things that are small yet wise, and things that are stately in their gait. Arrogance is again the major sin that is directly or indirectly challenged. The traditional, partial instruction at the end teaches that reverence before God should remove arrogance from the human heart.

Theology

God in this sixth collection is seen in two contrasting ways. For Agur, the sage of the East, God does not reveal to humans a direct knowledge of his ways and power, and no human, regardless of how arrogant or powerful, has ever succeeded in obtaining the gift of divine wisdom and the power to create and sustain the cosmos. By contrast, the traditional sages who appended the remainder of the collection to the wisdom of Agur in verses 1–4 conclude that the divine word always proves true and suggest that they are the recipients of this knowledge. God is the one to whom the pious sage turns for food and to avoid the arrogance that leads to blasphemy and the denial of the Almighty. Overall, God is revealed to the pious sage, rules the world in justice, and maintains its order through righteous oversight. Human arrogance is the sin that is largely of concern in both Agur's teaching and the appended sections. Only God has the power to rule the cosmos and human society through the just system of retribution (Boström, *God of the Sages,* 90–140).

The Seventh Collection

"The Words of King Lemuel of Massa,Which His Mother Taught Him"

PROVERBS 31:1–9

Date and Provenance

The "words of King Lemuel" in Prov. 31:1–9 comprises the seventh collection of the book of Proverbs (Crenshaw, "A Mother's Instruction to Her Son," 383–95). The instruction comes from the mother of Lemuel, most likely the queen mother, who instructed her royal son, newly installed as king, with a brief teaching dealing with just rule (Andreason, "Role of the Queen Mother," 179–94). As noted in the commentary on the preceding collection, the "words of Agur," Massa is likely an Arabian tribe located in the East. The name appears to refer to a migratory Arabian tribe that first appears in Assyrian sources as Mas'aia in the late eighth century B.C.E., having as its possible territory migratory routes to the east of Israel, in Arabia, Edom, the Transjordan, or beyond Seir (see Gen. 25:14; 1 Chron. 1:30). Thus Lemuel is a non-Jewish ruler from the East who is instructed by his queen mother in the ways of proper rule (see 1 Kings 4:29–34 = Heb. 5:9–14; Job and his friends Eliphaz, Bildad, and Zophar).

Queen mothers, while possessing great influence because they bore and reared the male heir apparent to the throne, rarely ever came to sit on the thrones of the ancient Near East. In Israel, one exception was Athaliah, who took the throne after the death of her son, Ahaziah (2 Kings 11:1). She ruled for seven years until Joash, her grandson and a descendant of David, was placed on the throne by a palace and temple coup. She was executed by the captains of the army at the command of the chief priest Jehoiada (1 Kings 11). In the New Kingdom (the eighteenth dynasty), Queen Hatshepsut of Egypt (1490–1469 B.C.E.) may have been a similar case. She assumed the throne when her half brother and husband Thutmose II died, leaving a male child,

Thutmose III, as his heir. The youth of the new pharaoh allowed his aunt and stepmother Hatshepsut to become senior co-regent and ultimately king, a position held until her death when her senior co-regency ended and Thutmose III was mature enough to rule Egypt alone. The queen mother in Egypt, Mesopotamia, among the Hittites, and in Israel and Judah had great influence in the kingdoms mentioned. In Judah, the queen mother likely was an official position, and she had a throne next to her son's (1 Kings 2:19). She is mentioned in connection with her ruling son (Jer. 13:18; 22:26; 29:2). There may have been a similar position in the North, that is, in Israel (1 Kings 14:21; 15:2, 10). Zeruah (1 Kings 11:26) and Jezebel (2 Kings 9:22) are the only queen mothers whose names are preserved in the Northern Kingdom.

Victor Turner has argued that instructions are often given during periods of transition (liminality) from one social status to another (*Ritual Process*). Thus it is not infrequently the case that there are royal instructions issued to kings newly installed or in the process of assuming the throne as a part of the rites of passage. It is during these occasions that the young ruler is most open to instruction and is thus provided guidance on the proper conduct befitting a king. In ancient Egypt, royal instructions have been found from the Old Kingdom continuing into the New Kingdom. These instructions consisted of two introductions: the first included a title giving the name of the writing (an instruction) and the titular and personal name of the teacher. The second inserted an introduction between the title and the instruction. The title was followed by an instruction proper, consisting of a series of admonitions and exhortations in the second person and, occasionally, third-person sayings that were used to support the truthfulness of what was taught. The presence of first-person speech may at times be detected. At times such instructions concluded with an epilogue or an exordium in which the scribe who wrote or copied the instruction spoke of the text he had transmitted and of himself. Two examples of this more simplified form are illustrated by the *Instruction of Hordedef* (*ANET,* 419–20) and the *Instruction for King Merikare* (*ANET,* 414–18). A more developed type of teaching inserted a prologue or narrative between the title and the instruction proper. This suggests that the narrative had a separate literary history but still served to provide the largely fictional setting for the teaching. Examples of this expanded type of teaching include the *Instruction of Ptah-hotep* (*ANET,* 412–14), the *Instruction of Amenemhet,* and the *Instruction of Amen-em-Opet* (*ANET,* 421–25). In providing a narrative setting, the biography usually speaks of a ruler or vizier who is about to enter or has just been installed in office, who receives counsel in the form of sapiential teaching. At times, royal instructions were

270

viewed as teachings from dead rulers, who thus legitimated the reign of their successors. These instructions may have been read during the New Year's enthronement festival that inaugurated the new king's rule.

In Israel and Judah, two examples of royal instructions may be discerned within the literary corpus of the Old Testament: the "Testament of David" (1 Kings 2:1–12) and the "Words of Lemuel" (Prov. 31:1–9). In the example of David, he is now grown old and approaching his death. He undertakes to instruct his successor and co-regent, Solomon, in how to rule the United Kingdom wisely and well. In the teaching before us, the "Words of Lemuel," the queen mother warns her son against the dangers of loose women and of strong drink. In addition, she emphasizes his role in maintaining justice in general and especially for the weaker members of society. While no narrative exists to provide concrete details about the setting of the instruction, it may be surmised that the context is the instruction of a newly installed king by his mother; or at least he is about to assume the throne, during a ritual of passage from being a crown prince to becoming the ruler of the tribe. Perhaps his royal father has recently died, and Lemuel is replacing him as king. Perhaps one should add here that the form and teaching of these instructions are quite similar to Egyptian grave biographies and Jewish testament literature.

Literary Structure and Interpretation

The literary structure of "the words of Lemuel" consists of two major parts: the superscription (v. 1) and the instruction proper (vv. 2–9). The instruction proper consists of an autobiographical warning (v. 2), a prohibition against liaisons with loose women (v. 3), a more lengthy section consisting of prohibitions and admonitions about strong drink (vv. 4–7), and a section comprised of admonitions exhorting the new ruler to rule righteously and especially to speak out for the rights of the poor and destitute.

The queen mother in verse 2 issues an autobiographical warning consisting of two prohibitions (*mâ, mâ,* = literally, "what") in synthetic parallelism. The Hebrew interrogative pronoun *mâ,* "what," may be used as an emphatic rhetorical negative (Judg. 11:12; 2 Sam. 16:10; 19:23; 1 Kings 17:18; 2 Kings 3:13; 2 Chron. 35:21; Jer. 2:18; 23:28). This use of "what" expects "no" or "nothing at all" for an answer from the son. The term also underscores the shock the mother would experience if the behavior she repudiates in her teaching were incorporated in her son's character. In other words, what follows in the instruction is fitting neither for the wise nor for royal rule. Three times

271

she addresses the recipient of her instruction as her "son," leading one to conclude unreservedly that, in agreement with the superscription, her biological son is being addressed. The son is called first the "son of my womb," a common expression for the woman's uterus (Gen. 25:23–24; 38:27; Job 10:19; Eccl. 11:5; Ps. 139:13; Hos. 12:4). The term for "son" (*bar*) is the Aramaic equivalent of Hebrew *bēn* (see Ezra 5:1–2; 6:10, 14; 7:21; Dan. 5:22; 6:25). This does not suggest a late date for the text necessarily, since Aramaic was a common language in the ancient Near East, especially in non-Israelite circles during the period before the establishment of the Israelite monarchy in the eleventh century B.C.E. Aramaic texts exist in abundance from the tenth and ninth centuries B.C.E. It was a commonly used language in the Assyrian kingdom from the eleventh to the late sixth century B.C.E.

The expression in synthetic parallelism to the above is "son of my vows" (see Clifford, *Proverbs*, 270). A vow in ancient Israel was a promise to God to perform some act in return for either divine protection or a gift. Examples include Jephthah's promise to sacrifice whoever would be the first to meet him from his house after battle, in exchange for a victory against the Ammonites (Judg. 11:30–31); Absalom's worship of Yahweh in exchange for being accepted back by his father David (2 Sam. 15:7–12); and Jonah's sailors casting him into the sea and offering sacrifices and making vows to Yahweh (Jonah 1:6). The closest example to that of Lemuel's mother, however, is Hannah's prayer to God for a son. In return for receiving a boy, she pledged that she would devote him to temple service at Shiloh (1 Sam. 1:11). It may be that the queen mother is alluding to this type of vow, which she would have made with her deity in exchange for the gift of a son who would become eventually the crown prince destined to rule over the tribe of Massa.

Verse 3 is a prohibition in which the queen mother warns the new king not to give his strength to women, to those who have the power to destroy his kingship. The term "strength" refers to the "ability or efficiency" of a person, usually intimating moral worth. The term is found in Prov. 12:4 and 31:10 to refer to a woman whose moral integrity is of great benefit to her husband. Though the term may also refer to wealth (Gen. 34:29; Num. 31:9; Deut. 8:17–18; Job 5:5; 15:29; Prov. 13:22) or to a military force (Exod. 14:4, 9, 17, 28; 15:4) or to physical strength (1 Sam. 2:4; Ps. 18:32 = Heb. 18:33, 39 = Heb. 40; Job 21:7; Eccl. 10:10), it appears that the queen mother has in mind more the moral worth of her son, the new ruler, whose integrity is not to be sacrificed in pursuing liaisons of intimacy with women. Perhaps the best contrast is Solomon, whose huge number of wives and concubines, including foreigners who were devotees of other gods, led to his building for them sanctuaries to engage in worship of strange deities. The Deuteronomistic History explains that this was the major reason for Solomon's apostasy and the breakup of the United Kingdom through revolution against the house of David after Solomon's demise (see 1 Kings 11–12). This prohibition fits a common theme in Proverbs involving the "strange" woman, whose fornication or prostitution was a major temptation leading to the entrapment of youthful school boys (see Proverbs 7). Thus the queen mother warns her son, who has recently become king, not to lose his integrity in the pursuit of women who have the power to destroy his kingship.

Verses 4–7 comprise the next section of this instruction. It elaborates the common theme in Proverbs to avoid "strong drink." The drinking of wine was usually viewed with disdain in the Old Testament. The drunken Noah in Gen. 9:20–27, the condemnations of wine and its misuse in the prophets (Isa. 5:11; Hos. 4:11; Micah 2:11; and Hab. 2:5), and especially Proverbs (20:1; 21:17; 23:20–21, 31–35; 26:4–5) all indicate the treachery of wine and its abuse. In part, this frequent condemnation was due to the evil effects of the substance, and perhaps it was even a reaction against the Canaanites, who grew vineyards to produce wine to drink and to use as libations in the worship of their fertility deities. In reaction to the Canaanites, the Nazirites (Num. 6:3; Judg. 13:4, 7, 14), and the Rechabites abstained from wine (Jer. 35:6–7). Used in moderation, however, wine was praised by some writers as the gift of Yahweh (Gen. 27:28; Ps. 104:15; Eccl. 10:19; Amos 9:13; Zech. 10:7). The warning of the queen mother to her son to avoid altogether the drinking of wine is based on the evil effects of the drug and the state of drunkenness that attended its overuse. Since wine had a deleterious effect on the wise and righteous thought and behavior of kings, she counseled Lemuel to avoid its use. The drink should be reserved for the dying, those in great distress, and the poor, in order to ease their pain and to forget their misery.

Finally, in verses 8–9, the queen mother instructs her son, the new ruler, to defend human rights and especially those of the poor, who have no one else to speak out on their behalf. The ruler especially had the responsibility for the establishment and maintenance of justice in the land. In the Old Testament, Yahweh is often described in legal terminology as the one who is righteous, that is, the judge who upholds the rights of all citizens (Pss. 9:4, 8; 50:6; 96:13; 99:4; Isa. 5:16; 58:2; Jer. 11:20). Yahweh's justice is redemptive acts to maintain the rights of Israelite citizens and strangers (Ps. 40:10; 51:14; Isa. 61:10). The poor and downtrodden in particular were the ones whom Yahweh and

273

his representatives, especially the Israelite kings, were to save, protect, and defend (Psalm 72). In this way, order as justice permeated society and enabled the community to live in concert with cosmic righteousness, the force used by God in creating and maintaining the world. Failure to maintain justice, especially for the poor, led to the undermining of human rule and the punishment of the community.

Conclusion

The "words of King Lemuel" are part of a rite of passage for a new ruler who is assuming or has just assumed the throne. The queen mother issues her son an instruction on how to rule properly, wisely, and justly in his new position. The sages borrowed this teaching from the Arabian tribe of Massa and incorporated it into their collections, to be passed down through the generations. The universality of wisdom was recognized by Israelite and Jewish sages who stressed that wise teachings, especially those derived from the East, could be borrowed, issued, and disseminated as authentic wisdom that could be adapted to Israelite and Jewish use.

The date of this collection is difficult to determine, although it would best fit a period when kingship was a living institution in Israel and/or Judah. Thus it is probably a teaching from the eighth or seventh century B.C.E. that was issued as an exemplar for young rulers, especially in the house of David, to study and to incorporate in their behavior, particularly when they came to the throne. Other students learned what was to be expected of their rulers once they assumed the position of king.

Theology

While there is no mention of God in the instruction, there is considerable interest in the justice of the ruler, who in Israel and Judah ruled on behalf of God. Justice was the goal to be reached in the ruler's reign in order that the community might be permeated with righteousness and learn to live in concert with world order. Particularly striking here and in the "words of Agur" is the recognition of Israel's and Judah's sages that wisdom is a universal phenomenon accessible to all. God is implied, therefore, to be the cosmic ruler who grants his wisdom to all peoples. Although Israelites and Jews liked to compare themselves favorably as the special reservoir of divine wisdom (see especially Sirach 24), all peoples could come to a knowledge of God and the rule of justice through their access to divine teachings (see Rankin, *Israel's Wisdom Literature*, 9–15).

The Eighth Collection

The Ideal Wise Woman

PROVERBS 31:10–31

Date and Provenance

This acrostic poem on the "woman of worth" (NRSV "capable wife") is probably a postexilic wisdom text that originated in Judah (see Camp, *Wisdom and the Feminine in the Book of Proverbs*). The evidence for this late dating is largely indirect; there is, however, no reference here to the Israelite or Judahite monarchy or kingdom. The "woman of worth" herself assumes certain royal attributes, including strength and dignity in verse 25 (see v. 17) and charity to the poor and needy (v. 20). In addition, the household is the major social institution, not the larger community. The household has a long and storied history as an Israelite and Jewish institution and could fit almost any biblical period, but the lack of any reference to the larger social framework may suggest that the kingdom had ceased to exist and had been replaced by Judah's colonial status in the Babylonian and possibly the Persian empires.

The household as the central social institution in Israel has many continuous characteristics (Perdue et al., *Families in Ancient Israel*). First, most households in ancient Israel were rural and agrarian, though the larger structures of the clans and tribes are characterized by the existence of small villages of related families whose farmland existed adjacent to the community of dwellings for human occupation. Households in ancient Israel and Judah were multigenerational and usually consisted of two or three families related by kinship and marriage. Households were normally patrilineal (descent was through the male line), patrilocal (the wife joined the household of her husband), and patriarchal, that is, the "father" was the major authority in ruling the household. This did not mean women were insignificant in the family; on the contrary. The wife of the senior male had important familial roles and great authority, as this poem indicates (Perdue et al., *Families in Ancient Israel*, 182–89).

Households were largely economic institutions. Their members provided the labor force necessary for even a subsistence-level existence. Thus the households were largely self-sufficient in the producing of shelter, food, and raw materials for clothing and pottery. Excess in productivity led to cottage industries and a barter and even more expanded trade system by which needed products, such as food and pottery, but also luxury items could be obtained.

The central value in the core of the family values of ancient Israel and Judah was the strong ethical concept of solidarity deriving from the interdependence of household members, which was necessary for the social unit to function as a viable entity. Thus members were responsible for one another's well-being, and the needs of the household took priority over those of the individual. This concept of solidarity was not limited to household members related by blood and marriage but extended also to marginals who, as day laborers, servants, concubines, and slaves, were included within the system of labor and care of the larger family.

The religion of the household included two major factors. First, the teaching of God's election of the founding ancestors, who produced through their offspring the clans and tribes that came to comprise the nation of Israel, was at the basis of household traditions, although this theological affirmation is absent in Proverbs. Second, however, was the different theological basis for the household that Proverbs introduces, namely God as Creator and Sustainer of the cosmos and of the family and individual person. The divine commandment to care for the poor, both within and outside the immediate family, was carried out by networks of families who provided for their kinsmen and kinswomen the necessary victuals for life, including food, shelter, and clothing. The worship of the household in Proverbs was grounded in the sapiential emphasis on the "fear of Yahweh," that is, faith in God as the Creator and Sustainer of the family. With the monarchy, the allegiance to the family shifted in part toward the royal household. The absence of any reference to royalty and royal institutions in 31:10–31, however, suggests that the monarchy had ceased to exist and to compete for the allegiance of people over and against their immediate household.

Literary Structure and Interpretation

276

Proverbs 31:10–31 is an acrostic poem devoted to praising the "woman of worth" (see Murphy, *Wisdom Literature*, 82). This expression could refer to a variety of characteristics attributed to a woman in the Old Testament: strength (1 Sam. 2:4; Ps. 18:32 = Heb. 18:35; 40 = Heb. 39), wealth (Gen. 34:29), and ability, especially in regard to moral worth (Ruth 3:11; 1 Kings 1:42, 52; and especially Prov. 12:4). The last alternative seems to fit best what the poet has in mind in describing this married woman.

There are several acrostic poems in the Old Testament. Other examples are Psalms 9—10, 24, 34, 37, 111, 119, and Lamentations 1—4. The acrostic may have been a mnemonic device in remembering the poem, a way of teaching the alphabet, or a literary device that one would expect of scribes accustomed to the use of language. The fact that it is most frequent among the sapiential literature of wisdom poems (Psalms 34, 37, 111, 119) supports the last understanding as the major explanation.

Apart from the acrostic device, there appears to be no demarcation of major literary structures in the poem, especially strophes or units of thought extending beyond one line. Instead, one finds throughout this poem the existence of synthetic sayings of one line, where the second half line extends the thought of the first.

This is largely an economic text dealing with production and consumption, although reproduction, nurture, education, and judicial features of the household, exemplified in the behavior and relationships of this woman, are other important characteristics of the poem and its subject, the "woman of worth."

The economic setting and the activities of the woman of worth dominate the entire acrostic poem. In a village, agrarian society, the economic functions of the household were a pragmatic focus for survival. The household of the woman in the poem includes a husband, children, and servant-girls; apparently it is a rather large and affluent household (cf. the household of Micah in Judges 17—18). Presumably the males would have worked with the herds and the fields, while the women, including the one here, who is probably the senior female married to the head of the household, engaged in a variety of economic tasks. The senior female's chief role was that of manager of the household, not only within the physical structure of the family dwellings but beyond into the fields. Her organizational tasks included the assigning of duties to servant-girls and children, the two primary groups over which senior women had authority. She saw to it that sheep were sheared to provide wool and that flax was grown to provide the major raw materials from which clothing was made.

It appears she had available to her resources beyond the family household's flocks and crops which provided raw materials. These

277

resources could also be bartered in order to obtain luxuries used for the production of clothing for her family. Indeed, the average household would have had only natural colors, but she produced clothing of crimson for her family, which indicated royalty or noble heritage. Even fine linen and purple provided the materials for her own clothing as well as that of her family, indicating that she possessed or at least had access, through the productivity of the household, to significant wealth. Linen produced from flax was available not only to Egyptian households but also to others in the ancient Near East. Flax was raised also in Israel (Josh. 2:6). Through a complicated and lengthy process, it was transformed into fibers of linen that spinners used to make the threads that were then taken by weavers to produce cloth. The "woman of worth" is said to have the talent of spinning materials into cloth and of making clothing. While bleached linen was the stuff from which clothing was made, colored linen, an expensive luxury, appears to have been used at least for decoration, if not for the making of the entire garment (see 1 Chron. 4:21). Imported linen was a great luxury, especially that which came from Egypt. All manner of clothing items were crafted from linen: tunics, headgear, and underclothing, as well as sails for ships, bedsheets, and curtains. Purple was the most valued dye in the ancient world, deriving from Mediterranean mollusks, and it was used for coloring woven cloth in various shades of purple and red. It may well have been imported to Israel (Ezek. 27:16, 27), indicating that the household of the "woman of worth" was especially wealthy. Purple therefore signified wealth and royalty (see Lam. 4:5; Ezek. 23:6). In addition to the making of linen garments, the woman of worth sells excess clothing and sashes in an example of a household industry that supplemented the family income. The metaphor is used of this woman being clothed with two royal or noble characteristics ("strength and dignity," v. 25).

In addition to the making of garments and to obtaining raw stuffs for their creation, the woman of worth's economic activities extend to the purchasing of fields, the planting of vineyards, and the providing and preparing of food for her family. She works well into the night and does not "eat the bread of idleness!" (vv. 18, 27). Thus she is not a pampered lady cared for by servants but instead engages in her own acts of labor and industry. Because of the intensity and productivity of her labors, she is the object of praise in the city gates, a place where commerce and news, in addition to judgment, are carried on.

278　　　The poem on the "woman of worth" provides a striking inclusion to the book of Proverbs, which opens with poems dealing with Woman Wisdom in chapters 1, 8, and 9 and now concludes with the concrete

example of the wise woman incarnate in an Israelite or Jewish housewife and mother, who, while admittedly wealthy, engages in the sapiential virtues of care, hard labor, wisdom, and the "fear of Yahweh."

The "woman of worth" is also known for teaching (see Prov. 1:8;
6:20), presumably not only the wisdom of the sages but also directions
to the children on how to labor, to girls on how to become wives and
mothers, and to the family on the proper use of language. She teaches
the "law of kindness" or steadfast love (v. 26), in this context a term
that probably refers to the bond of solidarity that holds the household
together and enables it to transcend individual greed and well-being
for the collective good of the entire social unit. Education, even for
girls and young women, went beyond the pragmatics of how to man-
age a household, cook, sew, and mother to include social customs,
moral values, and religious beliefs. This role of the woman as teacher
is found in cosmic wisdom in Prov. 1:20–33 and is suggested in Prov.
10:1; 15:20; 20:20; 23:22, 25; 28:24; 30:11, 17. This does not mean that
most adults, including women, were literate, but a few were, and especially among the wealthy and noble one finds literacy to have flourished (see Lemaire, "Schools and Literacy in Ancient Israel and Early
Judaism").

Finally, while custom and tradition did not normally permit
women to engage in acts of judgment, it is clear that the husband of
this woman of worth was not only known and respected in the city
gates but there took his place to serve as one of the elders of the land.
The "people of the land" and their elders were apparently a political
force in Israel that presented the interests of the agrarian communities
even during the monarchy and that had its origins in the predynastic
period and continued on (see Jer. 26:17) as a legal entity that had
importance in clan and tribal jurisprudence and other significant areas.

The praise of the "woman of worth" would have continued not
only during her lifetime but also beyond. This was because the household was comprised of both living and deceased members. The dead
were usually buried in a family tomb, and their memories were celebrated by later generations.

Conclusion

The acrostic poem on the "woman of worth" is probably an early
postexilic text that originated after the end of the Israelite and Judahite
monarchies. It probably was created when nobles, but not rulers, were
present in Judah. The woman of worth belongs to a wealthy household
and engages in many tasks that are worthy of admiration, if not

emulation by poorer women who lived in economically deprived families; on the margins of households as servants, concubines, and slaves; and as the extremely poor who existed on the charity of those like this wealthy but hard-working wife.

Theology

The poem provides an appropriate inclusion for the entire book of Proverbs, not only in dealing with the incarnation of wisdom in a female form—a noble housewife—but also in the reference toward the end of the poem that describes her "fear of Yahweh" (31:30; cf. 1:7). Her wealth, wisdom, and success are attributed to her faith. She believes, like all true sages, that the beginning of wisdom is the belief in God as Creator and Sustainer. As a result, all the accoutrements of human desire that are noble are hers.

BIBLIOGRAPHY

For Further Study

Albright, W. F. "The Goddess of Life and Wisdom." *American Journal of Scientific Languages and Literature* 36:258–94, 1919/20.

Aletti, Jean-Noël. "Séduction et parole en Proverbes I–IX." *Vetus Testamentum* 27:129–44, 1997.

Amsler, Samuel. "La sagesse de la femme." In *La Sagesse de l'Ancien Testament*, edited by Maurice Gilbert, 112–16. Gembloux: Ducolot, 1981.

Barré, Michael L., ed. *Wisdom, You Are My Sister: Studies in Honor of Roland E. Murphy, O. Carm., on the Occasion of His Eightieth Birthday.* Catholic Biblical Quarterly—Monograph Series 29. Washington, D.C.: Catholic Biblical Association of America, 1997.

Barucq, André. *Le Livre des Proverbes.* Sources bibliques. Paris: Gabalda, 1964.

Baumann, Gerlinde. *Die Weisheitsgestalt in Proverbien 1–9.* Forschungen zum Alten Testament 16. Tübingen: J. C. B. Mohr (Paul Siebeck), 1966.

Baumgartner, Walter. *Israelitische und altorientalische Weisheit.* Tübingen: J. C. B. Mohr (Paul Siebeck), 1933.

Begrich, Joachim. "Sōfēr und Mazkir." ZAW 58:1–29, 1940/41.

Blenkinsopp, Joseph. *Wisdom and Law in the Old Testament: The Ordering of Life in Israel and Early Judaism.* Rev. ed. Oxford: Oxford University Press, 1995.

Brenner, Athalya, ed. *A Feminist Companion to Wisdom Literature.* Sheffield: Sheffield Academic Press, 1995.

Camp, Claudia V. "The Female Sage in Ancient Israel and in the Biblical Wisdom Literature." In *The Sage in Israel and the Ancient Near East*, 185–203. Winona Lake, Ind.: Eisenbrauns, 1990.

———. "Woman Wisdom as Root Metaphor: A Theological Consideration." In *The Listening Heart*, edited by Kenneth G. Hoglund, Elizabeth F. Huwiler, Jonathan T. Glass, and Roger G. Lee, *et al.*, 45–76. Journal for the Study of the Old Testament—Supplement Series 58. Sheffield: JSOT Press, 1987.

Collins, John J. "The Biblical Precedent for Natural Theology." *Journal of the American Academy of Religion* 45, Supplement B:35–67, 1977.

———. *Jewish Wisdom in the Hellenistic Age.* Old Testament Library. Louisville, Ky.: Westminster/John Knox Press, 1992.

Crenshaw, James L. "Poverty and Punishment in the Book of Proverbs." In *Urgent Advice and Probing Questions,* edited by James L. Crenshaw, 396–405. Macon, Ga.: Mercer University Press, 1995.

_____, ed. *Urgent Advice and Probing Questions: Collected Writings on Old Testament Wisdom.* Macon, Ga.: Mercer University Press, 1995.

Fontaine, Carole R. "Wisdom in Proverbs." In *In Search of Wisdom,* edited by Leo G. Perdue, Bernard Brandon Scott, and William Johnston Wiseman, 99–114. Louisville, Ky.: Westminster/John Knox Press, 1993.

Gammie, John G., Walter A. Brueggeman, W. Lee Humphreys, and James M. Ward, eds. *Israelite Wisdom: Theological and Literary Essays in Honor of Samuel Terrien.* Missoula, Mont.: Scholars Press, 1978.

Gaspar, Joseph W. "The Social Background of Wisdom Literature." *Hebrew Union College Annual* 18:77–118, 1944.

Gemser, Bernard. "The Rib- or Controversy-Pattern in Hebrew Mentality." *Vetus Testamentum Supplements* 3:120–37, 1955.

_____. *Sprüche Salomos.* 2d ed. Handbuch zum Alten Testament 10. Tübingen: J. C. B. Mohr (Paul Siebeck), 1963.

Gilbert, Maurice. "Le Discours de la sagesse en Proverbes 8." In *La Sagesse de l'Ancien Testament,* edited by Maurice Gilbert, 202–18. Gembloux: Duculot, 1981.

_____, ed. *La Sagesse de l'Ancien Testament.* 2d ed. Gembloux: Duculot, 1990.

Greenfield, Jonas C. "The Wisdom of Ahiqar." In *Wisdom in Ancient Israel,* ed. John Day, Robert P. Gordon, and H. G. M. Williamson, 43–52. Cambridge: Cambridge University Press, 1995.

Hadley, Judith M. "Wisdom and the Goddess." In *Wisdom in Ancient Israel,* ed. John Day *et al.,* 234–43. Cambridge: Cambridge University Press, 1995.

Hoglund, Kenneth G., Elizabeth F. Huwiler, Jonathan T. Glass, and Roger W. Lee, eds. *The Listening Heart: Essays in Wisdom and the Psalms in Honor of Ronald E. Murphy, O. Carm.* Journal for the Study of the Old Testament—Supplement Series 58. Sheffield: JSOT Press, 1987.

Knierim, Rolf P. "Cosmos and History in Israel's Theology." *Horizons in Biblical Theology* 3:59–123, 1981.

Küchler, Max. *Frühjüdische Weisheitstraditionen.* Orbis biblicus et orientalis 26. Freiburg: Universitätsverlag, 1979.

Lang, Berhard, ed. *Anthropological Approaches to the Old Testament.* Issues in Religion and Theology 8. Philadelphia: Fortress Press, 1985.

Leclant, Jean. *Les Sagesses de Proche-Orient Ancien.* Paris: Presses Universitaires, 1963.

Lemaire, André. *Les Écoles et la formation de la Bible dans l'ancien Israël.* Orbis biblicus et orientalis 39. Freiburg: Universitätsverlag, 1981.

_____. "The Sage in School and Temple." In *The Sage in Israel and the Ancient Near East,* edited by John G. Gammie and Leo G. Perdue, 165–81. Winona Lake, Ind.: Eisenbrauns, 1990.

Lindenberger, James M. *The Aramaic Proverbs of Ahiqar.* Baltimore: Johns Hopkins University Press, 1983.

Marcus, Ralph. "The Tree of Life in Proverbs." *Journal of Biblical Literature* 62:118–120, 1942.

McKane, William. *Prophets and Wise Men.* London: SCM, 1983.

_____. *Proverbs: A New Approach.* Old Testament Library. Philadelphia: Westminster Press, 1970.

Morgan, Donn F. *Wisdom in the Old Testament Tradition.* Atlanta: John Knox Press, 1981.

Murphy, Roland E. "The Kerygma of the Book of Proverbs." *Interpretation* 20:3–14, 1966.

_____. "Wisdom's Song: Proverbs 1:20–33." *Catholic Biblical Quarterly* 49:456–60, 1987.

Murphy, Roland E., and Elizabeth Huweiler. *Proverbs, Ecclesiastes, Song of Songs.* New International Biblical Commentary. Peabody, Mass.: Hendrickson, 1999.

Noth, Martin, and D. W. Thomas. *Wisdom in Israel and in the Ancient Near East.* Vetus Testamentum, Supplements 3. Leiden: E. J. Brill, 1955.

Oesterley, W. O. E. *The Book of Proverbs.* London: Methuen, 1929.

Perdue, Leo G. "The Testament of David and Egyptian Royal Instructions." In *Scripture in Context II: More Essays on the Comparative Method,* edited by William W. Hallo, James C. Meyer, and Leo G. Perdue, 79–96. Winona Lake, Ind.: Eisenbrauns, 1983.

_____. *Companion to the Old Testament.* Oxford: Basil Blackwell, forthcoming, 2000.

Perry, T. A. *Wisdom Literature and the Structure of Proverbs.* University Park, Pa.: Pennsylvania State University Press, 1993.

Plöger, Otto. *Sprüche Salomos: Proverbia.* Bibel und Kirche 17. Neukirchen-Vluyn: Neukirchener Verlag, 1984.

Preuss, Horst-Dietrich. *Einführung in die alttestamentliche Weisheitsliteratur.* Urban Taschenbücher 383. Stuttgart: W. Kohlhammer, 1987.

Ringgren, Helmer. *Sprüche.* Das Alte Testament Deutsch 16. 3d ed. Göttingen: Vandenhoeck & Ruprecht, 1981.

Schmid, Hans Heinrich. *Altorientalische Welt in der alttestamentlichen Theologie.* Zurich: Theologischer Verlag, 1974.

_____. "Creation, Righteousness, and Salvation." In *Creation in the Old Testament,* edited by B. W. Anderson, 102–17. Issues in Religion & Theology 6. Philadelphia: Fortress Press, 1984.

Sheppard, Gerald T. *Wisdom as a Hermeneutical Construct.* Beihefte zur *Zeitschrift für die altestamentliche Wissenschaft* 151. Berlin and New York: Walter de Gruyter, 1980.

Shupak, Nili. *Where Can Wisdom Be Found?* Orbis biblicus et orientalis 130. Freiburg: Universitätsverlag, 1993.

Simpson, W. Kelly. *The Literature of Ancient Egypt.* 2d ed. New Haven, Conn.: Yale University Press, 1973.

Steiert, Franz-Josef. *Die Weisheits Israels—Ein Fremdkörper in Alten Testament?* Freiburger Theologische Studien. Freiburg: Herder, 1990.

van Leeuwen, Raymond C. "Liminality and Worldview in Proverbs 1–9." In *Paraenesis: Act and Form,* edited by Leo G. Perdue and John G. Gammie, 111–14. *Semeia* 50, 1990.

Weeks, Stuart. *Early Israelite Wisdom.* Oxford Theological Monographs. Oxford: Clarendon Press, 1994.

Westermann, Claus. *Roots of Wisdom.* Louisville, Ky.: Westminster John Knox Press, 1995.

Whybray, R. N. *Proverbs.* New Century Bible. Grand Rapids: Eerdmans, 1994.

Wilken, Robert, ed. *Aspects of Wisdom in Judaism and Early Christianity.* Notre Dame, Ind.: University of Notre Dame Press, 1975.

Yee, Gale A. "An Analysis of Prov. 8:22–31 according to Style and Structure." *Zeitschrift für die altestamentliche Wissenschaft* 94:58–66, 1982.

Works Cited

Albertz, Rainer. *A History of Israelite Religion.* Vol. 1. Old Testament Library. Louisville, Ky.: Westminster John Knox Press, 1994.

Andreason, N. A. "The Role of the Queen Mother in Israelite Society." *Catholic Biblical Quarterly* 45:179–94, 1983.

Bauer-Kayatz, Christa. *Studien zu Proverbien 1–9.* Wissenschaftliche Mongraphien zum Alten und Neuen Testament 22. Neukirchenvluyn: Neukirchener Verlag, 1966.

Berquist, John L. *Judaism in Persia's Shadow: A Social and Historical Approach.* Minneapolis: Fortress, 1995.

Blenkinsopp, Joseph. "The Social Context of the 'Outsider' Woman in Proverbs 1–9." *Biblical Interpretation* 42:457–73, 1991.

Boström, Lennart. *The God of the Sages.* Coniectanea Biblica, Old Testament Series 29. Stockholm: Almqvist & Wiksell, 1990.

Brichto, Herbert C. *The Problem of "Curse" in the Hebrew Bible.* Philadelphia: Society of Biblical Literature and Exegesis, 1963.

Brown, William P. *Character in Crisis: A Fresh Approach to the Wisdom Literature of the Old Testament.* Grand Rapids: Wm. B. Eerdmans Publishing Co., 1996.

Brueggemann, Walter. *The Land.* Overtures to Biblical Theology 1. Philadelphia: Fortress Press, 1977.

_____. "The Social Significance of Solomon as a Patron of Wisdom." In *The Sage in Israel and the Ancient Near East,* edited by John G. Gammie and Leo G. Perdue, 117–32. Winona Lake, Ind.: Eisenbrauns, 1990.

Camp, Claudia. *Wisdom and the Feminine in the Book of Proverbs.* Bible and Literature Series 11. Sheffield: JSOT Press/Almond Press, 1985.

Clements, Ronald. *Wisdom in Theology.* Grand Rapids: Wm. B. Eerdmans Publishing Co., 1992.

Clifford, Richard J. *Proverbs: A Commentary.* Old Testament Library. Louisville, Ky.: Westminster John Knox Press, 1999.

Collins, John J. "Marriage, Divorce, and Family in Second Temple Judaism," *Families in Ancient Israel,* 104–62. Louisville, Ky.: Westminster John Knox Press, 1997.

Crenshaw, James L. "The Birth of Skepticism in Ancient Israel." In *The Divine Helmsman: Studies on God's Control of Human Events,* edited by James L. Crenshaw, 1–19. New York: Ktav, 1980.

_____. "Clanging Symbols." In *Urgent Advice and Probing Questions,* edited by James L. Crenshaw, 371–82. Macon, Ga.: Mercer University Press, 1995.

_____. *Education in Ancient Israel: Across the Deadening Silence.* Anchor Bible Reference Library. New York: Doubleday, 1998.

_____. "The Human Dilemma and Literature of Dissent." In *Tradition and Theology in the Old Testament,* edited by Douglas A. Knight, 235–58. Philadelphia: Fortress, 1977.

_____. "A Mother's Instruction to Her Son (Proverbs 31:1–9)." In *Urgent Advice and Probing Questions,* edited by James L. Crenshaw, 383–95. Macon, Ga.: Mercer University Press, 1995.

285

_____. *Old Testament Wisdom: An Introduction.* Revised and enlarged. Louisville. Ky.: Westminster John Knox Press, 1998.

_____. "Poverty and Punishment in the Book of Proverbs." In *Urgent Advice and Probing Questions,* edited by James L. Crenshaw, 396–405. Macon, Ga.: Mercer University Press, 1995.

_____. "Prolegomenon." In *Studies in Ancient Israelite Wisdom,* 1–45. New York: KTAV Publishing House, 1976.

_____. "Wisdom and Authority: Sapiential Rhetoric and Its Warrants." In *Urgent Advice and Probing Questions,* edited by James L. Crenshaw, 326–43. Macon, Ga.: Mercer University Press, 1995.

Davies, G. I. "Were There Schools in Ancient Israel?" In *Wisdom in Ancient Israel,* edited by John Day, *et al.,* 199–211. Cambridge: Cambridge University Press, 1995.

de Boer, P. A. H. "The Counsellor." *Vetus Testament Supplements* 3:42–71, 1955.

Fontaine, Carole R. *Traditional Sayings in the Old Testament.* Bible and Literature 5. Sheffield: Almond Press, 1982.

Gammie, John G., and Leo G. Perdue, eds. *The Sage in Israel and the Ancient Near East.* Winona Lake, Ind.: Eisenbrauns, 1990.

Gerstenberger, Erhard. "Covenant and Commandment." *Journal of Biblical Literature* 84:38–51, 1965.

Hanson, Paul. *The Dawn of Apocalyptic.* Philadelphia: Fortress Press, 1975.

Hausmann, Jutta. *Studien zum Menschenbild der älteren Weisheit.* Forschungen zum Alten Testament 7. Tübingen: J. C. B. Mohr (Paul Siebeck), 1994.

Hermisson, Hans-Jürgen, and Eduard Lohse. *Faith.* Biblical Encounter Series. Nashville: Abingdon Press, 1978.

Kalugila, Leonidas. *The Wise King: Studies in Royal Wisdom as Divine Revelation in the Old Testament and Its Environment.* Coniectanea Biblica, Old Testament Series 15. Lund: Gleerup, 1980.

Koch, Klaus, ed. *Um das Prinzep der Vergeltung in Religion und Recht der Alten Testaments.* Wege der Forschung 125. Darmstadt: Wissenschaftlich Buchgesellschaft, 1972.

Kovacs, Brian. "Is There a Class-Ethic in Proverbs?" In *Essays in Old Testament Ethics,* edited by James L. Crenshaw and John Willis, 171–90. New York: KTAV Publishing House, 1974.

Lang, Bernhard. *Wisdom and the Book of Proverbs: An Israelite Goddess Redefined.* New York: Pilgrim Press, 1986.

Lemaire, André. "Schools and Literacy in Ancient Israel and Early Judaism." In *Companion to the Old Testament,* edited by Leo G. Perdue. Oxford: Basil Blackwell, forthcoming 2000.

Malherbe, Abraham J. *Moral Exhortation: A Greco-Roman Source-book.* Library of Early Christianity. Philadelphia: Westminster Press, 1986.

Marböck, Johann. *Weisheit im Wandel.* Bonner biblische Beiträge 37. Bonn: Peter Hanstein, 1971.

Meyers, Carol. "The Family in Early Israel." *Families in Ancient Israel,* 1–47. Louisville, Ky.: Westminster John Knox Press, 1997.

Mullen, E. Theodore. *The Assembly of the Gods.* Harvard Semitic Studies 24. Missoula, Mont.: Scholars Press, 1980.

Murphy, Roland E. *The Tree of Life: An Exploration of Biblical Wisdom Literature.* 2d ed. Grand Rapids: Wm. B. Eerdmans Publishing Co., 1996.

_____. "Wisdom and Eros." *Catholic Biblical Quarterly* 50:600–603, 1998.

_____. *Wisdom Literature.* The Forms of Old Testament Literature 13. Grand Rapids: Wm. B. Eerdmans Publishing Co., 1981.

Perdue, Leo G. *The Collapse of History: Creation, Text, and Imagination in Old Testament Theology.* Overtures to Biblical Theology. Minneapolis: Fortress Press, 1994.

_____. "Cosmology and the Social Order in the Wisdom Literature." In *The Sage in Israel and the Ancient Near East,* edited by John G. Gammie and Leo G. Perdue, 457–78. Winona Lake, Ind.: Eisenbrauns, 1990.

_____. "The Death of the Sage and Moral Exhortation: From Ancient Near Eastern Instructions to Graeco-Roman Paraenesis." In *Paraenesis: Act and Form,* edited by Leo G. Perdue and John G. Gammie, 81–109. *Semeia* 50, 1990.

_____. "The Household, Old Testament Theology, and Contemporary Hermeneutics." *Families in Ancient Israel,* 223–257. Louisville, Ky.: Westminster John Knox Press, 1997.

_____. "Liminality as a Social Setting for Wisdom Instructions." *Zeitschrift für altestamentliche Wissenschaft* 93:114–26, 1981.

_____. "Paraenesis and the Epistle of James." *Zeitschrift für die neutestamentliche Wissenschaft* 72:241–56, 1981.

_____. "The Riddles of Psalm 49." *Journal of Biblical Literature.* 93 (1974):533–542.

_____. "The Social Character of Paraenesis and Paraenetic Literature." In *Paraenesis: Act and Form,* edited by Leo G. Perdue and John G. Gammie, 5–39. *Semeia* 50, 1990.

_____. "Wisdom in the Book of Job." In *In Search of Wisdom: Essays in Memory of John G. Gammie,* edited by Leo G. Perdue, Bernard Brandon Scott, and William Johnston Wiseman, 73–98. Louisville, Ky.: Westminster John Knox Press, 1993.

_____. *Wisdom and Creation*. Nashville: Abingdon Press, 1994.

_____. *Wisdom and Cult: A Critical Analysis of the Views of Cult in the Wisdom Literatures of Israel and the Ancient Near East.* Society of Biblical Literature Dissertation Series 30. Missoula, Mont.: Scholars Press, 1977.

_____. "Wisdom Theology and Social History in Proverbs 1–9." In *Wisdom, You Are My Sister. Studies in Honor of Roland E. Murphy, O. Carm., on the Occasion of His Eightieth Birthday,* edited by Michael L. Barré, 78–101. Catholic Biblical Quarterly—Monograph Series 29. Washington, D.C.: Catholic Biblical Association of America, 1997.

Perdue, Leo G., Joseph Blenkinsopp, John J. Collins, and Carol Meyers. *Families in Ancient Israel.* The Family, Religion, and Culture. Louisville, Ky.: Westminster John Knox Press, 1997.

Preuss, H. D. *Old Testament Theology.* Vols. 1 and 2. Old Testament Library. Louisville, Ky.: Westminster/John Knox Press, 1991, 1993.

Pritchard, J. B., ed. *Ancient Near Eastern Texts with Supplement.* 3d ed. Princeton, N.J.: Princeton University Press, 1969.

Rankin, O. S. *Israel's Wisdom Literature.* Edinburgh: T. & T. Clark, 1936.

Ringgren, Helmer. *Word and Wisdom: Studies in the Hypostatization of Divine Qualities and Functions in the Ancient Near East.* Lund: H. Ohlssons, 1947.

Roth, Wolfgang. *Numerical Sayings in the Old Testament.* Vetus Testamentum Supplements 13. Leiden: E. J. Brill, 1965.

Skehan, Patrick. *Studies in Israelite Poetry and Wisdom.* Catholic Biblical Quarterly—Monograph Series 1. Washington, D.C.: Catholic Biblical Association of America, 1971.

Turner, Victor. *The Ritual Process.* Ithaca, N.Y.: Cornell University Press, 1967.

van Leeuwen, Raymond. *Context and Meaning in Proverbs 25–27.* Society of Biblical Literature Dissertation Series 96. Atlanta: Scholars Press, 1988.

_____. "The Book of Proverbs." In *The New Interpreter's Bible,* 5: 17–264. Nashville: Abingdon Press, 1997.

_____. "Proverbs 30:21–23 and the Biblical World Upside Down." *Journal of Biblical Literature* 105: 599–610, 1986.

_____. "Wealth and Poverty: System and Contradiction in Proverbs." *Hebrew Studies* 33:25–36, 1992.

von Rad, Gerhard. "The Joseph Narrative and Ancient Wisdom." In *The Problem of the Hexateuch and Other Essays,* 292–300. New York: McGraw-Hill Book Co., 1966.

_____. *Old Testament Theology.* Vol. 1. New York: Harper & Row, 1962.

_____. *Wisdom in Israel.* Nashville: Abingdon Press, 1972.

Washington, Harold. *Wealth and Poverty in the Instruction of Amenemope and the Hebrew Proverbs.* Society of Biblical Literature Dissertation Series 142. Atlanta: Scholars Press, 1994.

Weinfeld, Moshe. *Deuteronomy and the Deuteronomic School.* Oxford: Clarendon Press, 1972.

Westermann, Claus. *Blessing in the Bible and the Life of the Church.* Philadelphia: Westminster Press, 1978.

_____. *Creation.* Philadelphia: Fortress Press, 1974.

Whybray, R. N. *The Intellectual Tradition in the Old Testament.* Beihefte zur Zeitschrift für die alttestamentliche Wissenschaft 135. Berlin and New York: Walter de Gruyter, 1974.

_____. *Proverbs.* New Century Bible. Grand Rapids: Wm. B. Eerdmans Publishing Co., 1994.

_____. *Wealth and Poverty in the Book of Proverbs.* Journal for the Study of Old Testament—Supplement Series 99. Sheffield: JSOT Press, 1990.

_____. *Wisdom in Proverbs.* Studies in Biblical Theology 45. Naperville, Ill.: Alec R. Allenson, 1965.

Williams, James G. *Those Who Ponder Proverbs: Aphoristic Thinking and Biblical Literature.* Biblical Literature Series 2. Sheffield: Almond Press, 1981.

Wolff, Hans Walter. *Anthropology of the Old Testament.* Philadelphia: Fortress Press, 1974.

Wright, Christopher J. H. *God's People in God's Land: Family, Land, and Property in the Old Testament.* Grand Rapids: Wm. B. Eerdmans Publishing Co., 1990.